Connecticut 169 Club:

Your Passport & Guide to Exploring Connecticut

Connecticut 169 Club:

Your Passport & Guide to Exploring Connecticut

Martin Podskoch, Editor & Author

David Hayden, Asst. Editor

Contributors:

Ables, Kay
Armstrong, William
Atwell, Sarah
Beaumont, Robert
Bergeron, Ruth
Bergonzelli-Graham, Shana
Borysiewicz, Tom
Boughton, Kathryn
Bouley, Jane
Bowley, Joanie
Boyle, Doe
Bradley, Eliza
Brecher, Jeremy
Breor, Barbara
Brinton, William L.
Bucceri, Louis J.
Buchheit, Eileen
Burdick, Fred
Caliandri, Sallie
Callinan, Tom
Camposeo, Joe
Carpenter, Jennifer S.
Carso, Donald
Carvalho, Maria
Cheney, Glenn Alan
Christensen, Linda
Cilio, John
Clark, Sandra
Coolidge, Natalie L.
Coughlin, Martin
Coykendall, Betty
Crescimanno, Terry
Crowley, John
Davidge, Carol
Davis, Lauren
Dean, Mary
Deluca, Reed
DePold, Hans
Deveau, Mary Rose
Dodds, Khara
Dooling, Michael C.
Dunphy, Sharon
Eberhardt, Nancy
Ermenc, Christine
Fahy, Lynn
Failla, Kathleen
Farrish, Kate
Fiedler, Lisa
Fields, Cathy
Fisher, Chris
Forristall, Rhonda
Foster, Kit
Foulke-Green, Laurie
Fox, Linda
Foy, Betsy
Fuller, Marcy
Gagliardi, Ron
Geary, Nancy
German, Martha
Giannelli, Karen
Giguere, Judy
Gillotti, Laurel
Gilson, Verna
Goodman, Florence
Goulden, Teresa
Groth, Joanne
Guertin, Brigid
Gurski, Carol
Guy Shadford, Jackie
Hall, Anne
Hall Kuchta, Elizabeth
Hampton, Barbara J.
Hart, Paul
Havemeyer, Ann
Haynes, Wes
Healy, Anastasia Mills
Helander, Joel E.
Hemingway, Chris
Hinchman, Walter
Horan, Rose
Howard, Nora O.
Hulten, Julie
Jobbagy, Bill
Johnson, Craig
Kathan, Rev. Boardman W.
Kelmelis, Judy
Kennedy, Amy
Kerz, Leslie
Krenesky, Michael A.
LaCombe, Gert
Lamothe, Zachary
Langner Griggs, Bianka
Lantiere, Stephanie
Lauria, John
Leach Franco, Janis
Leff, David
Lentz, Thomas L.
Le Shay, Kitty
Lindley, Joe
Lobner, Jessica
LoPresti, Eliza H.
LoRusso, Jo-Ann C.
Loser, Debbie
MacGregor, Victoria
Magdziarz, Robert
Mahler, Kenneth E.
Malloy, Elizabeth
Marchesseault, Ron
Mariano, Bridget
Markham, Dean
Mazzone, Gary
McCue, Stephen
McDaniel, Ronald K.
McDougall, Bob
McEachern, Mark
McGarry, Michael
McGory, Megan
McMorran, Monica
McQuaid, Richard
Miller, Michael
Moss, Marven
Naumann, Kathy
Neary, Rebecca
Newington H.S. & Trust
Nielsen, Sarah
Nielson, Douglas
Northrop Wittorff, Amy
Nye, Robert M.
O'Keefe, Marian
Old Saybrook Historical Society
Old Saybrook Chamber of Commerce
Palmer, Mark A.
Pease, Kimberly
Petrella, Joyce
Phillips, Susan
Pierce, Dizck
Plaskett, Rog
Podskoch, Martin
Ponte, Rose
Potts, Eve
Preli, Grace
Purmont, Jon E.
Qian, Shu
Reinhard, Ginny
Rice, Robin
Rinaldi, Pamela
Ring, Kevin
Roesler, Karen
Roloff, Kira
Salsedo, Beth
Sanders, Allison
Santoro, Frank
Savilonis, Melissa
Schuler Hull, Cary
Schultz, William
Schwarzmann, Violet
Sholtys, Pauline
Shutts, Beth
Smith, Marge
Stankovics, Denise J.
Stellitano, Kathryn
Stowe, Arthur
Stub, Lorraine
Todd, Henry
Torgeson, Linda
Tortorigi, Sheila
Tulimieri, Kevin J.
Upson, Jeannine
Van Tuyl, Elizabeth
Vincent, Wendy M.
Walsh, John
Waters, Elizabeth C.
Weiss, Cathy
Westervelt, William & Ruth
Wierzbinski, Jean
Wilson, Ellen
Wilson, Terri
Wismar, Greg
Wood, Ingrid
Wooding, Phil
York, Bev
Youngblood Laban, Carolyn
Zak, Mary Anne

East Hampton, Connecticut

Connecticut 169 Club

Published by
Podskoch Press, LLC
43 O'Neill Lane
East Hampton, CT 06424

podskoch@comcast.net
https://martinpodskoch.com/

First Printing Oct. 2018
Second Printing Jan. 2019
Third Printing, Revised Edition Oct. 2019
Fourth Printing Dec. 2021
Fifth Printing, Revised Edition Feb. 2023

ISBN 978-0-9971019-6-6

Manufactured in the United States of America

654321

Cover Photo by ©Mark Bowie
Design by Amanda Beauchemin of Ford Folios
Photos by Jerry Dougherty and Maps by Paul Hartmann
Index by Mary Pelletier Hunyadi

TABLE OF CONTENTS

FOREWORD

Nothing defines Connecticut better than its 169 towns.

From the beginning of settlement, we have been a "hiving off" people, settling here, reaching out there, one town becoming the parent of many towns, each fiercely independent, with its own home-grown character, history, and special sense of self.

We are a state of exceptional geographic diversity, too, so our towns are extraordinarily beautiful and breath-takingly varied. From the Gold Coast to the Quiet Corner, the Litchfield Hills to the Long Island Sound, Connecticut has 169 kinds of picture-book perfection, from bustling cities to postcard-worthy village greens.

You owe it to yourself and your family to see them all. Because in Connecticut, the sum of the parts truly is greater than the whole.

This wonderful book is your invitation to do just that. Join the Connecticut 169 Club. Visit every town. See the sights. Hear the stories. Eat the foods. Meet the people. You'll be glad you did. And, you'll either be prouder than ever to be a Connectican, or you'll wish you were one!

–Walter W. Woodward, State Historian

Introduction

Since 2008, I have traveled to most of the 169 towns and villages in Connecticut gathering stories for my book on Connecticut's Civilian Conservation Corps Camps. In my travels I have gotten to meet many wonderful people and have seen so many interesting places that most people will never experience.

After I finished publishing my CT CCC book I decided to do a travel book as I had done in 2014 called *Adirondack 102 Club: Your Passport and Guide to the North Country*. I wrote it because I had traveled throughout the six-million-acre Adirondack Park gathering stories for my five books on the Adirondack fire towers, Civilian Conservation Corps camps, and illustrated Adirondack stories books. I got to see all of the beautiful Adirondacks and I wanted to get other people to have this great experience.

I got the idea for the travel club in the Dec. 11, 2005 issue of American Profile Magazine. It had a story about the Vermont 251 Club that was started in 1954 when Dr. Arthur W. Peach suggested the idea of an informal group, the 251 Club, to veer off the beaten path "to discover the secret and lovely places that main roads do not reveal." He felt that every part of Vermont had beauty, history, attractions, traditions, and interesting people.

I then decided to start a similar club for the Adirondacks. My club was different from Vermont because they charged a membership fee and just gave out a map of Vermont and said have fun. My club would have a book filled with maps, history of each town, and interesting places to visit.

I then contacted town official, historians, historical societies, or residents to write the short descriptions of their towns. They knew their town better than I. By June 2014, I had all 102 town and village summaries completed. Most of the writers were the town historians but there were also town supervisors, assessors, chambers of commerce, historical societies, and residents who contributed.

Sallie Way, my sister-in-law and art teacher at Shenendehowa High School (NY), suggested that I make the book like a passport where visitors would get their book stamped or signed by a resident in each town. She even designed a logo for the club.

This book was to be a guide to the travelers in their quest to visit all 102 towns and villages. Members learned about the history and fascinating places in the Adirondacks. By getting their book signed or stamped by a resident, they got to know the friendly locals and be able to ask questions such as where was a good place to eat or an interesting local attraction. Hopefully they would thereby get to know the real Adirondacks.

There was no membership fee for the club, just a desire to experience the whole Adirondack region. Adults and children of all ages became members. What a great adventure for families, grandparents and their grandchildren or by themselves. Most members traveled by car while others might use a bike, motorcycle, walk, or maybe a canoe!

Once a member reached their goal of all 102 towns and villages they then received the "Vagabond Award." I chose this name because there was a group of influential men: Thomas Edison, Henry Ford, Harvey Firestone, and John Burroughs who took automobile camping trips in the Adirondacks and other sojourns throughout America to get away from their busy lives.

So now people in Connecticut will experience what people in Vermont and the Adirondacks have been experiencing for years. You will have a guide to each town and city, some history, many annual events, and interesting places to visit. In the book there is a place to journal about your visit, and a place to get a stamp, sticker, or signature from a resident. In the back of the book there is a check-off list to record the date of your visit.

When the quest is finished, send a copy of the check-off list with dates you visited each town (inside back cover) to podskoch@comcast.net or by U.S. mail to 43 O'Neill Lane, East Hampton, CT, 06424 to receive a "Leatherman Award" patch. It is named after a man who first appeared in Connecticut during the Civil War wearing a head-to-toe stitched leather suit. He devoted his daily life to walking a 365-mile, 34-day-long, clockwise trip through southwestern Connecticut and adjacent sections of lower New York State till his death in 1889.

Each year a dinner will be held in a different Connecticut town. Anyone can attend. Members will share their stories and adventures. The highlight will be awarding the Leatherman patch to those who have visited, and had their passport book signed or stamped in all 169 towns.

Now begin your quest as a member of the Connecticut 169 Club to not only visit all the towns and villages but get to know the people of this beautiful state of Connecticut. Let's all take the road less traveled!

– Marty Podskoch

The Third Annual Gathering of members of the CT 169 Club was held at the Manchester Country Club. After the luncheon members who had visited all 169 CT towns were given the "Leatherman Award" patch. Lynn Podskoch

NOTE: All photo credits are in italics after the photo caption.

ACKNOWLEDGEMENTS

I would like to thank my wife, Lynn, for her encouragement and patience over the past year of research and writing; my children and their families, Matthew, Kristy & Matthew Roloff, and Ryan & Jenna Podskoch for their encouragement; my parents, Martin & Joan Podskoch; my son-in-law, Matthew Roloff, who helped me with computer problems; and my remarkable granddaughters, Kira and Lydia Roloff, for going on research trips with me and Ryan's wife Jenna for her beautiful twin daughters: Anna & Lily who when older will do exploring with 'Poppa Podskoch'.

A special thanks to Dr. Arthur W. Peach, who in a 1954 issue of *Vermont Life* magazine proposed an informal group to be known as the 251 Club after a reader asked him: "How can I come to know the real Vermont?" He invited local folk and newcomers alike to veer from the beaten path "to discover the secret and lovely places that the main roads do not reveal." He felt that all of Vermont had history, beauty, traditions, and interesting people. This is also true of the entire state of Connecticut.

I'd also like to give a special thank you to the following:

The 183 writers and co-writers for their time and effort spent helping me showcase their town or city.

My dedicated editor, David Hayden, who was always there to correct and guide me through the writing and editing of each town and city description. I never would have completed this book without his insightful questions and suggestions.

Jerry Dougherty, who let me choose photos from the thousands on his website that he had taken when he visited all 169 Connecticut towns and cities.

My sister-in-law, Sallie Way, for her passport idea.

Amanda Beauchemin for her excellent layout of this book, its cover, and the 'Connecticut 169 Club' and 'Leatherman Award' logos.

Special thanks to Barry Ford for helping out during the final weeks of organizing the book and his insights and encouragement.

Walter Woodward for his dedication and hard work as Connecticut's State Historian and for his insightful Foreword for this book.

Mark Bowe for his timely and beautiful photo for the cover.

Thank you to the people and businesses that provided photos of their town.

Fairfield
County
SHERMAN
NEW FAIRFIELD
BROOKFIELD
DANBURY
BETHEL
NEWTOWN
MONROE
RIDGEFIELD
REDDING
SHELTON
EASTON
TRUMBULL
WESTON
WILTON
STRATFORD
BRIDGEPORT
FAIRFIELD
NEW CANAAN
WESTPORT
NORWALK
STAMFORD
DARIEN
GREENWICH

CHAPTER 1

FAIRFIELD COUNTY

Bethel

Thomas Borysiewicz, Bethel resident and librarian at Woodbury Public Library

Bethel is a quiet community in northern Fairfield County. The area was settled in the early 1700s with the oldest homes dating to the 1730s. In 1759 the residents, finding it difficult to travel to Danbury for church services, petitioned for a separate parish. Bethel, which means 'House of God,' did not become a town until May of 1855 when it split from Danbury. Today Bethel is a diverse community of more than 19,000 residents. It has three main commercial areas: downtown Bethel, Greenwood Ave. (Rt. 302), and Stony Hill, (Rt. 6). With easy access to I-84 and service by Metro North RR and Housatonic Area Regional Transit many of the residents are able to commute into NYC.

Danbury is known as 'Hat City,' but at various points in its history there were actually more hat factories in Bethel. While little remains of that industry, many of the houses on the west end of town are former 'hatters' houses and are excellent examples of Victorian architecture. Today Bethel is known for more high-tech industries with Duracell and the Eaton Corp. both headquartered here. Smirnoff vodka was first distilled in Bethel in the early 1930s, the first vodka distillery in the U.S.

Bethel was the hometown of many interesting individuals, the most famous of whom was showman P.T. Barnum, who was born in Bethel on July 5, 1810. The house he grew up in still stands.

Bethel has an excellent school district made up of five schools housed on the 140-acre Educational Park. There are several public parks throughout the town: Meckauer and Parloa both have sports fields and playgrounds while Overlook Park offers hiking trails. The state maintains several properties in Bethel: the more than 1000-acre Huntington State Park, the 170-acre historic site Putnam Memorial State Park, and East Swamp in downtown Bethel. The Connecticut Agriculture Extension for the area is on Stony Hill and holds a seasonal farmers' market every Saturday, June thru November.

Interesting Places

The Bethel Historical Society Museum. It contains many items attributed to her most famous citizen, P.T. Barnum, who lived in Bethel from 1810 to 1835.

Bethel Historical Society.

Huntington State Park. Hiking trails and canoeing.

Putnam Memorial State Park. Maj. Gen. Israel Putnam chose this site for his encampment in the winter of 1778/1779. It is the oldest Connecticut state park created in 1887. There is a hiking trail and historic museum celebrating colonial life and the Revolutionary War.

Blue Jay Orchards. Offers seasonal apple picking and fresh cider, home-baked fruit pies, local produce, famous cider donuts, and more.

Holbrook Farm. Offers local fruits, vegetables, dairy products, and more at their family farm.

Sycamore Drive-In Restaurant. Classic Car Hop Restaurant with a "cruise night" every Saturday in the summer. Try their homemade root beer or a Dagwood burger.

One of the popular places to eat in Bethel is the Sycamore Drive-In, a Classic Car Hop restaurant. Tom Borysiewicz

NOTES

This statue of Abraham Lincoln reading a book while riding a horse was sculpted by Anna Hyatt Huntington. It is in front of the Bethel Public Library. Jerry Dougherty

The Bethel Historical Society is located in the 1842 Second Meeting House at 40 Main Street. The Bethel Historical Society Museum contains many items attributed to her most famous citizen, P.T. Barnum. Jerry Dougherty

ADDRESS BOOK

Town Site
www.bethel-ct.gov

Bethel Public Library
189 Greenwood Ave.
203-794-8756

Bethel Historical Society
40 Main St.
203-794-1050
www.bethelhistoricalsociety.com

Blue Jay Orchards
125 Plumtrees Rd.
203-748-0119
www.bluejayorchardsct.com

Holbrook Farm
45 Turkey Plain Rd.
203-792-0561
www.holbrookfarm.net

Huntington State Park
Sunset Hill Rd.
www.ct.gov/deep

Putnam Memorial State Park
Putnam Park Rd.
203-938-2285
www.putnampark.org

Sycamore Drive-In Restaurant
282 Greenwood Ave.
203-748-2716
www.sycamoredrivein.com

[Passport Stamp / Signature & Date Here]

Bridgeport

By Bridgeport History Center Staff

The city of Bridgeport is in Fairfield Co. in the southwestern part of the state on Long Island Sound. It is Connecticut's most populous city: 145,936 in 2016. Settled in the mid-17th century as part of the township of Stratford, Bridgeport incorporated as a town in 1821 and a city in 1836.

While early settlers farmed and fished, they soon took advantage of the Bridgeport and Black Rock harbors and shifted from an agrarian community to a mercantile and manufacturing hub. When the railroad opened in 1840, the city became a booming industrial center and produced everything from ammunition to sewing machines.

During the 19th century, there were still many farms in the city, especially on the North End. Buildings in downtown Bridgeport, especially along Main St. and State St., have undergone extensive restorations for commercial and residential space in recent years as part of a long term, multi-phase redevelopment project. But many of these "historic buildings" stand where earlier structures built in other styles once existed. The 20th century and especially the period after WWII saw a massive expansion of suburban housing and apartments throughout the North End and other neighborhoods.

Entrepreneur and one-term Mayor of Bridgeport, P.T. Barnum, helped establish Washington Park on the East Side as the first, modern city park and many more followed, including Seaside and Beardsley Parks, both designed by famed landscape architect Frederick Law Olmstead. For a city that occupies a compact area of land, Bridgeport has a large number of parks, small and large.

While today's Bridgeport hosts some manufacturers, industry has shifted to health care and service fields. Courts, banks, law offices, and trade-related shops are prevalent and, as always, many small businesses and entrepreneurs continue to establish themselves. The city's large immigrant population remains one driving component of Bridgeport's economic engine. Both Housatonic Community College and the University of Bridgeport call the city home. There are numerous artists' studios located throughout Bridgeport, making use of old industrial facilities and an artists' residence is situated in the center of downtown.

Interesting Places

Bridgeport Library History Center. A local history collection covering Bridgeport and the surrounding region. Materials include books, manuscript material, newspapers, photographs, genealogy information, and special collections on P.T. Barnum and the circus.

Discovery Museum and Planetarium. Entertaining and educational programs that promote a lot of hands-on interaction.

The Adventure Park. Behind Discovery Museum, 5 acres of wooded area, zip lines, bridges, aerial trails, and more.

Total Mortgage Arena. Entertainment complex with more than 100 different acts a year.

Barnum Museum. Circus giant P.T. Barnum lived in Bridgeport for 40 years and once served as mayor. Museum gallery, currently installed in the People's United Bank Gallery behind the historic Museum building, features artifacts that belonged to P.T. Barnum and Tom Thumb, pieces of historic Bridgeport, and a few extraordinary surprises! Open for viewing and tours from 11 AM-3 PM on Thurs. and Fri., year-round.

Beardsley Zoo. Explore all five sections.

Seaside Park. Features lawns, fields, and beaches along the three miles of coastline.

Black Rock Harbor Light. "Fayerweather Island Light."

Notes

Southeast end of Fayerweather Island. Barnum Blvd.

Captain's Cove Seaport. Marina with restaurant & bar, a boardwalk with local vendors, a maritime museum, a sailing school, and more.

Bijou Theatre. Film and live performances.

City Lights Gallery. Local, regional and emerging artists.

Sterling Block-Bishop Arcade. 19th century downtown, early "mall" with iron and glass ceiling, restored.

Harborview Market. Store in Black Rock neighborhood with delicious baked goods, breakfast & lunch.

Bloodroot. A feminist restaurant-bookstore with a seasonal vegetarian menu.

Address Book

Town Site
www.bridgeportct.gov

The Adventure Park
4450 Park Ave.
203-690-1717
www.discoveryadventurepark.org

Barnum Museum
820 Main St.
203-331-1104
www.barnum-museum.org

Beardsley Zoo
1875 Noble Ave.
203-394-6565
www.beardsleyzoo.org

P. T. Barnum funded and used his land for a building to house the work of the Bridgeport Scientific Society and the Fairfield County Historical Society. The museum was completed in 1893. The Barnum Museum is the leading authority on P.T. Barnum's life and work, and contains more than 60,000 artifacts relating to Barnum, Bridgeport, and 19th century America. Jerry Dougherty

Young learners interacting with the 'Dare to Discover' exhibit at the Discovery Science Center & Planetarium. Derek Sterling

Bijou Theatre
275 Fairfield Ave.
203-296-2875
www.bijoutheatrect.net

Bloodroot
85 Ferris St.
203-576-9168
www.bloodroot.com

Bridgeport Library History Center
925 Broad St.
203-576-7400
www.bportlibrary.org/hc

Captain's Cove Seaport
1 Bostwick Ave.

City Lights Gallery
265 Golden Hill St.
www.citylightsgallery.org

Discovery Science Center and Planetarium
4450 Park Ave.
203-416-3521
www.discoverymuseum.org

Downtown Cabaret Theatre
263 Golden Hill St. #3
203-576-1636
www.dtcab.com

Harborview Market
218 Harborview Ave.
www.harborviewmarket.com

Seaside Park
1 Barnum Dyke

Sterling Block-Bishop Arcade
993-1005 Main St.

Total Mortgage Arena
600 Main St.
203-345-2300
www.totalmortgagearena.com

[Passport Stamp / Signature & Date Here]

Brookfield

By Carol Gurski and Shana Bergonzelli-Graham, Brookfield Historical Society

Brookfield was founded in 1788 with a land contribution from Danbury, New Milford, and Newtown. The town was named in honor of Reverend Brooks, who was ordained and installed as permanent minister of the town in 1757, and who had guided its destiny for 30 years.

Brookfield is a friendly suburban town with easy access to New York City and the Connecticut shore. It has maintained its small town charm and rural character while providing residents with ample amenities. We have convenient shopping with big box stores like Costco and B.J.'s as well as many smaller shops and boutiques. We have an abundance of good restaurants and banks.

Brookfield is small enough to be friendly and large enough to offer most of the services anyone needs or wants. Danbury and New Milford Hospitals (both less than nine miles away) offer excellent medical services.

Candlewood Lake with boating, swimming, and fishing borders Brookfield, as does Lake Lillinonah. The Still River starts in Danbury and flows north through Brookfield until it empties into the Housatonic River in New Milford. Hiking trails are abundant, and the YMCA is centrally located and available to all.

Brookfield is home to several churches representing various denominations. Our schools are top-notch. The real estate market is active, offering a selection of apartments, condos, and single family houses. Brookfield has designated several sections of land as "open space" (never to be developed) for passive recreation.

Interesting Places

Brookfield Museum and Historical Society (BHS). Offers a snapshot of our history, with exhibits and programs that highlight where we have been and where we are going. The gift shop offers a wide variety of Brookfield-related gifts and crafts. The museum is open every Saturday from Noon-4 PM and by appointment.

Williams Open Space and Gurski Homestead. On 200-acres in Brookfield's historical center. The property features woodlands, streams, wetlands and hay fields. The main entrance is on Rt. 25 across from the town library. Trails from here lead to the Town's clay tennis courts, hay fields and the wooded hilltop. To the south is the Merwin Brook Cemetery, Gurski Homestead with its barn and forge and the Community Gardens. Parking is available at the main entrance and at the Gurski Homestead on Rt. 133.

Happy Landings Protected Open Space. A town-owned 55 acres of open fields and approx. 19 acres of woodlands with ample parking on the property. It is a lovely place to hike or walk one's dog.

Brookfield Craft Center. A 501(c)(3) not-for-profit organization, founded in 1952 and incorporated in 1954 "to teach and preserve the skills of fine craftsmanship, and to enable creativity and personal growth through craft education." A fine gift shop offering pottery, glasswork, woodcraft, jewelry, and other hand-crafted items is located on site. The craft center also offers the community many classes and workshops taught by acclaimed

Brookfield Museum and Historical Society. BHS

Notes

artisans and teachers. The historic 2.5-acre campus is located on the banks of the Still River, including the historic Grist Mill of the former Brookfield Ironworks district.

Still River Greenway. A 2.25-mile multi-use pedestrian/bicycle trail. One entrance is located on Silvermine Rd. and the other entrance located on Federal Rd. The trail features a 10-foot-wide paved surface, and a 170-foot bridge over the Still River (the longest footbridge in the state). It provides a safe place for everyone to exercise: biking, walking, rollerblading, and running. It is stroller friendly with no motorized vehicles permitted.

Brookfield Library. Offers programs for all ages along with up-to-date technology. Rt 25; across from Williams Park.

DiGrazia Winery. Founded in 1978 it features many varieties, from dry to sweet. It is one of the original six wineries on the Connecticut wine trail and offers guided tours and wine tasting. There is also a country gift shop on site and a large picnic area on the patio.

Old Gurski Homestead at Williams Park. Carol Gurski

Address Book

Town Site
www.brookfieldct.gov

Brookfield Craft Center
286 Whisconier Rd.
www.brookfieldcraft.org

Brookfield Museum and Historical Society
165 Whisconier Rd.
www.brookfieldcthistory.org

Brookfield Library
182 Whisconier Rd.
www.brookfieldlibrary.org

DiGrazia Winery
131 Tower Rd.
203-775-1616
www.digraziavineyards.com

Happy Landings Protected Open Space
55 Whisconier Rd.

Williams Open Space and Gurski Homestead
26 Obtuse Hill Rd.

[Passport Stamp / Signature & Date Here]

Danbury

By Brigid Guertin, Director of Danbury Museum and Historical Society

Since its foundation in 1684, Danbury has been a place of opportunity for all individuals.

When the first settlers arrived in Danbury from the Norwalk area, they brought with them the dream of creating a prosperous farming community. Through the next several decades they successfully grew crops, raised families, welcomed more residents, and by the mid-1700s the Town had become relatively prosperous; farmers grew more than they needed and traded their excess foods for important goods with their neighbors in the south and the newly formed communities surrounding Danbury.

Many changes occurred in Danbury with the onset of the Revolutionary War. The community was torn with patriotic feelings, on behalf of the Tories and the newly formed American army. Danbury was designated as a supply depot by the revolutionary forces who built it into a major way station for goods destined to fortify American troops. Although the British did attack the supply depot and cause damage to the town, the depot was soon back in service supplying the troops with many necessary items, like food and leather goods, especially shoes!

The 19th century saw the citizens take advantage of new skills, inventions, and the freedom of a young America to create several manufacturing industries within the town. One major industry, hatting, soon distinguished itself and so created significant job opportunities for residents and new immigrants. By the 1850s, with the new railroad station and advances in machinery, Danbury distinguished itself as the center of the hatting trade. Immigrants from across the world and throughout the country were attracted by the industry and work available in Danbury.

Although the hatting industry faded, and then eventually ended in the late 1980s, its demise gave rise to the many new industries and companies that transitioned to the Danbury area and have provided the community with many levels of employment through the late 1900s and into the 21st century.

Opportunity, in the form of education and work has abounded for over 320 years. Throughout challenging times of change and growth the Danbury community has persevered, grown stronger, and built a great foundation on which to prosper in the next 320 years.

Interesting Places

The Danbury Museum. The Danbury Museum & Historical Society (DMHS) preserves these historic buildings: the John and Mary Rider House (c.1785), the Dodd Hat Shop (c.1790), the Marian Anderson Studio, the old King Street Schoolhouse, the Little Red Schoolhouse, and the Charles Ives Birthplace. Huntington Hall, a modern exhibit building contains a research library. Open Tues.-Sat. 10 AM-4 PM

Charles Ives House (1780), aka "Charles Ives Birthplace." An internationally recognized composer in the early 20th century.

Danbury Railway Museum. Housed in the former Union Station (1903). Has a collection of heritage railcars in the neighboring

The studio where world-renowned contralto Marian Anderson rehearsed for the 50 years she lived in Danbury. DMHS

Notes

railyard. Features train rides, guided tours, turntable, gift store, library, and model train exhibit.

Danbury Public Library. The heart of the community for information including books, movies, music, and downloadables. Also activities and programs.

Candlewood Lake. Man-made 8.4 sq. mi. lake in Fairfield and Litchfield counties. It is the largest lake in Connecticut and borders Brookfield, Danbury, New Fairfield, New Milford, and Sherman.

Tarrywile Park & Mansion. A 23-room Victorian-era mansion features gardens, trails, ponds & picnic areas. 722-acre municipal park that once was an active dairy farm and fruit orchard and is now home to 21 miles of hiking trails, 2 ponds, a lake, and several picnic areas.

This 1907 Boston & Maine Class B-15 Mogul #1455 steam locomotive is on display at the Danbury Railway Museum. Carolyn Taylor.

Address Book

Town Site
www.danbury-ct.gov

Charles Ives House
7 Mountainville Ave.
203-743-5200

The Danbury Museum
43 Main St.
203-743-5200
www.danburymuseum.org

Danbury Public Library
170 Main St.
203-797-4505
www.danburylibrary.org

Danbury Railway Museum
120 White St.
203-778-8337
www.danburyrailwaymuseum.org

Tarrywile Park & Mansion
70 Southern Blvd.
www.tarrywile.com

[Passport Stamp / Signature & Date Here]

Darien

By William Armstrong, writer, former Darien resident

The original inhabitants of this small coastal village of incredibly fortunate destiny were the Siwanoy, members of the Wappinger Confederacy, who lived in the lands stretching from present day Bronx, NY to Norwalk, CT.

The first English settlers were pioneer farmers who established their homesteads on the Noroton, Goodwives, and Five Mile rivers. This was in 1641. In 1672 an old Siwanoy trail began use as a mail route between Boston and New York. It was known simply as the Country Road, then Old King's Highway, and now the Boston Post Road. By 1772 stagecoaches ran regularly between New York and Boston. Several severe winters necessitated the building of a church as parishioners were freezing to death journeying to Stamford services. Reverend Moses Mather was hired as minister in 1744 and continued in this position until his death in 1806. He was the spiritual and moral focal point around which the fledgling town clung and grew.

During the Revolutionary War, Mather was a staunch patriot in a town divided into passionate Tories and Rebels. Rebel sentiment prevailed and many of the town's Tories removed to Long Island to conduct raids across Long Island Sound which the Patriots did as well. In one such raid, Rev. Mather and 26 other men were taken hostage and held in British prisons in New York City until they were redeemed after five months. Several of the hostages died.

After the war, and until after the Civil War, Darien remained a small village of artisans, fishermen, farmers, and tradesmen who sailed or rode to New York to trade. With the coming of the railway and with the natural beauty and seclusion of its coast and inlets having caught the eye of various wealthy New Yorkers, Darien moved into the final chapter of its destiny as a pastoral haven for the wealthy whose fortunes are primarily made in Manhattan.

Darien was recently determined to be the richest town in the United States. It has an extraordinary public school system and its public library, built entirely from private funds, is a state of the art institution.

Interesting Places

Darien Public Library. From its automatic book sorter to its digital media lab to the sustainable architecture and geothermal heating system, the library puts the "edge" in cutting edge practices. But make no mistake; behind all the bells and whistles is an absolutely first rate staff of librarians and paraprofessionals. It is their work that wins the awards!

The Darien Historical Society. Dedicated to collecting, preserving, and exhibiting materials of local historical value and focuses on educating the community about Darien's heritage. It supports, maintains, and operates the c.1736 Bates-Scofield House Museum, the 1827 Scofield Barn Exhibit Hall, and the Darien Historical Archives and Resource Library.

Shopping. High end shops such as the Darien Sport Shop, Seasons Too, Helen Ainson, and the Darien Thrift Shop offer the visitor a consumer's delight.

Beaches and Parks. Though small in size, Darien has numerous parks. Beaches are immaculately kept.

The eight-acre Tilly Pond Park at 38 West Ave. has a beautiful stone pavilion. Jerry Dougherty

Notes

Cherry Lawn Park. Features community garden, nature center, playground, sports fields & tennis courts.

Stony Brook. Wonderfully hidden and meditative with hiking trails, benches and a waterfall.

Tilley Pond Park. Pure serenity located just walking distance from the downtown shops on Post Rd. The 8.651 acres park has walking/jogging paths, benches, garden area, trees and ornamental plantings.

Pear Tree Point. The beach features swimming, picnic tables and grills, a beautiful gazebo, a bathhouse, concession stand, boat launch ramp, and two beautiful beaches. Off Pear Tree Point Rd. at the mouth of the Goodwives River.

Weed Beach. Features bathing and picnic areas, 6 tennis courts, 5 paddle tennis courts, children's play areas, a bathhouse, a fit trail with equipment, and concession stand.

The Sugar Bowl. Since 1950 the Sugar Bowl has been the culinary staple keeping Darien from floating into the economic stratosphere. Every town in America has its breakfast and burger joint and the Sugar Bowl can hold its own against any of them. Great burgers, pancakes, French toast; you know the rest. We're all one in our love of a good shake and some fries.

The c.1736 Bates-Scofield House Museum at 45 Old Kings Hwy. in N. Darien is operated by the Darien Historical Society. William Armstrong

Address Book

Town Site
www.darienct.gov

Cherry Lawn Park
120 Brookside Rd.

Darien Public Library
1441 Post Rd.
203-655-1234
www.darienlibrary.org

The Darien Historical Society
45 Old Kings Hwy., North Darien
www.darienhistorical.org

Pear Tree Point
Pear Tree Point Rd.

Stony Brook
Ledge Rd.

The Sugar Bowl
1033 Boston Post Rd.
203-655-1259
www.sugarbowlofdarien.com

Tilley Pond Park
38 West Ave.

Weed Beach
155 Nearwater Ln.

[Passport Stamp / Signature & Date Here]

Easton

By Eliza Bradley, Easton Historical Society

First settled in 1757, Easton, along with neighboring Weston, was originally part of the town of Fairfield. Weston incorporated in 1787, followed by Easton in 1845. Today Easton, which is on the National Register of Historic Places, remains relatively unchanged. There are no streetlights, malls, or mainstream shopping. There is no grocery store. Blink once and you'll miss the town center, which consists of the Post Office and Greiser's General Store with a gas station that predates World War II. Down the road beyond Town Hall and the library is Easton Village Market, where you can pick up coffee and some of the best deli sandwiches around.

Across the street is the Easton Fire Station, where every August a carnival is hosted by the fire department. This is small-town living at its best, very reminiscent of the Norman Rockwell days of a bygone era.

In the 17th century farming began in this very rural area but by the middle of the 19th century it began to fade as the industrial revolution began to take hold. The Easton of the 19th century was a much busier place in terms of commerce than it is today. Easton's mills were scattered around on the streams that powered the town's early economy. Cottage industries morphed into factories. Wagons were supplanted by railroads. Farmers sought larger farms in New York, Vermont, and in the Midwest. Easton's mills had outlived their functionality shortly after the Civil War. The availability of jobs in nearby Bridgeport in particular changed Easton's population.

The waterpower of Easton's streams and rivers was replaced with steam engines and later gasoline and diesel engines and electric motors. The small village shops of Easton that had produced shoes and iron implements, clothing, and foodstuff were being replaced by much larger factories and larger farms elsewhere.

Although Easton is a sleepy town, it has had its share of famous residents and weekenders. Helen Keller made Easton her home toward the end of her life (the town's middle school is named after her). Other notables have included Jessica Tandy and Hume Cronyn, Ann Baxter, Edna Ferber and Dan Rather. Ernest Hemingway allegedly wrote A Farewell to Arms in the house adjacent to the old water mill on Old Redding Rd.

Places of Interest

In modern times as the industrial revolution has moved beyond Easton, farming is again the main form of industry. Silverman's Farm is a tourist attraction during the fall where people come to pick the apples and pumpkins.

Further up Rt. 59 is Sport Hill Farm. Here customers can pick up a wide variety of seasonal produce, eggs, dairy, and some meat products. Sport Hill Farm supplies many of Fairfield County's most prestigious restaurants.

A little further up the road is Snow's Farm, which specializes in gardening products and lawn care, has been around for more than 100 years.

Follow Rt. 59 further north and you'll come to an intersection, just beyond which is Union Cemetery, established in the 1700s and

The 1816 Bradley Hubbell House is one of two historic properties maintained by the Easton Historical Society. It is located at 535 Black Rock Turnpike in Easton. Kelly Higgins

Notes

purported by numerous books and documentaries to be the country's "most haunted" cemetery. Legend has it The White Lady walks the cemetery at night.

Maple Row Farm, a little further up the road, is a mecca for families wanting the unique Christmas experience of cutting their own trees.

On the other side of town on Rt. 58, not far from the town's second oldest cemetery, Gilbertown Cemetery, is the town's one and only restaurant. The Olde Bluebird Inn is known locally for its hearty and delicious New England breakfasts. Rumor has it that in its very early days it was a speakeasy for the locals who did not distill their own.

The nearly 400-year old Union Cemetery near the Easton Baptist Church is allegedly one of the most haunted spots in the country where people have claimed to have seen a White Lady with black hair, wearing a white gown and standing in the middle of Rt. 59. Kelly Higgins

Address Book

Town Site
www.eastonct.gov

Aspetuck Valley Apple Barn
714 Black Rock Tpke.
203-268-9033
/AspetuckAppleBarn

Bradley Hubbell House
535 Black Rock Tpke.

Greiser's Coffee & Market
299 Center Rd.
203-220-9424
www.greisers.com

Maple Row Farm
229 Sepney Rd.
www.mrfarm.com

The Olde Bluebird Inn
363 Black Rock Tpke.
/BlueBirdInnEastonCT

Silverman's Farm
451 Sport Hill Rd.
www.silvermansfarm.com

Snow's Farm
550 Sport Hill Rd.
www.snowsfarm.com

Sport Hill Farm
596 Sport Hill Rd.
www.sporthillfarm.com

[Passport Stamp / Signature & Date Here]

Fairfield

By Jennifer S. Carpenter, Deputy Chief of Staff to the Fairfield First Selectman

As Connecticut's fourth oldest town, Fairfield is a charming coastal community rich in history. Founded in 1639 by immigrants from England who wanted to build a farming village based on Puritan religious values, Fairfield's original boundaries included what are now the communities of Easton, Redding, Weston, and Westport, and parts of Bridgeport.

Fairfield prospered during the 1700s as farmers found markets for their goods in the West Indies, New York, and Boston. In 1779, the British burned most of Fairfield, but the town's spirit and resilience never wavered. Using Benjamin Franklin mile markers, some of which still exist today, George Washington later visited Fairfield to survey Revolutionary War damage. Washington presumably spent the night at the Sun Tavern, one of the colonial buildings situated on the Town's beautiful historic green. At the nearby Burr Mansion, John Hancock got married, and the likes of John Adams and his cousin Sam Adams conducted business.

In the 1800s, the town's picturesque village of Southport became known as the "Onion Capital" of Connecticut. Local farmers raised the Southport Globe Onion prized for its mild taste and inability to easily spoil during long winter voyages. It's said that General Ulysses S. Grant once sent an urgent message to the War Department that he wouldn't move his army without onions because they prevented scurvy.

The arrival of the railroad in 1848 enticed New Yorkers to visit Fairfield's beautiful beaches and fancy hotels, including one purchased by President Grover Cleveland's brother. After WWII, the town's population grew quickly transforming what was once a tiny village of English Puritans into a vibrant and diverse community.

Interesting Places

Fairfield Museum and History Center (FMHC). Explore the history of the region through changing exhibitions and educational programs. See the remains of the pond where women accused of witchcraft were "dunked." Tour historic sites including The Burr Mansion (739 Old Post Rd.) which can be rented for weddings and other festivities and the 1750 Ogden House (1520 Bronson Rd.), a typical mid-18th century colonial farmhouse where you can learn to make honey.

Pequot Library. Bringing Literature, Music, Art, Science & the Humanities to the Community. Home to New England's largest book sale.

Traditional Town Events

Celebrate Fairfield resident Gustave Whitehead's "First in Flight." Predating the Wright brothers' flight, every Aug. 14th on Sherman Green (Post & Reef Rds.), site of summer concerts and winter skating.

Participate in the Annual Wiffle Ball Tournament. Commemorating its 1953 invention in Fairfield.

Dogwood Festival. Revel in the beauty of blooming Dogwood trees each Mother's Day weekend, 1045 Old Academy Rd.

For over 125 years the Pequot Library in Southport has brought literature, music, art, science, and the humanities to our community. American architect Robert H. Robertson designed the building which was erected in 1893. The auditorium is one of the most stunning architectural spaces in New England. © Francis Dzikowski/OTTO

Notes

Celebrate Fourth of July. Along Fairfield's five miles of beaches.

Southport. Watch the Southport Street Parade, then shop and stroll through Southport Village, picnic at Southport Harbor and bike past old sea captains' homes.

Join our town's mailing list at www.fairfieldct.org to receive announcements for Restaurant Week, Holiday Shop & Stroll, Summer Sidewalk Sales and more!

October's Taste of Fairfield and January's Winterfest.

Clam Clinic. Dig for clams at Southport Beach. 203-256-3071.

Once a practice site for the NY Giants, Fairfield abounds in recreational activities at its parks, ballfields, two public golf courses, walking trails and Lake Mohegan. Enjoy the annual Pumpkin Festival at the town's last working farm. Visit one of Fairfield's five beaches to kayak, sail, or simply enjoy the view of L.I. Sound where the "haunted" Penfield Reef Lighthouse sits.

The Burr Mansion (c.1732) was built by Peter Burr, chief justice of the Superior Court of Connecticut. It was rebuilt in 1790 after the original homestead was burned in the British attack on Fairfield during the Revolutionary War. During the 1800s it was remodeled and enlarged. Today it is owned by the Town of Fairfield and managed by the Fairfield Museum and History Center. Fairfield Museum

Address Book

Town Site
www.fairfieldct.org

The Audubon Center
2325 Burr St.
203-259-6305
www.ctaudubon.org/fairfield-home

Birdcraft Museum
314 Unquowa Rd.
203-259-0416
www.ctaudubon.org/birdcraft-home

Edgerton Center for the Performing Arts
5151 Park Ave.
203-371-7908
www.edgertoncenter.org

Fairfield Museum and History Center
370 Beach Rd.
203-259-1598
www.fairfieldhistory.org

Fairfield Theatre Company
70 Sanford St.
203-259-1036
www.fairfieldtheatre.org

Parks and Recreation
www.fairfieldct.org/recreation

Pequot Library
720 Pequot Ave., Southport
203-259-0346
www.pequotlibrary.org

Public Libraries
1080 Old Post Rd.
1147 Fairfield Woods Rd.
203-256-3155
www.fairfieldct.org/library

Quick Center for the Arts
1073 North Benson Rd.
203-254-4010
quickcenter.fairfield.edu

[Passport Stamp / Signature & Date Here]

Greenwich

By Anastasia Mills Healy, travel writer and author of ***Secret Connecticut: A Guide to the Weird, Wonderful, and Obscure***

The Gateway to New England, Greenwich is the first town in Connecticut when crossing the New York border. Founded in 1640, it has a long history of prosperity, attracting scions of industry who leveraged a busy port and business-friendly proximity to New York City. While Greenwich is known for mansions built on rolling lawns, high-end stores, and restaurants, the town has much history and culture, including a destination-worthy museum and rousing polo matches.

Interesting Places

The Bruce Museum is an art, science, and natural history museum with a permanent collection that includes everything from a Native American wigwam to glow-in-the-dark geodes; rotating exhibitions feature well-known artists such as Andy Warhol, Toulouse-Lautrec, and Alfred Sisley. There's a great playground across the street. Tues.-Sun. 10 AM-5 PM. Admission: adults $20, seniors & students $15, children under 5 free. The museum is scheduled to complete a multi-year building project in April 2023.

The c.1730 Bush-Holley House, a National Historic Landmark, was first the home of a prosperous merchant and later the site of the first American Impressionist art colony. The house is interpreted in both eras and is part of the campus of the Greenwich Historical Society, which also operates an art gallery and a museum with rotating exhibitions and hosts many events relating to art and history. Admission: $10 adult, $8 seniors, under 18 free. Wed.-Sun. Noon-4 PM. Bush-Holley House Tours Wed.-Sun., 1, 2, and 3 PM or by appointment.

If your taste is contemporary art, schedule a visit to the Brant Foundation Art Study Center, a small museum on the gorgeous property of billionaire Peter Brant. Mon.-Fri., 10 AM-4 PM by appointment only. Free.

The New England version of Rodeo Drive, a stroll down Greenwich Avenue (from West Putnam Ave. to Railroad Ave.) takes you past retailers like Lily Pulitzer and Saks Fifth Avenue as well as home-grown stores such as Hoagland's and Vineyard Vines. Restaurants and coffee shops are dotted throughout.

If you're visiting on a Sunday afternoon in June, July, or September, check to see if there's a polo match at the Greenwich Polo Club, a spectacular site for high-goal polo. Bring your own picnic, purchase from food vendors, or buy a VIP ticket for reserved space and other amenities. $40 per car.

Other events include Art to the Avenue in May and June's Greenwich International Film Festival. In December, head to Sam Bridge Nursery for the Greenwich Reindeer Festival with live reindeer and photos with Santa.

The town's beaches are for residents only but there are many parks and preservation areas that are open to the public, including Pomerance Park at 101 Orchard St.; Cognewaugh Trails begins at Cognewaugh Rd. in Greenwich and continues to Merriebrook Ln. in Stamford; Babcock Preserve between North St. & Lake Ave.; and Montgomery Pinetum, at 150 Bible St., Cos Cob.

The c.1730 National Historic Landmark Bush-Holley House is the centerpiece of the Greenwich Historical Society's campus, which also includes museum galleries, a café, a library, and an education center. The House was the setting for the first American Impressionist art colony. Greenwich Historical Society

Notes

Greenwich Audubon Center manages seven public nature sanctuaries in Greenwich totaling 686 acres. The main one at 613 Riversville Rd. in western Greenwich opened in 1943 and became the National Audubon Society's first environmental education center. There are seven miles of trails that wind through and around fields, forests, lakes, and ponds on 285 acres. The wonderful Kimberlin Nature Education Center building houses a children's area, exhibition space, coffee lounge, and store.

Greenwich is known for its mansions, many which can be viewed from the water. Anastasia Mills Healy

High goal polo is played in Greenwich many Sunday afternoons in season. Anastasia Mills Healy

Address Book

Town Site
www.greenwichct.org

Babcock Preserve
Between North St. & Lake Ave.

Brant Foundation Art Study Center
941 North St.
203-869-0611
www.brantfoundation.org

The Bruce Museum
1 Museum Dr.
203-869-0376
www.brucemuseum.org

Cognewaugh Trails
Begins at Cognewaugh Rd., Greenwich & continues to Merriebrook Ln., Stamford

Greenwich Audubon Center
613 Riversville Rd.
www.greenwich.audubon.org

Greenwich Avenue
West Putnam Ave. to Railroad Ave.

Greenwich Historical Society Museum Bush-Holley House
47 Strickland Rd.
203-869-6899
www.greenwichhistory.org

Greenwich Polo Club
1 Hurlingham Dr.
203-561-1639
www.greenwichpoloclub.com

Montgomery Pinetum
150 Bible St., Cos Cob.

Pomerance Park
101 Orchard St.

[Passport Stamp / Signature & Date Here]

Monroe

By Marven Moss, Monroe resident and freelance writer

Monroe is a bucolic suburban Fairfield Co. community (pop. c.20,000) between Bridgeport and Danbury. Settled formally in 1762 as an ecclesiastical authority called the New Stratford Society, the town was incorporated as a municipality in 1823 and named after the fifth president of the U.S., James Monroe, 1758-1831.

Many of the early saltboxes and post-and-beam style residences with their Colonial barns still stand with contemporary updating in the Monroe Historic District and the neighborhoods known as the East Village, Stevenson, Stepney, and Upper Stepney (or Birdsey's Plain). While the classic rustic New England appeal remains, the agricultural character of the town has been transformed. Grassy expanses that once supported dairy and poultry farms, apple and pear orchards and lush fields of strawberries, blueberries and raspberries have been redeveloped into sidewalk-less streets of carefully-groomed residential lawns and homes of fashionable architecture inhabited by commuters.

By 2018, barely 500 acres of working farms survived, leaving church-sponsored apple and strawberry festivals in season on the Town Green as a heritage of tillage. Now the residential layering extends out from Rt. 25 (Main St.) and Rt. 111 (Monroe Turnpike), state highways that form a V-shaped commercial corridor lined with specialty shops and restaurants offering reasonably-priced cuisine. And the past has been preserved by the Monroe Historical Society (est. 1959) in three buildings that are virtual museums filled with the farm implements of yesteryear, antique furniture, and period clothing: Eliot Beardsley Homestead (c.1780), Methodist Meeting House (c.1811) and the Old Schoolhouse (c.1790).

Today 18 aluminum roadside markers, collectively known as the Stepney Heritage Trail, depict sites like the Stepney Railroad Depot of bygone days, the old toll roads, and one-room schoolhouses that have been converted into residences.

For outdoor recreation, Monroe offers an expansive patchwork of parklands and easy-to-walk trails. Five footpaths crisscross 131-acre Webb Mountain Park with 10 campsites (basic overnight permit, $10, available from the Monroe Parks and Recreation Department). One path is an ascent to a landmark called Goat Rock that affords a captivating view of the Housatonic River Valley. An additional 171 acres of wooded open space is available contiguously in the Discovery Zone where 26 learning stations provide education exhibits with environmental themes. At the Chalk Hill Nature Preserve, two abandoned mine shafts, where men with picks and shovels once dug for quartz and possibly silver, are accessible for limited exploration and the trail leads past a massive boulder called Whale Rock where a fissure looks like the gaping mouth of a behemoth.

William E. Wolfe Park is an outstanding 215-acre recreational complex with trout-stocked Great Hollow Lake and a sandy beach as a centerpiece. The park contains four baseball diamonds, football and soccer fields, a 25-meter, six-lane outdoor swimming pool, eight tennis courts (two reconfigured for pickleball), basketball and

Lake Zoar was completed in 1919 with the building of the Stevenson Dam on the Housatonic River. It provides electricity and recreation for residents. Cargill Photography

Notes

volleyball courts, walking paths, provision for outdoor summer theater and layouts for devotees of bocce, horseshoes, and shuffleboard, all bordered by a section of the Rails-to-Trails hiking and bicycling route cutting 4.2 miles through forestland. Another footpath, the Paugussett Trail, also known as the Blue Blaze or Blue Dot Trail, runs past the stone ruins of a waterwheel-driven factory that produced hoopskirts and twine in the 1800s.

With three other communities, Monroe shares a shoreline on Lake Zoar, a 975-acre reservoir for boating, swimming, and fishing for bass, walleye, and trout, created when the Stevenson Dam was built in 1917-19 as a hydroelectric generating station and remaining today one of the few dams in the U.S. traversed by a state highway (Rt. 34). Below the dam, the Housatonic River shoreline is a habitat for nesting eagles.

Other points of interest in town are Washington Lodge of the Masonic Temple off the Town Green (est. 1791) in a majestic building erected in 1904, architecturally resembling part of the White House, and WMNR Fine Arts Radio (88.1 FM), a volunteer-driven 5,000-watt nonprofit that broadcasts classical, big band, and jazz music from studios on Main Street.

Famous Figures

Mike Gminski, 6' 11" NBA player.

Mary O'Hara (1885-1980), author of *My Friend Flicka*.

The majestic 1904 Washington Lodge of the Masonic Temple on Fan Hill Rd. in Monroe. John Babina

Address Book

Town Site
www.monroe.ct.gov

Eliot Beardsley Homestead
31 Great Ring Rd.

Methodist Meeting House
433 Barn Hill Rd.

The Old Schoolhouse
311 Wheeler Rd.

Washington Lodge of the Masonic Temple
1 Fan Hill Rd., off the Town Green

William E. Wolfe Park
285 Cutlers Farm Rd.

WMNR Fine Arts Radio
731 Main St.
203-268-9667
www.wmnr.org

[Passport Stamp / Signature & Date Here]

New Canaan

By Nancy Geary, Executive Director, New Canaan Museun & Historical Society

The area that is now New Canaan was originally settled around 1715 as part of the towns of Norwalk and Stamford. In 1731, the Connecticut legislature approved a new Congregational Parish to accommodate families who lived far from existing parishes and named it Canaan Parish. New Canaan was finally incorporated 70 years later in May 1801.

Agriculture and milling were the town's primary industries. Shoe manufacturing, first introduced in 1818, rapidly expanded to become the town's dominant industry. Its growth led to the establishment of the downtown area as new roads were laid out and land subdivided for development. The height of the shoemaking boom was in 1850, but failure to install new automatic sewing machines right before the Civil War did not allow the shoemakers to keep up with the wartime demand. The last shoemaker closed in 1913.

To attract new businesses and new employment opportunities, local businessmen financed the construction of a railroad spur from Stamford in 1866. The New Canaan Railroad eventually became part of the New York, New Haven & Hartford railroad in 1890. The increased accessibility made the town desirable as a vacation retreat. Large summer estates were constructed. Many of the summer people decided to become permanent residents and encouraged their friends and families to relocate. The New Canaan Historical Society was founded in 1889. By the end of World War II, the town had developed a vital downtown area with a bustling suburban community.

Then in the late 1940s and early 50s, New Canaan attracted a group of modern architects who had studied at Harvard University's School of Architecture under Walter Gropius, the founder of the Bauhaus School of Design. These young architects, Eliot Noyes, John Johansen, Landis Gores, Philip Johnson, and Marcel Breuer, became known as "The Harvard Five." Throughout New Canaan, many of these ground-breaking mid-century modern houses designed by members of The Harvard Five and others still stand, including three in the National Register of Historic Places: The Glass House, The Gores Pavilion, and The Hodgson House.

New Canaan today is a vibrant town of approx. 20,000. Its walkable business district is filled with shops and restaurants that are open year-round. The active Chamber of Commerce publishes a full calendar of events. Visitors will find the locals friendly and welcoming.

Interesting Places

New Canaan Museum & Historical Society. Its museums include a 1764 residence, two one-room schoolhouses, a tool museum, a mid-century modern pavilion, New Canaan's first pharmacy, and the Rogers Studio, New Canaan's first designated National Landmark building and home to the largest collection of John Rogers' sculptures in the country. Its lectures and exhibits are open to the public.

The Glass House. Tours of Philip Johnson's iconic home, grounds, and art collection run from May through November.

Waveny House. The former

The Hanford-Silliman House in New Canaan. NCHS

NOTES

Fairfield Hills Campus. Originally Fairfield Hills State Hospital, an asylum constructed in the 1930s and closed in 1995. The hospital was used as the set of the juvenile facility in the film "Sleepers." It fell into disrepair and is reputed to be haunted. It was purchased by the town in 2001. In addition to Newtown's new municipal office, the campus offers public walking trails and a community garden. The plan for the campus includes retail stores, offices, restaurants, banks, and sports and cultural activities. Many of the original buildings are boarded up awaiting renovation.

Castle Hill Farm. Castle Hill Farm offers lots of fun fall activities: pick-your-own pumpkins, 7-acre corn maze, hay rides, petting zoo, and pony rides, as well as an annual Ukrainian Festival in September!

The Orchard Hill Nature Center. The park has hiking trails through diverse habitats and contains two historical mills and dams, which date back to the early part of the 19th century.

Eichler's Cove Beach and Marina. This park offers the only public access to Lake Zoar. The park has a marina, boat launch, picnic area, and a small beach. A park permit is required.

Ferris Acres Creamery. Seasonal ice cream shop on a true family farm with three generations involved. Sit and watch the cows graze in the pastures while you enjoy a treat.

Newtown is the only town in Connecticut with a steel flagpole in the middle of its main street. So be careful driving since there is no traffic light. Pam Rinaldi

ADDRESS BOOK

Town Site
www.newtown-ct.gov

Castle Hill Farm
40 Sugar Ln.
www.castlehillfarm.net

Edmond Town Hall
45 Main St.
203-270-4285
www.edmondtownhall.org

Eichler's Cove Beach and Marina
11 Old Bridge Rd.
www.newtown-ct.gov

Fairfield Hills Campus
3 Primrose St.
203-270-4282
www.fairfieldhills.org

Ferris Acres Creamery
144 Sugar St.
203-426-8803
www.ferrisacrescreamery.com

Matthew Curtiss House Museum
44 Main St.
203-426-5937
www.newtownhistory.org

Newtown Meeting House
31 Main St.
203-270-8293
www.newtownmeetinghouse.com

Orchard Hill Nature Center
20 Huntingtown Rd.
www.newtown-ct.gov

[Passport Stamp / Signature & Date Here]

Norwalk

By Richard McQuaid, Norwalk Town Clerk

The history of the City of Norwalk predates its consolidation in 1913 by 273 years when on Feb. 26, 1640, Roger Ludlow entered into a treaty with the Norwalk tribe and purchased "all lands lying between the Saugatuck and Norwalk rivers, to the middle of said rivers, and from the sea, a day's walk into the country." This was what is now, East Norwalk.

Another portion of early Norwalk was the central portion comprising "the meadows and uplands adjoining, lying off the west side of the Norwalk River. It was purchased by Daniell Patrick.

In these early deeds and other references, Norwalk was spelled either Norwalke or Norwake. Sometimes even Northwalk or Norrwake. Early on, it was believed that the name Norwalk came from "north walk," which was a day's walk to the northern edge of the land. Its derivation, more likely, comes from an early native word, "naromake" or "naramake."

On Feb., 15, 1651, the western part of the lands was purchased by 12 men and added to the area of Norwalk which included Rowayton and the Norwalk Islands.

More settlers made their way to the new lands from Hartford and the north to East Norwalk where they began to settle. This end point was marked with the "Founder's Stone" in 1896 which was placed at the corner of East Avenue at Fitch Street by the Norwalk chapter of the DAR. It began:

"Norwalk founded A.D. 1649. Its earliest homes were planted in the vicinity of this stone."

In 1651 Norwalk became a town. In 1836 it was reincorporated as a borough and as a city in 1893. It was 20 years later, in 1913, that its "consolidation" created the current City of Norwalk.

Interesting Places

Maritime Aquarium. Home to over 2,000 fish and marine mammals, including sharks, turtles, river otters, and seals all of which are housed in natural habitats from the area of Long Island Sound.

The Lockwood-Mathews Mansion Museum. Built by railroad baron LeGrand Lockwood in the 1860s, it is filled with exquisite Gilded Age interiors and antique furniture and features several excellent exhibits.

Stepping Stones Museum for Children. Has many educational-based exhibits, displays, and programs. It features several hands-on interactive exhibits that encourage children to explore, discover, inquire, and learn.

SoNo (South Norwalk Historic District). Originally a settlement called Old Well, South Norwalk is today a colorful, bustling area home to over 30 restaurants, buzzing bars and nightclubs, trendy stores and boutiques, an array of museums, theaters, and galleries, and sightseeing attractions. It also has beautiful scenic walks along the Norwalk River and Harbor, which visitors can explore by bike or on foot, as well as an array of beer gardens, pubs, and wine bars.

The SoNo Switch Tower Museum. The 1896 Switch Tower showcases the history of the "towers" that housed the mechanism used to switch trains from one track to another. The museum delves into the story of "Signal Station 44" and

The Maritime Aquarium is in SONO with more than 30 freshwater & saltwater exhibits, including a touch tank, IMAX theater, and cafe. Bob McDougall

Notes

its 88-year-old history, as well as the people behind the operation of switching the tracks.

Sheffield Island Lighthouse (1868) and Nature Trail. Visitors can explore the lighthouse and the beautiful surrounding area on a guided walk that offers a fascinating insight into the history and heritage of the lighthouse.

Norwalk Historical Society Museum. Manages and operates the Norwalk Historical Society Museum and Mill Hill Historic Park.

The 62-room Lockwood-Mathews Mansion Museum, a Second Empire style country house at 295 West Ave. Norwalk, was built in 1864-68 by railroad and banking magnate LeGrand Lockwood. Bob McDougall

Address Book

Town Site
www.norwalkct.org

Lockwood-Mathews Mansion Museum
295 West Ave.
203-838-9799
www.lockwoodmathewsmansion.com

Maritime Aquarium
Mathews Park (303 West Ave.)
203-852-0700
www.maritimeaquarium.org

Norwalk Historical Society Museum
141 East Ave.
203-846-0525
www. norwalkpubliclibrary.org

Sheffield Island Lighthouse and Nature Trail
40 N. Water St., Seaport Dock
203-838-9444

SoNo Switch Tower Museum
77 Washington St., South Norwalk.
203-246-6958

Stepping Stones Museum for Children
Mathews Park (303 West Ave.)
203-899-0606
www.steppingstonesmuseum.org

[Passport Stamp / Signature & Date Here]

Redding

By Thomas Borysiewicz, former resident & librarian at Bethel Public Library

The Town of Redding was first settled in the late 1600s as Northfield, part of Fairfield. The town eventually came to be known as Reading, later changed to Redding. While stories differ as to the origin of the name most people claim the town is named for one of its largest landowners, John Read, who is depicted on the town seal purchasing the land from Chicken Warrups, a Native American possibly from the Mohawk tribe. Warrups Farm, operated by descendants of John Read, is near the land owned by Chicken and John Read.

During the Revolutionary War over 3000 men were encamped during the winter of 1778-1779 at three different camps spread across the town. The main encampment was at what is known today as Putnam Memorial State Park, which maintains a museum and several reconstructed buildings.

Redding is a very peaceful town, bounded mostly by the Aspetuck and Saugatuck rivers, which flow south to Long Island Sound. An idyllic country setting, Redding is often voted one of the best places to live. The Town Center maintains a quintessential New England feel with a large Town Green and Church Steeple. While the town retains much of its colonial charm, with several houses dating to the time of the Revolution, it has seen many modern advances and updates. An active Land Trust preserves open space in the town and maintains many wonderful trails for hiking and recreation.

Redding has been home to many notable people from politicians to artists. Joel Barlow, a noted Poet and Diplomat, was born in the town and the High School is named for him. Anna Hyatt Huntington, a sculptor known for her equestrian statues, most notably of El Cid, had her studio and home in town. Upon her death, her property was donated to the State and made into Huntington State Park. Samuel Clemens made his home in Redding for a short time and was integral to the founding of the Mark Twain Library.

Interesting Places

Lonetown Farm. Home of the Redding Historical Society and Museum.

Huntington State Park. Named after Collis Potter Huntington (1821-1900), the railroad tycoon. who became one of the wealthiest men in the country in the late century by his promotion and completion of the first transcontinental railroad. Hiking trails and canoeing.

Putnam Memorial State Park. Maj. Gen. Israel Putnam chose this site for his encampment in the winter of 1778-1779. It is the oldest Connecticut state park, created in 1887. There is a hiking trail and an historic museum celebrating colonial life and the Revolutionary War.

Mark Twain Library. A center for intellectual, educational, social and cultural enrichment, providing a wide variety of materials, resources, and programs for all ages.

Saugatuck Falls Natural Area. Forested park bisected by the Saugatuck River, offering 5+ miles of trails. Across from John Read Middle School off Rt. 53, 491 Redding Rd.

Top Stone Park. Forested 280-acre park with a picturesque lake used for swimming and kayaking, plus nature trails.

The Mark Twain Library (1908) named after its founder Samuel Clemens. Sara Zimmerman

Notes

Noted sculptor Anna Hyatt Huntington's Wolves statue welcomes visitors at the entrance to Huntington State Park. www.stateparks.com

General Israel Putnam shouted a warning to his men to retreat before they were surrounded. The British pursued and fired at Putnam who fled on his mount. Putnam and horse plummeted down a steep flight of stone steps to the valley floor making their escape. The statue stands at the entrance of Putnam Memorial Park and Visitor Center Museum. DEEP

Address Book

Town Site
www.townofreddingct.org

Huntington State Park
Sunset Hill Rd.
www.ct.gov/deep

Lonetown Farm
43 Lonetown Rd.
reddinghistoricalsociety@gmail.com

Mark Twain Library
439 West Redding Rd., West Redding
203-938-2545
www.marktwainlibrary.org

Putnam Memorial State Park
Putnam Park Rd. (Rt. 58)
203-938-2357
www.putnampark.org

Top Stone Park
72 Topstone Rd.
www.townofreddingct.org

[Passport Stamp / Signature & Date Here]

Ridgefield

By Kay Ables, Monica McMorran, and Sharon Dunphy, Ridgefield Historical Society

Ridgefield is comprised of 35 square miles, bordered on the north by Danbury, south by Wilton, east by Redding, and west by Westchester Co., NY.

In the latter years of the 17th century the town of Norwalk sent surveyors north to search for land to settle a new plantation. They found a land with gently rolling hills and exceptional beauty set on three north/south ridges which the Native Americans called "Caudatowa," meaning "high land." Ridgefield was founded in 1708 by the Congregational Society of Norwalk, on land purchased from the Ramapo tribe. In November of 1708 at a meeting of the Proprietors, a lottery was held to give 25 settlers 2-1/2 acres of home lot land facing the newly planned Towne St. Immediately after each Proprietor was given additional farm land.

Ridgefield was primarily an agricultural community. Small industries such as blacksmithing, tanneries, clothing manufacturers, and candle making provided the necessities of life.

Ridgefield was divided between remaining loyal to the King or joining the patriots. At first the citizens voted to remain with the King, but on the 17th Dec. 1775 they voted to transfer their loyalty to the Continental Congress.

In April, 1777, British commander General Tryon, landed at Compo Beach in today's Westport, and marched his men north to destroy provisions being stored in Danbury. After burning and looting the town the army proceeded south through Ridgefield on its way back to the ships. The only inland battle in Connecticut ensued, with American forces led by Generals David Wooster, Gold Selleck Silliman and Benedict Arnold engaging the enemy at a hastily built barricade on Ridgefield's Main St. Today the 'Battle of Ridgefield' is still remembered with reenactments and parades.

Not long after that battle Benedict Arnold turned traitor. He gave the plans of West Point to British Major John Andre to deliver to British headquarters in New York City. Along the way Andre was stopped by men who discovered the plans and turned him over to the Americans stationed in South Salem, NY. The officer in charge was Joshua King. During his captivity King and Andre became friends, and King walked with Andre to his execution.

After the war Joshua King, settled in Ridgefield, married the minister's daughter and became a leading citizen. His descendants became major landowners. In the latter part of the 19th century the Kings sold parcels of land on High Ridge to New York City friends who came to build summer cottages, and the era of the "summer people" began. After a devastating fire in 1895 that burned much of the business area of town, a much-needed fire department was formed, wooden buildings were rebuilt with brick; electricity, water, telephones and a sewer system were formed, all with the help and money of the summer people.

Ridgefield was the home of two brothers, Phineas and George Lounsbury, who both became governors of the state. Notable writers, politicians, artists, and actors made their homes here. The studio of J. Alden Weir, (an impressionist painter) and 60 acres

The Ridgefield Historical Society has its headquarters in the restored 1714 David Scott red saltbox house at 4 Sunset Ln. Kay Ables

NOTES

of land have become a National Historic Site. Eugene O'Neill wrote "Desire Under the Elms" here; opera singer Geraldine Farrar and, actors Robert Vaughn and David Cassidy were also residents.

Today we are blessed with a beautiful, tree-lined Main St. graced with historic mansions, stately churches, museums, unique boutiques, and sidewalk cafes.

INTERESTING PLACES TO VISIT

The Museum in the Streets. A heritage discovery trail for the community and visitors featuring permanent markers at 32 "stations of history."

Keeler Tavern Museum. An 18th century revolutionary tavern and inn with a cannonball still lodged in its side.

Keeler Tavern Museum c.1772 provides educational and cultural programs on colonial life. There are exhibitions and public events in its carriage house, and a garden for hosting special events. Kay Ables

Weir Farm National Historic Site. A National Park Service property that preserves the farm/studio of the American impressionist painter J. Alden Weir.

Aldrich Contemporary Art Museum. A world-famous modern art museum.

Ridgefield Playhouse. Features live concerts and events.

Prospector Theater. A state of the art movie theater that creates jobs for disabled adults.

Lounsbury House (1896). The home of former governor Phineas Lounsbury is in the National Historic Register and functions as our Community Center.

Peter Parley Schoolhouse. A charming red schoolhouse museum.

The Ridgefield Historical Society. The Society is in a red saltbox house from 1714.

ADDRESS BOOK

Town Site
www.ridgefieldct.org

Aldrich Contemporary Art Museum
258 Main St.
www.aldrichart.org

Keeler Tavern Museum
132 Main St.
www.keelertavernmuseum.org

Lounsbury House
316 Main St.
www.lounsburyhouse.org

Peter Parley Schoolhouse
Intersection of West Ln. & Rte. 35
203-438-5821
www.ridgefieldhistoricalsociety.org

Prospector Theater
25 Prospect St.
www.prospectortheater.org

Ridgefield Historical Society
4 Sunset Ln.
203-438-5821
ridgefieldhistory@sbcglobal.net

Ridgefield Playhouse
80 E. Ridge Rd.
www.ridgefieldplayhouse.org

Weir Farm National Historic Site
www.nps.gov/wefa

[Passport Stamp / Signature & Date Here]

Shelton

By Martin Coughlin, President Shelton Historical Society

In the 1690s, English settlers from Stratford felt the pinch of overcrowding and began moving north, settling along the current Long Hill Ave. They named the area Corum. By 1717, there were 50 families living in Corum and they petitioned the Colonial government to incorporate Corum into a town named Ripton Parish. The town was primarily an agricultural community. By 1789 the town had grown large enough to reorganize itself under the name of Huntington, named for Samuel Huntington who was the governor of Connecticut. The people took advantage of its location on the Housatonic River and began building ships. Soon the town, along with Derby on the other side of the river, became a major seaport trading up and down the eastern United States and down to the West Indies.

Shipbuilding dwindled after the War of 1812 and farmers turned to the production of goods such as milk, butter, fruit, and vegetables which could be sold locally and in New Haven, Bridgeport, and as far away as New York City. All that changed when in 1870 the Ousatonic Water Co. built a dam across the river. Abundant cheap water power and local canals sparked the industrialization of the downtown area. By 1896, more than 25 manufacturers lined the canal. Shelton greeted visitors with a sign: "Welcome to Shelton, Home of a Mile of Factories." Plentiful jobs attracted immigrants from Germany, Ireland, Italy, and the Slavic countries to the downtown area. The growth of the area caused Huntington to incorporate as a city and rename itself Shelton after one of its major industrialists, Edward Shelton.

During the 1900s the heavy industries that dominated the city died off, and the town reinvented itself. The completion of Rt. 8 in 1975 made Shelton convenient to Bridgeport and Waterbury. With open land and low taxes Shelton became a magnet for post-industrial businesses. Today Shelton continues to be an attractive business and residential community.

Points of Interest

Shelton History Center. The restored 1913 Brownson Farm House, the Wilson Barn Museum, Trap Fall School House, and the Carriage House. Buildings and grounds are open for tours.

Jones Family Farms and Winery. The home for pick-your-own strawberries, blueberries, pumpkins, and Christmas trees. The farm offers its own wines and wine tasting on weekends.

Shelton Memorial Park and River Walk. Walk along the scenic Housatonic River in downtown Shelton and stroll past monuments dedicated to Shelton veterans who died in American wars from the Civil War to those of today.

Shelton Farmer's Market. Offers locally grown foods and flowers. Open Sat. 9 AM-1 PM from May to Nov. and Wed. from 3-5:30 PM.

Long Hill Burying Grounds 1720. The oldest cemetery in town and burial site of many of the founding families of the community.

Shelton Trails. 15 miles of gentle walking trails. These well-maintained trails are open to all hikers.

The Shelton History Center consists of the c.1822 Brownson House, the c.1860 Wilson Barn, the one room c.1872 Trap Fall School, a carriage barn housing a collection of horse-drawn vehicles, a corncrib, and an outhouse. Deborah G. Rossi

Notes

The Rinks at Shelton. The Rinks offers ice skating, a golf driving range, miniature golf, and an entertainment arcade for children and adults.

Indian Well State Park. Offers swimming, boating and picnicking during the summer months. Off Rt. 110 along the Housatonic River.

At the Jones Family Farms you can pick strawberries, blueberries, pumpkins, etc., or you can cut your own Christmas tree. You can then enjoy a glass of wine made from their vineyard. Deborah G. Rossi

Address Book

Town Site
www.cityofshelton.org

Indian Wells State Park
1 Indian Wells Rd.
www.ct.gov/deep

Jones Family Farms and Winery
606 Walnut Hill Rd.
203-929-8425
www.jonesfamilyfarms.com

Long Hill Burying Grounds
246 Long Hill Ave., near the intersection with Constitution Ave.

The Rinks at Shelton
784 River Rd.
203-929-6500
www.rinksatshelton.com

Shelton Farmer's Market
100 Canal St.
www.sheltonctfarmersmarket.com

Shelton History Center
70 Ripton Rd. & Cloverdale Ave.
203-925-1803
www.sheltonhistoricalsociety.org

Shelton Trails
To find more information and to access maps: www.sheltonconservation.org/recreation/shelton_trails.html

[Passport Stamp / Signature & Date Here]

SHERMAN

By John Cilio, Sherman resident and author, www.vintageflyer.com

Sherman is a picturesque, rural New England town that has been named "Best Small Town in Connecticut" by *Connecticut Magazine* more than once. It offers miles of wooded trails, a small historic district, a vibrant JCC entertainment venue, a seasonal Playhouse, a delightful set of shops, and an award-winning winery. Sherman is the northernmost and least populated town of Fairfield County, situated in the Litchfield Hills. It's the county's only town with an 860-area code.

Approximately 90 minutes from Manhattan, Sherman was the 111th town to be incorporated in the state. It is named for former resident Roger Sherman, one of America's founding fathers. In 1787, he suggested a compromise for the developing U.S. Congress, where representation in the House of Representatives would be according to state population and in the Senate by equal numbers for each state.

Sherman's public school supports Pre-K through Grade 8 giving students and their parents a choice of neighboring town high schools. According to the 2021 census, Sherman is one of the more educated communities in America with 60% of its adults having a college or an advanced degree compared to the national average of 39%.

INTERESTING PLACES

Sherman offers an eclectic collection of interesting indoor and outdoor places to visit, including its two restaurants. A delightful mainstay is The American Pie Company. It's a busy, family restaurant with a full bakery where everything is homemade daily on the premises. It is consistently voted Connecticut's Best Pie by *Connecticut Magazine*. Our other restaurant, The Painted Lemon featuring old-world Italian, is open for dinner only. It's designed to excite all of your senses with impeccable selections and service.

Visit the family operated boutique winery, White Silo Farm and Winery, offering award-winning wines including a specialty, Sangria. Its revolving art gallery will temp your senses as do the cheese platters or the gourmet picnic lunch boxes. For instant picnics, stop by the IGA deli for an incredible sandwich made on demand. Or maybe you are into a cup of coffee? We're blessed to have Sacred Grounds Coffee Roasters, a small batch roastery where you can select from several fresh brewed delights or take home a special package of freshly roasted coffee.

Happy Rainbows is a most interesting "new age" shop in Sherman. The proprietress is an herbalist who, since 1997, operates the store replete with herbs, tinctures, natural remedies, essential oils, crystals and handmade jewelry.

Active trail hikers will enjoy the Appalachian Trail which goes through the northern end of Sherman or Squantz Pond State Park in the south of town. Also in Sherman is Connecticut Audubon Society's Deer Pond Farm. It's an 850-acre nature preserve with 15 miles of trails through forests, meadows, and wetlands. It's open to the public every day from dawn to dusk for self-guided hikes, with guided programs offered throughout the month. It's a great place to hike, snowshoe, cross-country ski or sit and watch for wildlife.

Historically speaking, in 1991, the Sherman Historic District joined the National Register of Historic Places. The Sherman Historical Society features two treasures: The Northrop House (1829) and the Sherman Old Store Museum and Gift Shop (1802). The Federal era Northrop house has served as a public house/tavern where one could find a bed, food, and drink. The second-floor ballroom was a general meeting place while today it hosts the Roger Sherman Learning Center which is open by

Notes

appointment only. The property still includes the cow barn and a lovely pasture with an adjoining forest hiking trail. The Old Store Museum and Gift Shop (3 Rt. 37 Center) is housed in the town's first mercantile exchange. Today it features a large selection of men's and women's gifts, handbags and surprises for every age group. They like to say, "We have a little of a lot." The building also features a store museum reminiscent of 1867.

The Sherman Library offers public Wi-Fi, a revolving art exhibit, and a peaceful place to read. Visit their website for event, artists and book sale dates. Speaking of books, in visiting Sherman, maybe you'll experience the ghost featured in the Graham Masterton's novel, Spirit, set in Sherman during the 1940s and 1950s.

All of these locations are a place you can get your Connecticut 169 Club book signed or stamped for having visited Sherman.

The 1802 Old Store Museum and Gift Shop was acquired by the Sherman Historical Society in 1998 with the intent of preserving the building and its tradition of being a store. SHS

Address Book

Town Site
www.townofshermanct.org

The American Pie Company
29 Rt. 37 Center
860-350-0662
www.americanpiecompany.com

Connecticut Audubon Deer Pond Farm
57 Wakeman Hill Rd.
860-799-4074
www.ctaudubon.org/deerpondfarm

Happy Rainbows
11 Rt. 39 #4
860-355-4959
www.happyrainbows.com

Old Store Museum & Gift Shop
3 Rt. 37 Center
860-350-3475
www.shermanhistoricalsociety.org

Sherman Historical Society
10 Rt. 37 Center
860-354-3083
www.shermanhistoricalsociety.org

The Sherman Library
1 Rt. 37 Center
860-354-2455
www.shermanlibrary.org

White Silo Farm & Winery
32 Rt. 37 East
860-355-0271
www.whitesilowinery.com

[Passport Stamp / Signature & Date Here]

Stamford

By Wes Haynes, Co-Director, External Partnerships Connecticut Trust for Historic Preservation and Reed Deluca, Stamford resident

The City of Stamford, in southwestern Fairfield Co. is the state's third most populous city (c.130,000 in 2016). First settled as Rippowam in 1641 by Congregationalists from the Wethersfield colony after what may have been a religious disagreement, it was renamed Stamford the next year after the English town in Lincolnshire. The agricultural settlement grew slowly over the next two centuries, with Anglicans settling by the 1720s and several men serving in the British army in 1756 during the French and Indian War. Although local loyalties were split during the War of Independence, Stamford was the launching point of Major Benjamin Tallmadge's successful "whale boat" nighttime raid on loyalist supplies at Lloyd's Neck across the sound, and a place of supply, training and encampment for American forces.

The arrival of the railroad in 1848 transformed Stamford from an agricultural town (incorporated as a borough in 1830) with small scattered mill villages to an industrial center along the shoreline incorporated as a city in 1893. Known primarily for Yale locks, Phillips Milk of Magnesia, extracts, and later postage meters, the first neighborhoods for immigrant workers were close to factories in the Cove, South End, Waterside and downtown. In the twentieth century, former farmland and mill villages beyond this area were gradually re-developed with new neighborhoods (West Side, Hubbard Heights, Belltown, Turn of River, Springdale, Glenbrook, East Side and Shippan) in the early 1900s. After World War II, urban renewal replaced much of the industrial downtown with office towers occupied (in 2017) as headquarters for four Fortune 500 and nine Fortune 1000 corporations. Stamford, the "Gateway to Connecticut," is 48 minutes by MetroNorth to Manhattan.

Interesting Places

Stamford Downtown. Over 80 restaurants and clubs, 100s of stores and services, movies and live theatres, galleries and special events. Nightlife centers on the city's historic core.

Alive @ 5 / Summer Concert Series. Live music attracts after-work crowds to Columbus Park. Thursday summer nights have great music, great dancing, and great times.

Cove Island Beach and Park. A city park with two sandy beaches, a 1-mile loop walking/running trail, children's play area, a rollerblade/cycling path, and expansive lawn areas for kite-flying, all developed from the site of the Stamford Manufacturing Company (1844-1919).

Palace Theatre. An incredible concert and 1927 vaudeville theatre venue that brings the world's best in arts and entertainment.

The Stamford Museum & Nature Center. An art, history, nature, and agricultural sciences museum it is home to a 10-acre working farm, a museum and gallery which hosts exhibitions, an interactive nature center, 80 acres of outdoor trails, and a large planetarium.

The Ferguson Library. With its Georgian Revival portico (1913), the library provides information, programs, and activities.

Stamford History Center. Exhibits on history of Stamford and a research library.

The 83-acre Cove Island Beach and Park on Long Island Sound is great for picnics, swimming, walking, fishing, or just relaxing. Reed Deluca

NOTES

Public Golf Courses: Sterling Farms. An 18-hole public facility laid out over 144 acres, the facility is rated the #1 public golf course in Fairfield Co. year after year. The E. Gaynor Brennan. Features 5,935 yards from the longest tees for a par of 71.

The "Fish Church." The First Presbyterian Church of Stamford, designed by architect Wallace K. Harrison and nicknamed Fish Church for its unusual shape, is a unique example of modernist architecture, and an architectural landmark.

Curtain Call. With year-round performances in The Kweskin Theatre and The Dressing Room Theatre in historic barns of the Sterling Farm, and an annual free outdoor Shakespeare production. At least 12 full-scale productions each year.

Mianus River Park. Nearly 400-acre forest with dramatic landscapes, includes the Mianus River and its tributary streams, hiking trails, wetlands, a wildflower garden, and even a cave. Merribrook Lane.

Bartlett Arboretum. A 93-acre sanctuary of ecosystems for generations to explore and enjoy. It provides comprehensive environmental, horticulture and plant science educational programs for children and adults.

The Ferguson Library is a pleasant place for research and reading with a helpful staff. It also has a coffee shop and used bookstore. Jerry Dougherty

ADDRESS BOOK

Town Sites
www.stamfordct.gov
www.stamford-downtown.com

Bartlett Arboretum
151 Brookdale Rd.
www.bartlettarboretum.org

Cove Island Beach and Park
www.stamfordct.gov

Curtain Call
1349 Newfield Ave.
www.curtaincallinc.com

E. Gaynor Brennan Golf Course
www.brennangolf.com

The Ferguson Library
One Public Library Plaza
www.fergusonlibrary.org

The Fish Church
1101 Bedford St.
www.fishchurch.org

Mianus River Park
www.friendsofmianusriverpark.org

Palace Theatre
61 Atlantic St.
203-325-4466
www.palacestamford.org

The Stamford Museum & Nature Center
39 Scolfieldtown Rd.
www.stamfordmuseum.org

Stamford History Center
1508 High Ridge Rd.
www.stamfordhistory.org

Sterling Farms Golf Course
www.sterlingfarmsgc.com

[Passport Stamp / Signature & Date Here]

STRATFORD

By Mary Dean, Director of Economic Development in Stratford

Founded in 1639, Stratford is a community rich in history, and abundant in natural beauty.

Situated on Long Island Sound, and bounded to the east by the Housatonic River, Stratford has long viewed its waterfront as an important natural resource. The Town's location on Long Island Sound affords residents and visitors alike with two public bathing beaches, five marinas, several fishing piers, and two public boat-launching facilities.

Within an hour's drive of New York City, Stratford is the easternmost town in Fairfield County, Connecticut's 'Gold Coast.' Major highways I-95, Rts. 8 & 25, and the Merritt Parkway bisect Stratford, and provide convenient access to the entire Northeast corridor. Sikorsky Memorial Airport, located in the Lordship section of Stratford, provides commuter service to other cities in the northeast. Rail service provided by Metro North with connections to Amtrak further round out an excellent array of transportation choices.

Stratford has a long association with the aviation industry. Stratford became the birthplace of the American helicopter industry, when in 1939 Russian immigrant, Igor Sikorsky, successfully flew the first helicopter at this Stratford-based aircraft plant. More than a half-century later, Lockheed Martin-Sikorsky Aircraft, the world's leading helicopter manufacturer, still designs and produces state-of-the-art helicopters for both military and commercial applications at its sprawling manufacturing facility on Stratford's north side. Drawn by a highly skilled and productive work force, excellent access to transportation, and a large inventory of affordable housing, it's no surprise that many businesses have chosen to call Stratford home.

The diversity of Stratford's resources is as rich as its cultural heritage, ranging from the 250-acre, town-owned Roosevelt Forest to the Great Meadows Salt Marsh, one of the largest unditched salt in New England and now a portion of the Steward B. McKinney National Wildlife Refuge.

INTERESTING PLACES

Connecticut Air & Space Museum. Located near Sikorsky Memorial Airport, provides education on Connecticut's unique aviation heritage.

Perry House. Stratford's oldest structure at the gateway to Main Street and the historic town center.

Sterling House. Founded in 1932, offers educational, recreational, and social programs to the community.

Boothe Memorial Park & Museum. 32-acre site on the Housatonic River, listed on the National Register of Historic Places.

The Captain David Judson House. Built about 1750 by Capt. David Judson on the site of his great-grandfather William's 1639 stone house, it was home to nine Judson generations until 1888 when the house was sold to John Wheeler. In 1891 the house was sold to Celia and Cornelia Curtis and in 1925 was willed to the Stratford Historical Society. The Society authentically restored the house to its 18th century condition The house is open to the public and is operated as a historic house museum and research library by the Stratford Historical Society, and is located at 967 Academy Hill in Stratford.

Two Roads Brewing Company on Stratford Ave. draws thousands of visitors each year to their brewery for tours, to taste their excellent varieties of beer, and for private parties. Mary Dean

Notes

Two Roads Brewing Company. Features an extensive lineup that takes a unique twist on classic beer styles.

Stratford Library Association (1896). The building is of classic Romanesque design with walls of St. Lawrence granite. It has copper gutters and a roof of specially made brown glazed tiles.

Mellow Monkey. Ecclectic gifts and home décor.

Year-Round Events

Restaurant Week. April. Local restaurants feature special 'prix fixe' menus.

Stratford Main Street Festival. In June from Stratford Center to West Broad Green. Fun, food, entertainment, crafts. Rain or shine.

Blues on the Beach. Sat. in July. Music, dancing, and food.

Latin Music Festival. Sunday in Sept. Celebrates Hispanic Heritage month with Latin music, food, folk dances, and more.

Pumpkin Festival. Sat. in Oct. Hayrides, costume parade, pumpkin carving, games, and food.

Address Book

Town Site
www.townofstratford.com

Boothe Memorial Park & Museum
5774 Main St.
www.townofstratford.com

Connecticut Air & Space Museum
595 Main St.
203-345-1559
www.ctairandspace.com

Captain David Judson House
967 Academy Hill

Great Meadows Salt Marsh
Meadowview Ave. & Philo St.
www.townofstratford.com

The Stratford Point Lighthouse is a private residence and not open to the public except on special occasions. You may view the lighthouse and/or photograph it, from the Stratford Point property on the east of the lighthouse.
Mary Dean

Mellow Monkey
360 Sniffens Ln.
888-300-0631
www.mellowmonkey.com

Perry House
1128 West Broad St.
www.perryhousestratford.org

Roosevelt Forest
700 Peters Ln.
www.rooseveltforest.info

Sterling House
2225 Main St.
www.sterlinghousecc.org

Stratford Library Association
2203 Main St.
203-385-4160
www.stratfordlibrary.org

Two Roads Brewing Company
1700 Stratford Ave.
203-335-2010
www.tworoadsbrewing.com

Events

Blues on the Beach
701 Short Beach Rd.

Latin Music Festival
16 Paradise Green
www.celebratestratford.com

Pumpkin Festival
12 Boothe Memorial Park
www.celebratestratford.com

Restaurant Week
www.stratfordrestaurantweek.com

Stratford Main Street Festival
www.stratfordctfestival.com

[Passport Stamp / Signature & Date Here]

Trumbull

By John Lauria, Trumbull Historical Society

When English settlers arrived the area was occupied by the Pequonnock branch of the Paugussett Native American tribe which had an agricultural based society. The word Pequonnock means "cleared field" in the native language and is also the name of Trumbull's major water source, the Pequonnock River.

In 1639, 17 Puritan families settled in what is now Stratford near the mouth of the Housatonic River. Some land within the present bounds of Trumbull was laid out and surveyed in 1670. By the 1690s homes were built in what is now Trumbull; the first was built for Abraham Nichols who had over 1,000 acres of farmland carved out of the wilderness known as "Nichol's Farms." Soon additional families moved into the area, roads were constructed, and sawmills and gristmills sprang up along the Pequonnock River.

By May of 1725 there were enough inhabitants in this outpost of Stratford to petition the General Assembly to form a separate parish called Unity. In October of 1744, the farmers living in the Long Hill district of the adjoining Parish of Stratfield merged with Unity. The reorganized parish was renamed the Society of North Stratford. Today's town boundaries remain unchanged from those established in 1744.

The eastern section of the town of Trumbull was pioneered by families from Stratford; the western section was settled from the village of Stratfield. Each of the farm settlements was established as a church parish with local burial grounds. As the town grew, parishes gave way to school districts that bear the names Nichols (1852), Long Hill (1854), White Plains (1856), Daniels Farm (1857), and Chestnut Hill (1859).

On Oct. 12, 1797, after 11 years of petitioning, the inhabitants of North Stratford won the right to become an independent town. The new town was named Trumbull after Jonathan Trumbull, Connecticut's colonial governor from 1769-1784, who was an ardent supporter of the revolutionary cause.

After the Revolutionary War, over time, two paper mills and a wool knitting mill were constructed on the Pequonnock River, the Housatonic railroad was built, two different factories began making shirts and underwear, Parlor Rock amusement park was established, a tungsten mine was built, as well as carriage shops, ice houses, and several cigar factories. In 1989 two special events occurred: the Trumbull Little League won the 1989 Little League World Series when they beat Tiawan and the Pequonnock Valley State Park was established.

Prior to the end of World War II, Trumbull's major industry was dairy farming with a population of about 7,500. After the war Trumbull's population increased dramatically as almost all the farms were transformed into residential areas. Today Trumbull's population is about 36,000 (2010 census). Over 8% of Trumbull's land is comprised of town and state parks.

Notable people who have lived in Trumbull include: early American scientist Benjamin Silliman, actor Will Geer, helicopter inventor Igor Sikorsky, professional hockey player Chris Drury, submarine inventor Simon Lake, comedian Lisa Lampanelli, Goodwill Industries founder Reverend Henry Morgan, pull-chain light switch inventor Harvey Hubble, musician/singer Michael Bolton, professional baseball player Craig Breslow, and actor/fitness instructor Tony Horton.

Places of Interest

Pequonnock Valley State Park. A 382-acre park on the east side of the Pequonnock River can be easily accessed from the commuter parking lot on Park St. near the

NOTES

southbound Exit 9 ramp of Rt. 25. From the lot take a short walk to the end of Park St. to the park's eastern entrance.

Housatonic Railroad Rails-to-Trails Bike Path. This 12.8-mi. trail runs from Bridgeport Harbor to the Newtown Line. An easy starting point is Tait Rd. near the Helen Plumb building where parking is available. The smooth crushed-stone portion of the trail here follows the original Housatonic rail bed along the west side of the Pequonnock River.

Tashua Knolls Golf Course and Recreation Area. The 18-hole Tashua Knolls and 9-hole Tashua Glenn golf courses are open to the public, including clubhouse, restaurant, driving range, and practice greens.

Westfield Trumbull Mall. 5065 Main St. (Rt. 111) at Merritt Pkwy., Exit 48.

Plasko's Farm and Creamery. A family-owned farm that grows and sells seasonal produce, plants, and ice cream.

Since its founding in 1964, the Trumbull Historical Society Museum at 1856 Huntington Turnpike has displays and offers events to educate the community about their town's history. John Lauria

ADDRESS BOOK

Housatonic Railroad Rails-to-Trails Bike Path
www.traillink.com/trail/pequonnock-river-trail

Pequonnock Valley State Park
vizettes.com/pequonnockvalley

Plasko's Farm and Creamery
670 Daniels Farm Rd.
www.plaskofarm.com

Tashua Knolls Golf Course and Recreation Area
40 Tashua Knolls Lane
203-452-5186
www.tashuaknolls.com

Westfield Trumbull Mall
5065 Main St. (Rt. 111)
www.westfield.com/trumbull

[Passport Stamp / Signature & Date Here]

Weston

By Kathleen Failla, Trustee of the Weston Historical Society

Weston's rich history is anchored in the birth of Colonial America. Originally, the town was part of Fairfield. In 1671, the early settlers of Fairfield to the south started dividing up communal lands to create individually-farmed lots. The farmland was laid out in "long lots" which extended from Fairfield's center. Land was distributed according to the needs of individual families and, although there were boundary disputes, an initial survey in 1726 reassured residents that the land they had cleared and farmed did indeed belong to them. This was the catalyst that propelled Weston's founding.

As property lines were drawn for the "long lots" that extended 12 miles north of Fairfield's "mile common," farmers began to settle the back country in what is now Weston. They were called "outlivers" and were the younger sons who inherited the poorer-quality land of rocky Weston to till. Their names, Banks, Bradley, Coley, Lockwood, Godfrey, and Smith, to name a few, are prominent in town history and today some even mark town roads. Weston resident Christopher Plummer helped immortalize the settlement of Weston in the film, "The Outlivers."

The initial step in independence from Fairfield occurred in 1757 when residents formed their own ecclesiastical society called the Norfield Society, the name of which appears today with the presence of the Norfield Congregational Church, Norfield Road, and the Norfield Historic District. In 1787, the Connecticut General Assembly incorporated Weston as a town over Fairfield's objections.

Today, Weston retains something of its early days in the formation of its government, the town meeting, held annually to approve the budget. Weston's location near the New York metropolitan area along with its award-winning school system, and small town New England charm are the reasons residents find the town so attractive. The population in 2010 was 10,025.

Weston Attractions

Weston Historical Society. On the former Coley Homestead which dates back to the early 19th century. The family farm once included more than 100 acres. Today the homestead is 3.7 acres and features the Coley farmhouse (c.1841), a large barn and cattle shed (c.1880), a carriage house (c.1880), several small outbuildings, and a new facility that contains space for the archives, exhibits, meetings and lectures. The Society is restoring the Coley house and barn, and will feature exciting new exhibits in these buildings in the near future.

The Lucius Pond Ordway/Devil's Den Preserve. Encompasses 1,746 acres and is one of the larger preserves in the New York metropolitan area and the largest in Fairfield Co. The preserve derives its name from Weston lore: local charcoal makers said that a hoof-like mark in a boulder was the footprint of the Devil. Run by the Connecticut chapter of the Nature Conservancy, the park is popular with hikers who enjoy the diversity of its many trails, which are open from dawn to dusk.

Saugatuck Reservoir. Straddles the border between Weston and Redding. Its creation is intertwined with Weston history as it forced

The Coley Homestead, home of the Weston Historical Society, dates to the early 19th century. Today it is a lively venue for historic and current events and established permanent exhibits. Kathleen Failla

Notes

the displacement of the Valley Forge village in Weston. The village was flooded in1938 to create the reservoir, which supplies water to surrounding towns. Tailrace fishing is allowed in the Weston end of the reservoir, where there is a handicapped-access area. Anglers must obtain a permit from the Aquarion Water Co. before fishing. The Saugatuck is the largest of the eight reservoirs that comprise Aquarion's greater Bridgeport water system. It holds approx. 12 billion gallons of water. The scenic road that encircles the reservoir is a beautiful drive especially in autumn.

Places to Eat

Peter's Weston Market. For deli, prepared foods, and bakery.

Lunch Box. Serving breakfast, lunch, and dinner; ice cream, beer, and wine.

The Weston Public Library at 56 Northfield Rd. provides a broad range of informational, educational, and recreational resources to serve the diverse needs of the community. Jerry Dougherty

Address Book

Town Site
www.westonct.gov

The Lucius Pond Ordway/ Devil's Den Preserve
33 Pent Rd.

Lunch Box
190 Weston Rd.
203-227-4808
www.lunchboxweston.com

Peter's Weston Market
190 Weston Rd.
203-227-2066
www.peterswestonmarket.com

Saugatuck Reservoir
100-198 Newtown Tpke.

Weston Historical Society
104 Weston Rd.
www.westonhistoricalsociety.org

[Passport Stamp / Signature & Date Here]

Westport

By Eve Potts, Advisory Council member, Westport Museum of History and Culture

Located in Fairfield Co. on Long Island Sound, 46 miles from Manhattan, Westport lies between I-95 and the Merritt Parkway and has frequent rail service to two stations including Saugatuck Village and Greens Farms. Saugatuck Village and downtown/Main St. both lie on the beautiful Saugatuck River, once of key importance to Connecticut's maritime, manufacturing, and commercial history. The two locations are replete with fine dining and shopping, beautiful strolling areas, and historic structures.

Though not incorporated until 1835 from parts of neighboring towns, Westport actually grew from a farming community in the 1600s, to a shipping center in the 1800s, to a renowned artist's mecca in the 1920s, to a sophisticated suburban town. Drawn to Westport's lovely shoreline, generations of families have found a welcoming atmosphere and excellent schools close to New York City.

Interesting Places

Westport Museum of History and Culture. Has year-round exhibitions, research facilities, and a gift shop. The property includes Bradley-Wheeler House, built in 1795, outdoor space with Wi-Fi, and the Cobblestone Barn, a one-of-a-kind octagonal structure. Tues.-Sat., 10 AM-4 PM and Sun., Noon-4 PM.

The Westport Library. A nationally-acclaimed resource and busy multimedia community center, containing one of the first Maker Spaces. A lighted walkway and garden area features benches, picnic tables, and river views.

Westport Arts Center. A visual and performing arts organization. Changing contemporary art exhibitions, chamber and jazz music concerts. Mon.-Sat., 10 AM-5 PM.

Levitt Pavilion for the Performing Arts. An outdoor performance venue providing a variety of free musical entertainment throughout the summer.

Westport Country Playhouse. Originally an 18th century leather tannery turned country barn, the Playhouse hosts notable stage presentations and offers a full performance schedule plus an on-site restaurant.

Earthplace. This nature center maintains a 62-acre wildlife sanctuary with two miles of trails. Grounds open from dawn to dusk. Main building open 9 AM-5 PM daily.

Wakeman Town Farm. Town-owned sustainability center, preserving and teaching local agriculture to children and adults. Popular attractions include chickens, rabbits, and goats.

Outdoor Activities

Sherwood Island. Connecticut's first State Park and public beach located on what was originally a 17th century farming community. The Nature Center offers educational programs. Park also contains the CT 9/11 Living Memorial. Sherwood Island Connector. Daily fee and hours at www.ct.gov/deep.

Compo Beach. Famed as the landing site for British troops arriving to quell rebellion during the Revolutionary War, Compo

The Levitt Pavilion is on the banks of the Saugatuck River. Robert Mitchell

NOTES

is a popular bathing spot offering handicapped-accessible facilities, boardwalk, pavilion, picnic areas, concession stand, pickleball and volleyball courts, skate park, playground, bathrooms, and lockers. Lifeguards. Memorial Day to Labor Day. Daily fee and hours at www.westportct.gov.

Minute Man Monument. Commemorates the patriots' engagement of British troops landing in Westport to march to Danbury in 1777 where they burned American supplies, engaging in the Battle of Ridgefield on the way back.

Longshore Club Park. Public park, inn and golf course on 169 waterfront acres. Restaurant, 18-hole course, tennis courts, swimming pool, and winter skating rink.

In addition, Westport contains several nature preserves for walking and hiking. Dogs are especially welcome at downtown Winslow Park. Kayak, paddle board, and sailboat rentals are available on the river in Saugatuck and at Longshore Sailing School on the Sound.

1795 Bradlee Wheeler House at 25 Avery Place. Westport Museum of History and Culture

ADDRESS BOOK

Town Site
www.westportct.gov

Earthplace
10 Woodside Ln.
203-557-4400
www. earthplace.org

Levitt Pavilion for the Performing Arts
40 Jesup Rd.
203-602-4122
www.levittpavilion.com

Longshore Club Park
Compo Rd. South (Rt. 136)
www.westportct.gov

Minute Man Monument
281 Compo Rd. South

MoCA Westport
51 Riverside Ave.
203-222-7070
www.mocawestport.org

Wakeman Town Farm
134 Cross Hwy.
www.wakemantownfarm.org

Westport Country Playhouse
25 Powers Ct.
203-227-4177
www.westportplayhouse.org

Westport Library
20 Jesup Rd.
203-291-4800
www.westportlibrary.org

Westport Museum of History and Culture
25 Avery Pl.
203-222-1424
www.westporthistory.org

[Passport Stamp / Signature & Date Here]

WILTON

By Allison Sanders, former Co-Director, Wilton Historical Society

The first settlers arrived in Norwalk in 1651, and by the end of the 17th century, the Norwalk Proprietors began to sell off the northern lands for settlement. In 1726 a petition created Wilton Parish, "a village enjoying parish privileges" but still part of the town of Norwalk.

As soon as the first meetinghouse was built in 1726, Wilton had a "center" of town. The Revolutionary War came to Wilton briefly in 1777 when the British retreated through the village after their invasion of Danbury. Although several Wilton houses were set afire, none were destroyed. In 1802, despite Norwalk's objections, the people of Wilton sought and were granted separate Town government status.

The Civil War had little impact on Wilton, except that the continued success of local businesses was due largely to the demands of the war effort. The coming of the railroad in 1852 did not bring many advantages to a community of home industry and farming. About 30% of the population was lost between 1860 and 1900 due to westward migration. Beginning in the 1910s, abandoned farms were discovered by New Yorkers for summer homes. Its proximity to New York City, and improved transportation systems, as well as the suburbanization movement transformed it into a rapidly growing, middle class community. Beginning about 1910 and most particularly after 1918, the development of modern transportation and communication facilities brought about the possibility of many urban workers separating their place of residence from their place of work. The influx of part-time residents was the greatest economic boon to the town during the first third of the 20th century. From 1920 to 1940, its population increased with professionals commuting to New York City accounting for most of the increase.

INTERESTING PLACES

Wilton Historical Society. Visitors are welcome to the Museum Complex, consisting of the Betts-Sturgis-Blackmar House built on-site c.1740; the c.1840 Burt Barn Gallery; the Sloan-Raymond-Fitch House built c.1770; the c.1860 Abbott Barn, c.1890 Blacksmith Shop, plus a c.1895 two-seat privy. A new permanent exhibition, Connecticut's History, Wilton's Story tells the history of the town through objects and artifacts. Visitors may tour the historic houses and stroll in the 1750 Colonial Herb Garden. Changing exhibitions. Tue.-Sat., 10 AM-4 PM. Betts Store Museum Shop. Farmer's Market on Wed., Noon-5 PM, June-Oct.

Weir Farm National Historic Site. Visit the home and studio of America's most beloved Impressionist, J. Alden Weir. Set amidst more than 60 acres of painterly woods, fields, and waterways, Weir's farm is a national legacy of American Impressionism. Visitor center and museum store: May-Oct., Wed.-Sun., 10 AM-4 PM. Grounds open daily, sunrise to sunset, year-round.

Quarry Head State Park. The 33-acre park is the site of Wilton's most notable quarry. During the 18th century, the quarry produced millstones for grinding rye and corn in local gristmills, and later for steps and foundations for buildings. Evidence of quarrying can be seen in slabs of stone with drill holes

The c.1770 Sloan-Raymond-Fitch House on Wilton Historical Society Museum Campus at 224 Danbury Rd. (Rt. 7). Alex von Kleydorff

Notes

and huge granite ledges. Well-developed trails for hiking. Open daily year-round, sunrise to sunset.

Food

Scoops. Ice cream and candy shop. Open Noon-8 PM.

Heibeck's Stand. Ice cream, sandwiches, and lobster rolls. Open 11 AM-8 PM.

Gofer Ice Cream. Noon-10 PM.

Orem's Diner. Classic diner fare. Daily 6 AM-Midnight.

Little Pub. Burgers, soups, salads, and more. Open daily 11:30 AM-9:30 PM.

Bianco Rosso. Creative Italian Cuisine. Mon.-Sat., 11:30 AM-10 PM, Sun., 5-9 PM.

Shops

Open House Gifts. Fashion and home accessories. Mon.-Sat., 9:30 AM-5:30 PM.

B Chic. For women and teens. The go-to store for denim, apparel, and accessories.

The Sunken Garden with lilacs in bloom and Burlingham House Visitor Center at Weir Farm National Historic Site at 735 Nod Hill Rd., Wilton. Weir Farm National Historic Site

Address Book

Town Site
www.wiltonct.org

B Chic
78 Old Ridgefield Rd.
203-210-7037

Bianco Rosso
151 Old Ridgefield Rd.
203-529-3800
www.biancorossorestaurantandbar.com

Gofer Ice Cream
379 Danbury Rd. (Rt. 7)
203-210-5546
www.gofericecream.com

Heibeck's Stand
951 Danbury Rd. (Rt. 7)

Little Pub
26 Danbury Rd. (Rt. 7)
203-762-1122
www.littlepub.com

Open House Gifts
9 Center St.
203-762-3868
www.openhousegiftshop.com

Orem's Diner
167 Danbury Rd. (Rt. 7)
203-762-7370
www.oremsdiner.com

Quarry Head State Park
Entrance 760-764 Ridgefield Rd.

Scoops
92 Old Ridgefield Rd.
203-834-1100
/ScoopsWiltonCT

Weir Farm National Historic Site
735 Nod Hill Rd.
www.nps.gov/wefa

Wilton Historical Society
224 Danbury Rd. (Rt. 7)
www.wiltonhistorical.org

[Passport Stamp / Signature & Date Here]

Litchfield County

CHAPTER 2

LITCHFIELD COUNTY

Barkhamsted

By Paul Hart, Barkhamsted Historical Society

Barkhamsted is a rural town in northwest Connecticut. Our town history is a lot shorter than most Connecticut towns because Barkhamsted was one of the last areas settled in the state. The town was incorporated in 1779. Why so late? Good farm land was not abundant in Barkhamsted, so many bypassed the town in favor of more fertile areas. Also, the town is not located near the ocean or on a big river. Transportation was difficult due to steep, rocky hills, numerous streams, and thick woods. As settlement progressed sawmills, gristmills, and other water-powered mills were soon up and running. Most early residents were farmers for family consumption with any surplus traded at market.

The population grew fairly rapidly in town until about 1830. But then a 100-year decline began, primarily because of two factors: better farmland available to the west, and the growth of urban factory jobs in other towns. Barkhamsted had some small factories, including the famous Hitchcock Chair Co., but never developed a robust manufacturing base. The railroad eventually came through town but there were no railroad depots in Barkhamsted.

In the 1930s a pressing need for more drinking water for Hartford led to the construction of the Saville Dam and Barkhamsted Reservoir. The reservoir had a huge impact on the town. A section called Barkhamsted Hollow was flooded and much of the watershed land was reserved. Farms, small villages, and the town's municipal center were displaced. In addition, two large State Forests were established in Barkhamsted. Today, almost half the land area of Barkhamsted is devoted to Peoples State Forest, American Legion State Forest, and the water company land, limiting economic development but insuring open space, a rural character, and the beauty of our town.

Interesting Places

Historic Squires Tavern Museum. Operated by the Barkhamsted Historical Society. Exhibits, historic photos of Barkhamsted, restored tavern and farmhouse. Hours: Wed. 9 AM-Noon, Sun. 1-4 PM.

Peoples State Forest. Main area located on East River Rd. about one mile north of Pleasant Valley and one of Connecticut's most beautiful state forests. Excellent trout fishing, canoeing, and tubing in the Farmington River which is designated as a Wild & Scenic River. Miles of hiking trails (many with excellent vistas), snowmobile trails, picnic areas along the river, and a nature museum.

Peoples State Forest Nature Museum. A stone-faced building originally built by the Civilian Conservation Corps in 1935. Information on native flora and fauna, animal mounts and skulls, minerals and insect specimens. Also displays about area pioneers, Native Americans, logging, quarrying, and the Civilian Conservation Corps.

American Legion State Forest. Offers fishing, hunting, canoeing, and kayaking. There are also 30 camp sites in the Austin Hawes Campground that is in a wooded setting. Season begins in mid-April and ends Labor Day.

Saville Dam. One can walk on the dam to see beautiful water vistas. Free parking.

The beautiful stone-faced Peoples State Forest Nature Museum built by the Civilian Conservation Corps in 1935. Podskoch

Notes

Village of Riverton. A charming New England village with historic Hitchcock Chair Company, (Hours: Tues.-Sat., 10 AM-4 PM) glassblower shop, general store, and other quaint shops. Riverton Fair on second weekend in October. On Rt. 20 in the northwest part of Barkhamsted.

Pleasant Valley Drive-in Theater. One of the few remaining in Connecticut – a classic Americana experience. Snack bar available. Has operated since the 1940s.

The Peoples State Forest Museum has displays on native flora and fauna, animal mounts and skulls, minerals, and insect specimens. Podskoch

Address Book

Town Site
www.barkhamsted.us

American Legion State Forest
www.ct.gov/deep/americanlegion

Hitchcock Chair Company
13 Riverton Rd.
860-738-9958
www.hitchcockchair.com

Historic Squires Tavern Museum
100 East River Rd.
860-738-2456
www.barkhamstedhistory.us

Peoples State Forest
106 East River Rd., off Rt. 44
Office: 860-379-2469
www.ct.gov/deep/americanlegion

Peoples State Forest Nature Museum
Greenwoods Rd.
860-379-2469
www.peoplesstateforestmuseum.org

Pleasant Valley Drive-in Theater
47 River Rd. (Rt. 181)
860-379-6102
www.pleasantvalleydriveinmovies.com

Saville Dam
Intersection of Rts. 318 & 219

Village of Riverton
Rt. 20

[Passport Stamp / Signature & Date Here]

Bethlehem

By Barbara J, Hampton, historian, writer, lawyer, and librarian

The little town of Bethlehem, like many colonial era towns, was named after a famous Biblical town. Originally a farmland district of "Ancient Woodbury," it became a separate town in 1787. It is in the southeastern part of Litchfield County, at the intersection of Rts. 47 and 61, just north of its mother town, Woodbury. Of all the progeny of Ancient Woodbury, Bethlehem has retained more of its rural character. Local farms produce fruit, vegetables, flowers, Christmas trees, dairy products, chicken, turkeys, beef, pork, and lamb. The annual Bethlehem Agricultural Fair features exhibits and competitions in dozens of traditional and modern categories with entries from northwestern Connecticut and beyond, musical performances, and midway entertainment.

In the early twentieth century, interest grew in having Christmas mail postmarked in the town. In 1938, the tradition began of creating an annual hand-carved cachet stamp for these items. The religious art of the popular Bethlehem painter, Lauren Ford, helped make the nickname, "The Christmas Town" stick. The growing Catholic community's new church was named "The Church of the Nativity." In 1947, nuns fleeing war-torn France founded the Abbey of Regina Laudis and inspired the popular 1949 Christmas movie, "Come to the Stable." The nuns have recorded three albums of Gregorian chants and ancient Christian music. Hundreds of people gather at the town green for the annual Christmas Town Festival, with crafts, foods, sleigh rides, caroling, and a visit with Santa Claus.

Well-known for its traditions of country food and fun, Bethlehem also has a long history in education, extending beyond the district common schools. Its first minister, Rev. Joseph Bellamy, was pastor of the Bethlehem Congregational Church. Bellamy founded America's first theological school (1738-1789) here. Aaron Burr and Jonathan Edwards II were students. In addition to his pastorate Rev. Bellamy led the "New Light" movement across Connecticut and published 22 theological books. The University of Aberdeen (Scotland) awarded him a Doctorate of Divinity degree.

Rev. Bellamy's successor, Rev. Agel Backus, opened a boys' college preparatory school, with students from across the original 13 states. Rev. John Langdon also operated a school in the early 1800s, and the Episcopal rector, Rev. Alonzo had a boys' boarding school in the mid-1800s. Bertha Harrison Follensby had a school for girls in the late1800s. The Bethlehem Fair raises thousands of dollars in scholarships for local students. Two modern private special education schools are also in town, Woodhall School (gr. 9-12, boys) and Arch Bridge School (gr. 1-12, coed).

Points of Interest

Bellamy-Ferriday House and Garden. Home of the first pastor of Bethlehem Congregational Church; site of the first theological school in America.

Abbey of Regina Laudis. Community of contemplative Benedictine nuns; visitors welcomed at church and chapel, farm, art shop, and theater.

Old Bethlehem Historical Society.

The Bellamy-Ferriday House decorated for Christmas in Bethlehem. It was the home of the first pastor of Bethlehem's Congregational Church. Barbara J. Hampton

Notes

Northeast corner of town green with town history collections; District #1 Schoolhouse.

March Farm. Pick-your-own blueberries, apples, pumpkins; corn maze; petting zoo; hay rides; snack shack, store, and bakery; fresh produce.

Bethlehem Post Office.

Events

Truck Show. Antique Truck Club of America.

Bethlehem Fair. Weekend after Labor Day.

Garlic & Harvest Festival. Early October.

Christmas Town Festival. First weekend in December.

Lauren Ford, a revered Connecticut artist, created this Nativity Creche that is in a small farm shed near the Lower Benedictine Abbey Chapel in Bethlehem. Mary and Joseph are dressed in Colonial clothes. Barbara J. Hampton

Address Book

Town Sites
www.bethlehemct.org
www.ci.bethlehem.ct.us

Abbey of Regina Laudis
273 Flanders Rd.
www.abbeyofreginalaudis.org

Antique Truck Club of America Truck Show
Rt. 20
/AntiqueTruckClubOfAmericaCT yankeechapter

Bellamy-Ferriday House and Garden
9 Main St. North
www.ci.bethlehem.ct.us/bellamy_ferriday

Bethlehem Post Office
34 East St.

March Farm
160 Munger Lane
www.marchfarm.com

Old Bethlehem Historical Society
4 Main St. North, Rt. 61
www.ci.bethlehem.ct.us/obhsi

Events

Bethlehem Fair
384 Main St. North
www.bethlehemfair.com

Garlic & Harvest Festival
www.garlicfestct.com

Christmas Town Festival
www.christmastownfestival.com

[Passport Stamp / Signature & Date Here]

Bridgewater

By Eileen Buchheit, Town Historian

Bridgewater, a town northeast of Danbury in Litchfield Co., got its name from "a bridge between two waters" as it is bordered by Lake Lillinoah and the Shepaug River.

Bridgewater traces its origins back to the settlement of New Milford in 1702. Then known as "The Neck," the name was first used by the General Assembly of Connecticut in 1803 when they established the Ecclesiastical Society. It got the name from the shape of the land jutting out into the Housatonic River. Called the County of the Wyantenock, it was the principal seat of the Native Americans in Litchfield Co. It was also called the "Sheep Pasture" because of numerous flocks in the area.

The travel between New Milford and Bridgewater to attend Sunday services was difficult. Residents constructed a meeting house in 1807 and followed with St. Mark's Episcopal Church in 1810. The connection to New Milford continued until 1856 when the elders of the Congregational Church petitioned for the construction of a new church in Bridgewater and the creation of a separate town, known as Bridgewater.

Agriculture was strong in the early days of Bridgewater, with tobacco serving as what they called the "Christmas Crop," which made enough cash to pay for holiday gifts and feasts. In 1823 Glover Sanford began making hats, an industry which spread throughout the area. In Southville, in the southern end of town, numerous businesses flourished. In addition to a tannery, a textile plant, hat factories, country stores, a chapel, a church, a post office, and a little red schoolhouse. In 1849 Bridgewater and Brookfield incorporated the Toll Bridge Co. that operated a bridge over the river.

Now, Southville is a distant memory as it lies beneath the waters of Lake Lillinoah. By the 1930s, Southville was almost a ghost town. When the plan was made for the flooding of the lake, the few remaining homes were either torn down or burned. By then, the industries which had employed the people of Bridgewater had all but disappeared. A few active farms remain in this mainly residential community.

Where five schools once operated, now a combined school, the Burnham School, takes their place. The town is part of a consolidated middle and high school, Region 12, which will become an AGSTEM school in the coming year.

Interesting Places

The Bridgewater Historical Society's Peck House (c.1820). Built by Elijah Peck, it was moved in 1910 to just south of the Town Hall. Visitors will be impressed with its old-world look. A private tour can be scheduled by calling the phone number on the door or by email.

The Town Hall is open on weekdays. Be sure to note the small window and closet-like space to the right of the door. It once served as the ticket office for the programs which were offered on the stage on the second floor.

The Village Store (1899). Owner Charles B. Thompson founded the first mail order business in his general store. It has changed over the years from rock candy, snuff,

The historic 1820 Elijah Peck House is the home of the Bridgewater Historical Society. Eileen Buchheit

Notes

and ice cream sodas to gourmet chocolate, fine teas, and refreshing beverages. It is a focal point of the community.

Scenic Views. At the scenic overlook on Rt. 67 and the view from Rt. 133 of the Litchfield Hills.

Burnham Library (1904). Is also a hub of the community and hosts art shows and openings, fundraising events, educational programs, and group meetings.

Sunny Valley Preserve. The Nature Conservancy has several hiking trails in Bridgewater. Maps available at Town Hall.

Lake Lillinoah. Formed in 1955 by impoundment of the Housatonic and Shepaug rivers by the Shepaug Dam built by the Conn. Light and Power Co. Bridgewater has a park on the lake for picnics, fishing, and boat launch.

Notable People

Celebrities have lived here for many years, largely because the residents respect their privacy. From award-winning authors Van Wyck Brooks and Theodore White to actors such as Mia Farrow, many have found a place of quiet contentment in Bridgewater.

Burnham Library was founded in 1926 at the bequest of Captain William Dixon Burnham. The Neo-classical structure stands in the center of town, a center of information and technology. Chris Fisher

Address Book

Town Site
www.bridgewater-ct.gov

Bridgewater Historical Society's Peck House
48 Main St. South
bridgewaterhistorical@yahoo.com
www.bridgewaterhistoricalsocietyct.com

Bridgewater Town Hall
44 Main St. South
860-354-2731

Burnham Library
62 Main St. South
860-354-6937
www.burnhamlibrary.org

Lake Lillinoah
Maps available at Town Hall
(44 Main St. South)

Scenic Views
Overlook, Rt. 67
View from Rt. 133

Sunny Valley Preserve
Maps available at Town Hall
(44 Main St. South)

The Village Store
27 Main St. South
www.bridgewatervillagestore.com

[Passport Stamp / Signature & Date Here]

Canaan

By Henry Todd, Town of Canaan First Selectman

The Town of Canaan (Falls Village) is in the northwest corner of Litchfield Co., close to both the New York and Massachusetts borders. Historically, it contains the communities of Falls Village, Lime Rock Station, South Canaan, and Huntsville.

In 1738, the area known as Canaan was sold at auction in New London as part of the Western Lands sale. One year later, in 1739, the town became official, having established a Congregational Church with the requisite elders who governed the village.

The town prospered in the ensuing years but, in 1858, was separated into two towns: Canaan to the south and North Canaan. No one knows exactly what the impetus was for the 'great schism.' From the "Scrapbook of North Canaan," it is noted, "...Taxes, paupers, town indebtedness, the distribution of political settlement, all or in part, seem to have figured in the calculations..."

Thus started the great name confusion. Locally, many refer to us as Falls Village, since our post office serves the 06031 zip code, despite also serving parts of Cornwall and Salisbury. North Canaan, in local parlance, is referred to as simply Canaan. Hence, our town website is CanaanFallsVillage.org.

The name Falls Village refers to the majestic Great Falls on the Housatonic River which borders our town.

The village itself was designated a National Historic District in 1971 and contains excellent examples of Italianate, Greek Revival, and Queen Anne architecture. When stopping at the village, stroll around and spend some time in our newly streetscaped center.

Interesting Places

Appalachian Trail. The trailhead is on Water St.

Mohawk Trail. The trailhead starts on Warren Turnpike.

Falls Village-Canaan Historical Society. On Railroad Street in the old Housatonic Railroad Depot.

South Canaan Meeting House. Beautifully restored wooden church, fabulous for weddings.

Falls Village Inn. Architectural treasure across from the Historical Society and a great place to grab a libation and a great meal.

Toymaker's Café. Voted best breakfast in Connecticut.

Beebe Hill Schoolhouse. One of the oldest one-room schoolhouses in the United States.

D. M. Hunt Library. Built in 1890, with Mercer Tile Fireplaces in a brick building.

Mountainside Café. Astride the Mohawk Trail on Rt. 7.

Great Mountain Forest. Wonderful walking trails that stretch all the way to Norfolk. Hidden amidst it is an adjunct to The Yale School of Forestry with classes held there in the less inclement months.

Music Mountain. Venue hosting mostly classical musical events on weekends all summer long.

Great Falls and Housatonic River. Great view, picnic areas, and one of the best trout streams east of the Mississippi.

Great Falls on the Housatonic River in Falls Village. Courtesy Lakeville Journal

Notes

David M. Hunt Library in Falls Village. Henry Todd

Address Book

Town Site
www.canaanfallsvillage.org

Appalachian Trail
Trail Head on Water St.

Beebe Hill Schoolhouse
Beebe Hill Rd. and Railroad St.

D. M. Hunt Library
63 Main St.
www.huntlibrary.org

Falls Village - Canaan Historical Society Museum
44 Railroad St.
www.fallsvillage-canaanhistoricalsociety.org

Falls Village Inn
33 Railroad St.
www.thefallsvillageinn.com

Great Mountain Forest
www.greatmountainforest.org

Mohawk Trail
Trailhead on Warren Tpke.

Mountainside Café
251 Rt. 7
www.mountainsidecafe.com

Music Mountain
225 Music Mountain Rd.
www.musicmountain.org

South Canaan Meeting House.
Intersection of Rts. 7 & 63

Toymaker's Café
85 Main St.

[Passport Stamp / Signature & Date Here]

Colebrook

By Laurie Foulke-Green of Sandisfield, Mass. & former assistant to Colebrook Historian Robert Grigg, and Alex Green

The Town of Colebrook is in the foothills of the northwest section of Litchfield Co. It was the last colonial town settled. The first person to build a home here was Benjamin Horton of Springfield, Mass. in 1765. The town was incorporated in 1779.

It was thought to be named after "Colebrooke" in Devonshire, England, but there could be a connection to the town named "Colnbrook," 35 miles northwest of Birmingham, England. More research is needed to determine this.

Colebrook's land consists of 21,000 acres, with scenic hills and woodlands, and several streams and lakes. There are many old farms, stonewalls, and wildlife to enjoy. Its elevation ranges from 560' foothills, to Pond Mountain at 1,552 feet.

The town was made up of seven districts: Sandisfield Road, Beech Hill, Colebrook River, Old Forge, Pinney, Hart's, and Porter's. Colebrook had many industries in the 18th and 19th centuries. A large cotton mill located in Colebrook River district employed 200 people. There was an abundance of sawmills and gristmills. The two iron forges aided the Patriots in the American Revolution. Other industries included: a chair factory, a creamery, a cheese factory, and a potashery. The countryside consisted of many farms with dairy cows, oxen, merino sheep, horses, and chickens.

The most tragic event in Colebrook was the creation of two dams and reservoirs on the West Branch of the Farmington River, which was conducted by the Metropolitan District Commission between 1930 -1964. They bought up the land and disrupted the people's lives who lived in the hamlet of Colebrook River. Old family homes and graves had to be relocated.

There are two churches in Colebrook: the Congregational Church, built in 1842 in the town Center .and the Baptist Church, built in 1794 which is located in North Colebrook, and is now named Church in the Wildwood. For those searching for their ancestors there are several cemeteries throughout Colebrook: Center, Cobb City, Prock Hill, Hitchcock, Hemlock, South, and Beech Hill.

There are many notable citizens of Colebrook including Ammi Phillips (1788-1865) a self-taught portrait painter and Captain William Swift (1769-1858) a master builder, who was the architect of the Colebrook Store in 1792. Richard Smith was a Boston merchant who established the Robertsville Forge in 1770. Henry Hart Vining (1890-1974) was a writer who contributed to the magazine "Lure of the Litchfield Hills." Mr. Robert Laffin Grigg (1932-2016) was the Town Historian and President and Curator of The Colebrook Historical Society. He contributed greatly to the research of the town and wrote many articles that can be found at www.colebrookhistoricalsociety.org under Bob Grigg's "Bytes of History."

Interesting Places

The Colebrook Store (1792). Old-time charm, great sandwiches, and wonderful people.

Colebrook River Lake. Boating and fishing.

The 1792 Colebrook Store. Laurie Foulke-Green

Notes

Algonquin State Forest. Hiking and hunting.

Sandy Brook. Trout fishing.

Colebrook Historical Society (CHS). Est. 1953. The Society's museum is housed in an 1816 building in the center of town that was an inn and later housed the Town Hall from 1953-2003. The Society holds many events from June thru Dec.

Rock School House. 1779-1911. Museum owned and operated by the Colebrook Historical Society. Open to the public and used for learning by Colebrook school children.

Rock Hall Inn (c.1912). A luxurious B&B.

Camp Jewell YMCA.

Yearly Events

Firemen's Steak Roast at Maasser Park, held in July.

4th of July Celebration in the center of Colebrook at the Congregational Church. Events, with lunch on the Green and homemade pies.

Labor Day Fair located in the Center of Colebrook on the Saturday before Labor Day. Crafts, vendors, car show, frog-jumping contest, and the Cardboard Boat Regatta.

The Christmas Fair in the Center of Colebrook in early Dec.

William Underwood, a prominent Colebrook citizen, commissioned master builder William Swift to design and construct this 1816 inn as a wedding present for his daughter, who ran it as the Seymour Inn for many years. Today it is the home of the Colebrook Historical Society. CHS

Address Book

Town Site
www.townofcolebrook.org

Algonquin State Forest
Sandy Brook Rd., White Trail
Maps available at www.ct.gov

Camp Jewell YMCA
www.campjewellymca.org

Colebrook Historical Society (CHS)
www.colebrookhistoricalsociety.org

Colebrook River Lake
On the Farmington River

The Colebrook Store
559 Colebrook Rd.
860-379-5031
www.colebrookstore.net

Rock School House
Rt. 20
www.colebrookhistoricalsociety.org/rockschoolhistory

Rock Hall Luxe Lodging
19 Rockhall Rd.
info@19rockhallroad.com

Sandy Brook
Maps available at www.ct.gov/deep

EVENTS

4th of July Celebration
Congregational Church,
471 Smith Hill Rd.

The Christmas Fair
Center of Colebrook

Firemen's Steak Roast
Maasser Park, Rock Hall Rd.

Labor Day Fair
Center of Colebrook

[Passport Stamp / Signature & Date Here]

Cornwall

By Jeremy Brecher, Historian & Documentary Filmmaker and Bianka Langner Griggs, Resident

Those who visit Cornwall can find evidence of its past ranging from stone walls to the remains of mills and factories to farmsteads to the very layout of the town, with its scattered village centers and its two commercial towns along the track of the railroad.

In 1738, a century after the founding of Puritan Connecticut, the colony auctioned off what became Cornwall. The purchasers were seeking not holiness but land. Unlike earlier Connecticut settlers, they did not establish a town residential area centered around the church; rather, they established isolated farms scattered around the township. These gradually developed into villages, often referred to as the six (or seven or eight) Cornwalls. They established a church, a town meeting, and a school. At its peak in 1855 there were 17 schoolhouses spread around town.

Almost all Cornwall's early residents were farmers, though some doubled as ministers, lawyers, and millers. They cut down forests, plowed the soil where they could, and piled stones into walls.

Around 1810 agriculture started a long decline. Many Cornwall residents migrated west or developed small-scale manufacturing. Mills and factories appeared almost everywhere that a waterfall provided a source of energy, processing raw materials from the region to make charcoal, scissors, shears, stoves, vinegar, lumber, cheese, and tanned hides. The Housatonic Railroad reached Cornwall in the 1840s, and the railroad stops of Cornwall Bridge and West Cornwall became the commercial centers of the town. West Cornwall's 1864 covered bridge remains in service today.

Later in the 19th century industry declined but the railroad made possible a large dairy industry producing milk for distant cities. Cornwall's picturesque scenery and rural way attracted those seeking a respite from city life, many of whom boarded in local homes and farms. In the 1920s boarders were replaced by "summer people" who bought homes in Cornwall. Cornwall became a center of literature and culture, represented by such names as James Thurber, Carl and Mark Van Doren, Henry Seidel Canby, and Lewis Gannett. It remains dense with writers and artists to this day.

Cornwall in general confuses the average visitor with its three current town centers and its variety of other Cornwalls tucked away in the surrounding hills. A local map generally available at the Cornwall Country Market in Cornwall Bridge or The Wish House in West Cornwall may come in handy. The Cornwalls are not just a historical gem. They offer a vast array of recreational opportunities such as quiet back roads that invite a leisurely stroll, a challenging bicycling terrain for the pro, and hiking trails through woodlands and fields all with views, vistas, and environments unimaginably magical. For local hiking trails, visit www.cornwallconservationtrust.org.

Cornwall has always attracted Artists, Writers, and Intellectuals such as James Henry Moser, Robert Andrew Parker, Tim Prentice, Philip Taaffe, and others.

Morning fog over a field in Coldsfoot Valley. Lazlo Gyorsok

Notes

Interesting Places

West Cornwall Covered Bridge (c.1864). Oldest continuously used covered bridge in the U.S. at the foot of the bucolic town center of West Cornwall.

Clark Outdoors. Watersports outfitter and tour guides.

Housatonic River Outfitters.

Housatonic Angler Guide Service.

Mohawk Mountain. Snowmaking was invented here. Hiking and skiing.

Cornwall Library. Offering events, talks, and children's programs.

The Wish House. Gifts, clothing, and home accents.

Cornwall Country Market. Sandwiches and market.

RSVP. French restaurant.

Pearly's Farmhouse Café. Breakfast and lunch venue. Dinners served Thurs.-Sun.

Souterrain Gallery.

Toll House Gallery. By the Covered Bridge in W. Cornwall.

Ian Ingersoll Cabinetmakers. Residential furniture manufactory specializing in one of a kind hand built furniture.

West Cornwall Covered Bridge. Lazlo Gyorsok

Address Book

Town Site
www.cornwallct.org

Clark Outdoors
163 Rt. 7 • 860-672-6365

Cornwall Country Market
25 Kent Rd. • 860-619-8199
www.cornwallcountrymarket.com

Cornwall Library
30 Pine St.

Housatonic River Outfitters
24 Kent Rd. • 860-672-1010

Housatonic Angler Guide Service
860-672-4457
www.housatonicanglers.com

Ian Ingersoll Cabinetmakers
422 Sharon-Goshen Tpke.
www.ianingersoll.com

Mohawk Mountain
46 Great Hollow Rd.
www.mohawkmtn.com

Pearly's Farmhouse Café
421 Sharon-Goshen Tpke.
860-248-3252
www.pearlysfarmhousecafe.com

RSVP
7 Railroad St. • 860-672-7787
www.rsvp-restaurant.com

Souterrain Gallery
413 Sharon-Goshen Tpke.
860-672-2969
www.souterraingallery.com

Toll House Gallery
860-672-6334

The Wish House
413 Sharon-Goshen Tpke.
www.wishhouse.com

[Passport Stamp / Signature & Date Here]

Goshen

By Barbara Breor, Goshen Town Clerk

Nestled in the Northwest Hills of Connecticut you will find Goshen. The breathtaking landscape is mostly hilly with outcroppings of glacial deposits and picturesque lakes. You will find about 1400 acres of Mohawk State Forest, and a part of the Appalachian Trail passes through the area. The Connecticut Wine Trail makes a path through the once prosperous farming community. State Rts. 63 & 4 meet at the center of town to form a traffic rotary, and Rts. 272 & 263 meet in the northeast corner of town. The Goshen Fairgrounds hosts numerous events from April to October, including the Goshen Fair held annually on Labor Day weekend.

Originally known as New Bantam, Goshen was later renamed by the General Assembly in 1737. The lands were auctioned off in New Haven in 1737, with bids going as high as £60 per right. The original settlers from the auction came from Wethersfield, Farmington, and New Haven. The first settlements started in 1738. The town was incorporated in October 1739. The first town meeting was held on Dec. 6, 1739.

Lewis M. Norton made the famous "Pineapple" cheese, which was shaped to look like a pineapple. It was patented in 1810. He originally made the cheese from his own herd. As demand grew he bought milk from area farmers and made a factory by his house in 1844, one of the first established cheese factories in the country.

Other claims to fame include the distinguished astronomer, Asaph Hall, who was born in Goshen in 1829. Mr. Hall discovered the outer and inner satellites of Mars, as well as a moon of Saturn. Gunsmith, Medad Hills, had a contract with the government to make muskets that were used to fight the Red Coats in the Revolutionary War. Also, Hervey Brooks, a red earthenware potter, had his home and shop in Goshen.

Goshen's other early industries included: clock making, ash oars, bedsteads, cheese boxes, butter tubs, muskets, cutlery, sash and blinds.

Some residents of Goshen left to establish the Western Reserve or New Connecticut, now known as Ohio, in particular Hudson, Ohio. These settlers were led by David Hudson, who came to Goshen from Branford at the age of 4.

The Goshen Land Trust has been instrumental in preserving valuable land in Goshen and creating a scenic hiking trail system. The trails wind through Goshen on Town property and Land Trust property extending nearly from one end of town to the other.

A wonderful event that has become renowned is the Annual Goshen Turkey Trot. This 10k race takes place every year on Thanksgiving morning, leaving the fairgrounds on a circuitous route to Dog Pond and back to the fairgrounds. Neighbors and volunteers often set up along the roadside to cheer on the runners.

Points of Interest

Action Wildlife. Animal attraction located at the Goshen-Torrington town line on Rt. 4.

Goshen Fairgrounds.

Goshen Historical Society. In the Old Academy building.

Thorncrest Farm & Milk House that sells milk products and chocolates. Kimberly Thorn

Notes

Milkhouse Chocolates. Thorncrest Farm & Milk House. Wonderful assortment of freshly made chocolates and cheese.

Miranda Vineyards. Winery.

Nodine's Smokehouse.

Mohawk Bison Farm. Bison and bison meat.

Old Barn Farm. Blueberry Farm, pick your own or buy.

Sunset Meadow Vineyards. Located near the Litchfield town line.

Sunset Meadow Vineyards is one of the largest in Connecticut and hosts wine tasting. Sunset Meadow Vineyards

Address Book

Town Site
www.goshenct.gov

Action Wildlife
337 Torrington Rd.
www.actionwildlife.org

Goshen Fairgrounds
116 Old Middle St.
(Rt. 63, S of the rotary)
www.goshenfair.org

Goshen Historical Society
21 Old Middle St.
(Rt. 63, S of the rotary)
www.goshenhistoricalct.org

Milkhouse Chocolates
280 Town Hill Rd.
860-304-2545
www.milkhousechocolates.net

Miranda Vineyards
42 Ives Rd.
/MirandaVineyard

Mohawk Bison Farm
47 Allyn Rd.
www.mohawkbison.com

Nodine's Smokehouse
39 North St. (Rt. 63, N of the rotary)
www.nodinesmokehouse.com

Old Barn Farm
300 Bartholomew Hill Rd.
www.oldbarnfarmct.com

Sunset Meadow Vineyards
599 Old Middle St. (Rt. 63)
www.sunsetmeadowvineyards.com

[Passport Stamp / Signature & Date Here]

Harwinton

By Rog Plaskett, Municipal Historian, Town of Harwinton

Harwinton is in the northwestern section of Connecticut in Litchfield Co. with the Naugatuck River on its western boundary. It is approx. five miles SE of Torrington. The population in 2000 was 5,283. The town's name is a blend of Hartford and Windsor (Har-Win-ton).

In 1732 Daniel Messenger was the first to settle here. Incorporated in 1737 Harwinton would soon become primarily an agricultural community with many industries carried on in conjunction with farming. Products produced included pitchforks, clocks, bricks, lumber, tin ware, bricks, hats, cutlery, whetstones, and barrels.

Today the town boasts two historic districts and one historic property which include some lovely houses from the early 18th century and more modern homes that blend in with the rural character of the town. There is a land trust which manages over 170 acres of open space that includes hiking trails and wildlife observation areas.

Harwinton was the birthplace of Collis P. Huntington, who would become one of the greatest American railroad builders.

Theodore A. Hungerford was also born here and became a very successful publisher in Chicago and New York. He left a trust which was used to build and maintain the town's first library. The beautiful Carnegie-style building is now used to house the T. A. Hungerford Memorial Museum.

In 2012 Harwinton celebrated its 275th birthday. Over those years the landscape has certainly changed but one thing that will never change is the community spirit of a New England small town and its beautiful stone walls that grace the town's farms and homes.

Interesting Places

Harwinton Historical Society. It has two buildings: a restored one-room Schoolhouse and Barn Museum. They are located on the grounds of the Harwinton Consolidated School on Rt. 118.

Theodore A. Hungerford Memorial Museum. Formerly the Harwinton Public Library.

Harwinton Land Trust. Owns over 170 acres of open space. There are numerous hiking trails and wildlife observation areas around town.

Bull Pond Preserve. It is across from the Harwinton Fairgrounds on Locust Rd. Accessible either from the paved drive leading to the pond (by courtesy of the Harwinton VFD) or by parking alongside the road and using the path starting at the "Heflin" sign that leads to a wildlife observation deck next to the pond. There are also nearly two miles of hiking trails.

Annual Harwinton Fair. A three-day event held on the first weekend in October. It is the oldest country fair in New England, which celebrated its 150th anniversary in 2005.

The 1840 one-room schoolhouse has been restored and maintained by the Harwinton Historical Society. Rog Plaskett

Notes

T. A. Hungerford Memorial Museum named after Theodore A. Hungerford who was born in Harwinton and became a very successful publisher in Chicago and New York. He left a trust that built and maintained the town's first library. The beautiful building houses the T. A. Hungerford Memorial Museum. Rog Plaskett

Address Book

Town Site
www.harwinton.us

Harwinton Historical Society
115 Litchfield Rd.
www.harwintonhistory.com

Harwinton Land Trust
www.harwintonlandtrust.org

Theodore A. Hungerford Memorial Museum
50 Burlington Rd. (Rt.4)
860-485-1555

Bull Pond Preserve
Across from Fairgrounds on Locust Rd.
860-304-2545

Events

Annual Harwinton Fair
150 Locust Rd.
www.harwintonfair.com

[Passport Stamp / Signature & Date Here]

KENT

By Marge Smith, Kent Historical Society Curator

The Town of Kent, nestled in the northwest hills of Litchfield Co. has a complex and proud history dating back to 1738. From its first decades as a colonial frontier town settled by intrepid adventurers, through the smoky industrial times of iron manufacturing, followed by the pastoral days of dairy farming, to the present era as a quintessential New England town tourist destination, Kent has remained a healthy and vibrant community of around 3000 people.

Main Street is still a classic, lined with shops, restaurants, and art galleries. There is no other "industry" in Kent, though the town is home to three good private high schools: Kent School, South Kent School, and the Marvelwood School. There is also the Kent Community Nursery School. A few small farms provide organic produce and meat, continuing the agricultural life that dominated Kent 100 years ago.

Kent's children attend the Kent Center School through 8th grade and then join students from five other towns at the Housatonic Valley Regional High School in Falls Village. Three churches meet the needs of Kent's Christian population, with synagogues in nearby Amenia or New Milford in NY.

Outdoor recreation is a big part of life in Kent. The Appalachian Trail runs the length of the town, and various other public trails are scattered throughout. Several lakes and the Housatonic River welcome boaters of all kinds.

Interesting Places

Eric Sloane Museum & Kent Iron Furnace. On the National Register of Historic Places. Houses a replica of artist Eric Sloane's studio as well as his extensive collection of early American tools. Ruins of the Kent Iron Furnace are on the grounds.

CT Antique Machinery Association. Adjacent to the Eric Sloane Museum. Home of the famous Antique Machinery Fall Festival at the CT Museum of Mining and Mineral Science.

Kent Memorial Library. A community hub in the center of town.

Kent Historical Society. Programs and exhibitions inspired by an extensive collection of objects and photographs documenting the town's history.

House of Books. Kent's Literary Landmark. This iconic bookstore is named by *CT Magazine* as one of the top ten independent bookstores in the state.

Appalachian Trail. Climbs along the western ridge above the Housatonic from South Kent to Cornwall Bridge. Great views! Kent is a favorite stop for through hikers to resupply and clean up.

Marble Valley Farm. Marble Valley operates a Community Supported Agriculture (CSA) program and a farm stand.

Walking trails. For resources, visit Weantinogue Heritage Land Trust at www.weantinogue.org, and Kent Land Trust on Facebook.

Kent Falls State Park. 295 acres along the cascading Kent Falls Brook. The original trails were created by workers of the Civilian Conservation Corps during the Depression, and have seen steady use ever since. A beautiful popular site for tourists and natives alike. Located Five miles north of town on Rt. 7.

The Kent Historical Society's 1751 Seven Hearths Museum houses furnishings (furniture, fittings, and other decorative accessories) that reflect phases of Kent history. Marge Smith

Notes

Macedonia Brook State Park. 2,300-acre park along Macedonia Brook, with high hiking trails and excellent fishing. Campground is temporarily closed, but the picnic grounds and trails are open with no admission fee.

Art Galleries. Morrison Gallery, Naples Studio, Good Gallery, Kent Art Association, Kathy Wismar Studio, Ober Gallery and many more. Check the Kent Chamber of Commerce website for more information about the individual galleries, restaurants, and shops: www.kentct.com.

Just 5 miles north of the Village of Kent on Rt. 7 are the beautiful Kent Falls that thousands visit each year.
Marge Smith

Address Book

Town Site
www.kentct.com

CT Antique Machinery Association
www.ctamachinery.com

Eric Sloane Museum & Kent Iron Furnace
31 Kent Cornwall Rd.
860-927-3849

House of Books
10 North Main St.
860-927-4104
www.houseofbooksct.com

Kent Falls State Park
Located on Rt. 7

Kent Historical Society
4 & 10 Studio Hill Rd.
860-927-4587
www.kenthistoricalsociety.org

Kent Land Trust
www.kentlandtrust.org
/KentLandTrust

Kent Memorial Library
32 North Main St.
www.kentmemoriallibrary.org

Macedonia Brook State Park
159 Macedonia Brook Rd.

Marble Valley Farm
170 Kent Rd.
www.kentlandtrust.org/marble-valley-farm

Art & Galleries

Morrison Gallery 60 North Main St.
Naples Studio 3 Landmark Ln.
Good Gallery 23 South Main St.
Kent Art Association 21 South Main St.
Kathy Wismar Studio 3 Landmark Ln.
Ober Gallery 6 North Main St.

[Passport Stamp / Signature & Date Here]

LITCHFIELD

By Cathy Fields, Director of the Litchfield Historical Society

Litchfield was founded in 1719, one of the last areas of the state to be settled. By 1750 the town had become the commercial center of the county and was named the County Seat.

Located at a crossroads, Litchfield was a central point on several routes between important Connecticut towns and the strategic military posts in the Hudson River Valley. As a result, during the American Revolution the town became a critical supply depot and as home for important Loyalist prisoners.

Following the Revolution the years between 1784 and 1834 were a time of growth and prosperity for the community. Litchfield was an active, growing urban center, and by 1800 the town had become the fourth largest in the state.

In addition to becoming a commercial center Litchfield grew to be an important intellectual hub of Federalist New England. The town became known for its educational institutions, including the country's first law school begun by Tapping Reeve in 1774. In 1792 Sarah Pierce founded the Litchfield Female Academy providing a rigorous academic education for young women.

Between 1774 and 1833 Tapping Reeve and his partner James Gould revolutionized the way law was taught in this country, educating over 1000 young men who became leaders in law, politics, education and business. The students at the Litchfield Law School played an important role in the foundations of American democracy. They produced two Vice-Presidents, three Supreme Court justices, 28 Senators and 10% of the U.S. Congress in 1800. They had a part in anything that took place in this country between 1800 and 1850.

In 1872, the Shepaug Railroad opened a passenger spur into Litchfield paving the way for the town's emergence as a resort community. In the last decades of the 19th century and into the early years of the 20th century, Litchfield and nearby Bantam Lake is a popular resort community.

In the 1960s Litchfield embraced the modernist movement and constructed homes and public buildings designed by noted architects Marcel Breuer, Richard Neutra, John Johansen, Eliot Noyes, Edward Durell Stone, and Edward Larrabee Barnes.

Today, Litchfield is a vibrant community. Residents and visitors alike treasure the historic character of the architecture and landscape. In the 1950s the state's first historic district was established in the center of Litchfield.

INTERESTING PLACES

The Litchfield Law School. America's First School of Law. Visitors are taken on a journey through the life of a real student from the early 19th century through role-playing, hands-on areas, and interpretive exhibits. Open: mid-April thru Nov. Tues.-Sat. 11 AM-5 PM, Sun. 1-5 PM.

Litchfield History Museum. Explore the evolution of a small New England town. Furniture, historic clothing, household objects, and paintings reveal Litchfield's history from its earliest European settlement to the present. The museum's 7 galleries hold the country's largest collection of paintings by 18th

Niles Golovin, owner of the Bantam Bread Company in Bantam, with some of the artisan breads that he baked. Bantam Bread Co.

Notes

century artist Ralph Earl including the iconic portraits of Benjamin Tallmadge and his wife Mary Floyd Tallmadge. Other highlights include artwork produced at the Litchfield Female Academy and a collection of Litchfield County furniture. Open: mid-April thru Nov., Tues-Sat. 11-5, Sun. 1-5.

White Memorial Conservation Center. A 4,000-acre wildlife sanctuary. Also, natural history museum and nature center. Displays of common animals found on property. Museum hours. Mon.-Sat. 9 AM-5 PM, Sun. Noon-5 PM. Also, hiking trails & 18 tent camp sites.

Bantam Bread Co. Artisan breads and pastries all freshly made from scratch and by hand using all-natural ingredients.

Topsmead State Forest. Former summer residence of Edith Morton Chase, daughter of Henry Sabin Chase, first president of the Chase Brass and Copper Co. Free tours of mansion. Consult website for time & dates. Hiking trails (on 600-acre estate) and picnic area.

Mount Tom State Park. Features: swimming, boating, fishing, picnicking, and hiking to fire tower.

Livingston Ripley Waterfowl Conservancy. Pre-eminent facility for breeding rare and endangered waterfowl. Tours available.

Boyd Woods Audubon Sanctuary. 102 acres of diverse habitat & many well-marked and managed hiking trails.

Arethusa Farm. Dairy, Café, and Arethusa al tavolo Restaurant. Dairy products, ice cream and farm-to-table cuisine.

The Litchfield History Museum contains furniture, clothing, household objects, and paintings that reveal Litchfield's history from its earliest European settlement to the present. It includes hands-on areas that help visitors discover the town's past. Litchfield History Museum

Address Book

Town Site
www.townoflitchfield.org

Arethusa Farm
556 S. Plain Rd.
www.arethusaaltavolo.com

Bantam Bread Co.
853 Bantam Rd. • 860-567-2737
www.bantambread.com

Boyd Woods Audubon Sanctuary
Rt. 254

The Litchfield Law School
82 South St. • 860-567-4501
www.litchfieldhistoricalsociety.org

Haight-Brown Vineyard
29 Chestnut Hill Rd. • 860-567-4045
www.haightvineyards.com

Litchfield Distillery
569 Bantam Rd.
www.litchfielddistillery.com

Litchfield History Museum
7 South St. • 860-567-4501
www.litchfieldhistoricalsociety.org

Livingston Ripley Waterfowl Conservancy
55 Duck Pond Rd. • 860-567-2062
www.lrwc.net

Mount Tom State Park
Rt. 202.
www.ct.gov/deep

Topsmead State Forest
46 Chase Rd.
www.ct.gov/deep

White Memorial Conservation Center
80 Whitehall Rd.
www.whitememorialcc.org

[Passport Stamp / Signature & Date Here]

Morris

By Laurel Gillotti, Executive Assistant, First Selectman, and "Pictorial History of Morris" by Ann & Bill Carr and Sally Irwin

The town of Morris is in Litchfield Co. in the northwest. It is home to 90% of Bantam Lake, the state's largest natural lake (approx. 947 acres). The town has an area of 18.9 sq. mi. The population in 2010 was 2,388.

The land was surveyed by Capt. John marsh in 1715 and was purchased for 15 pounds from the Bantam tribe of the friendly Pootatuck. The southern section of Litchfield was settled around 1723 and organized as the South Farms parish in 1767.

It was not until 1859 that Morris incorporated and became a separate town from Litchfield. It was named for Revolutionary War soldier, James Morris (1790-1820) who was born in the parish of South Farms. The town had opened its homes during the Revolution to quarter patriots traveling from other New England towns to battles in New York.

After the war James Morris established Morris Academy in 1790. A pioneer in co-education Morris taught both boys and girls in the same classrooms with the same lessons a practice unheard of in those days. The Academy lasted for almost 100 years before it closed in 1888.

In the early days there were many sections of town that had their own school and sometimes a general store. Some of the sections were: Morris Center, East Morris, West Morris including Smoky Hollow, and Lakeside which included Bantam Lake.

At first Morris was a farming town with numerous dairy farms. The Shepaug Railroad shipped milk and other freight from the Morris station in Smoke Hollow in West Morris during the late 1800s and early 1900s. There were also many mills including Kings Mill in East Morris, Burgess Mill in Smoke Hollow, and Troops Mill in Lakeside.

It was not until very recent times that many dairy farms were sold and divided into house lots. Today Morris has retained its rural nature and there are many homes and horse farms. Morris still has some 90 homes built before 1859.

Interesting Places

Bantam Lake. Features swimming at Morris Beach, fishing, waterskiing, and boating. There is a marina at the corner of Rt. 209 and Palmer Rd.

White Memorial Wildlife Sanctuary. On Marsh Point on Bantam Lake. Home to a wide array of birds.

Morris Public Library. Provides the community with the power of information through a wide range of materials and programs.

Camp Columbia State Park/ State Forest. It was the summer school for students of Columbia University that was started in 1885 and all Columbia engineering students were required to take classes here during the summer until 1964 when it then served as a summer training camp for the Columbia football team until the camp closed in 1983. In April 2000 the state purchased the property and use it as a historic park. Features hiking.

Apple Hill Trail. In the southwest portion of White Memorial, off East Shore Rd., this 2-mile trail through mountain laurel culminates

Morris Beach on Bantam Lake in Morris. Gary Hodge

NOTES

at the top of Apple Hill (1,200') with a great view of Bantam Lake from an observation platform.

Buddha Ariyamett Aram Temple.

Morris Historical Society. Maintains two buildings: the original 1861 Town Hall, and one-room Mill School, c.1772 that was moved to the site in 1980.

The White Barn at South Farms. Iconic New England family-run farm. Wedding venue, festivals, and events.

White Flower Farm. A must-see nursery with many display gardens set across several acres. Open between April & Nov.

The Stone Tower at Camp Columbia State Park/State Forest in Morris is one of the remains of Columbia University's School of Surveying that had classes for almost 80 years. Niles Golovin

RESTAURANTS & FOOD

Popey's Ice Cream Shoppe. Sandwiches, wraps & burgers, too.

West Shore Seafood. Seasonal seafood market on Bantam Lake.

The Restaurant at Winvian Farm. A truly luxurious, fine dining experience. Almost everything served is grown on premises.

Don Giovanni's Pizza Restaurant. Family owned and operated for over 20 years. Four corners of Rts. 109 & 63.

The Deli. Fresh deli meats, spreads, and salads.

ADDRESS BOOK

Town Site
www.townofmorrisct.com

Bantam Lake Marina
16 Palmer Rd.

Buddha Ariyamett Aram Temple
140 East St., Rt. 10

Don Giovanni's Pizza Restaurant
227 East St.
www.dongiovanniscatering.com

The Deli
7 West St.
860-567-1199

Morris Historical Society
12 South Rd.

Morris Public Library
4 North St.
www.morrispubliclibrary.net

Popey's Ice Cream Shoppe
7 West St. • 860-567-0504
www.popeysicreamshoppe.net

The Restaurant at Winvian Farm
155 Alain White Rd. • 860-567-8000
www.winvian.com

West Shore Seafood
449 Bantam Lake Rd. • 860-567-8000
www.westshoreseafood.com

The White Barn at South Farms
21 Higbie Rd.

White Flower Farm
167 Litchfield Rd., Rt. 63
www.whiteflowerfarm.com

White Memorial Wildlife Sanctuary
329 S. Plains Rd.

[Passport Stamp / Signature & Date Here]

New Hartford

By Anne Hall, Town Historian

On the eastern edge of the Berkshire Foothills, New Hartford includes two watersheds: the Nepaug and the Farmington rivers. Both have fertile flood plains and steep drops, suitable for water power. They are divided by the first rugged foothills that are steep enough to include names such as "Satan's Kingdom" or "Slasher's Ledges."

The Nepaug and the Tunxis occupied the area at the time of colonial settlement. The Nepaug area had several deposits of high quality soapstone, valued throughout prehistory. The Native American settlements lasted into the early 1800s as distinct villages.

Named in 1733 and officially incorporated in 1738, New Hartford began as a classic, agricultural hill town centered on Town Hill. By 1757 Town Hill boasted a school, the First Congregational Church, and a cemetery. The last town meeting was held on Town Hill in 1848. In 1912, the long vacant church became known as the 'The Church that Stabbed Itself' when the steeple, its bolts removed for inspection and never replaced, flipped backwards and plunged through the roof of the building. The only other remaining part of the center is the Town Hill Cemetery, dating back to the 1750s and still active.

Since the 1830s both the North End, located on the Farmington, and Nepaug Center, on the Nepaug, claimed to be the town center, and during the 1850s and 1860s the town meetings alternated between the two. Also growing were the villages of Pine Meadow, a quarter-mile down the Farmington from North End; and Baker(s)ville, located upstream on the Nepaug, which formed the 'South End.' North End and Pine Meadow won the argument for being the center of town, with the Town Hall officially established in the North End during the 1870s.

Water power changed New Hartford from an agricultural town to an agricultural-industrial hybrid. In the 1840s the Greenwoods Textile Co. built a dam across the Farmington. forming the two-mile-long Greenwoods Pond, used for power, ice production, and recreation. Another weir below the North End directed water into the canal that powered D.B. Smith's textile company and the Chapin Co. The Chapin Co. made fine carpentry tools such as planes, levels, and rulers. Today, the most prominent remains of the Chapin and Smith companies are the elegant houses that form the Pine Meadow historic district, many of which were built by the Chapin family, or the company foremen, or for the company workers.

The Greenwoods dam failed on March 18th, 1936 at 8:02 AM, destroying much of the Greenwoods Co. complex, and numerous buildings in the North End and Pine Meadow. Today the site of Greenwoods Pond is Greenwoods wildlife management area, owned by the MDC. The remains of the dam are next to the Hurley Industrial Park, the surviving portion of the once massive Greenwoods factory complex.

The South End has changed drastically, its farms becoming woods, reservoirs, and subdivisions. In 1912 work began on the Nepaug Reservoir, the first of three major reservoirs in the area: Nepaug, Lake McDonough, and Barkhamsted. Nepaug Reservoir flooded hundreds of acres of New Hartford, and subsequent land purchases to protect the quality and security of the water

The center of New Hartford on Rt. 44 has many stores, restaurants, and a government buildings. Anne Hall

Notes

closed hundreds more acres to any public access.

As industry and agriculture declined in the early 20th century, the town's recreational qualities came to the fore. West Hill Pond gradually became ringed with summer cottages and camps. In the 1960s, Ski Sundown on Ratlum Mt. was started. Meanwhile, the Farmington River boasts high quality trout fishing.

Interesting Places

Ski Sundown. 16 trails.

Hiking. Jones Mountain, Nepaug State Forest, Phillips Farm, and Brodie Park. The Metropolitan District (MDC) Nepaug Reservoir can be admired from the old road across the Nepaug Dam. MDC also maintains the Greenwoods management area on the West Branch of the Farmington River.

Farmington River & West Hill Pond. Public launch is in Barkhamsted, kayaking, fishing, and other water sports. A seasonal river tubing operation at Satan's Kingdom State Park.

Vineyards/Breweries/Farms. Jerram Winery, Brewery Legitimus, Grezcyk Farm, Barden Farm, Haywards Orchard, and other seasonal farm stands, including Christmas tree production.

Music. Parrott Delany Tavern, a summer concert series at Brodie Park, and the Beekley Library has a winter series "Nights at the Beekley."

One of the many canoers paddling down the Farmington River that flows through New Hartford. Many canoers, kayakers, and tubers begin their trip at the one-acre Satan's Kingdom State Recreation Area on the north side of the Rt. 44 bridge in New Hartford. Anne Hall

Address Book

Town Site
www.newhartfordct.gov

Barden Farm
45 Burgoyne Heights Rd.
860-379-8803
www.bardenfarm.com

Beekley Library
10 Central Ave.
860-379-7235
www.beekleylibrary.org

Brewery Legitimus
283 Main St., B3
860-238-7870
www.brewerylegitimus.com

Farmington River Tubing
Satan's Kingdom State Park
92 Main St.

Grezck Farm
860 Litchfield Tpke.
860-482-3925
www.grezckfarms.com

Hayward Farm Orchards
238 Hayward Rd.
860-489-9502

Jerram Winery
535 Town Hill Rd.
860-379-8749
www.jerramwinery.com

Parrott Delany Tavern
37 Greenwoods Rd.
860-379-0188
www.parrottdelanytavern.com

Ski Sundown
126 Ratlum Rd.
www.skisundown.com

[Passport Stamp / Signature & Date Here]

New Milford

By Chris Fisher, Historian

New Milford is the gateway to the Berkshires, split in half by the iconic Rts. 7 and 202, offering people access to beautiful foliage, history, and antique shops, the stuff of idyllic New England. The town is bordered on its west by Sherman; Kent on its north; Washington & Roxbury on its east; and Bridgewater & Brookfield on its south.

New Milford was first conceptualized by the Anglo mind in 1702 when a group of proprietors purchased from the Native Americans the parcel that we now call New Milford.

What happened next is a tale that every child in New Milford is taught. A girl of eight ventured into the forest with her father from Westfield, Mass. to settle and build a homestead. Others followed and a settlement was formed on the west side of what is now the historic district.

The settlement would eventually migrate to a naturally suited hill on the east bank of the Housatonic and would continue to grow. This growth was around a town green, which was used for grazing animals and was not the picturesque, well-manicured lawn it is today. The proprietors built a house of worship in 1716 on the center of our modern green. It was eventually razed and replaced with the Congregational Church that stands today.

New Milford grew around mill sites like many New England towns. Places like the Great Falls helped the town thrive in an era of water power. This would set the tone for the future and prepare it for the larger businesses that flourished in the 19th and 20th centuries, such as New Milford Hat Factory, Bridgeport Silex Factory, the Bleachery, and later Kimberly Clarke and Nestle.

At its core, New Milford had a focus on factories and small shops during most of the 1800 and early 1900s. In the river valley of the town, tobacco was king and several of the buildings downtown were dedicated to processing, sorting, and shipping the crop. The tobacco was then shipped out on the Housatonic Railroad to be sold in lots. The rocky hills and outskirts of the town were farmed in subsistence manner and later focused on dairy and cattle.

In 1926 plans for the flooding of what would become Lake Candlewood began by J. Henry Roraback. This would provide power to an increasingly power-hungry region. The lake changed the face of the community, offering new recreation, but also creating an atmosphere conducive to the building of weekend homes for those hoping to escape the stress of New York City.

Due to its large size, New Milford consists of a number of villages including Merryall, Northville, Lanesville, Park Lane, and Gaylordsville. Many of these villages, especially Northville and Gaylordsville, have maintained a unique identity and held on to their community cornerstones.

The late 20th and 21st century have brought challenges to New Milford including downtown businesses competing with big-box stores, the loss of many industrial jobs, and development of its farmland. However, it is meeting these challenges by focusing on its historic district, preserving open space, and wooing modern employment.

Interesting Places

The Green is the center of the New Milford community, hosting events such as fairs and concerts. The Green

The beautiful New Milford Green is in the heart of town surrounded by the library, churches, businesses, and residences. Chris Fisher

Notes

also has iconic symbols including several monuments, a tank, and the bandstand. Main St.

Historical Society and Knapp House. Has a museum and archive which reveal the greater history of New Milford through its citizens' artifacts. Of note is the Knapp house, which has recently been restored and the Boardman Store.

Theatreworks New Milford. Puts on high-caliber shows that have received acclaim throughout the county. Parking is available in the rear.

Lovers Leap State Park. The property has a number of trails and views of Lake Lillinonah as well as a restored lenticular bridge across the gorge. Across the street are the remnants of the Bridgeport Silex Factory with trails in and around the ruins. Open year-round from dawn to dusk.

New Milford's Barn Quilt Trail consists of eight colorful quilt patterns painted on large wood blocks hung on antique vintage barns around New Milford. Chris Fisher

The Elephant's Trunk. The flea market has gained notoriety in past years after being showcased on a number of television shows. It is open April through Dec., every Sun. 7 AM-3:30 PM.

Lake Candlewood. Bordering New Milford, Sherman, New Fairfield, Brookfield, and Danbury.

Famous People

Roger Sherman, signer of the Declaration of Independence called New Milford home and had a business here.

Historians Charles and Mary Beard spent the last years of their lives on a farm in town.

Notable actors found a respite in the Gateway to the Berkshires as well, such as Peter Gallagher, Eartha Kitt, and Fredric March.

Diane Von Furstenburg, fashion designer and philanthropist calls her estate Cloud Walk Farm.

Address Book

Town Site
www.newmilford.org

The Elephant's Trunk
490 Danbury Rd.
860-355-1448
www.etflea.com

Historical Society and Knapp House
6 Aspetuck Ave.
860-354-3069
www.nmhistorical.org

Lovers Leap State Park
Entrance is off Pumpkin Hill Ext.

Theatreworks New Milford
5 Brookside Ave.
860-350-6863
www.theatreworks.us

[Passport Stamp / Signature & Date Here]

Norfolk

By Ann Havemeyer, Norfolk Library and Historical Museum

Nestled in the northwest hills of Connecticut, Norfolk is not an old town by Connecticut standards, but because later 20th century development has largely passed it by, the town retains the architectural charm that was created around the turn of the 20th century when Norfolk was a popular summer resort. Today it is known for its cultural offerings and its natural resources which include three state parks, over 16 miles of hiking trails, and Great Mountain Forest.

The Village Green reflects Norfolk's colonial layout; the Church of Christ sat at the center of town, its white steeple rising above the shade trees that circled the Green. With the opening of the Greenwoods Turnpike (now Rt. 44) in 1800, the commercial and industrial district grew along the thoroughfare to the north. The railroad arrived in 1871, and Station Place became the town center and primary entrance to the village for summer visitors attracted by the pure mountain air and spring water.

The history of Norfolk is intimately entwined with the family of merchant Joseph Battell and his wife Sarah Robbins, daughter of the town's first pastor. Their descendants are responsible for many of the buildings that surround the Green. As a result of their patronage, Norfolk's Historic District encompasses the work of seven 19th and early 20th century architects of national standing. Ellen Battell Stoeckel and her husband Carl founded the Norfolk Music Festival, building the Music Shed in 1906. When she died in 1939, her 78-acre estate became the summer home of the Yale School of Music and Art.

Also formative in the town's architectural history is the work of Alfredo S. G. Taylor, a Beaux-Arts-trained New York architect who became a summer resident of Norfolk in 1902. He designed over three dozen houses and buildings in Norfolk, transforming Station Place into an attractive commercial center. His imaginative designs are now a National Register Thematic District.

Interesting Places

The Norfolk Library. Built in 1888 and designed by Hartford architect George Keller, this magnificent terra-cotta tile and brownstone building boasts a soaring wooden barrel-vaulted ceiling and Maitland Armstrong stained glass rose windows.

The Norfolk Historical Museum. Housed in the 1840 Norfolk Academy building with seasonal exhibitions and a country store with artifacts from Norfolk's mercantile past. Open Sat. & Sun., 1-4 PM, Memorial Day weekend thru the first weekend in Oct. Admission is free.

Norfolk Chamber Music Festival. World-class artists perform as part of a series of more than 30 concerts in the Music Shed each summer. Ellen Battell Stoeckel Estate.

Infinity Hall. Built in 1883 as a Village Hall, this historic theater has become a top Connecticut music venue.

Haystack Mountain State Park. A 34-foot high stone tower at the summit provides views of the Berkshires. From Rt. 44 take Rt. 272 N, parking on the left.

The Norfolk Chamber Music Festival, believed to be the oldest active summer music festival in North America, is held in the Music Shed that was built in 1906 and expanded in 1910. It is built of cedar and lined with redwood. Michelle Brummitt

Notes

Dennis Hill State Park. A 240-acre estate gifted to the state in 1935 by Dr. Frederic Dennis with a hilltop pavilion at 1627 feet and panoramic views. From Rt. 44 take Rt. 272 S and park will be on the left.

Campbells Falls State Park Reserve. Land protected and managed to preserve a particular type of habitat and its flora and fauna which are often rare or endangered. Features 50' falls from the Whiting River. Take Rt. 272 N from Norfolk center. Go left onto Old Spaulding Rd. Park on right.

Great Mountain Forest. Encompassing more than 6000 acres of contiguous forestland in the towns of Norfolk and Canaan, GMF's charitable mission is to educate about forests and forest management.

Walking Historical Norfolk Map and Guide. A self-guided walking tour through the town's Historic District is available at the Norfolk Historical Museum, the Norfolk Library, and Town Hall. It includes the Stanford White Fountain and Civil War Monument on the Green.

Norfolk Land Trust Trails. A network of over 16 miles of hiking trails.

Center Cemetery. The grave of James Mars, a slave who wrote his autobiography in 1868, is a site on the Upper Housatonic Valley African American Heritage Trail.

The Norfolk Library was designed by Hartford architect George Keller in 1888. A disciple of the renowned American architect Henry Hobson Richardson who was the architect of the Soldiers and Sailors Memorial Arch in Hartford's Bushnell Park, Keller used russet freestone and fish scale shingles below a roof of fluted Spanish tile. Babs Perkins

Address Book

Town Site
www.norfolkct.org

Center Cemetery
www.africanamericantrail.org

Great Mountain Forest
www.greatmountainforest.org

Infinity Hall
20 Greenwoods Rd. West
www.infinityhall.com

The Norfolk Historical Museum
13 Village Green
www.norfolkhistoricalsociety.org

Norfolk Chamber Music Festival
20 Litchfield Rd.
www.norfolk.yale.edu

Norfolk Land Trust
www.norfolklandtrust.org

The Norfolk Library
9 Greenwoods Rd. East
www.norfolklibrary.org

State Parks

Haystack Mountain State Park
Intersection of Rts. 44 & 272

Dennis Hill State Park
519 Litchfield Rd.

Campbells Falls State Park
117 Old Spaulding Rd.

[Passport Stamp / Signature & Date Here]

North Canaan

By Kathryn Boughton, Director of the Canaan History Center & Republican-American Correspondent

North Canaan is only half the town it was when it was sold at auction in New London in 1737/38. The town then encompassed the modern municipalities of North Canaan and Canaan, a tract of land almost completely bisected by Canaan Mountain.

The difficultly Canaan Mountain imposed on travel and communication between the north and south halves resulted in its formal separation in 1858 into North Canaan and Canaan. The northern half is familiarly known as Canaan and the southern is locally known as Falls Village for the business hamlet that grew up around the Great Falls.

North Canaan enjoyed early prosperity as an important center for iron production, especially along the Blackberry River, where Squire Samuel Forbes, a famed entrepreneur, established his iron dynasty.

Iron was king in Northwest Connecticut for almost 200 years, playing a major role in arming the Continental Army during the American Revolution and helping in the development of railroads in the 19th century.

The current village of Canaan did not develop until 1841 when the Housatonic Railroad first chugged into town. The advent of the railroad brought people and trade into the area and a lively business district grew up around it. During the late 19th century and the first half of the 20th century, the dairy industry was active in North Canaan and farmers brought their milk to the railhead where the Borden Milk Factory was. Milk was shipped twice a day to New York City.

Most of the small farms are now gone, as is the Borden plant, but five dairy farms continue to operate in Canaan, the highest such concentration in Litchfield County. One farm has more than 1,000 animals, reflecting the national trend to "industrial" farming.

A hotel, the Warner House, was built in the 1840s to act as a rail station. It served the growing town until 1872 when the Canaan Union Depot was built at the junction of the north-south and east-west rail lines. Until it was heavily damaged by fire in 2001, the depot was the oldest union depot in continuous use in the country. The depot has now been restored.

As the iron industry faded, other industry developed. Lime quarries have been a major part of Canaan's economy for more than a century. Other mining operations include sand and gravel operations throughout the town.

Points of Interest

Beckley Furnace (1847). A state-owned historic site preserving a 19th-century blast furnace on the north bank of the Blackberry River. It produced pig iron until 1918-19. The furnace has been restored and can be visited by the public. The park-like site is well-explained through signage, and volunteers act as guides on summer Saturdays.

The Canaan History Center. In the offices of former State Supreme Court Justice A.T. Roraback, founder of a legal dynasty in Canaan that continued until the death of his granddaughter, groundbreaking Civil Rights attorney Catherine Roraback in 2007. The History Center contains resources concerning the tristate region, including genealogical information, and is open every Friday from 9 AM-Noon and by appointment.

Douglas Library (1823). Reputed to be the fourth-oldest library in Connecticut, it has a small taxidermy museum on the second floor. It is open Mon. 1:30-8 PM, Wed. and Fri., 10 AM-8 PM, and Sat. 10 AM-1 PM.

Canaan Union Depot Railroading Museum. Has been restored

Notes

following the 2001 fire that destroyed large portions of the historic building. The building was restored in 2018, and now houses a number of businesses and offices, including a brewery, as well as a museum capturing the railroading past of the community.

The 1847 Beckley Furnace operated till 1918 producing pig iron. It is at 140 Lower Rd, in East Canaan. Jerry Dougherty

The 1872 Canaan Union Depot was at the junction between the two rail lines, making a right angle right at the crossover. The angle of the building was a 3-story tower, at the top of which sat the electric telegraph operator. The two 90-foot wings of the building were occupied by the two railroad companies. The second floor had a large restaurant that was especially important before the development of the dining car. Today the depot is a railroading museum. Christian Allen

Address Book

Town Site
www.northcanaan.org

Beckley Furnace
140 Lower Rd., East Canaan
www.beckleyfurnace.org

The Canaan History Center
115 Main St., Canaan Village
860-480-0307

Douglas Library
108 West Main St.
www.douglaslibrarycanaan.org

Canaan Union Depot Railroading Museum
1 Railroad Plaza
www.canaanunionstation.com

[Passport Stamp / Signature & Date Here]

Plymouth

By Judy Giguere, Plymouth Town Historian

Plymouth was originally part of the Mattatuck Plantation and called "Northbury." Henry Cook was the first settler arriving about 1728. The town includes Plymouth Center, Terryville, and Pequabuck.

The Plymouth Congregational Church (10 Park St.), the focus of Plymouth Green, was constructed in 1838. The large clock with its wooden clock movement dominates the steeple of the church and was built at Eli Terry's factory and donated by him. In front of the church is a Civil War memorial inscribed with "War of 1861" and "Abraham Lincoln" along with the names of several Civil War soldiers from Plymouth.

Across the street is the First Baptist Church of Plymouth (once St. Peter's Episcopal Church), a charming chapel constructed of local fieldstone donated by members of the community. The original St. Peter's Episcopal Church, built in 1796, was lost to fire in 1915 and was located in the northeast corner of the Green.

The original brick Plymouth Post Office building was built in 1782 and shared space with the town clerk's office. The present post office building was constructed in 1914-15.

A. C. Shelton & Tuttle carried on a successful carriage making business in Plymouth in the mid-19th century.

Ives Toys earned an international reputation for making toy trains. Ives also manufactured buttons for Union soldier's uniforms during the Civil War but moved on to making toys using clockwork mechanisms. The retaining pond on North Street was used for the Ives factory, and has recently been purchased by the town for passive recreation.

The northern section of Terryville is called "East Church," named during the Revolutionary War. Most East Church residents maintained their loyalty to the King of England and the English Church, much to the chagrin of Captain Wilson and the local branch of the Sons of Liberty. The woods of East Church contain a cave known as "The Tory Den" which was the hiding place for Tories when the Sons of Liberty were on the prowl.

St. Matthew's Episcopal Church was consecrated in 1795 and formed the heart of the little East Church community. Surrounding the small triangular green in front of the church are several historic homes dating from the early 1700s. St. Matthew's burying ground was first used in 1795 and contains more than 500 internments of both Tories and Revolutionaries.

Eli Terry initiated interchangeable parts and revolutionized the early clock-making industry. His son Andrew was one of the first in the new United States to produce quality malleable iron.

The waterwheel on Main St. in the Terryville section has been preserved and will be part of an industrial display promoted by Plymouth.

Eagle Bit and Buckle, later known as Eagle Lock, was one of the first companies to manufacture cabinet locks and it patented locks for mail bags.

Eli Terry built a bow-shaped dam on the Pequabuck River in 1851. It is called Horseshoe Falls. A bridge was built overlooking the falls and named for TV star Ted Knight, who was a former resident of Terryville. Judy Giguere

Notes

Address Book

Town Site
www.plymouthct.us

Blue Trails
www.ctwoodlands.org

Dorence Atwater Memorial
www.plymouthhistoricalsociety.orgh

Hancock Brook Lake
Rt. 262 S to S. Main St.

Horseshoe Falls
On the Pequabuck River

Lake Winfield
Off Seymour Rd.

The Lock Museum of America
230 Main St. (Rt. 6), Terryville
www.lockmuseumofamerica.org

Mattatuck State Forest
www.ct.gov/deep

Plymouth Land Trust
www.plymouthlandtrust.org

Interesting Places

Dorence Atwater Memorial. A Civil War cannon dedicated in honor of Dorence Atwater, a 19-year-old soldier in the Union Army. Atwater was captured and imprisoned at Andersonville where he made detailed records of the death of more than 13,000 prisoners, including a duplicate set. These records were used in the trial of the commander of the camp, Capt. Henry Wirz, toward his conviction for war crimes.

The Lock Museum of America. Extensive collection of locks primarily made in American with major display of over 1,000 locks and keys made by the Eagle Lock Company (est. 1833).

Blue Trails. Over 10 miles of Blue Trails offer paths for all levels of hikers.

Hancock Brook Lake. 721 acres with a 40-acre reservoir for kayaking, canoeing, and fishing. Contains a soccer field, hiking trails, and dog walking. From Plymouth, take Rt. 262 S to S. Main St. to lake.

Horseshoe Falls. A bow-shaped dam on the Pequabuck River built by Eli Terry.

Lake Winfield. Has walking path, and kayaking/canoeing off Seymour Rd.

Mattatuck State Forest. It meanders through Plymouth/ Terryville with nearly 900 acres. Rock climbing, hiking, bird watching.

St. Matthew's Church at the intersection of East Plymouth and Marsh Road had many followers loyal to the King of England. Many were harassed by the Sons of Liberty and some are buried in the cemetery. Judy Giguere

Plymouth Land Trust. 75+ acres in Plymouth and Terryville offering a variety of hiking trails.

Additional information is available at the Town of Plymouth municipal website: www.plymouthct.us.

[Passport Stamp / Signature & Date Here]

Roxbury

By Barbara Hampton, Historian, Librarian & Lawyer

Rocks, minerals, and gems have defined Roxbury for most of its three centuries. In 1713, settlers from early Woodbury migrated to the plains of the Shepaug (Mohican: "rocky water") River and began harvesting the rich crop of granite to build walls and foundations. Quarries developed on Mine Hill and became an important industry, supplying granite to build Grand Central Station, the Statue of Liberty, and the Brooklyn and the 59th Street bridges in New York City.

Roxbury cousins Ethan Allen, Seth Warner, and Remember Baker proved themselves as tough as Roxbury granite. They led the 'Green Mountain Boys' in Revolutionary battles, including Fort Ticonderoga, Bennington, and Quebec.

Some miners sought wealth from silver and lead deposits, but these weren't commercially viable. In the 1800s, focus turned to iron deposits. Tunnels, furnaces, a rolling mill, and a rail bed at Mine Hill sent Roxbury steel to a growing nation. Geologists know Roxbury for its garnet outcroppings at Roxbury Falls and in the hills near the Southbury border. Industrial garnets were once mined for use as abrasives. Later, rock hounds explored a private garnet mine, but this site is now closed.

Today, Roxbury's hidden gems are the many celebrities who have chosen this tranquil community in the Litchfield Hills at the intersection of Rts. 67 and 317, including: actors Dustin Hoffman, Denis Leary, Daniel Day-Lewis, Richard Widmark, Marilyn Monroe, Sylvia Sydney; writers Mercer Mayer, Billy Steers, Frank McCourt, William Styron, Candace Bushnell, Arthur Miller, Nancy Tafuri; musicians Stephen Sondheim, Debbie Harry; athletes Lindsey Jacobellis, Joseph Paul Wanag, and artists Alexander Calder, Inge Morath. Roxbury residents respect the privacy of their famous neighbors, making the town a welcome change from the glare of the spotlight.

Interesting Places

Roxbury Falls. Roxbury Land Trust's Rivers Edge Preserve, Sherman Park, and Lower Falls Road. Scenic rapids, and Shepaug River cascades.

Mine Hill Preserve. (National Register of Historic Places) off Mine Hill Rd. Nature trails.

Minor Memorial Library. Excellent collection of local history and biography, many programs and speakers; intermediate maquette (a small model or study in three dimensions for either a sculptural or an architectural project) by Alexander Calder for the sculpture "Mountain" displayed outside.

Seth Warner Monument. Obelisk honoring Lt. Col. Warner, 1743-1784. Seth was second in command of the Green Mountain Boys at the capture of Fort Ticonderoga on May 10, 1775. Located at the intersection of North St. and Wellers Bridge Rd.

Toplands Farm. Working farm producing meat and eggs sold at a farm stand, home of "DD" Dudley Diebold and the Living History Farm. It is dedicated to the preservation of early farming techniques and lifestyles through display, demonstration, and

The c.1860 Henry Randall Store & Post Office at the Roxbury Station is the headquarters of the Roxbury Land Trust. Barbara Hampton

Notes

education. Maintains the largest collection of restored antique tractors and farm equipment in the Northeast. Open for tours from Apr. 1 thru Nov. 1 by appointment only.

Roxbury Market & Deli. Popular meeting place, coffee stop, and general store featuring wide variety of local specialty foods as well as kitchen staples.

Mine Hill Distillery. Craft distillery located in historic buildings at Roxbury Station.

An obelisk monument on the Roxbury Green marks the burial site of Seth Warner (1743-1784), a Roxbury native and an American Revolution hero. Barbara Hampton

Mamie's Restaurant. Breakfast, lunch, and dinner; select menu featuring local produce, on-site bakery.

Events

Roxbury Pickin' & Fiddlin' Contest. One of the biggest Bluegrass music festivals in July, attracting individuals and groups from many states to compete for awards and prize money; proceeds benefit Roxbury Volunteer Fire Dept.

Roxbury Kitchen Tour. Tour of interesting private kitchens ranging in style from antique colonial to contemporary; fundraiser for Minor Memorial Library.

Annual Old Fashioned Beef Barbecue. August.

Address Book

Town Site
www.roxburyct.com

Mamie's Restaurant
162 Baker Rd.
www.mamiesrestaurant.com

Mine Hill Distillery
5 Mine Hill Rd.
www.minehilldistillery.com

Mine Hill Preserve
www.roxburylandtrust.org/minehill

Minor Memorial Library
23 South St.
www.minormemoriallibrary.org

Roxbury Falls
www.roxburylandtrust.org

Roxbury Market & Deli
26 North St.
www.the roxburymarket.com

Toplands Farm
102 Painter Hill Rd.
860-354-0649
www.toplandsfarm.com

Events

Annual Old Fashioned Beef Barbecue
24 Church St.
860-355-1978

Roxbury Kitchen Tour
26 North St.

Roxbury Pickin' & Fiddlin' Contest
Hurlburt Town Park, 14 Apple Ln.

[Passport Stamp / Signature & Date Here]

SALISBURY

By Louis J. Bucceri, Chairman, Salisbury Association Historical Society

Salisbury is the most northwestern town in Connecticut. Massachusetts lies on its northern border, and New York on its western. Though the peak of Mount Frissell is in Massachusetts, its south slope is Connecticut's highest point at 2,380 feet. In marked contrast is Salisbury's Lake Wononscopomuc, which, at 102 feet, is the deepest lake in the state. The Housatonic River flows along the eastern edge of town and the Great Falls of the Housatonic provides power both physically and spiritually. From 14 different school districts in the late 19th C., five population centers have emerged: the villages of Salisbury and Lakeville and the hamlets of Amesville, Lime Rock, and Taconic.

Before the arrival of European settlers the area was at the southeastern corner of the Mohican tribal lands, used mostly as seasonal hunting grounds. In 1720, a couple of Dutch families migrated from the Hudson River Valley and acquired land along the Housatonic. By 1731, a large deposit of iron ore was discovered and settlement of the land by people of English heritage increased dramatically. The town charter was granted and the first town meeting convened in 1741. Ethan Allen came from Cornwall as part of a group that built the area's first iron blast furnace in 1762. It was this same furnace that, under the direction of Governor Jonathan Trumbull, cast more than 800 cannons for use by Continental and State forces during the American Revolution. Iron fueled the economy of the town for nearly 200 years, but economic forces outside the area reduced demand for Salisbury iron and the town transitioned to education and tourism. As a result, the name of 'Furnace Village' was changed to Lakeville.

Today, Salisbury boasts about its public elementary school, Salisbury Central, and its three independent schools, Hotchkiss, Salisbury, and Indian Mountain. What has become the Scoville Memorial Library was established in 1771 through public donations. In 1810, after adding the Bingham Library for Youth, the nation's first public children's collection of its kind, the library received $100 from town funds to expand the holdings, making it the oldest tax supported library in the United States.

Norwegian immigrants began teaching locals to ski jump in the 1920s. Their first competition took place in 1927. Since then the group has become the Salisbury Winter Sports Association and has conducted the Eastern National Ski Jumping Championships every February since 1952. Lime Rock Park, "The Road Racing Center of the East," built in 1956 to showcase state-of-the-art road and highway safety principles, is the oldest continuously operated road racing venue in the country. The Appalachian Trail traverses the northern part of town and a number of other hiking and nature trails are scattered throughout the area.

INTERESTING PLACES

Salisbury Winter Sports Association. Fosters ski jumping, and holds Jumpfest and the Eastern National Ski Jumping Championships in early Feb. on Satre Hill.

Lime Rock Park. Racing venue.

The Scoville Memorial Library at 38 Main St. was established in 1771. It is the oldest tax-supported library in the country. The present stone building was built in 1893. Jerry Dougherty

Notes

Scoville Memorial Library. Open Tues. thru Sun. Check website or call for hours.

Hiking trail information. Open Mon. thru Fri. 9 AM–1 PM or by appointment.

Salisbury Association. Rotating history and environmental exhibits.

The Salisbury Town Hall at 27 Main St. has been on this site since 1752. The current building was built in 1988, replacing one that was destroyed by fire. Jerry Dougherty

Lime Rock Park at 60 White Hollow Rd. in Lakeville is a natural-terrain motorsport road racing venue. It was built in 1956 and is the nation's oldest continuously operating road racing venue. Lime Rock Park

Address Book

Town Site
www.salisburyct.us

Lime Rock Park
60 White Hollow Rd., Lakeville
860-435-5000
www.limerock.com

Salisbury Association
24 Main St.
860-435-0566
www.salisburyassn.org

Salisbury Winter Sports Association
80 Indian Cave Rd.
860-850-0080
www.salisburyisjumping.com

Scoville Memorial Library
38 Main St.
860-435-2838
www.scovillelibrary.org

[Passport Stamp / Signature & Date Here]

Sharon

By Marge Smith, former Sharon Historical Society Curator

Sharon, a town in Litchfield County in the 'Northwest Corner' of the state, is surrounded by Salisbury on the north, the Housatonic River on the east, Kent on the south, and Duchess County, N.Y. on the west. The population in 2010 was 2,782.

Sharon was founded in 1739 by settlers primarily from eastern and southern parts of the colony who were drawn by the high-quality of resources found in abundance, iron ore, wood, and water power. Young men hankering for their own domains left comfortable homes behind to rough it in the woods of the Litchfield Hills. Their bet paid off! In a mere 60 years, the population of Sharon reached 2,300 people. Manufacturing of iron goods was the driving force for generations. The monkey wrench was invented in Sharon, as well as an early rifled canon; and high-demand artillery shells were made during the Civil War by the Hotchkiss family. A unique mousetrap, made with iron wire, put Sharon on the map (mid-1800s) as the 'Mousetrap Capital of the Western World.'

For a fascinating history of the people and places involved in Sharon's Iron Age, visit the Sharon Historical Society at sharonhist.org.

The iron industry consumed most of the trees for charcoal manufacture, and the blast furnace fires were extinguished forever by the turn of the 19th century. Undaunted, Sharon turned quickly to dairy farming, an occupation still practiced to a lesser degree today in the Sharon area. Sharon has a long history of medical practice, beginning with Dr. Simeon Smith (1735-1804), an early proponent of the controversial smallpox vaccination. Today Sharon is home to the venerable Sharon Hospital, which was founded in 1909. Thanks in part to the proximity of the Metro-North Railroad, Sharon is also home to New York City residents who have weekend escapes nestled in the hills and valleys of the town.

Sharon's children are well-educated, beginning with one Sharon Day Care, and then Sharon Center Elementary School, after which the students are bused to the Housatonic Valley Regional High School in Falls Village. Several private schools near Sharon offer an alternative to both public education.

Interesting Places

Audubon Sharon. A nature center with live animal exhibits, a nature store, 11 miles of hiking trails, butterfly and herb gardens and raptor aviaries.

Hotchkiss Library. The Northwest Corner's most beautiful library. Relax by the fireplace in a reading room.

Sharon Historical Society. Programs and exhibitions inspired by an extensive collection of objects that dates back to the region's early settlers.

Appalachian Trail. Meanders through the southeastern corner of Sharon.

Sharon Playhouse. Musicals and dramas during the summer and special events and concerts in the Bok Gallery year-around.

Open-to-the-public Produce Parms: Ellsworth Farm and Berry Orchard. Paley's Farm Market. Q Farms.

Sharon Playhouse is a not-for-profit summer theatre, at the foot of the Berkshires that features musicals and dramas. Sharon Historical Society

Notes

Walking/Hiking Trails. See www.sharonlandtrust.org.

Housatonic Meadows State Park. Recreation area covering 452 acres along Housatonic River offering: camping, hiking, picnicking, canoeing, and fly-fishing.

Darren Winston Bookseller.

Blacksmith. William Trowbridge at Wild Iron Forge.

Here is the beautiful Sharon countryside with a dairy farm and Sharon Reservoir from Grandview Lane. Sharon Historical Society

Address Book

Town Sites
www.sharonct.org
www.sharonlandtrust.org

Audubon Sharon
325 Cornwall Bridge Rd.
860-364-0520
www.ct.audubon.org

Darren Winston Bookseller
81 Main St.
www.darrenwinstonbookseller.com

Ellsworth Farm and Berry Orchard
461 Cornwall Bridge Rd.
www.ellsworthfarm.com

Hotchkiss Library
10 Upper Main St.
www.hotchkisslibrary.org

Housatonic Meadows State Park
90 Rt. 7 North
www.ct.gov/deep

Paley's Farm Market
230 Amenia Rd.
www.paleysmarket.com

Q Farms
63 Jackson Hill Rd.
www.qfarms.net

Sharon Historical Society
18 Main St.
www.sharonhist.org

Sharon Playhouse
49 Amenia Rd.
www.sharonct.org

Sharon Land Trust
www.sharonlandtrust.org

Wild Iron Forge
23 Lucas Rd.

[Passport Stamp / Signature & Date Here]

Thomaston

By Robert Magdziarz, President of the Thomaston Historical Society

The Town of Thomaston is located in the Naugatuck Valley. The Village is situated on the Naugatuck River. The town contains 8,606 acres, making it a medium-sized township. It is shaped like a wedge and lies between the towns of Litchfield, Watertown, Plymouth, Harwinton, Waterbury, and Morris.

Thomaston was originally part of the Farmington proprietors purchase in 1684 of the Mattatuck Plantation.

The Thomaston area achieved its independence in 1739, being set off as Northbury Parish.

In 1780 Northbury separated to become Plymouth with the Thomaston section called Plymouth Hollow.

Thomaston was a small farming community when Seth Thomas came to Plymouth and purchased the Heeman Clark Clock Factory in Plymouth Hollow and continued to manufacture wall clocks and then shelf clocks.

Twenty years later in 1834 Seth Thomas bought his second factory, a cotton mill on Elm Street. Then in 1838 came a big change in the clock industry. Chauncey Sharon began to manufacture clocks out of stamped brass parts that were less expensive to make.

Thomas drew the New York, New Haven, & Hartford Railroad to start a regular run through Plymouth Hollow. Thomas then built his own brass mill in 1850 and called it the Seth Thomas Manufacturing Co. He then built houses on Chapel and Railroad Streets for his workers.

In 1860, due to the problem of getting cotton from the South, Thomas changed the cotton mill to a clock movement shop. In 1863 the sawmill owned by Aaron Thomas, son of Seth Thomas, became the main shop where the clock movements were assembled.

In 1866 Main St. started to change its appearance. American Hall became the first building made of brick from the Thomas Brick Yard.

On July 6, 1875 the separation of 'Thomas Town,' as it was called in memory of Seth Thomas, was confirmed by the State Legislature. The town had changed from a small farming community to a good-sized industrial community. There were now five more brick buildings: the Morris Block in 1876, the Bradstreet Block 1877, the Town Hall 1883, the railroad station 1881, and the East Side School in 1882.

Interesting Places

In 1738 on the Cannon Park site, Northbury Proprietors built a meetinghouse and church. From 1830 to 1851 a public school stood there. 10 Park St.

The Thomaston Town Hall. Built in 1883 contains the Opera House, Old Fire House, and Historical Society.

The Historical Society is open Saturday, Noon-3 PM from May-Dec.

There are three beautiful clock towers: the Town Hall Tower, Congregational Tower (135 Main St.), and Seth Thomas Building Tower.

Seth Thomas-Bradstreet House. It was built by Marvin Blakeslee and purchased by Seth Thomas in 1838. It is the only house left owned by Seth Thomas. Guided tours run from 11 AM-2 PM, on Saturdays from June thru October.

Railroad Station. Built in 1881, now houses the Railroad Museum of New England.

Notes

The Thomaston Historical Commission has restored the 1938 Seth Thomas-Bradstreet House on 237 Main St. It is a museum open to the public. Bob Magdziarz

The Thomaston Public Library is noted for its friendly and helpful staff that provides information and educational programs. Cindy Killian Thomaston Library

Address Book

Town Site
www.thomastonct.org

Black Rock Tavern & Restaurant
78 Main St.
860-283-4447
www.blackrocktavern.com

Mona Lisa Ristorante
66 Main St.
860-283-4422

Patti's Place
4 Park St.
860-283-0103

Railroad Museum of New England
242 East Main St.
860-283-7245
www.rmne.org

Seth Thomas-Bradstreet House
237 Main St.
/Seth-Thomas-Bradstreet-House

Thomaston Town Hall at Thomaston Opera House
158 Main St.
860-283-4421

[Passport Stamp / Signature & Date Here]

Torrington

By Mark McEachern, Executive Director, Torrington Historical Society

Torrington is on the northern end of the Naugatuck River in scenic Litchfield County. It was established as a daughter town of Windsor in 1732 and was incorporated in 1740 when there were just 12 families living here. Torrington's hills on either side of the river valley provided the best agricultural land for the early settlers and their agrarian lifestyle.

Torrington was the birthplace of the abolitionist, John Brown (1800). He moved with his family to Ohio while still a young boy. Nevertheless, Torrington was a center of abolitionist activity and Brown visited here often. The Litchfield County Anti-Slavery Society was established here and at least one home was a stop on the Underground Railroad.

Industrial growth began here in 1813 with the construction of a water-powered woolen mill on the Naugatuck River. This was the beginning of a village that today is downtown Torrington, a National Register Historic District. By 1835 there were two brass mills operating here. This was the start of the brass industry in Torrington, an industry that would later be synonymous with the entire Naugatuck River Valley. Immigration swelled the population in the late 19th and early 20th centuries. New arrivals, mostly from Europe, came here to work in the growing mills and factories that produced: brass, woolen cloth, machinery, needles, bicycles, wooden products, hardware, ice skates, and much more.

During the late 1920s and early 1930s, the downtown district experienced a facelift, which reflected the Art Deco and Art Moderne architectural themes of that period. Beautiful examples of that architecture are visible today in downtown Torrington, now home to a lively arts, culture, and restaurant scene.

Interesting Places

Hotchkiss-Fyler House Museum. An outstanding early 20th c. house museum with elaborate woodwork and decorative arts. The house museum is furnished as it was in 1956 and is operated by the Torrington Historical Society.

Torrington History Museum. The museum features an award-winning permanent exhibit of Torrington's history with objects and photographs from the collection of the Torrington Historical Society.

John Brown Birthplace. This 40 acre site includes the location where the John Brown house once stood and a two-thirds mile walking trail loop.

Five Points Gallery. A not-for-profit art gallery showcasing professional regional, national, and international visual artists. Five Points has earned the reputation as one of Connecticut's outstanding contemporary art venues.

KidsPlay Museum. A place where children between the ages of 1 and 8 can learn through hands-on and multi-sensory activities. Exhibits and programs include science, arts, and literacy.

The Torrington Historical Society operates the beautiful early 20th century Hotchkiss-Fyler House Museum. The home has elaborate woodwork and decorative arts furnished as it was in 1956. Mark McEachern

Notes

Warner Theatre. A beautiful art deco movie house now operated as a performance venue and arts education center by the NW CT Association for the Arts.

Burr Pond State Park. Located between Torrington and Winsted on Burr Mountain Rd: hiking, canoeing, and swimming. The park includes the site of the Borden condensed milk factory.

Sunny Brook State Park. Located on Newfield Rd. between Torrington and Winchester Center: numerous hiking trails along and near the East Branch of the Naugatuck River.

Burr Pond State Park lies between Torrington and Winsted. The park features swimming, fishing, picnics, and hiking around Burr Pond, an 85-acre man-made body of water. DEEP

Address Book

Town Site
www.torringtonct.org

Burr Pond State Park
Burr Mountain Rd.

Five Points Gallery
33 Main St.
www.fivepointsgallery.org

Hotchkiss-Fyler House Museum
192 Main St.
www.torringtonhistoricalsociety.org

John Brown Birthplace
John Brown Rd.
www.torringtonhistoricalsociety.org

KidsPlay Museum
61 Main St.
www.kidsplaymuseum.org

Nodine's Smokehouse
65 Fowler Ave., Torrington
860-489-3213
www.nodinessmokehouse.com

Sunny Brook State Park
Newfield Rd.

Torrington History Museum
208 Main St. www.
torringtonhistoricalsociety.org

Warner Theatre
68 Main St.
www.warnertheatre.org

[Passport Stamp / Signature & Date Here]

Warren

By Rebecca Neary, Vice President, Warren Historical Society

Warren, a few miles east of Kent in Lithchfield Co., was first settled in 1737 as part of the Town of Kent. In 1750 a separate ecclesiastical society, East Greenwich, was formed, and in 1786 Warren was incorporated as a separate town. On the recommendation of local Revolutionary War veteran Eleazer Curtiss, the new town was named after Joseph Warren, a military and political leader whose life was cut short at the Battle of Bunker Hill.

For most of its history Warren has been an agricultural community, with other early residents employed in the local iron industry. By 1810 Warren was also an educational center, with seven district schools and an Academy graduating ministers and educators – notable for a town of its size. Warren's Brick School is known as the longest continuously operating schools in the state – from 1784 until 1924.

Warren retains much of its original rural character. Its hilly landscape features farmland and forests, as well as the secluded Upper Shepaug Reservoir and a substantial portion of Lake Waramaug's shoreline. The town is traversed by Routes 45 and 341, intersecting at Warren's historic Congregational Church. Residents are drawn to the town's unpretentious charm; notable residents have included artists Herbert Abrams, Cleve Gray, Alexander Liberman, and Eric Sloane; film director Milos Forman; and writers Francine du Plessix Gray, Scott Peck, and Philip Roth. Charles Grandison Finney, a leader of the 19th Century Second Great Awakening and President of Oberlin College, was born and educated in Warren.

Over the last two and a half centuries Warren's population has fluctuated widely. By 1810 the town's population grew to 1100, but by 1930, with the decline of agriculture and the iron industry, it declined to 303 inhabitants. Today, residential development and the recreational facilities of Lake Waramaug have boosted the population to almost 1400, although it remains one of Connecticut's smallest towns.

Interesting Places

Warren Congregational Church. Well-preserved example of Federal architecture. Built in 1818; added to National Register of Historic Places in 1991.

Warren Historical Society. Houses a collection of documents and other historical artifacts. Self-guided walking tour of historic sites are available. Open Mondays 9 AM-Noon.

Warren Land Trust Trails. Four preserves with trails featuring diverse landscapes and terrain.

Mattatuck Trail. Excellent hiking on part of the state's blue-blazed trail system.

Above All State Park. Site features remnants of a Cold-War-era military radar installation operational from 1957 to 1968.

Warren Woods – Warren Fall Festival. Park with pond and walking trails. Columbus Day Weekend Festival – classic small-town New England country fair with music, food, vendors, tractor pull, lumberjack contests.

Hopkins Winery. Local wine to taste and purchase, shop, live music.

Hopkins Inn and Restaurant. Quaint lodgings and Austrian cuisine overlooking the lake; outdoor patio.

The Brick School (1784), also called North West School, is on Brick School Rd. Jerry Dougherty

Notes

Warren General Store. Country store and café. Gourmet coffee, meals and treats. Eat in or take out.

Lake Waramaug. Pristine rural lake surrounded by hills. Contact info@warrenlandtrust.org for suggested driving route and viewpoints. Town Beach; residents-only parking.

Old Burying Ground. Graves dating from the Colonial era.

The Warren Fall Festival's pumpkin patch at Warren Woods on Brick School Rd. Rebecca Near

The 1818 Warren Congregational Church at the intersection of Rt. 341 and Sacette Hill Rd. Jerry Dougherty

Address Book

Town Sites
www.warrenct.org
www.warrenlandtrust.org

Above All Road
Off Rt. 431
info@warrenlandtrust.org
www.ctvisit.com/listings/above-all-state-park

Hopkins Inn & Restaurant
22 Hopkins Rd. • 860-868-7295
www.thehopkinsinn.com

Hopkins Vineyard
25 Hopkins Rd. • 860-868-7295
www.hopkinsvineyard.com

Mattatuck Trail
Entrance on Valley Rd.
www.ctwoodlands.org/blue-blazed-hiking-trails/mattatuck-trail
info@warrenlandtrust.org

Old Burying Ground.
Cornwall Rd.
warrenhistorian@outlook.com

Warren Congregational Church
4 Sackett Hill Rd.
www.warrencongregationalchurch.org

Warren General Store
10 Cornwall Rd.
www.warrentowncenter.com

Warren Historical Society
Warren Community Center
7 Sackett Hill Rd.
www.warrencthistoricalsociety.org

Warren Woods – Warren Fall Festival
Brick School Rd.
www.warrenct.org/town-facilities/slideshows/warren-woods

[Passport Stamp / Signature & Date Here]

WASHINGTON

By Barbara J. Hampton, Historian, Librarian & Lawyer

The village names in the town of Washington tell the story of its people through their religion, farming, quarrying, crafts, and recreation: Judea, Washington Depot, New Preston, Marbledale, Lake Waramaug, and Romford. Early settlers in 1734, formed Judea, the northern-most district of Ancient Woodbury. The town was incorporated in 1779, adding portions of the surround settlements to Judea. As that date suggests, the town was named after George Washington. Today, the town is more often associated with strong schools, rich culture, and the preservation of its natural resources.

The colonial-era districts have maintained their identities. On the town green at Rt. 47 and Kirby Rd., the founding Congregational Church of Judea (now known as the First Congregational Church of Washington) continues as a center of faith, community, and culture, with a popular preschool and many music programs open to the public. The current church was built in 1801-1802. Nearby are the Gunnery School and Gunn Memorial Library, named after Frederick Gunn, a minister, abolitionist, outdoorsman, educator, and father of recreational camping.

About a mile downhill is Washington Depot, originally a manufacturing center using the power of the headwaters of the Shepaug River. A horrific flood resulting from the hurricane of 1955 erased many of the mills and factories, and killed William and Maud Foulois. Today, it is the town government and commercial center.

Early manufacturing developed around the steep falls at the outlet of Lake Waramaug, the headwaters of the East Aspetuck River in New Preston. Today, its 19th century buildings are transformed into restaurants and boutiques, a shopping destination popular with residents and visitors. Many lovely homes, inns, and bed & breakfasts overlook the lake from the surrounding steep hillsides and farmland. Summertime brings sailboats, racing sculls, and other small boats out on the lake.

CULTURE AND EDUCATION

Hickory Stick Bookshop. Sophisticated independent bookstore with frequent author events and programs for readers.

Washington Art Association. Gallery, juried art shows, and educational programs.

Gunn Memorial Library & Museum. Extensive local history and genealogy collections; designed by Erhick Rossiter, with stunning ceiling mural by H. Siddons Mowbray and stained glass window by Frederick Stymetz Lamb.

Washington Dramalites. Community theater founded by Frederick Gunn.

Hill Historic District and Hill Church "Stone Church" (1824). Rare stone meetinghouse, still used for special celebrations and occasional worship.

Institute for American Indian Studies. Museum with cultural artifacts and recreated 16th century Algonkian wigwam village; guest speakers and workshops.

Gunnery School. (Gr. 9-12). Founded 1850, welcoming boys and girls, international students, and students of color. 22 Kirby Rd. www.gunnery.org.

Rumsey Hall. (K-Gr. 9). 201 Romford Rd. www.rumseyhall.org.

A replica of a bark covered Algonkian Sachem Wigwam is on display at the Institute for American Indian Studies in Washington. Barbara Hampton

Notes

Washington Montessori School. (18 mo.- Gr. 8). 240 Litchfield Tpke. www.washingtonmontessori.org.

Food and Drink

Grace Mayflower Inn and Spa. Luxury hotel, restaurant, landscaped gardens.

The Smithy Café at 9 Main. Breakfast, lunch, and specialty baked goods.

White Horse Country Pub. Lunch, dinner.

Flemming's Hidden Valley Restaurant. Breakfast, lunch, dinner; menu features local ingredients.

G.W. Tavern. Brunch, lunch, and dinner in colonial-era house.

Norimaki. Traditional Japanese cuisine.

Hopkins Vineyard. Award-winning reds, whites, and sparkling wines; across the street from Hopkins Inn and Restaurant.

Averill Farm. Since 1746, over 100 varieties of apples and pears, including many heirloom varieties; cider, hard cider, cider wine and other delicious treats.

Parks

Mount Bushnell State Park. Overlooking west shore of Lake Waramaug; hiking, undeveloped.

Mount Tom State Park. Observation tower, hiking, swimming, boating.

Steep Rock Preserve. Largest of 5 natural spaces of the non-profit Steep Rock Association, preserved from development by architect Erich Rossiter; hiking, riding, mountain biking, cross-country skiing, and snowshoeing; camping (permit required).

Address Book

Town Site
www.washingtonct.org

Averill Farm
250 Calhoun St. • 860-868-2777
www.averillfarm.com

Grace Mayflower Inn & Spa
118 Woodbury Rd. • 860-217-0869
www.gracehotels.com/mayflower

Gunn Memorial Library & Museum
5 Wykeham Rd. • 860-868-7586
www.gunnlibrary.org

Hickory Stick Bookshop
2 Green Hill Rd. • 860-868-0525
www.hickorystickbookshop.com

Hill Historic District & Hill Church "Stone Church"
New Preston Hill Rd. & Gunn Rd.

Institute for American Indian Studies
38 Curtis Rd. • 860-868-0518
www.iaismuseum.org

Washington Art Association
4 Bryan Hall Plaza • 860-868-2878
www.washingtonartassociation.org

Washington Dramalites
/WashingtonDramalites

Food & Drink

G.W. Tavern
20 Bee Brook Rd. • 860-868-6633
www.gwtavern.com

Flemming's Hidden Valley Restaurant
88 Bee Brook Rd. • 860-619-0027
www.flemingshvrestaurant.com

Hopkins Inn & Restaurant
22 Hopkins Rd. • 860-868-7295
www.thehopkinsinn.com

Hopkins Vineyard
25 Hopkins Rd. • 860-868-7295
www.hopkinsvineyard.com

Norimaki
4 Green Hill Rd. • 860-868-0555

The Smithy Café at 9 Main
9 Main St. • 860-619-0699
www.thesmithystore.com

White Horse Country Pub
258 New Milford Tpke. • 860-868-1496
www.whitehorsecountrypub.com

Parks

Mount Bushnell State Park
Tinker Hill Rd.

Mount Tom State Park
Mount Tom Rd., off Litchfield Tpke.

Steep Rock Preserve
2 Tunnel Rd.
www.steeprockassoc.org

[Passport Stamp / Signature & Date Here]

WATERTOWN

By Stephanie Lantiere, Watertown Town Historian

In 1739, Watertown was part of the original Mattatuck Plantation known as Westbury. The oldest house (1735) still standing is the Belden House at the intersection of Rts. 63 and 73. Westbury was renamed Watertown when it was incorporated in May of 1780.

In 1740 an area on Main St. was set aside as a burial ground. The stones for the burial ground wall were obtained from Matoon farm. In the early 1700s, several members of the Scott family were killed by Native Americans, and Jonathan was captured and taken to Canada. He returned with one of his sons and built the first sawmill in the Greenville section of Westbury.

Michael Dayton and his wife, Mehitable, moved to Watertown c. 1750. The family owned a large tract of land and had 13 children. Dayton served in the Revolutionary War and died on Sept. 22, 1776. On Nov. 15, 1985, the new bridge on French St. was dedicated with a plaque to the Dayton family.

The First Congregational Church was formed in Westbury in May 1739. In 1740, John Trumbull was ordained pastor of the new parish, and the church's building, the First Watertown Meeting House, was completed in 1741on the corner of the cemetery on Main Street. The building was demolished in 1772, and a new house of worship was built near where the current Watertown Post Office stands. In 1914, the DAR placed a plaque in the stone wall at the corner of Main and French Streets. The current DAR is responsible for the upkeep of the cemetery.

The First Episcopal Church was erected in 1765 on the southeast corner of Main & French Sts. It was taken down in 1794, when the Second Episcopal Church was built on the green.

In 1910, plaques listing some of the 48 Revolutionary War soldiers from Watertown buried in the old cemetery were placed on each side of the front gate by the DAR. On May 10, 1920, a monument was dedicated to the young men and a few nurses from Watertown who saw action in World War 1.

Soon after World War II, Oakville (part of Watertown) built a monument, complete with cannon, by the bridge across Steel Brook. After a beautiful park was developed nearby, the monument and cannon found a new home. Also in the park in the center of Oakville a monument was dedicated on October 10, 1908, to the 130 men from Watertown who served in the Civil War.

PLACES TO VISIT

Nova Scotia School House. An 1853 Greek Revival school that closed in 1929. It was disassembled and reconstructed in Munson Park on DeForest St. It is maintained by the historical society.

Black Rock State Park. Harley F. Roberts, from Taft School, donated land to Black Rock Association in 1925 and other parcels were added. The site of Civilian Conservation Corps work in 1930s. Features swimming, fishing, and hiking. Directions: From Rt. 8 N take Exit 38. Turn left off exit ramp to first traffic light. Turn left at traffic light

The 1853 Nova Scotia Schoolhouse. Stephanie Lantiere

Notes

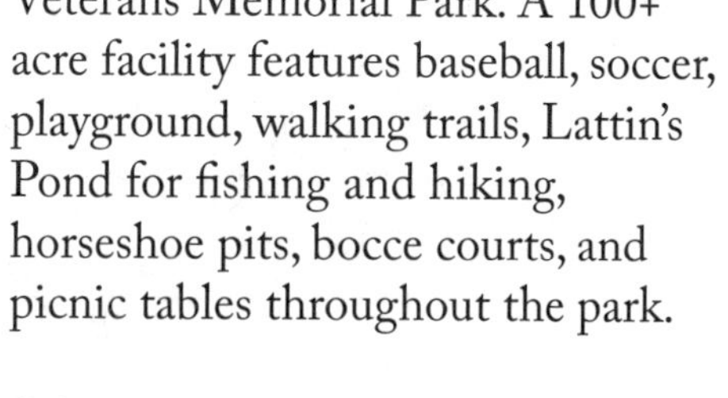

onto Rt. 6 W. Park entrance is a 1/2 mile on the right.

Mattatuck State Forest. Many parcels are spread out over many towns including Watertown.

Watertown Library. Source for information, activities, and programs.

Oakville Library.

Taft School (1890). A private, coeducational school on a 226-acre campus.

Leatherman Cave. Park at Black Rock State Park or Bidwell Hill Road off Rt. 6 and access the cave by walking east along the Mattatuck Trail.

Crestbrook Park. Features a golf course, tennis, a 34-acre lake, fishing, swimming, etc.

Veterans Memorial Park. A 100+ acre facility features baseball, soccer, playground, walking trails, Lattin's Pond for fishing and hiking, horseshoe pits, bocce courts, and picnic tables throughout the park.

Sylvan Lake Park. Swimming. Intersection of Frost Bridge Rd. and Echo Lake Rd. in Oakville.

Marion Munson Plaque. Near the Munson House.

Walking Tour of the Historic District. For information, visit: watertownhistoricalsociety.org.

Phoenix Stage Co. at Clockwork.

Evergreen Cemetery & New Evergreen Cemetery, 165 North St.; Old Cemetery, 851 Main St.; Mt. St. James Cemetery, 97 Porter St.; Mt. Olivet Cemetery, Platt Rd.

The 1735 Belden House; the oldest house in Watertown. Stephanie Lantiere

Address Book

Town Sites
www.watertownct.org
www.watertownctrecreation.com

Crestbrook Park
834 Northfield Rd.
www.crestbrookpark.com

Nova Scotia School House
22 DeForest St.
www.watertownhistoricalsociety.org

Oakville Library
55 Davis St.

Phoenix Stage Co.
133 Main St., Oakville
www.phoenixstagecompany.org

State Parks
Black Rock State Park
Mattatuck State Forest
www.ct.gov/deep

Sylvan Lake Park
Intersection of Frost Bridge Rd. and Echo Lake Rd.

Taft School
110 Woodbury Rd.

Veteran's Memorial Park
580 Nova Scotia Hill Rd.

Watertown Historic District
www.lhdct.org/district/watertown-historic-district

Watertown Library
470 Main St.
860-945-5360
www.watertownlibrary.org

[Passport Stamp / Signature & Date Here]

Winchester

By Verna Gilson, retired genealogist at Beardsley Library

The Town of Winchester and the City of Winsted are located in scenic Litchfield County. Winchester was named for the cathedral town in Hampshire, England and was settled in 1750. It became a town in 1771, the same year that Winsted settled along the Mad and Still Rivers. Winsted was named for Win-chester and neighboring Barkham-sted. It became a borough of Winchester in 1858 and a city within the town in 1917.

Winchester's landscape ranges from rocky, grass-covered hills to steep mountains and valleys. The higher elevations provide panoramic views of the surrounding region. Woodlands, wildlife, and waterways abound, and there are countless outdoor recreations, including bicycling, hiking, and watersports. Highland Lake, a popular year-round attraction and one of Connecticut's largest lakes, offers public beaches and a state boat launch.

In the early 19th century, several turnpikes opened this region to travel and trade, and Winchester and Winsted embarked upon a century of remarkable growth and prosperity. Winchester's grassy slopes proved ideal for cattle-breeding and dairy-farming, and water power proved ideal for manufacturing. Winsted became a major industrial community producing tools, clocks, hardware, textiles, thread, etc. for domestic and foreign markets. When the railroads and trolleys arrived, Winsted's cultural venues and countless amenities attracted tourists, and it became an important commercial center. Winsted is called The Laurel City, for its abundant mountain laurel, and the Green District, Main Street, and Soldiers' Monument are among the historic sites.

As with most mill towns, Winsted's economy was affected by world affairs in the first half of the 20th century, and its workforce declined, along with business, industry, and farming. When a devastating flood struck Winsted in 1955, lives, businesses, industries, and homes were lost, but the community rallied and moved forward.

Winsted is experiencing a renaissance in the 21st century. Its historic structures are being converted into museums, studios, shops, and housing, and business and industry is thriving. Winsted and Winchester are known for their majestic churches, diverse architecture, old burying grounds, and memorial monuments, as well as the unique year-round events they sponsor to celebrate their past. With their idyllic landscape and convenience to highways and international airports, they are attractive year-round destinations. This quintessential New England city and town beckon visitors to take a closer look at their captivating past and enduring charm.

Interesting Places

American Mural Project. An impressive hand-painted mural, at Whiting Mills, honors American workers.

American Museum of Tort Law. Ralph Nader, Winsted native and consumer-advocate, developed this noteworthy museum in 2015. Open 10:30 AM–5 PM, except Tues.

Beardsley Library. Built in 1898, this 20th century library has 19th century charm.

Winsted native and consumer-advocate, Ralph Nader, founded the American Museum of Tort Law. Verna Gilson

Notes

Gilson Café and Cinema. This former vaudeville theater shows films in a bistro setting.

Northwestern CT Community College. Founded in 1965, this was Connecticut's first community college. Park Place East. www.nwcc.commnet.edu.

Soldiers' Monument. This remarkable Civil War monument was dedicated in 1890.

Sue Grossman Still River Greenway. This walking trail connects Winsted and Torrington.

Whiting Mills Studios. This historic mill houses studios and retail shops.

Winchester Historical Society. The Solomon Rockwell House showcases Winchester's history.

The Soldiers' Monument honoring those who fought in the Civil War was dedicated in 1890. Verna Gilson

Address Book

Town Site
www.townofwinchester.org

American Museum of Tort Law
654 Main St.
860-379-0505
www.tortmuseum.org

Beardsley Library
40 Munro Place
860-379-6043
www.beardsleylibrary.org

Gilson Café and Cinema
354 Main St.
860-379-5108
www.gilsoncafecinema.com

Soldiers' Monument & Memorial Park
Crown St. • P.O. Box 322
www.soldiersmonumentwinsted.org

Solomon Rockwell House
226 Prospect St.
www.townofwinchester.org

Sue Grossman Still River Greenway
18 Lanson Dr.

Winchester Historical Society
Solomon Rockwell House
226 Prospect St.
860-379-8433

Whiting Mills Studios
210 Holabird Ave. Studio #418
860-738-2240
www.whitingmills.com
www.americanmuralproject.org

[Passport Stamp / Signature & Date Here]

Woodbury

By Barbara J. Hampton J.D., M.L.S., resident of Southbury

Woodbury is at the southern tip of Litchfield County, along U.S. Rt. 6, the Grand Army of the Republic Highway. It includes Hotchkissville, Woodlake, Flanders, and Good Hill.

"Ancient Woodbury" is what historians call the area that 17 families from Stratford purchased from the Pootatucks, the Native American tribe on the Housatonic River with whom they traded. Beginning in 1662, they purchased the land that would become today's towns of Woodbury (1673), Southbury (1787), Bethlehem (1787), Roxbury (1796), and Judea (now Washington) (1779).

Without inland roads, settlers used canoes to reach the "Pomperaug Plantation," the fertile fields on the Pomperaug River. The first settlers wrote "Fundamental Articles," a unique town constitution. Stores and workshops came next. The Jabez Bacon store (c.1760) and home (c.1762) were built for Jabez Bacon, Connecticut's first millionaire. Dozens of other buildings over two centuries old remain, many housing antique dealers as part of the Connecticut Antiques Trail.

Among the notable residents of Woodbury over its more than 300-year history is Leroy Anderson (1908-1975), a world-renowned conductor and composer of over one hundred works of light orchestral music, including the popular melody, "Sleigh Ride," which Anderson conceived during a July 1946 heat wave in Woodbury.

More than a dozen restaurants offer options from coffee breaks to pizza to gourmet dining.

Points of Interest

Canfield Corners Pharmacy (1876). Old-fashioned drug and sundries store; still jerking soda, scooping ice cream, and serving up floats at classic soda fountain. Regular business hours.

Colonial Milestones. Remain on Main St. and Flanders Rd. along the main path taken in colonial days to Litchfield (the county seat).

Flanders Nature Center. Art, nature center, and preserves with nature trails.

Frazier Farm. Riding lessons & shows.

Glebe House (1750) and Gertrude Jekyll Garden. Seabury Society museum; site of election of first Episcopal bishop in U.S.; summer hands-on history program for kids; holiday programs; special events.

North Congregational Church (1816). Designed by Asher Benjamin, "America's first architect."

Old Woodbury Historical Society. Maintains local archives and historic buildings, including South Center District School #2 (1867), 423 Main St. South, a one-room schoolhouse and museum; Hurd House, a 17th century home.

Orenaug Park Observation & Fire Tower (1911). Impressive views of the Pomperaug valley; trail to Bethel Rock, site of early settler's church services. Travel via Orenaug Park trail from Park Rd. Trail begins behind Woodbury Library parking lot.

Walk Woodbury. Contains list of walks and maps for the town.

The c.1750 Glebe House. Barbara Hampton

Notes

See woodburyparksandrec.com.

Woodbury Public Library. Local events, history and biography information; "Walking Tours of Historic Woodbury."

Woodbury Ski Area. Now closed. A site for downhill skiing, tubing, summer sports, and concerts.

Events

Community Theater at Woodbury. Year-round at Woodbury's Historic Town Hall.

New Morning Songwriter's Series. Year-round at New Morning Market.

2nd Connecticut Heavy Artillery. Civil war re-enactors, year-round, and various locales.

Woodbury Restaurant Week. Showcases local eateries. In some years the week begins in late Feb. while others are in early March.

Main Street Ballet Summer Performance.

Hollow Park Summer Concert Series & theater. Events have various sponsors. Most are listed on the "Community Events Calendar" on the town's website.

Woodbury Arts Festival in June, Easrth Day Celebration in April, Fall Festival in October, Christmas Eve Luminaria Celebration in December.

Address Book

Town Sites
www.woodburyct.org
www.woodburyparksandrec.com
www.woodburyct.myrec.com

Canfield Corners Pharmacy
2 Main St. North

Community Theater at Woodbury
5 Mountain Rd.
www.ctaw-ct.org

Flanders Nature Center
596 Flanders Rd.
www.flandersnaturecenter.org

Frazier Farm
335 Middle Road Tpke.
www.frazierfarmct.com

The 1876 Canfield Corners Pharmacy. Barbara Hampton

Glebe House
49 Hollow Rd.
www.glebehousemuseum.org

Hurd House
25 Hollow Rd.

Main Street Ballet
124 S. Pomperaug Ave.
203-263-5107
www.mainstreetballet.com

North Congregational Church
11 Main St. North
203-263-2410
www.northchurchwoodbury.org

South Center District School #2
423 Main St. South

Woodbury Public Library
3269 Main St. South
www.woodburylibraryct.org

Woodbury Ski Area
785 Washington Rd.
www.woodburyskiarea.com

Events

Hollow Park Summer Concert Series
Hollow Park on Hollow Rd.
www.woodburyct.myrec.com

Main Street Ballet Summer Performance
www.mainstreetballet.com

New Morning Songwriter's Series
129 Main St. North

Woodbury Earth Day
www.woodburyearthday.org

Woodbury Restaurant Week
www.wowbury.org

[Passport Stamp / Signature & Date Here]

New Haven County
WOLCOTT
WATERBURY
MIDDLEBURY
SOUTHBURY
NAUGATUCK
PROSPECT
CHESHIRE
MERIDEN
WALLINGFORD
BEACON FALLS
OXFORD
BETHANY
HAMDEN
NORTH HAVEN
SEYMOUR
WOODBRIDGE
NORTH BRANFORD
MADISON
ANSONIA
DERBY
NEW HAVEN
EAST HAVEN
GUILFORD
ORANGE
WEST HAVEN
BRANFORD
MILFORD

CHAPTER 3

NEW HAVEN COUNTY

Ansonia

By Pauline Sholtys, lifelong Ansonia resident and local history buff

Ansonia is bisected by the Naugatuck River, which powered the factories of historic importance to the community. Located 12 miles northwest of New Haven, the city has rail service to New York City, and Rt. 8 connects to major interstate highways.

Ansonia was part of Derby until the late 1800s. The first English settlers, who came to Derby from Milford in 1654 to grow hops for brewing, built their houses on land now mostly in Ansonia; some of the foundations still exist. These settlers were still obliged to attend and support the Milford church. In 1672 they organized their own church, and in 1675 the area became a plantation named after Derbyshire, England.

In 1844, Anson G. Phelps purchased land along the east side of the river for an industrial village within Derby, creating the name "Ansonia" from his first name. In 1864 Ansonia was chartered as a borough of Derby. In 1889 the state incorporated it as a town, and in 1893, as a city.

"The Copper City" became known for manufacturing. Besides copper and brass products, Ansonia produced heavy machinery, rubber and plastics products, molding and tubing, iron castings, sheet metal, electric supplies, automatic screw machines, silk goods, foundry products, and the famous Ansonia Clocks.

On Aug. 19, 1955, the Naugatuck River flooded, submerging the downtown area under ten feet of water. Two hurricanes within a week dumped 20 inches of rain on Connecticut, causing tributaries to swell and overflow, sending several feet of rushing water downstream. In Ansonia, many buildings were destroyed, and a wall of water and debris washed away the Maple Street Bridge. Electric and telephone services were down for days, and city water was unsafe for a month. While cleanup was still under way, the Naugatuck flooded again on October 16. Following this disaster, a concrete flood wall was erected along the east bank of the river. The U.S. Army Corps of Engineers built flood control dams on the upper Naugatuck and its tributaries.

With Ansonia's gradual transition from a manufacturing hub to a suburb, Main Street waned as shoppers left for area malls, but in recent years it has been invigorated by new businesses. In 2000, the National Civic League named the Lower Naugatuck Valley, including Ansonia, as an "All-America City."

Interesting Places

Ansonia Nature & Recreation Center. This 150-acre park offers hiking trails, a two-acre pond, a soccer field, a baseball field, a playground, and educational programs and workshops. The Visitor Center is an octagonal stone and glass building (1977). A calendar of events is on the website. Open Sun.-Sat., 9-5. Free admission.

Ansonia Public Library. This Richardsonian Romanesque structure (1892) features a square clock tower with a pyramidal roof and an entrance hall with a stone mosaic floor picturing Pegasus and Bellerophon. The Anna Sewell Memorial Fountain, including a water trough once used by horses, is on the grounds. On the National Register of Historic Places. Open Mon.-Thu., 9-7; Fri., 9-4; Sat., 9-1; Sun., closed.

General David Humphreys House. The birthplace of David Humphreys,

Humphreys House (1698). Pauline Sholtys

Notes

aide-de-camp to George Washington, is the oldest structure in Ansonia (1698). Restored to its 18th-century appearance, it is a museum of local history and Derby Historical Society headquarters. On the National Register of Historic Places. Open Mon.-Fri., 1-4. Groups of 8 or more, call in advance.

Ansonia Historic District. Besides the Humphreys House, the Historic District includes several privately owned pre-1800 houses.

Richard Mansfield House. This privately owned 18th-century saltbox is on the National Register of Historic Places.

Pork Hollow Monument. This honors a 1777 incident in which military provisions were moved to a secure location before the British could seize them.

Ansonia Riverwalk Park and Walkway. This paved section of the Naugatuck River Greenway connects to the Derby Greenway at Division St. Free parking near the trail entrance.

Events

Memorial Day Parade. May.

Midsummer Fantasy Renaissance Faire. June-July.

Festa! Italian Festival. August.

Rock the Valley, a day of music, art and family fun! August.

Ansonia Harvest Festival. September.

Tree Lighting and Holiday Marketplace. December.

Ansonia Nature & Recreation Center was once a 150 acre dairy farm that has reverted to its natural ways. Trails wind through young forests, meadows, streams, and an upland swamp. Its unique visitor center houses classrooms and an assortment of small animals. Pauline Sholtys

Address Book

Town Site
www.cityofansonia.com

Ansonia Nature & Recreation Center
10 Deerfield Ln.
203-736-1053
www.ansonianaturecenter.org

Ansonia Public Library
53 South Cliff St.
203-734-6275
www.ansonialibrary.org

General David Humphreys House
37 Elm St.
203-735-1908
www.derbyhistorical.org

Richard Mansfield House
35 Jewett St.
www.derbyhistorical.org

Events

Ansonia Harvest Festival
253 Main St.
203-305-9255

Annual Tree Lighting
Veterans Park

Festa! Italian Festival
Holy Rosary Church Grounds

Memorial Day Parade

Midsummer Fantasy Renaissance Faire
Warsaw Park, 119 Pulaski Highway
www.mfrenfaire.com

Rock The Valley
/RockTheValleyAnsonia

[Passport Stamp / Signature & Date Here]

Beacon Falls

By Michael A. Krenesky, Beacon Falls Selectman and President of the Beacon Falls Historical Society

The Town of Beacon Falls is one of the smallest towns in Connecticut being only 9.9 sq. mi. Beacon Falls was first settled in c. 1678 when it was part of Derby. The name of Beacon Falls first appears in 1864 when a joint school district was formed out the Towns of Bethany and Oxford. The town was incorporated shortly thereafter in June 1871 out of the towns of Bethany, Naugatuck, Oxford and Seymour, the largest sections of land coming from Bethany and Oxford.

Early in its history it was both agricultural and a 'company' town. Like most of Connecticut, it was inhabited by Native American tribes, primarily Algonquian, who lived along the Naugatuck River, which when translated from Algonquian means "Lone tree along the fishing place."

Its industrial base began c.1848 with textiles and in the 1850s the establishment of the American Hard Rubber Co., c.1854, which used the invention of vulcanized hard rubber by Charles Goodyear to manufacture multiple products, such as buttons, buggy whips, and powder flasks. At this time a canal was built that ran behind the mill buildings. There is a short section of that canal behind the buildings today. Several years later the rubber company moved to Long Island, NY. The 100 acres that comprised the mill and the hill above the factory buildings became the location of the Home Woolen Co. which made blankets and shawls used by Union Troops in the Civil War. The mill complex is listed on the National Register of Historic Places. During 1870-71 when the Town petitioned for recognition by the State, the name was suggested to be "Home." Beacon Falls was the final designation in 1871.

The mill buildings would experience their greatest output with the opening of the Beacon Falls Rubber Shoe Co. in 1899. Started by George Lewis and his son Tracy, the company would grow from several hundred employees to over two thousand. When George Lewis died in 1914, Tracy became President. During the next seven years the company expanded the most. Tracy had a vision of building a fully self-sufficient community that included its own electric company, a community center, movie house, and bowling alley amongst other improvements. The town band would play during lunch in the summer months. Its 'fire company' would become the roots of the current fire department, Beacon Hose Company No. 1.

Tracy's vision ended in 1921 when he died unexpectedly. US Rubber Company would buy the company in 1931, adding the last major holdout of independently owned rubber companies into the so-called "American Rubber Trust."

Beacon Falls grew slowly, but steadily during the 20th century to the current 6,020 residents. It merged into a regional school system in 1969 with the town of Prospect. In the fall of 2001, after 30 years of debate and several failed attempts to approve building a high school, the regional school district opened Woodland Regional High School on the eastern-most portion of the Matthies Park site.

Interesting Places

Matthies Park. 300-acre park purchased in 1971 from Bernard Matthies with the intent of building a high school on the property. Carrington Pond in the center has a

Volunteer Park is on Main St. behind the firehouse. It is perfect place to read or watch the river run by. Michael Krenesky

NOTES

man-made island with the summer home of Bernard Matthis. Hiking, fishing, and canoe/kayaking in the warmer months.

Toby's Pond. Developed by O&G Industries as a sand & gravel operation along the Naugatuck River, the Town took possession in 2009. The site includes a nearly one-mile long pond. Fishing, canoeing, kayaking, and hiking.

High Rock State Park/Naugatuck State Forest. Also known as Clara O'Shea State Park. Hiking trails with small waterfalls along brook. This the former site of High Rock Grove, a recreation area developed by the Naugatuck Railroad from 1880 through the early 1900s. It had upwards of 10,000 visitors a year who came to ride the carousel and to canoe on the Naugatuck River.

Naugatuck River. 40-mile river passing North to South through the center of town. One of only several authorized river access points for canoe and kayaking on the river. The two access areas are one at Riverbend Park, and the other at Volunteer Park behind the firehouse on North Main Street. There is also catch and release fishing of salmon and trout.

There are 300 acres in Matthies Park including the placid Carrington Pond and an island cottage that belonged to the Matthies family. In 1971 the town purchased the property which features fishing, hiking, canoeing, kayaking, and picnics. Michael Krenesky

ADDRESS BOOK

Town Site
www.beaconfalls-ct.org

High Rock State Park / Naugatuck State Forest
Cold Springs Rd.

Matthies Park
Pines Bridge Rd.
203-729-4340

Toby's Pond
601-895 S. Main St.

Volunteer Park
45 N. Main St.

[Passport Stamp / Signature & Date Here]

Bethany

By William L. Brinton, Town Clerk of Bethany & Bethany Historical Society

Bethany is in central New Haven County, 6 mi. north of Woodbridge and 12 mi. south of Waterbury. In the 2020 census, the population was listed as 5,297.

Bethany was home to Native Americans for thousands of years before Europeans arrived. Samuel Downs was one of the first recorded inhabitants in 1717. In 1784 the Town of Woodbridge was incorporated, including the area of present-day Bethany. The northern half broke off in 1832 to form the Town of Bethany.

Like most of Connecticut, forests were cleared in the 18th century to make way for agriculture. In the 19th century Bethany was mostly subsistence farms, but a few individuals constructed small mills along watercourses while others established hotels, blacksmith shops, and other commercial ventures. The two churches in town, Congregational and Episcopal, were both built in the 1800s, replacing earlier structures.

The early population of Bethany peaked in 1840 at 1,170 residents, and then began a long decline due to sections being annexed by adjacent towns as well as an overall migration out West. In the late 19th century, the New Haven Water Co. began buying up large tracts of land, building reservoirs, and replanting forests. The population bottomed out in 1920 at 411 people and didn't exceed the 1840 peak until 1950.

In the early 20th century, many families converted their land to cash-based businesses, primarily dairy farms. The dawn of the automobile age also brought new people to town, some of whom built summer cottages to escape the heat of the city while others settled permanently and commuted to New Haven or other towns for work.

The old Bethany Airport holds a unique position in town history. The field was established in 1923, one of the first in New England, and many pioneers of aviation visited. The airport was in operation for 42 years, closing in 1965.

After World War II, the town grew rapidly and many new homes and roads were built. The population nearly tripled in size between 1950 and 1970, increasing to 3,857. This prompted the town to construct a total of six additions to the elementary school as well as enlargements to the town hall and firehouse.

As the town grew, the desire to protect Bethany's irreplaceable rural character increased. The Bethany Land Trust was incorporated in the 1960s to accept donations of property. Also, a land acquisition fund was established in the 1970s to purchase important parcels. In the 1990s, the town, land trust, and water company all accelerated acquisition of open space. Today, over 6,000 acres are publicly or quasi-publicly owned, totaling about 45% of the town. Bethany has the smallest population density in New Haven Co. and is one of only three towns in the county still considered "rural." In 2007, Bethany was named Connecticut's #1 Small Town by *Connecticut Magazine*.

Places to Visit

Bethany Historical Society. Housed in former 1914 Town Hall, renamed the Stanley Downs Memorial Building.

First Church of Christ, Congregational (1831).

The former 1914 Bethany Town Hall was renamed the Stanley Downs Memorial Building to honor a former First Selectman. It has been restored and is the home of the Bethany Historical Society.
William L. Brinton

Notes

Christ Episcopal Church (1809).

Clover Nook Farm. 250 year-old family farm. Fresh vegetables, fruits, beef and other products.

Naugatuck State Forest. Hiking, hunting, mountain-biking, bird-watching, snowmobiling, and cross country skiing.

Old Bethany Airport. Town owned and used for recreation, such as horse shows, soccer, etc.

Quinnipiac Trail (18.3 mi). Oldest in the Connecticut Blue-Blazed Hiking Trail System.

Regional Water Authority recreation trails. Take Rt. 69 to Hatfield Hill Rd. for Lake Bethany trails or Sperry Rd. for Lake Chamberlain trails.

www.rwater.com/recreation

Russell Homestead. A 200 year-old farm museum operated by the Bethany Historical Society.

Veteran's Memorial Park. Features, swimming, picnics, playground, tennis courts, boating, hiking, Lakeview Lodge event facility and pavilion.

West Rock Ridge State Park. Fishing, hiking, picnicking, mountain-biking and horseback riding.

Whitlock's Book Barn. Selling used books, old maps, and ephemera since 1948.

Woodhaven Country Club. A 9-hole public course.

Founded in 1930 the Clark Memorial Library provides services, materials, programs, and activities. It has been enhanced with a large two story addition in the rear that has a beautiful children's section.
William L. Brinton

Address Book

Town Site
www.bethany-ct.com

Bethany Historical Society
512 Amity Rd. • 203-393-1832
www.bethanyhistory.com

Bethany Land Trust
www.bethanylandtrust.org

Bethany Town Hall
40 Peck Rd. • 203-393-2100
www.bethany-ct.com

Christ Episcopal Church
526 Amity Rd. • 203-393-3399
www.christchurchbethany.org

Clark Memorial Library
538 Amity Rd. • 203-393-2103
www.bethanylibrary.org

Clover Nook Farm
50 Fairwood Rd. • 203-393-2929
www.clovernookfarm.com

First Church of Christ, Congregational
511 Amity Rd. • 203-393-3116
www.bethanyfirstchurch.org

Old Bethany Airport
755 Amity Rd.

Russell Homestead
20 Round Hill Rd.

Veteran's Memorial Park
265 Beacon Rd.

Whitlock's Book Barn
20 Sperry Rd. • 203-393-1240
www.whitlocksbookbarn.com

Woodhaven Country Club
275 Miller Rd. • 203-393-3230
www.woodhavengolf.org

[Passport Stamp / Signature & Date Here]

Branford

By Jane Bouley, Branford Town Historian

The first settlers of New Haven purchased a tract of land from the Mattabesech Indians in December 1638 which included the territory of "Totokett" later called Branford. The Totoket Indians who lived here retained the peninsula known as Indian Neck. Before the English came, the Dutch set up a trading post at the mouth of the Branford River and the name Dutch Wharf remains today.

In 1643 the New Haven Colony granted to Mr. William Swayne and others of Wethersfield the plantation of Totokett whose boundaries were the Stony River and Great Pond (Lake Saltonstall) north to the Wallingford line (including the present-day North Branford and Northford). In the 1660s the plantation known as Totokett or Totoket became Branford.

The early settlers were concerned with dividing the land, building homes and fences, and branding livestock. Farming was the mainstay of Branford family life for over two hundred years. Branford was also an accessible port and many boats traded along the eastern seaboard and to the West Indies exporting lumber, livestock, brooms, and produce in return for molasses and rum. The shipping era in Branford ended in the early 20th century. Today, hundreds of pleasure boats are moored along Branford's shoreline with its easy access to Long Island Sound.

The railroad was built through Branford in 1852 which brought the Industrial Age. The Branford Lock Works was organized at the lower end of Main Street in 1862 making door and window hardware. The other large companies were the Malleable Iron Fittings Co. (1854) on the Branford River and the Atlantic Wire Co. (1906). These factories provided employment to many European immigrants.

The railroad and later the trolley opened Branford's shore to summer tourism. Branford became a popular summer resort and 19 summer hotels lined the shore. The most famous of these were the Indian Point House in Stony Creek, the Sheldon House in Pine Orchard, and the Montowese House in Indian Neck. The summer resort period ended after World War I due to the Depression, changing lifestyles, and increased mobility made possible by the automobile.

Today Branford, approx. 7 miles east of New Haven, is a residential community (pop. 30,000) offering superb location and recreational facilities.

Interesting Places

Harrison House Museum. Owned by Branford Historical Society, features period furnishings, gardens, and local artifacts. On the National Register of Historic Places. Sat. 1-4 PM, June-Sept. or by appointment.

Shoreline Trolley Museum. Tracks run through Branford. Oldest continuous running trolley line in the U. S. On the National Register of Historic Places.

Branford Town Center. Across from the train station. Features shops, restaurants, a beautiful New England Green, and an annual Festival and concert attracting 10,000 people every Father's Day weekend. www.branford-ct.gov

Branford Land Trust. Many miles

One of the 23 Thimble Islands in Long Island Sound in and around the harbor of Stony Creek in the southeast corner of Branford. Carol Highsmith

Notes

to walk with hundreds of acres and trails including Supply Pond, Youngs Pond, Beacon Hill, Stony Creek Quarry, and more.

Stony Creek Museum. Local artifacts and exhibits. Open seasonally. Open year round by appointment.

Seaside Home & Gifts. A unique boutique with nautical style. Shop in-store or online.

Thimble Island Boat Tours. Several tour companies offer trips and narrative. May-Oct., weather permitting.

Breweries. Branford has a thriving brewery scene including Stony Creek Brewery, and Thimble Islands Brewing Co.

The 1820 Academy is the oldest building on the Branford Green. It was a very select school till 1871 when it was sold to the Masons. In 1971 it was deeded to the town. Bill O'Brien

Address Book

Town Site
www.branford-ct.gov

Branford Land Trust
17 River St., East Haven
www.branfordlandtrust.org

Harrison House Museum
124 Main St.
203-488-4828
www.branfordhistoricalsociety.org/harrison-house.html

Seaside Home & Gifts
172 Thimble Island Rd.
203-208-0521
www.seasidehomeandgifts.com

Shoreline Trolley Museum
17 River St., East Haven
www.shorelinetrolley.org

Stony Creek Museum
84 Thimble Island Rd.
203-488-4014
www.stonycreekmuseum.org

Stony Creek Brewery
5 Indian Neck Ave.
www.stonycreekbeer.com

Thimble Islands Boat Tours
www.thimbleislandcruise.com
www.thimbleislander.net
www.thimbleislands.com

Thimble Island Brewing Co.
16 Business Park Dr
203-208-2827
www.thimbleislandbrewery.com

[Passport Stamp / Signature & Date Here]

Cheshire

*By Ron Gagliardi, author of **Images of America: Cheshire** and former editor of **Cheshire Magazine** and Municipal Historian Emeritus of Cheshire*

Cheshire is the "daughter town" of Wallingford, which is the "daughter town" of New Haven.

Cheshire was "born" in the late 1600s when the first settlers moved into "Ye Fresh Meadows" and began to hunt and farm. In 1705 English transplant, Thomas Brooks, called the settlement "Cheshire" after a county in his homeland. His own name survives today in Brooksvale, a section in the southern part of town.

These "West Farmers" established a school by 1719, a Congregational Church in 1724, and St. Peter's Episcopal Church in 1760. 1794 saw the founding of an Episcopal Academy now known as Cheshire Academy.

1780 was our incorporation year when Cheshire's 2,015 citizens were finally officially recognized by the State Legislature. In 1801 Cheshire's main street became a turnpike for the Hartford-New Haven stagecoach. The Farmington Canal arrived around 1828 and survived summer's droughts and winter's freezes until the New Haven and Northampton Railroad laid its tracks along the Canal's towpath in 1848. Today the Linear Park travels where the rails had been, past the lock and the Raimon Beard Lock 12 Museum. The Linear Park is on the National Register of Historic Places. The trail will be part of the East Coast Greenway that will eventually stretch from Florida to Canada.

Cheshire's agricultural roots are embodied in our state-bestowed title, the "Bedding Plant (a plant set into a garden bed or container when it is about to bloom) Capital of Connecticut," but we also had copper mines, first found in 1712 and barite mines from 1838 through 1877. Many of the miners came from a district in Cornwall, England, expanding the numbers of the local Methodist Church, founded in 1834. We even had an unsuccessful oil well drilled near what is now Dodd Middle School. There is a rumor of an unexplored silver vein under the appropriately named Copper Valley Country Club, but that has been declared to be unlikely by a local geologist, Dr. Charles Dimmick.

Industry continues to prosper here in our Industrial Park, following in the footsteps of the Cheshire Manufacturing Co., founded in 1850, later known as the Ball & Socket Co. and currently being resurrected by the Ball & Socket Arts group as a center for art and artists. Our Watch Factory complex is the home of numerous successful businesses. It was originally the home of the Cheshire Watch Co., a company whose watches were so likely to break that they are now rarities because owners felt it was better to discard them than to throw good money after bad trying to repair them.

In 2018 Cheshire was named to a list of the safest communities in the United States at number 45.

Interesting Places

Raimon Beard Lock 12 Museum. Collections include tools and implements of the canal era and wares manufactured in Cheshire during that time. The museum is open on the first or second Sunday of every month and by appointment.

The Barker Character, Comic & Cartoon Museum. Home of 80,000 antique toys and collectibles. Open Wed.-Sat. Noon-4 PM.

Cheshire Canal, Lock 12. Cliff Scofield post card from Ron Gagliardi

Notes

Audubon Society's Riverbound Farm and Sanctuary. Open on the third Sunday of the month from spring through the fall.

SAGE Mini Museum Multiplex. A hybrid art gallery and educational museum. Open to the public by invitation or appointment only.

The Cheshire Historical Society's Hitchcock-Phillips House. Keeps and shares the storied past of Cheshire. Open to the public every Sunday, 2-4 PM.

Artsplace Art Center. Many activities and special events involve not only the fine arts, but also the performing arts, literary arts, and outreach programs. Open Mon.-Thurs. 9 AM-4 PM.

Roaring Brook Falls. A difficult to reach, but inspiring waterfall. It is the highest single-drop waterfall in CT. Open daily 8 AM-6 PM.

Historic District. Contains 56 buildings in the center of town in the area of the Church Green. The principal axis of the Cheshire Historic District is South Main and Main St.

"Muffler Man" Paul Bunyan Statue. Stands 26' tall at House of Doors.

Address Book

Town Sites
www.cheshirect.org
www.cheshirepedia.org

Artsplace Art Center
1220 Waterbury Rd.
203-272-2787
www.artsplacecheshirect.org

Audubon Society's Riverbound Farm and Sanctuary
1881 Cheshire St.
203-634-1911
www.quinnipiacvalleyaudubon.org

Sweet Claude's is the first tenant in the renovated Ball and Socket Art complex. Ron Gagliardi

The Barker Character, Comic & Cartoon Museum
1188 Highland Ave., Bldg. B
203-699-3822
www.barkermuseum.com

The Cheshire Historical Society's Hitchcock-Phillips House
43 Church Dr.
203-272-2574
www.cheshirehistory.org

Extreme Air Trampoline Park
540 West Johnson Ave.
203-439-0280
www.extremeairfunusa.com

Historic District
South Main and Main St.

"Muffler Man" Paul Bunyan Statue
540 West Johnson Ave.

Museum of Celebrated Cartoonists and Illustrators (MOCCAI)
615 West Johnson Ave., Ste. 202

Raimon Beard Lock 12 Museum
487 N. Brooksvale Rd.
203-272-2743

Roaring Brook Falls
857 Roaring Brook Rd.

SAGE Mini Museum Multiplex
615 West Johnson Ave., Ste. 202
203-699-2633

Sweet Claude's Ice Cream
493 W. Main St.
203-272-4237
www.sweetclaudesicecream.com

[Passport Stamp / Signature & Date Here]

Derby

By John Walsh, former President of Derby Historical Society

Derby is the smallest of the state's 169 towns at 5 sq. mi. Chartered in 1675, it was once a much larger city including Ansonia, Oxford, and Seymour. Derby's location at the confluence of the Naugatuck and Housatonic rivers has allowed it to reinvent itself many times throughout its history

It has been marked with great military leaders like Commodore Isaac Hull, commander of the U.S.S. Constitution (Old Ironsides), and Fightin' Joe Wheeler who grew up in Derby but became a general in the Confederate Army.

Derby has also been home to ambassadors and inventors such as the first ambassador to Spain (David Humphreys) and the first Afro-American to serve as an ambassador to any country, Ebenezer Bassett, Haiti. Henry Sanford Shelton served as ambassador to Belgium and is considered the father of the citrus industry in the United States. Pierre Lallement took the first American bike ride here and J. Newton Williams invented the first American vertical lift machine (helicopter) here.

Water power from two rivers and the building of the Housatonic Dam made Derby a thriving industrial center after the decline of its ship building and maritime trade. Following the tragic flood of 1955 and the decline of heavy industry, Derby has been part of one of the greatest environmental cleanup stories in U.S. history, the cleanup of the Naugatuck River and is poised for its next great reinvention.

Interesting Places

Derby's Two Greens. Founders Commons. The old colonial town green, is located on the east side of town and Birmingham Green is a classic New England town green in the center of town.

Kellogg Environmental Center. Offers workshops, exhibits, nature activities, and lectures for the public.

Osborne Homestead Museum. Encompasses the house and grounds of the former Frances Osborne Kellogg Estate. Open May thru Oct. Free admission.

Osbornedale State Park. Offers hiking, fishing, picnics and visits to nearby Osborne Homestead Museum. Open 8 AM-8 PM.

Gilder Boat House. Yale has been rowing in Derby since 1852 and the Gilder Boat House, on Housatonic Lake, is one of the finest in the world.

Derby Greenway. The popular 1.7 mile path sits atop the flood walls along the Housatonic and Naugatuck rivers.

Derby Hall of Fame. Situated at the Division Street entrance to the Derby Greenway, the Hall of Fame surrounds the restored 1906 National Humane Alliance Fountain.

Olde Uptown Burial Ground. Possibly the oldest public burial ground in the country, its first burial took place in 1687. On Derby Ave. at the base of Academy Hill.

Memorial Day Parade. Derby continues to honor those who fell in service to our country with its annual parade that meanders through Derby and Shelton.

Osborne Homestead Museum Garden. John Walsh

NOTES

"Dueling" Fourth of July Fireworks. Fourth of July is especially festive as both sides of the Housatonic River erupt with spectacular fireworks and there are free concerts as Derby and Shelton celebrate our country's independence.

Commodore Hull Thanksgiving Day 5K Road Race. Thanksgiving starts early in Derby and Shelton as runners pound the pavement between Derby and Shelton in a 5K race.

Valley Heritage Driving Tour. Tourists can take a self-guided driving tour of the area. The tour begins in Derby and travels through Shelton, Ansonia, Seymour, Beacon Falls, Oxford and back to Derby.

Derby Greenway trail along the Housatonic and Naugatuck rivers. John Walsh

ADDRESS BOOK

Town Sites
www.derbyct.gov
www.electronicvalley.org/derby

Derby Hall of Fame
1 Elizabeth St.

Kellogg Environmental Center
500 Hawthorne Ave.

Olde Uptown Burial Ground
Derby Ave. & Division St.

Osborne Homestead Museum
500 Hawthorne Ave.
203-734-2513

Osbornedale State Park
555 Roosevelt Dr.

Gilder Boat House
280 Roosevelt Dr.

EVENTS

Commodore Hull Thanksgiving Day 5K Road Race
www.hullrace.org

"Dueling" Fourth of July Fireworks
On the Housatonic

[Passport Stamp / Signature & Date Here]

East Haven

By Chris Hemingway, Librarian at Hagaman Memorial Library

East Haven is a town on the southern shoreline in New Haven County (pop. 2010 c.29,000). It is part of the greater New Haven area between Boston and New York City.

The area now known as East Haven was first obtained on Nov. 29, 1638, by Puritan settlers, Reverend John Davenport and Theophilus Eaton. The Foxon section of East Haven was purchased from Chief Montowese on Dec. 11, 1638. In 1639, settlers started moving into the "center" of present-day East Haven. The first Connecticut ironworks was established in 1655, and the area became known as Iron Works Village. In 1675, villagers petitioned to be a separate town, but land issues and a feud with the Governor stalled the process for years.

During the time of the American Revolution, British forces, led by General William Tryon, attacked East Haven at a fort called Black Rock. General Marquis de Lafayette and revolutionary forces also visited the town and encamped on the Green. East Haven finally became an incorporated town in May 1785.

The War of 1812 saw a new threat by the British so the government decided to re-fortify Black Rock Fort, which was renamed Fort Nathan Hale, after the Connecticut patriot. During the war, the fort successfully defended the area from several British raids.

In 1863, during the Civil War, Fort Nathan Hale II was constructed to defend against raids by the Confederacy, but the fort did not see any action.

In 1892, there was a fire that destroyed much of the Town Hall and several businesses. In 1899, a volunteer fire department was formed. The new East Haven continued to grow. A growing Italian population emerged as a result of an influx of immigrants at the turn of the century. A new Town Hall was built in 1927 and a new library in 1928. During World War II, many East Haven men volunteered for the war.

The post-war era saw massive population growth and the construction of I-95. Retail stores and fast food franchises arose. The downtown area was redeveloped in the 1970s with more commercial centers and housing units in the Center and Foxon sections. A new police station was built in 1973.

Since 2004, the downtown area has been revitalized with new sidewalks and period lighting. Hispanic immigrants have settled in East Haven. In the 2010 census, Hispanics made up about 10 percent of the population.

Interesting Places

East Haven Green Historic District. The Green is located in the center of town across from the East Lawn Cemetery. An original Civil War cannon from Fort Nathan Hale is on the grounds as well as a marker where General

The 1909 Hagaman Memorial Library at 227 Main St. Jerry Dougherty

Notes

Lafayette and his troops encamped. Filled with a rich history, the Green continues to play an important role in hosting concerts, festivals, and town events.

Hagaman Memorial Library. The East Haven Library (1909) is an important community and research center, with a collection exceeding 70,000 volumes along with hosting concerts, programs, children's activities, and much more. Mon. 10-5, Tue.-Thur. 10-8, Fri. 10-5, Sat. 10-5.

Trolley Museum. The oldest operating trolley museum in the U.S. Daily 10:30 AM-4:30 PM.

First Congregational Church of East Haven. One of the oldest stone churches in the U.S. rightfully nicknamed "Old Stone Church." Jacob Hemingway, one of the first Yale University students, served as the first pastor from 1704-1754. The new building was constructed 1772-1774. Sunday services are at 10 AM. It hosts seasonal events, craft fairs, a day-care center, and a nursery school.

The Margaret Tucker Park and the 1774 Old Stone Church at the corner of Main and High streets. Jerry Dougherty

Address Book

Town Site
www.townofeasthavenct.org

Hagaman Memorial Library
227 Main St.
www.hagamanlibrary.org

Trolley Museum
17 River St.
www.shorelinetrolley.org

First Congregational Church of East Haven
251 Main St.
www.oldstonechurchucceasthaven.org

[Passport Stamp / Signature & Date Here]

Guilford

By Joel E. Helander, Guilford Town Historian

Guilford is a charming and largely rural suburban town bordering Long Island Sound in south-central Connecticut. Interstate I-95 and the AMTRAK rail line provide convenient transportation to or from Boston and New York City in less than two hours.

The town was settled by an oppressed, but optimistic, band of Puritans under the leadership of Reverend Henry Whitfield in 1639, making it the seventh oldest town in our great state. During the 18th century, both ship-building and the West Indies cattle/rum trade prospered around the port of Sachem's Head and West River. During the 19th century, the industrial revolution gave rise to tomato canneries and the celebrated Beattie Granite Quarry, where every block of granite in the pedestal of the Statue of Liberty was quarried. Light industries and commercial enterprises such as rose growing, fruit/vegetable farming, book publishing, brass foundries, poultry raising, and fishing blossomed during the 20th century.

The heart of Guilford is the 8-acre Village Green, surrounded by small businesses and boutique shops, four churches, town hall, free library, and art galleries – yet it is a living neighborhood with one of the largest number of Colonial-era homes in Connecticut. The town is proud of the manner in which it balances economic development and tourism with preservation of cultural resources. There are nearly 800 dwelling houses that are older than 100 years, four National Register districts, two local historic districts, and several thousand acres of protected open space, including two town swimming beaches (Lake Quonnipaug & Jacob's) and waterfront parks (Chittenden Beach, Chaffinch Island, Shell Beach). Special events of all kinds are staged on the Green, such as Memorial Day exercises (May), High School graduation (June), Sunday summer concerts, Little Folks Fair (June), Strawberry Social (June), Arts Center Expo (July), Shakespearean Theater (August), Jewish Festival (August), Taste of the Shoreline (August), Harvest Festival (September), October Fest (October) and tree/menorah lighting (December).

Shopping, dining, and exploring Guilford offer stimulating opportunities for residents and tourists alike, including five museums. The Henry Whitfield State Museum (1639-40) is Connecticut's oldest house and New England's oldest stone house. The Dudley Farm Museum (1844) in picturesque North Guilford maintains two large barns and outbuildings, farm animals, gardens, and a seasonal farm market. The Hyland House Museum (1713) is completely furnished with an exceptional collection of 17th and 18th century furniture and artifacts. The Medad Stone Tavern Museum (1803), with its ten fireplaces, contains many original furnishings and is sited on a large property with horse pasture and community gardens. The Thomas Griswold House Museum (1764) is a classic New England saltbox dwelling with a working blacksmith shop and other outbuildings.

Four miles offshore, in Long Island Sound, the state's second oldest lighthouse, Faulkner's Island Light (1802) remains an active aid

Emily Ott (L), a lineal descendant of several founding fathers of Guilford, and friend, Kaitlin Worden, by the historical marker on the Town Green. Joel E. Helander

Notes

to navigation maintained by the U.S. Coast Guard. The landmark island is a beautiful wildlife refuge owned by the U.S. Fish & Wildlife Service, which co-sponsors an annual "open house" shortly after Labor Day.

Other recreational opportunities include two yacht clubs, boat launching ramp and mooring slips at the Town Marina, a sightseeing tour boat that departs from the Guilford Lobster Pound Dock, historic walking and bus tours, senior citizens programming, and a 9-hole golf course.

During the third weekend of September, the Guilford Agricultural Society hosts a magnificent country fair on its grounds off Lover's Lane. Be sure to visit the town's Information Kiosk at 32 Church St. in the parking lot of the Greene Community Center.

Built in 1802, Faulkner's Island Lighthouse is Connecticut's second oldest lighthouse and the state's only active light station on an island. Joel E. Helander

Address Book

Town Sites
www.guilfordct.gov
www.guilfordpreservation.org

Breakwater Books
81 Whitfield St.
203-453-4141
breakwaterbooks.indielite.org

Dudley Farm Museum
2351 Durham Rd.

Grass Island Cruises
505A Whitfield St.
203-245-7208
www.grassislandcruisesct.com

Guilford Lakes Golf Course
200 N. Madison Rd.
203-453-8214
www.guilfordlakesgolf.com

Guilford Walking Tours
203-233-1026
www.guilfordpreservation.org

Henry Whitfield State Museum
248 Old Whitfield St.
203-453-2457

Hyland House Museum
84 Boston Street

Medad Stone Tavern Museum
197 Three Mile Course

Thomas Griswold House Museum
171 Boston St.

[Passport Stamp / Signature & Date Here]

Hamden

By Beth Shutts, Archivist, Hamden Historical Society, Miller Memorial Library

Hamden is the 11th largest town in Connecticut, with a current population estimate of 61,000. It is urban at the southern end, bordering on New Haven. Northern Hamden is more rural and is home to Quinnipiac University and Sleeping Giant State Park.

Hamden was originally settled in 1638 as part of the New Haven Colony. In 1786 it was incorporated as a separate town, and was named after the English statesman John Hampden.

Hamden played a role in the Industrial Revolution, thanks to Eli Whitney, who invented mass production at his arms factory. The major thoroughfare through Hamden is Whitney Ave., named in honor of Eli Whitney, and it runs past Whitney's old factory, now the Eli Whitney Museum.

The Farmington Canal Heritage Trail runs through Hamden. Situated along the scenic 10 miles are Lock 13 and Lock 14, where there is a Lock Keeper's House and Museum. Culturally Hamden boasts many notable people. Thornton Wilder made Hamden his home and is buried here. Alice Washburn, one of America's first female architects, lived in Hamden and designed many homes in the area. Ernest Borgnine is from Hamden.

Places of Interest

West Rock Ridge State Park. Straddling Hamden and New Haven this park has great trails. There is a boat launch at Lake Wintergreen for kayaks and canoes.

Sleeping Giant State Park. Hike up the Tower Trail on a clear day and you will be rewarded with remarkable views. In Hamden, we love our Giant!

Brooksvale Park. This Hamden town park features a petting zoo, hiking trails, parking for access to the Linear Trail, and in the winter, a sledding hill.

Farmington Canal. Extending 10 miles through Hamden there are several parking lots. It is very popular on the weekends. Entrance at Todd Street, 350 feet west of its intersection with Rt. 10. www.farmingtoncanal.org

Sleeping Giant Golf Course. This scenic public golf course is at the base of the Sleeping Giant.

Eli Whitney Museum. This is an especially wonderful place to take children ages 5-12. Generally it is open only on weekends. From Thanksgiving to New Year's the American Flyer train exhibit attracts many visitors.

Quinnipiac University. York Hill Campus. The views of New Haven from this part of the QU campus are spectacular. With wind turbines and Adirondack chairs to lounge in, it's worth the side trip. The TD Bank Sports Center is located here.

Jonathan Dickerman House. Open only on summer weekends.

Hamden History Room. On Facebook as Hamden Historical Society History Room. Open only on Tuesdays from 10 AM-2 PM. 2901 Dixwell Ave. The History Room is located in the Miller Memorial Library and hours are limited. For current hours call the Library (203-287-2680).

Hamden High. Depicting the

Jonathan Dickerman House (c.1792) has been preserved by the Hamden Historical Society. www.ctvisit.com

Notes

history of Hamden, the murals in the lobby were commissioned as a WPA project and painted by Salvatore DiMaio. 2040 Dixwell Ave.

Memorial Town Hall. Listed on the National Register of Historic Properties, the rotunda boasts five stunning stained glass windows. 2392 CT-10.

Places to Eat

Playwright. A fine way to end an Irish-themed visit to Hamden.

Glenwood Drive-In.

Wentworth Homemade Ice Cream. Stop here for the perfect treat after a hike on the Giant. Closed on Sunday.

And for the Irish in You!

Ireland's Great Hunger Museum. It is part of Quinnipiac University and is located a short way from the main campus.

Lucky Ewe Irish Goods. This new shop is centrally located in town.

The Eli Whitney Museum is an experimental learning workshop for students, teachers, and families. The museum's main building was originally the Eli Whitney Armory, a gun factory erected by Eli Whitney in 1798. www.ctvisit.com

Address Book

Town Site
www.hamden.com

Brooksvale Park
524 Brooksvale Ave.
www.brooksvalepark.com

Eli Whitney Museum
915 Whitney Ave.
www.eliwhitney.org

Glenwood Drive-In
2538 Whitney Ave.
www.glenwooddrivein.com

Ireland's Great Hunger Museum
3011 Whitney Ave.
www.ighm.org

Jonathan Dickerman House
3217 Whitney Ave.

Lucky Ewe Irish Goods
2371 Whitney Ave.
www.luckyeweirishgoods.com

Playwright
1232 Whitney Ave.
www.playwrightirishpub.com

Quinnipiac University
305 Sherman Ave.
www.qu.edu

Sleeping Giant Golf Course
3931 Whitney Ave.
www.sleepinggiantgc.com

Sleeping Giant State Park
200 Mount Carmel Ave.
www.ct.gov/deep/sleepinggiant
For trail maps: www.sgpa.org

Wentworth Homemade Ice Cream
3697 Whitney Ave.
www.wentworthicecream.com

[Passport Stamp / Signature & Date Here]

Madison

By Doe Boyle, Trustee of the Madison Historical Society and the author of two travel guides to her native state of Connecticut

Europeans early in the 1600s. First the home of the indigenous Hammonasset people, it was known as East Guilford throughout the 18th century, after Puritans founded its "mother-town" of Guilford in 1639. Incorporated as a separate town in 1826, it was named for James Madison – primary author of the Bill of Rights and fourth president of the nation.

In its first two centuries, Madison shared the agrarian, mercantile, and maritime roots of its neighbors. Fisheries, shipbuilding wharves, oyster beds, and a robust coastal trading scene kept its docks busy as Madison products traveled to New York, Boston, and beyond. By the 19th century, small industries dotted Madison's woods, riverbanks, and shore, in the form of gristmills, sawmills, paper mills, a crayon factory, charcoal pits, and lumberyards. In the 20th century, the economics of Madison shifted to the business of leisure as vacationers thronged to its cottages and inns.

Today this suburb is at heart a small town, and its pulse is found on its picturesque Main Street. Commonly called "downtown," the portion of the Boston Post Road that lies between Britton Lane on the west and Scotland Road to the east is a cheerful hub of commerce, culture, and entertainment. This corridor includes the Madison Green National Historic District, one of the nation's best independent bookstores, a restored movie house, an intriguing string of independent retail establishments, and, new in 2022, the Madison Center for History and Culture, located in Lee's Academy on Madison's green. These features infuse this "village" of 18,000 inhabitants with an atmosphere of energy and neighborly pride.

Those willing to wander away from Main Street won't be disappointed by Madison's other thoroughfares. Eastward from Main Street, the Boston Post Road heads toward the Shoreline Greenway Trail within Hammonasset State Park, the longest public beach on the CT coast. At Hammonasset, the beach, the Meigs Point Nature Center, and the campground draw more annual visitors than to any other park in the state. Luckily, in this town that extends northward nearly 15 miles from the Sound to the border of Durham, development elsewhere in town is limited by such protected spaces as the town-owned Rockland Preserve, Bauer Park, and Salt Meadow Park, plus more than 1,700 acres under the stewardship of the Madison Land Conservation Trust.

When the sun goes down, travelers can settle in such peaceful places as the Scranton Seahorse Inn, a bed-and-breakfast in the heart of downtown, the Homestead Inn just outside the town center, and the Madison Beach Hotel, one of Connecticut's few shorefront hostelries. Madison may sometimes feel a bit removed from the rest of the world, but it's hard to resist the urge to enjoy life here with neighbors and friends, not too far from the waves upon the sand.

Interesting Places

Madison Green National Historic District. Walking tour guides at www.madisonhistory.org.

Lee's Academy. Madison Historical Society (MHS) administrative offices and non-circulating research library.

Allis-Bushnell House Museum. House museum operated by MHS.

Madison Mile. Outdoor sculptures downtown. Guided tours, Saturdays at 11 AM, May-Oct.

Shoreline Greenway Trail. 2.5 miles round-trip; parking lot east of Hammonasset Beach State Park entrance.

Hammonasset Beach State Park. Two-mile beach, swimming, fishing, bicycling, bird-watching.

Notes

Open year-round. 550 seasonal campsites.

Meigs Point Nature Center. In Hammonasset State Park. Ranger programs, touch tanks, live animals. Tues.-Sun. 10 AM to 5 PM (Mar. -Oct.) and Tues.-Sat.10 AM to 4 PM (Nov.-Feb.).

Rockland Preserve. Open year-round.

Madison Land Conservation Trust. Open year-round. Enjoy 23 hiking trails and geocaching.

Address Book

Town Site
www.madisonct.org

Allis-Bushnell House Museum
853 Boston Post Rd.
203-245-4567
www.madisonhistory.org

E.C. Scranton Memorial Library
801 Boston Post Rd.
203-245-7365
www.scrantonlibrary.org

Hammonasset Beach State Park
1288 Boston Post Rd.
203-245-1817

Homestead Inn
391 Boston Post Rd.
203-245-0212
www.homesteadmadison.com

Madison Beach Hotel
94 West Wharf Rd.
203-245-1404
madisonbeachhotel.curiocollection.com

Madison Center for History and Culture at Lee's Academy
14 Meetinghouse Ln.
203-245-4567
www.madisonhistory.org

Madison Land Conservation Trust
www.madisonlandtrust.org

Madison Sculpture Mile
Downtown Madison
www.hollycroftfoundation.org

Meigs Point Nature Center
203-245-8743
www.meigspointnaturecenter.org

R.J. Julia Booksellers
768 Boston Post Rd.
203-245-3959
www.rjjulia.com

Rockland Preserve
99 Renee Way
203-245-5623

Scranton Seahorse Inn
818 Boston Post Rd.
203-245-0550
www.scrantonseahorseinn.com

Shoreline Greenway Trail
www.shorelinegreenwaytrail.org

In October second grade students observing "History Day" by visiting the Congregational Church (1838) on the Madison Green. Bob Gundersen

[Passport Stamp / Signature & Date Here]

Meriden

By Karen Roesler and Janis Leach Franco, Meriden Public Library

Centrally located, between Hartford and New Haven and abutting a dramatic landscape composed of traprock ridges towering above hills, valleys and streams, Meriden offers a combination of suburban and city life. Originally a sector of Wallingford, Meriden incorporated as a town in 1806. Mills powered by the Quinnipiac River and its tributaries made the town an early manufacturing center for items such as cut nails and ivory combs. By the mid-1800s, Meriden boasted more than a dozen manufacturers of britanniaware and silver-plated products that were consolidated into the International Silver Company in 1898. The company's success and prosperity led to Meriden being dubbed "the Silver City of the World." In 1944 Meriden was named an "Ideal War Community" for its manufacturing in World War II.

With the decline in the silver industry and the rise in imported products, Meriden had to overcome the loss of manufacturing jobs. While a few of the oldest companies continue, many new technology firms have moved in and many old manufacturing sites have been revitalized. Recently a former site in the center of the City has been cleaned, structured to control downtown flooding, and converted into a public park. The "Meriden Green" has received numerous state and national awards and it joins the list of other beautiful and spacious public parks, including Hubbard and Giuffrida Parks.

Interesting Places

Castle Craig. Given to Meriden in 1900 by Walter Hubbard, Castle Craig is a stone observation tower set high on a traprock peak in Hubbard Park. The structure is 32 feet high and 58 feet in circumference. Since the tower is more than 1000 feet above sea level, it provides spectacular views of the countryside. The road up to Castle Craig is open April thru Oct., from 10 AM to 5 PM. Hiking trails to the tower are open year-around.

Hubbard Park. Located on the west side of Meriden, the 1,800-acre park was the gift of local industrialist Walter Hubbard and is on the National Register of Historic Places. Hubbard Park has it all: natural beauty, picnicking, hiking trails, a swimming pool, playground, ice skating, Castle Craig, and some fabulous festivals. The Daffodil Festival, held annually in late April, highlights over 600,000 daffodils planted throughout the park as a backdrop to the crafts, amusement rides, food, entertainment, and a fireworks display for all to enjoy. In December, the park becomes a wonderland of lights that adorn the trees and shrubs, and form animal shapes and other whimsies throughout the park.

Andrews Homestead. The Moses Andrews Homestead was built about 1760. During the Revolutionary War, and until 1810, Episcopal church services were held at the residence. The traditional New England salt-box house remained in the Andrews family until 1864. After that it had many uses and fell into periods of neglect and rescue. After 1940, the Meriden Historical Society gained control and completed a major renovation in 1954. Today, the City owns the building with the Meriden Historical Society maintaining the museum. The fully

The 1711 Solomon Goffe House is a museum that has tours led by volunteers dressed in period attire. Karen Roesler

Notes

furnished center has a fabulous permanent and rotating collection of "made in Meriden" objects. The museum has open house hours on Sundays in October and May.

Solomon Goffe House. Meriden's oldest structure was built by Solomon Goffe around 1711. Through the years it has had a succession of owners and uses, including several decades as a restaurant named the 1711 Inn. The house was vacant when the Napier Company presented it to the city in 1977. After extensive renovation, it was opened as a museum in 1986 and offers programs demonstrating life in the 18th and 19th centuries presented by costumed guides.

From the top of Castle Craig visitors have great views. On a clear day looking south is Long Island Sound and the outline of Long Island itself. To the north are the Berkshire Hills of Massachusetts. Karen Roesler

Address Book

Town Site
www.meridanct.gov

Andrews Homestead
424 West Main St.
203-639-1913
www.meridenhistoricalsociety.org

Castle Craig
Peak Dr.
www.meridenct.gov

Hubbard Park
999 West Main St.

Meridan Public Library
470 Lewis Ave.
203-630-4621
www.meridenlibrary.org

Solomon Goffe House
677 North Colony St.

[Passport Stamp / Signature & Date Here]

Middlebury

By Jo-Ann C. LoRusso, Library Director, Middlebury Public Library

Middlebury was incorporated in October 1807. This typical New England town is located in New Haven Co. Its population was 7,597 in the 2011-2015 census.

The town of Middlebury's name comes from its location in the middle of these three surrounding towns: Waterbury, Southbury, and Woodbury. It was known for its dairy farms and horse raising. Middlebury remains a country-like setting with rolling hills. A picturesque historical barn, known as Brookdale Farm, can be seen along Rt. 188. Trolley rails that connected Waterbury to Woodbury are now a greenway for walkers to enjoy. Lake Quassapaug, which is the home of Quassy Amusement Park established in 1952, remains a popular destination during the summertime.

Interesting Places

Middlebury Public Library. Contains approx. 75,000 volumes. Free programs and services promoting literacy for all ages are offered daily. Programs offered are computer classes, lectures on health and wellness, story time for early learners, 3D printing workshops, and local art exhibits. Visit our Connecticut History Room dedicated to preserving the history of Middlebury and surrounding towns neatly cataloged for accessibility. A mural of Fenn's Pond by local artist Sue Healey is proudly displayed.

Middlebury Historical Society. The building began as Center School, a two-room schoolhouse built in the 1800s, and later housed the Middlebury Public Library. Open most Mondays 2-5 PM.

Brookdale Farm. Called 'Fenn Farm' by the locals after the Fenn family that lived there since the 1800s. This property was purchased by the town to preserve its historic significance. Every fall, a farm tour is offered to the public. Refreshments are served and stories of the past are shared. Skating on Fenn Pond in the winter is as much fun as sledding down the hillside.

Middlebury Land Trust. Seeks to preserve those natural areas, including forests, meadows, swamps, marshes, ponds and streams which contribute to and enhance the rural nature of Middlebury. List of holdings.

The Middlebury Greenway. A 4.4-mile hilly walking trail was originally a trolley line built in 1908 that ran from Woodbury to the Waterbury town line. It runs from Straits Turnpike/Rt. 63 at Woodside Ave. to Quassapaug Field at Middlebury Rd.

Lake Quassapaug. "Big Pond" has been a summer destination since the 1908 installation of the trolley rail system connecting Waterbury to Woodbury. It offers swimming, fishing, and picnicking.

Quassy Amusement Park. Rides, especially the carousel, are popular attractions. The rides are updated and replaced to reflect the times while keeping with tradition. A waterpark overlooking the lake was recently added.

The Middlebury Historical Society is near the Green on Library Rd. The 1800s building began as Center School, a two-room school and later housed the Middlebury Public Library. Jerry Dougherty

NOTES

The Middlebury Public Library is at 30 Crest Rd. It was expanded in 2013. Jo-Ann C. LoRusso

The first town hall, a 2.5-story, frame, and Georgian Revival style, was built in 1896 and remodeled in 1916. In 1935 a fire destroyed by fire it and it was replaced with the present structure. Jerry Dougherty

ADDRESS BOOK

Town Site
www.middlebury-ct.org

Brookdale Farm
55 Artillery Rd.

Middlebury Greenway
Straits Tpke./Rt. 63 & Woodside Ave.

Middlebury Historical Society
Village Green on Library Rd.
203-758-9798
www.middleburyhistoricalsociety.org

Middlebury Land Trust
www.middleburylandtrust.org

Middlebury Public Library
30 Crest Rd.
203-758-2634
www.middleburypubliclibrary.org

Quassy Amusement Park
2132 Middlebury Rd.
203-758-2913
www.quassy.com

[Passport Stamp / Signature & Date Here]

Milford

By Arthur Stowe, Milford City Historian

Milford is on Long Island Sound, between Bridgeport and New Haven. It encompasses 23.7 sq. mi. with some 50,000 people.

Milford was settled in 1639 by Puritans seeking their own parish. The native people valued the area for its rich soil and the wealth of the sea. The Paugusset Indians had a large settlement here and in addition to farming they harvested oysters, clams and fish.

Our town has the longest shoreline of any CT town and one of the largest town greens in New England. Both the Merritt Parkway and I-95 pass through town along with the Metro North railroad.

Other sections of town are Devon to the west and the borough of Woodmont to the east. There are multiple beaches: Walnut Beach, Bayview, Point Beach, Fort Trumbull, Gulf Beach, and more. Milford also includes Silver Sands State Park, local parks and hiking trails at Eisenhower Park, Wilcox Park, Walker's Pond, the Solomon Property, Mondo Ponds and the Red Root Nature Trail. You can fish from piers at Gulf Beach, Walnut Beach and other spots along the shore. Golf at the municipal course, The Orchards, or the semi-private Great River Golf Club.

Events

From spring through the fall there are various fairs and festivals in Milford, usually on the Green.

Oyster Festival each August, St. Patrick's Day parade, the Children's Trout Derby in May, the Memorial Day Parade, Farmers Markets, Pirate Day, the Milford Rotary Lobster Bake, the Sand Sculpture Competition at Walnut Beach, Woodmont Day, the Fire Engine Muster, Oktoberfest, the Irish Festival, Veteran's Day Parade, and a Christmas Lamplighter Stroll.

Famous People

One of our founders, Robert Treat, went on to found Newark, NJ. Peter Pond was one of the earliest explorers in the Canadian northwest. Three Connecticut governors have come from our town. Simon Lake obtained over two hundred patents for advances in naval design vital to modern submarines. Catherine "Kay" N. Pollard was the first female Scoutmaster in the Boy Scouts of America.

Milford is home to the world Headquarters of Subway Restaurants.

Interesting Places

Milford Historical Society. Three furnished 17th and 18th century houses, the Claude C. Coffin Indian collection, and a gift shop. Open from Memorial Day through Columbus Day on Sat. & Sun. 1-4 PM or by appointment.

Milford Regional Chamber of Commerce. Open Mon.-Fri. 8:30 AM-4:30 PM.

Milford Lisman Landing Marina. Open every day May 15th through Columbus Day. Weekdays 7 AM-7 PM and weekends 7 AM-11 PM.

Silver Sands State Park. One half mile of shoreline and beaches and 3/4 mile boardwalk.

Milford Arts Council. Restored Civil War era railroad station on the National Historic Register. It offers a black box stage with beautiful acoustics, intimate seating

The Connecticut Audubon Society's Coastal Center at Milford Point with observation decks. www.ctvisit.com

Notes

for up to 110 in theater or café configuration. Every year the MAC presents community theatre, live music concerts with international, regional and local talent, exhibitions, classes, workshops, films and lectures.

Downtown Milford Business Association. Downtown has unique shops, award-winning restaurants, night life, and a full-service marina accommodating day trippers or overnight boaters.

Connecticut Audubon Society's Coastal Center at Milford Point. On 8.4-acre barrier beach, next to the 840-acre Charles Wheeler Salt Marsh and Wildlife Management Area at the mouth of the Housatonic River. Visitors to the center have access to the Sound and to tidal salt marshes, barrier beaches, tide pools, and coastal dunes. The Coastal Center is a bird-watcher's paradise, 315 species have been seen here, many rarities. Center Hours: Tue.-Friday 10 AM-4 PM. Sat. 10 AM-1 PM Sun., Noon-4 PM

The c.1700 Eells-Stow House, one of the oldest houses in Milford, is on Milford Historical Society property and forms part of the Wharf Lane complex of historic houses. MHS

Address Book

Town Site
www.ci.milford.ct.us

Connecticut Audubon Society's Coastal Center at Milford Point
1 Milford Point Rd.
203-878-7440
www.ctaudubon.org/coastal-center-home

Downtown Milford Business Association
40 Railroad Ave.
203-882-0969

Milford Arts Council
40 Railroad Ave.
203-882-0969
www.milfordarts.org

Milford Public Library
57 New Haven Ave.
203-783-3290
www.milfordlibrary.info

Milford Historical Society
34 High St.
203-874-2664
www.milfordhistoricalsociety.org

Milford Regional Chamber of Commerce
5 Broad St.
203-878-0681
www.milfordct.com

Silver Sands State Park
1 Silver Sands Pkwy.
203-735-4311
www.ct.gov/deep/silversands

[Passport Stamp / Signature & Date Here]

NAUGATUCK

By Sandra Clark and Bridget Mariano, Naugatuck Historical Society

Naugatuck, located on and named after the Naugatuck River, was incorporated as a town in 1844 and became a borough in 1893, becoming then the only consolidated town and borough in Connecticut.

Only one year earlier in 1843 Charles Goodyear, a Naugatuck resident, discovered the process of vulcanizing rubber. He persuaded his brother-in-law, William Deforest, and the Lewis family brothers to support him in using vulcanization to make rubber products. The Rubber Industry became a major employer in Naugatuck for the next 150 years. In 1850 Bronson B. Tuttle and John Howard Whittemore established The Naugatuck Malleable Iron Co., later known as the Eastern Malleable Iron Company, whose corporate offices are maintained in Naugatuck.

During the early part of the 20th century other industries that flourished in Naugatuck included Peter Paul Manufacturing Co., makers of Mounds and Almond Joy candy bars. The company was bought by the Hershey Co. and moved to Virginia in 2007. The Risdon Mfg. Company made beautiful lipstick cases, perfume bottles and sewing notions. The company moved to Watertown CT in 2000.

With a great deal of foresight town leaders created an Industrial Park in 1970, located on route 68. Today the Industrial Park is at capacity, small and midsize industries have become a significant portion of Naugatuck's tax base and source of employment for the Borough

Industrialist John Howard Whittemore left an architectural legacy to the town in his gifts of schools, churches, public monuments and a public library. All were designed by the foremost architects of the late 19th and early 20th century. Stanford White, Charles Eliot, Warren Manning, Henry Bacon, Evelyn Beatrice Longman, Theodate Pope and the Olmsted Brothers are the famous names that contributed to the treasures located in our town.

Today Naugatuck takes pride in its architectural heritage. The pre-eminent architectural firm of the 19th and early 20th centuries was that of McKim, Mead and White. The Naugatuck Town Green, designed by Warren Manning, landscape architect, is surrounded by important buildings. The John Howard Whittemore Jr. Memorial Library, Salem School, the Naugatuck Congregational Church and Hillside School were all designed by the firm of McKim, Mead and White. Other architectural gems include Hop Brook School designed by one of the first women architects in the United States, Theodate Pope, and the World War I Memorial designed by Evelyn Beatrice Longman.

INTERESTING PLACES

Naugatuck Walking Tour. The Naugatuck Historical Society offers a guided walking tour of the historic district which includes a collection of McKim, Mead and White buildings; also the Whittemore Bridge and the former Train Station, both designed by Henry Bacon, architect of the Lincoln Memorial in Washington D.C.

The Peter Paul Candy Manufacturing Co. was founded in New Haven by six immigrants led by Peter Halajian. In 1922 the company moved its plant to Naugatuck.and produced millions of Mounds and Almond Joy candy bars till the factory was moved by its new owner, the Hershey Co., in 2007. NHS Collection

Notes

Gunntown Passive Park and Nature Preserve.

Naugatuck State Forest. A great place for hiking along the many different trails.

Whittemore Glen State Park. This is an undeveloped public recreation and wilderness area for hiking and horseback riding located in the town of Naugatuck. It is also known as the Larkin Bridle trail.

The Bronson B. Tuttle Home. This Queen Anne Victorian mansion is the home of the Naugatuck Historical Society.

Places to Eat

The Corner Tavern. It boasts unique features of old taverns.

66 Church. Enjoy lunch at this popular restaurant.

The Station Restaurant.

The 1881 Tuttle Home was built by Bronson B. Tuttle, the co-founder of the Naugatuck Malleable Iron Co. It is the home of the Naugatuck Historical Society. Ken Hanks

The post card shows the station when it opened in 1911. The station is now used as a restaurant. NHS Collection

Address Book

Town Site
www.naugatuck-ct.gov

Bronson B. Tuttle Home
380 Church St.
www.naugatuckhistory.org

66 Church
66 Church St.
475-212-3992
www.66church.com

The Corner Tavern
178 N. Main St.
203-729-3640
www.cornertavernct.com

Gunntown Passive Park and Nature Preserve
Gunntown Rd.

Howard Whittemore Memorial Library
243 Church St.
203-729-4591
www.whittemorelibrary.org

Naugatuck State Forest
Hunters Mountain Rd.
www.ct.gov/deep

Naugatuck Walking Tour
203-729-9039
www.naugatuckhistory.org

The Station Restaurant
195 Water St.
203-714-6611
www.thestation.online

Whittemore Glen State Park
Route 63

[Passport Stamp / Signature & Date Here]

New Haven

By William Armstrong, writer and resident of New Haven

Glaciers withdrawing from what was to become New Haven revealed a wide sandy plain between two ridges of volcanic traprock known to the area's first recorded residents, the Quinnipiac, as Wappintumpseck (Dawn Mountain) and Mautumpseck (Evening Mountain), now known as East and West Rock. Human inhabitation of the area has been dated back 8,000 years. The Quinnipiac, who numbered around 250 in 1638, were ravaged by foreign diseases and suffered oppression by the Pequot. They were traders, farmers, and fishers, and by English accounts, formidable allies in battle.

When explorers from the Massachusetts colony arrived, Theophilus Eaton and John Davenport stood on top of East Rock, looked down upon the fertile plain, and saw a land to fulfill their vision of a New Heaven, where they might establish a community "pleasing in the eyes of God." They founded a theocratic society (the only one in American history) in which only church members could participate in governance. They signed agreements with the Quinnipiac yet despite those good relations, by the outbreak of the American Revolution the tribe had dispersed and few remained in the area.

Education was close to the colonists' hearts and in 1660 Edward Hopkins established the Hopkins Grammar School, one of the oldest in the country. Yale came to New Haven soon afterwards; established in 1701 in Saybrook, New Haven leaders convinced the school to move to New Haven in 1716. This was not a popular decision with Saybrook and a cart of books leaving town was set afire by angry residents. New Haven may be the ultimate college town; in addition to Yale there are six other colleges and universities in the immediate area.

Many of New Haven's Puritans were merchants and sought to open trade with England. They accumulated goods for trade, loaded a ship and set sail. It was never seen again, a crippling blow to their hopes. For years afterwards, colonists and their offspring saw visions of a ghost ship sailing in the offing. The New Haven colony persevered and in 1750 reached its height as a mercantile town, which they were able to sustain despite a raid by the British in 1779. In the mid-1850s, inventors such as Eli Whitney, Charles Goodyear, and Oliver Winchester turned New Haven into an industrial powerhouse.

Although New Haven's economic strength faded, the character of the town was well established. New Haven follows the traditions of America's great immigrant cities. Waves of German, Irish, African-American, Italian, and other immigrants have left their mark on New Haven, and secured her reputation as a welcoming haven to immigrants and refugees.

Points of Interest

The People. Come to New Haven and stroll around the nine central blocks of America's first planned city. The variety of people and languages you encounter brings to mind London or New York.

Arts and Culture. Yale Peabody Museum. One of the world's most impressive university museums of natural history, bursting with collections of ornithology, Incan and Egyptian artifacts, and dinosaurs. In the Broadway era, plays would premiere here to test their success with audiences. The Long Wharf

View of New Haven, from the Soldiers and Sailors monument atop East Rock. Ryan Pilot

Notes

Theatre, Yale School of Drama, Yale Repertory Theater, and the Schubert Theater have productions and premieres every year. New Haven is home to five(!) symphony orchestras and countless ensembles.

Food. New Haven is a foodie city. New Haven style pizza, "apizza"(pronounced ah-beetz), always ranks at the top of national polls. Modern, Pepe's, Sally's, and Bar are the four big names but it's hard to find a bad pie in town. The hamburger was invented at Louis Lunch in 1898; they're still making them the same way today. You'll find outstanding Southern American, Thai, French, Italian, Chinese, Spanish, Japanese, and Mediterranean restaurants on New Haven's abundant menu.

Architecture. Cass Gilbert designed our train station and public library. Louis I. Kahn designed the Yale Center for British Art, the largest collection outside of the U.K. Yale boasts many styles from their collegiate gothic buildings to stylistic triumphs such as the Beinecke Library. The 216' Harkness Tower was completed in 1921 was donated to Yale by Anna M. Harkness in honor of her recently deceased son, Charles William Harkness, an 1883 Yale graduate.

Walking distance. New Haven is a walking city; everything described above is a 20-min. walk from the Green.

The Saturday carillon concerts from Harkness Tower are sublime. Bring a chair.
William Armstrong

Address Book

Town Site
www.newhavenct.gov

BAR
254 Crown St.
203-495-8924
www.barnightclub.com

Harkness Tower
74 High St.

Ives Main Library / New Haven Free Public Library
133 Elm St.
203-946-8130
www.nhfpl.org

Louis Lunch
261 Crown St.
203-562-5507
www.louislunch.com

Modern Apizza
874 State St.
203-776-5306
www.modernapizza.com

Pepe's Pizzeria
157 Wooster St.
203-865-5762
www.pepespizzeria.com/new-haven

Sally's Apizza
237 Wooster St.
203-624-5271
www.sallysapizza.com

Yale Peabody Museum
170 Whitney Ave.

[Passport Stamp / Signature & Date Here]

North Branford

By Lauren Davis, Library Director, Atwater Memorial Library North Branford

North Branford, a small community in New Haven Co. with a population of 14,407 in 2010 has these sections: Totoket, Northford, South Queach, Ashley Park, and East Bradford.

The town was first settled in 1695 as the north farms of Branford. In 1638, Theophilus Eaton negotiated the land from the Mattabeseck, called Totoket, meaning "place of the tidal river" because of its access to the Branford River. By 1644 a permanent settlement was established, after which it was called Branford. As Branford continued to increase in prosperity and size, the people petitioned the state of Connecticut in 1831 to divide Branford into two distinct towns, resulting in the establishment of North Branford.

Agriculture was an important aspect of the town's early economy and remains a strong presence today. At a 1966 auction, Donald Augur sold his 72-animal dairy herd, the highest-producing Holstein herd on the continent of both milk and butterfat, for $627,750. Two Augur bulls were the highest-priced Holstein animals sold in North America at $108,000 each.

During the 19th century, mills were erected along the Farm River, promoting the growth of industry and manufactured goods. Resident Chapman Maltby earned first prize at the 1876 Philadelphia Centennial Exposition for his shredded coconut. In the 1870s, Northford was renowned as the Christmas card center of the world. The Stevens brothers created ornamental Christmas cards that were fancier than usual and met with success.

By the early 1900s, North Branford's supply of traprock, a material used for making roadways, made quarrying a growth industry for the town. In 1914, the New Haven Trap Rock Co. opened its quarry operation on Totoket Mountain, believed to be the largest, single-faced quarry in the world.

Approx. one third of the land of North Branford includes the Lake Gaillard watershed. The New Haven Water Co. purchased several homes from residents in 1923 to build a 13-billion-gallon reservoir on Totoket Mountain. Construction of the dam began in 1926 and was completed in 1929. Today, Lake Gaillard supplies drinking water to many communities surrounding North Branford.

Interesting Places

Little Red School House (1805). The oldest one-room schoolhouse still standing in New Haven Co. It was used as a school until 1890. The building in Northford was recently restored to become a museum maintained by the Totoket Historical Society. It is open to the public on predetermined dates or by appointment

Reynolds-Beers House. Built by Hezekiah Reynolds in 1786, the Reynolds-Beers House was acquired by the town of North Branford in 1997 and is maintained and operated as a museum and learning center for local history by the Totoket Historical Society. Also on the property is the Gordon S. Miller Museum. Built in 2002, the Miller Barn contains farm machinery and farm implements used in Northford/North Branford in the 18th, 19th, and early 20th centuries. Open to the public one Saturday a month from 9 AM to Noon during spring, summer, and fall months.

The 1805 Little Red School House in Northford was used as a school for 85 years and has been restored by the Totoket Historical Society. Lauren Davis

NOTES

HIKING TRAILS

North Farms Trails. As a lasting commemorative of the nation's bicentennial in 1976, a 77-acre tract of land on the Branford River was purchased for a park and, in a town-wide contest, was named North Farms, the original designation of the area. North Farms Park has three primary trails with varying degrees of difficulty. Total trails length: 1.59 mi.

Notch Hill Brook Trail. Created by the North Branford Land Conservation Trust, the "Red Trail" starts on town property and crosses a historic defunct trolley line. Once on land trust property, the trail becomes a loop in secluded and undisturbed woodland. Total trails length: 1.59 mi.

Big Gulph. A Regional Water Authority recreation area, the place for challenging hiking in untamed woodlands. Big Gulph features more than six miles of trails, ranging from flat to very steep with a variety of wildlife habitats, including streams, meadows, and forests. Total trails length: 7.8 mi.

Potato and Corn Festival. Annual family-oriented festival held at the Augur Farm (383 Forest Rd.) during the first weekend in August, featuring signature baked potatoes and local roasted corn as well as a 5 K race, crafts, music, food, contests and games, amusement rides, classic car and motorcycle show, entertainment, fireworks display, tractor pull, and hay rides.

The Atwater Memorial Library (L) at 1720 Foxon Rd. N. Branford and the 1786 Reynolds-Beers House is operated as a museum and learning center for local history by the Totoket Historical Society. Lauren Davis

ADDRESS BOOK

Town Site
www.townofnorthbranfordct.com

Atwater Memorial Library
1720 Foxon Rd.
203-315-6020
www.nbranfordlibraries.org

Big Gulph Recreation Area
Middletown Ave.

Edward Smith Library
3 Old Post Rd.
203-484-0469
www.nbranfordlibraries.org

Little Red School House
1740 Foxon Rd.
203-488-0423

North Farms Trails
Rt. 139

Notch Hill Brook Trail
Ciro Rd.

Potato and Corn Festival
Augur Farm, 383 Forest Rd.

Reynolds-Beers House
1740 Foxon Rd.

Totoket Historical Society
1740 Foxon Rd.
203-980-9828
www.totokethistoricalsociety.org

[Passport Stamp / Signature & Date Here]

North Haven

By Julie Hulten, former North Haven Historical Society Archives Manager

Originally inhabited by the Quinnipiac people, the area along the Quinnipiac River north of New Haven, quickly attracted the interest of the English colonists. Many of New Haven's early settlers sought opportunities for farming and business beyond the original settlement's boundaries. The navigable Quinnipiac River facilitated transport of raw materials, goods, and products. The settlers used the power of the river and the other waterways to run mills and develop small manufacturing concerns. They took advantage of the rich soil to feed themselves and to develop markets in area towns and villages.

First known as the Northeast Village, North Haven was incorporated in 1786. Throughout the 18th and 19th centuries farming remained the primary occupation although small businesses continued to develop. Of particular importance was the Clintonville Agricultural Works which engaged in inventing and manufacturing labor-saving agricultural tools and housed a printing company, among the first in the country to publish greeting cards. In the late 19th and early 20th centuries the established farms of early Yankee settlers became the "market gardens" of Italian immigrants. Some of those arriving from Italy used native expertise to gain employment in the growing industry of brick production. Clay was in such abundance that North Haven, at one time, sported the nickname of "Bricktown."

Throughout the early 20th century brickmaking was a major employer. The mid-20th century brought the expansion of highways: the Wilbur Cross Parkway and I-91, which facilitated the development of a commuter culture and the influx of larger industries like Pratt & Whitney. Today North Haven has developed commercially along US Rt. 5. It is home to one of Quinnipiac University's three campuses. While many of the older homes have made way for development, there are neighborhoods that offer a picture of earlier town life, including buildings designed by local architect, Solomon Linsley.

Interesting Places

North Haven Green. This typical New England center holds an "ancient" burying ground, monuments, and a gazebo. On the Green's east side sits St. John's Episcopal Church, dedicated in 1761. The houses along Trumbull Place typify early North Haven architecture. Weekly concerts occur during the summer. North Haven Fairgrounds. An annual agricultural Fair is held the weekend after Labor Day. A variety of other events are held throughout the year. Each June the fairgrounds hosts Connecticut's oldest Irish Festival. See www.ctirishfestival.com.

The North Haven Historical Society, headquartered in the North Haven Cultural Center is a non-profit, volunteer organization that preserves, collects, and researches North Haven history.

Hiking/Outdoor Pursuits. Available dawn to dusk.

Peter's Rock. Once a lookout for the indigenous people, the 'rock' is the highest spot in North Haven. It offers hiking trails, picnic areas, and seasonal events.

The 1834 St. John's Episcopal Church and cemetery on the North Haven Green. Ted Stockmon

Notes

Tidal Marsh Trail. This quiet walk along the Quinnipiac River affords opportunities for bird-watching or launching a canoe. Remnants of the Cedar Hill Rail Yard can be seen along the way.

Quinnipiac River State Park. The hiking trail is part of the Blue-Blazed Trail system and follows the Quinnipiac River.

North Haven Historical Society. Displays showcase aspects of North Haven's history. Archives are available to researchers.

The picnic area at the base of Peter's Rock. It is the highest point (373') and largest parcel of open space (220 acres) in North Haven. The view from the summit is expansive: to the north, you can see Sleeping Giant and the Hanging Hills of Meriden; to the east, Branford and North Branford; and to the south, New Haven harbor. North Haven Historical Society and Museum

Address Book

Town Site
www.northhaven-ct.gov

North Haven Fairgrounds
290 Washington Ave.
203-239-3700
www.northhaven-fair.com

North Haven Historical Society and Museum
27 Broadway
203-239-7722
www.northhavenhistoricalsociety.wordpress.com

Peter's Rock
133 Middletown Ave.
www.petersrockassociation.org

Quinnipiac River State Park
10 Banton St.
203-424-3200
www.ct.gov/deep

Tidal Marsh Trail
200 Universal Dr.
www.northhaventrails.org

[Passport Stamp / Signature & Date Here]

ORANGE

By Ginny Reinhard, Orange Historical Society

Ordinarily, a town springs up from nowhere and works its way to bigger and better – but bigger is not always a good thing. The history of Orange arises from the history of Milford with its settlement in 1639. Having been founded by Rev. Peter Prudden, Milford grew north as families and farms increased and the little town of Bryans Farms became a small community to itself. Richard Bryan bought 208 acres from the Paugusett sachem Ansantawae and when more families moved north, a little town called North Milford came into its own.

By 1804, North Milford, under the umbrella of Milford, became restless to seek its independence since travel to worship was getting more and more difficult. At one point, North Milford built a meetinghouse at the northern end of the Green and was allowed ministers on a limited basis. In 1822, North Milford spread its wings, taking the name Orange in honor of William of Orange, husband to Queen Mary, for his support of the Colony of Connecticut in 1689.

Today, the town of Orange is in New Haven County, approx. 10 miles west of New Haven. It's population listed at 13,956 in the 2010 census.

A community, with history at its fingertips, has a historic district surrounding the town Green with its early Congregational church standing proudly at its northern end. The Green hosts two historic buildings that have been restored by the Orange Historical Society and open to the public. The Stone-Otis House, built in 1830, hosts summer tours and events and is decorated for the holidays. The Academy, built in 1878 as a meetinghouse, is now a museum and antique shop giving tours and an opportunity for historical research in the Mary Woodruff Research Center. Each building is being cared for by the Orange Historical Society.

Nearby is the Orange School, known as the Mary L. Tracy School, that was built in 1909 gathering all five district schools into one. It is now being used for kindergarten and the Board of Education. In the area once known as Bryans Farms is the

The Bryan-Andrew House, a 1740 homestead, has been restored by the Orange Historical Society. It is the oldest house still standing in the town and open to the public by appointment.
Ginny Reinhard

The Orange Historical Society restored the 1830 Stone-Otis House and restored the furnishings and accessories of the two families associated with it.
Ginny Reinhard

Notes

Nathan Bryan-William Andrew House. Built in 1740, the house has been fully restored by the Orange Historical Society and is open to the public by appointment. This home has the ability to serve hearth-cooked dinners for family occasions.

The town has a comprehensive sports program easily accessible through the Park and Recreation Department. For all of its 17.4 sq. mi., the little Town of Orange is a unique place to live!

If one wants to leave the history and explore the today, the PEZ Co. has its factory and Visitor Center just off I-95, a worthwhile trip for families and scout groups. Here you can see an example of every PEZ container ever manufactured by this wonderful addition to Orange and if the timing is right, you can watch the PEZ candies being packaged.

So, if Orange sounds like a nice place, come for a visit and stay awhile. You decide!

The PEZ Visitor Center has the largest collection of PEZ memorabilia on public display in the world: the world's largest PEZ dispenser, viewing windows into the production facility, a factory store, an interactive time line, and much more. PEZ Candy, Inc.

Address Book

Town Site
www.orange-ct.gov

Nathan Bryan-William Andrew House
131 Old Tavern Rd.
203-795-3106
www.orangehistory.org

Orange Historical Society
www.orangehistory.org

PEZ Visitor Center
35 Prindle Hill Rd.
203-298-0201
www.us.pez.com

[Passport Stamp / Signature & Date Here]

Oxford

By Cathy Weiss, freelance writer
www.cathyweiss.info

Oxford is 14 miles NW of New Haven, Conn. with a population in 2010 of 12,683. The town includes these sections: Quaker Farms, Oxford Center, and Riverside.

Every summer I can often be found in Oxford at Rich Dairy Farm eating, in my opinion, the best ice cream in the state. Another reason I come here is because Oxford has had the highest amount of economic development of any town in Conn. from the years of 1985 -2006. I live in a small rural area near Oxford, without a post office, drug store, or supermarket, so ice cream notwithstanding, I frequently visit Oxford for necessities and good eats.

Dairy farming was an important industry for many years in Oxford. Despite its growth, Oxford still has many pastoral pockets of rural charm. In fact, it was first settled as a collection of farms in 1741. Originally part of Derby it separated and became incorporated by the general assembly in 1798.

In addition to agriculture Oxford was known for a variety of mills along the waterways. A sawmill, gristmill, and paper mill were located on what is now Southford Falls on Rt. 188 north of the Quaker Farms section of town.

Hospitality was another industry in town since the main thoroughfare, Oxford turnpike, now Rt. 67, was used to transport agricultural products. Two of the stops along the way were the Oxford House, still a popular restaurant in the center of town, and the Washband Tavern, a notable building overlooking the southern end of Rt. 67 that was a stop on the Underground Railroad.

My Favorite Eating Spots

Rich Farm and Ice Cream. So many interesting seasonal varieties of ice cream. Even sugar and dairy-free selections. Sit outside at the tables overlooking the real working farm (They even sell raw milk!) and pastoral hills. A great place for children of all ages!

My next-door neighbor always goes to the Oxford Baking Company, and why not? It has fresh seasonal pies, soups, and a stuffed bread schedule. This is a quaint post-and-beam building that was lovingly restored by its owners who have made it an important gathering place as it was many, many years ago. There is even an art gallery upstairs.

Fritz's Snack Bar. A family diner known for comfort food; Wednesday nights are cruise nights weather permitting from 5-7.

Then take a hike to burn off the calories at Larkin State Bridal Trail or at Southford Falls State Park, a beautiful recreation area in both Oxford and Southbury offering fishing, hiking, scenic waterfalls, picnicking, and a jaunt to a fire tower.

Actress Barbara Hershey was married in 1992 in her Oxford home.

Black Hog Brewing Co. Their tasting room offers flights, pints, games, and more.

Rich Farm and Ice Cream was established on July 3, 1994 by David and Dawn Rich. They make delicious ice cream daily. Dan Rich

Notes

Oxford Baking Company is in a restored 19th century harness shop and serves freshly made baked goods from scratch. Oxford Baking Co. Cathy Weiss

Address Book

Town Site
www.oxford-ct.gov

Black Hog Brewing Co.
115 Hurley Rd., Bldg. 9A
203-262-6075
www.blackhogbrewing.com

Fritz's Snack Bar
72 Oxford Rd.
203-888-9604
www.fritzssnackbar.com

Oxford Baking Company
451 Oxford Rd.
203-828-6219
www.oxfordbakingcompany.com

Oxford Historical Society
www.oxford-historical-society.org

Rich Farm and Ice Cream
691 Oxford Rd.
203-881-1040
www.richfarmicecream.com

Southford Falls State Park
175 Quaker Farms Rd., Southbury

[Passport Stamp / Signature & Date Here]

Prospect

By Rev. Boardman W. Kathan, former historian of the Prospect Congregational Church

In the early 1700s pioneers pushed into the area now known as Prospect. They came from Waterbury in the North and from Wallingford in the East. It was rocky and hilly terrain, the highest point in New Haven County. The western one-third of the area was part of Waterbury and was known as "South Farms." The eastern two-thirds was a part of Wallingford and was called "West Rocks" and later "Cheshire Mountain." When the people of "New Cheshire" petitioned Wallingford for their own church, founded in 1724, it was said "that settlers are increasing greatly over the west rocks where we expect a Parish will be made hereafter." Indeed, later in the 18th century the area was set aside as "Columbia Parish," winter privileges were granted, and a meetinghouse was built on what became the Prospect Green. In this early period the parish was famous for a visit by noted Methodist bishop, Francis Asbury, and the residence of counterfeiter Peter Gilkey.

When the town was incorporated in 1827, it was recognized that a town of Columbia already existed, so the name, Prospect, was chosen, since it was "the town with the extended view." The people in this new town were sturdy, independent and hard-working, and subsisted for generations on hardscrabble farming, modest orchards, water-powered manufacturing, and small "cottage industries." Dams were built on the streams, and mills were erected, producing a variety of tools, buttons, and even matches. The Ten Mile River begins in Prospect, and William Mix built a large mill in 1826 on one dam on the river, and invented a buffing wheel for the polishing of Britannia ware, until the enterprise was moved to Wallingford.

A turnpike, a railroad, and a trolley line ran through the northeastern corner of Prospect in the latter part of the 19th century or early in the 20th century. The goal was to find a more direct and accessible route between the growing industrial city of Waterbury and the population centers in central and southern Connecticut. First came part of the Plank Road turnpike in 1853, the only such road built of timber in Connecticut, In 1888 the Meriden, Waterbury and Connecticut River Railroad was extended. Finally, the Cheshire street railway or trolley was opened in 1905. The original trolley stop still stands on Plank Road.

By the beginning of the 20th century manufacturing had ceased and the town reverted to small-scale farming. However, the improvement of state highways and the coming of electricity transformed the town. Industry returned at the time of World War II, exemplified by the successful foam plastics products developed by Harry Talmadge and Eugene Lewis. In the 1960s Prospect was one of the fastest-growing towns in the State of Connecticut. The first supermarket (Olivers) was built in 1948, and the first drugstore (Neals) in 1954. In 1969 the town joined Beacon Falls to form the Region 16 school district, and built a middle school in town and a high school in Beacon Falls. The town was recognized as a "Bicentennial Community" by the American Revolution Bicentennial Administration, and it celebrated its 150th anniversary in 1977. Later that same year Robert Chatfield was elected Mayor, thus beginning the longest tenure of any town executive in Connecticut. The Reverend Philip Cascia of St. Anthony's Church really put the town on the map by organizing Intersport USA, an international educational and athletic program for young people.

Interesting Places

Hotchkiss House Museum. Built in 1818, it is maintained by the Prospect Historical Society, and visits can be arranged by calling Carol Brooks.

Notes

Prospect Green Historic District. Includes the 1844 Glebe house now a private residence, the1867 Center School, a 1886 Advent Chapel, a 1905 Meeting Place (the original library), and a 1907 Civil War monument, recognizing that Prospect sent more volunteers into the Civil War in proportion to its voting list than any other town in Connecticut. Also on the Green are the fourth building of the Prospect Congregational Church (1951) , the parsonage (built in 1941-42) , the Prospect Community Center (formerly a school built in 1936), the former Grange Hall, and the new public library (1991). North of the Green and across Route 68 is the Prospect Town Hall.

Kathan Woods. 82-acre nature preserve with hiking trails on an old wood road, the Quinnipiac Blue Trail, and an old town road.

The Prospect Historical Society maintains the 1818 Hotchkiss House on Waterbury Rd. Boardman W. Kathan

Address Book

Town Site
www.townofprospect.org

Hotchkiss House Museum
61 Waterbury Rd. (Rt. 69)
203-758-5503
www.prospecthistoricalsociety.org

Kathan Woods
1 Boardman Dr., off Plank Rd.
www.prospectlandtrust.blogspot.com

[Passport Stamp / Signature & Date Here]

SEYMOUR

By Marian O'Keefe, Seymour Town Historian

Seymour, 18 miles north of Bridgeport at the junction of Rts. 8 and 67, was part of the town of Derby from 1672 1850. In 1735 it was known as Chusetown, named for the Native American Pequot chief Joe Chuse. In 1804 it was called Humphreysville for Gen. David Humphreys, Aide de Camp to George Washington and America's first ambassador to a foreign country. Humphreys founded a paper mill in 1804 and also constructed New England's first successful (merino) woolen mill in 1806. Both of these mills were on the Naugatuck River in the center of Seymour.

In 1850 Humphreysville was incorporated as a separate town and renamed Seymour, after Connecticut Gov. Thomas Seymour. As more industries moved into town, Seymour transitioned from an agrarian and dairy economy to a manufacturing hub. Companies that set up operations included New Haven Copper (1846), Kerite Underwater Cable Manufacturer (1850), Seymour Manufacturing, Nickel Silver (1874), and Seymour Products (bicycle, luggage parts, and industrial products).

Another company was The Waterman Pen Co. Lewis Waterman invented the fountain pen in 1884 in New York. He asked the Day Rubber Pen company in Seymour to manufacture the pens. They agreed with a handshake and made the pens until 1946 when the Waterman Pen Co. bought the Day Pen Company. In 1983, Bic purchased the Waterman Co. and eventually sold the Pen Co to Nestles in France. Today "Waterman's of Paris" sells their fine pens across the world .

By the turn of the 20th century many more companies opened in Seymour. During the First and Second World Wars most of these companies made significant contributions to the U. S. War effort but by the 1970s the larger industries relocated due to an economic downturn. Seymour Manufacturing experienced many changes but in the end was forced to close its doors in 1992. Then Seymour Products and New Haven Copper (2009) closed, but Kerite survives and in business at its original site in Seymour.

In 1955 a massive flood caused by two hurricanes inundated the lower Naugatuck Valley. The damage to Seymour was incredible with loss of life as well as serious damage to property and infrastructure. Sadly, Seymour lost its library in the flood and with it many irreplaceable resources and artifacts. But the town came back from this disaster with diligent effort.

In 1991 the film "Other People's Money" was partly filmed in Seymour starring Gregory Peck and Danny DeVito. The story was based on the purchase of Seymour Mfg., then known as Seymour Specialty, by its employees in the early 1990s. Today the site is occupied by a large super market.

Today Seymour is a bedroom community with a population of over 16,000. The town has a thriving downtown antique marketplace with restaurants, a shopping center, a greenway, and nearby, a large industrial park. Other companies have moved into town. The library, rebuilt after the flood, is one of the best in the area.

Seymour's Downtown is home to six antique shops, a cake and confection shop, pubs, a tea house, and gift and specialty shops. Marian O'Keefe

Notes

Interesting Places

Seymour Historical Society. Open by appointment. Sunday programs eight times a year.

Tingue Fish Ladder. On Naugatuck River in center of town.

French Park. Activities year-round.

Greenway Path.

Broad Street Park. A donation-funded and volunteer-built park in Seymour that honors Seymour's veterans.

Keith Mitchell Forest.

Little-Laurel Lime Rock Park.

Shops at Seymour. A great day trip.

Downtown is home to 6 antique shops, a cake and confection shop, pubs, a tea house, and gift and specialty shops.

Strand Theatre. Variety of activities and films.

Events & Activites

Founders Day. Promotes the community and raises funds for a local charity. First Sunday in June.

Pumpkin Festival. French Park in October.

Christmas Parade. First Saturday in December.

Smoke in the Valley. Craft Beer Festival. Silvermine Park in October.

The $4.75 million Paul Pawlak, Sr. Bypass Channel and Park at Tingue Dam was completed in 2015 on the Naugatuck River in downtown Seymour. Now Atlantic salmon and shad can go around the Tingue Dam and migrate to prime spawning areas on the Naugatuck River in Beacon Falls and Naugatuck. Marian O'Keefe

Address Book

Town Site
www.seymourct.org

Broad Street Park
46 Broad St.

French Park
73 Spruce St.

Greenway Path
Naugatuck River
Rt. 67, Bank St.

Keith Mitchell Forest
Squatuck Rd., Rt. 188

Little-Laurel Lime Rock Park
Tibbets Rd.

Seymour Historical Society
59 West St.
203-888-7471

Seymour Public Library
46 Church St.
203-888-3903
www.seymourpubliclibrary.org

Shops at Seymour
Main & Bank Sts.

Silvermine Park
Silvermine Rd.

Strand Theatre
165 Main St.
203-881-5025

Tingue Fish Ladder
Spruce St.

[Passport Stamp / Signature & Date Here]

SOUTHBURY

By Barbara Hampton, Historian, Librarian & Lawyer

Southbury is at the northern tip of New Haven Co., bisected by Interstate 84. It includes South Britain, Southford, and Heritage Village.

Southbury is a "daughter" town of Ancient Woodbury. In 1673, families from Stratford landed their canoes on the banks of the Pomperaug River, the area now known as Settlers Park (349-479 Crook Horn Rd.) A rough-hewn stone and modern brass plaque marks the spot. This southern section of the Woodbury settlement became the town of Southbury in 1784.

The rich bottomland of the Pomperaug and its tributaries made farming a core of the local economy for its first two centuries. The rivers powered manufacturers including the Diamond Match Factory, now the site of Southford Falls State Park, and animal-trap manufacturer Hawkins Co. in South Britain.

Hydroelectric dams on the Housatonic River created Lake Lillinonah and Lake Zoar, large recreational lakes on the town's western border. Swimming, boating, and fishing drew city dwellers to summer cottages and eventually luxury year-around lakeside homes.

In 1923, Count Ilya Tolstoy (son of Leo Tolstoy) and author George Grebenstchikoff, established "Churaevka," also known as Russian Village, in Southbury's birch-lined woodlands at the mouth of the Pomperaug. Russian luminaries fleeing the Bolshevik Revolution found a comfortably familiar new home here. Many descendants and others who knew these immigrants from Russia remain in the area.

When the American wing of the Nazi party planned a youth training camp in Southbury in 1937, local pastors preached against Nazi bigotry and citizens rallied to enact a zoning ban on the activity. Bund camps were built across the country, but Southbury was the only town to successfully block one. A 2012 documentary, Home of the Brave: When Southbury Said No to the Nazis, tells the story.

The Southbury Playhouse presented summer stock theater in a classic barn from the 1950s to the 1980s. Playhouse actors included Southbury residents Ed Sullivan and Philip Charles Anglim. Continuing that tradition, a live stage was incorporated into a contemporary movie complex. Riverview Cinemas and Playhouse, 690 Main St. South.

Heritage Village, a large over-55 condominium community with nearly 4,000 residents, began in the 1960s on musician Victor Borge's farm. Some active farms remain, including several equestrian facilities.

NOTABLE PEOPLE

Don Troiani. Civil War artist. www.dontroiani.com

David Merrill. Landscape artist and muralist.

Gladys Taber. Author of Stillmeadow books and naturalist.

Sergei Rachmaninoff. Composer.

Igor Sikorsky. Invented the helicopter.

St. Sergius Russian Orthodox Chapel is in the Russian Village. Count Ilya Tolstoy, the son of Leo Tolstoy, discovered the area and led to the establishment of a community here. It was a seasonal cultural center for Russian writers, artists, musicians and scientists. Podskoch

Notes

Historical Sites

Bullet Hill School. Public school (1762-1942), now a living history museum.

Southbury Historical Society. Historical sites, museum, archives.

St. Sergius Russian Orthodox Chapel.

Parks and Recreation

Audubon Center Bent of the River.

Shepaug Dam Eagle Observation Site.

Southbury Land Trust.

State Parks

George C. Waldo State Park. On Lake Lillinonah. Undeveloped trails.

Larkin Bridle Trail. 10.3 miles for walkers, joggers, bikers, and hikers.

Kettletown State Park. On Lake Zoar offering swimming, camping, hiking, picnicking, and fishing.

Southford Falls. Scenic waterfalls and covered bridge.

Aldo Leopold State Wildlife Management Area.

Town Parks.
www.southbury-ct.org/parks

Southford State Park's dam and pond on Eight Mile Brook once powered the Diamond Match Co. (est. 1901-burned c.1923). It is a great place for picnics, hiking, and enjoying the picturesque waterfalls. Podskoch

Address Book

Town Site
www.southbury-ct.org

Aldo Leopold State Wildlife Management Area
Access points on Kuhne Rd., Purchase Brook Rd., East Flat Hill Rd., and Little York Rd.

Audubon Center Bent of the River
185 E. Flat Hill Rd.
www.bentoftheriver.audubon.org

Bullet Hill School
U.S. Rts. 6 & 202
www.southburyhistory.org

George C. Waldo State Park
457 Purchase Brook Rd.

Kettletown State Park
1400 Georges Hill Rd.

Larkin Bridle Trail
Trailhead on Kettletown Rd.

Shepaug Dam Eagle Observation Site
2225 River Rd.
www.shepaugeagles.info

Southbury Historical Society
624 South Britain Rd.
www.southburyhistory.org

Southbury Land Trust
www.southburylandtrust.org

Southford Falls
175 Quarker Farms Rd.

St. Sergius Russian Orthodox Chapel
85 Russian Village Rd.

[Passport Stamp / Signature & Date Here]

Wallingford

By Robert Beaumont, Wallingford Historical Society

Wallingford, named in 1670 for Wallingford, Berkshire, England, was the first interior town founded by New Haven, and was purchased more than once from the Quinnipiac Indians. It lies on the largest flat area in the state, along the sand plain surrounding the Quinnipiac River. Now a town of 45,000 within 39.8 square miles, it was once three times that size, which led to the daughter towns of Cheshire, Meriden and the eastern districts of Prospect.

Named the "Cradle of American Liberty" by the newspapers of the day after a meeting in January 1766 in which the freemen voted to fine anyone who used a stamp mandated by the infamous Stamp Act, and voted that "they would take the field," that is, would fight the British to stop the implementation of the Stamp Act. The Act was withdrawn two months later. When the American Revolution came a decade later, 475 of our men, at least 14 of whom were slaves, fought in numerous battles right through to Yorktown.

An agricultural town by necessity in the early years, Wallingford would later have many orchards and many types of farming. In addition, our 19th century entrepreneurs were active in many fields of manufacturing, from razor strops, tin ware, japanned ware, coffee pots, bayonets for Eli Whitney's military contract, to rubber clothing and, of course, silverware. Meriden may have been known as the Silver City, but Wallingford could easily have been known as the Silver Town, for its many silver and silver plate facilities.

Through the 20th and into the 21st centuries, Wallingford has maintained and increased its wide range of industrial and commercial establishments, due in no small part to having its own municipal electric utility, which provides reliable service at the lowest rates in Connecticut, and to having robust transportation access, what with being bisected by I-91 and the Wilbur Cross Parkway and having rail passenger service by AMTRAK and CT Rail, and freight service by Connecticut Southern.

Interesting Places

Wharton Brook State Park. On Rt. 5 on the Wallingford-North Haven town line.

Quinnipiac River Linear Trail. A scenic 2.1 mile wheel-chair accessible trail.

Lufbery Park. Noted for its disc golf course.

Toyota Oakdale Theatre. Noted for its top-tier music and comedy acts.

Dutton Park. A tribute to our military history.

Wallingford Historical Society. Known as 'Wallingford's Attic' with its collection of local memorabilia and manufactured and agricultural items.

American Silver Museum. A fine collection of silver items and period furniture.

Paul Mellon Arts Center. On the Choate Rosemary Hall campus and home to the Wallingford Symphony.

Choate Rosemary Hall. Internationally acclaimed preparatory school founded in 1890 for girls and in 1896 for boys. John F. Kennedy, Glenn Close, and Ivanka Trump graduated from this fine school.

Gaylord Specialty Healthcare. Founded in 1902 as a tuberculosis sanatorium, it is now known for its rehabilitation work with brain and spinal injuries.

The Wallingford Historical Society Museum is housed in the 1759 Parsons House at 180 South Main St. Robert Beaumont

Notes

Famous People

John Moss, Sr. Founder of both New Haven and Wallingford, he was the oldest male founder and lived to be our first centenarian.

Katherine Miles. Our oldest founder at 82 when she and her son's family ventured into the wilderness of Wallingford in 1670.

Lyman Hall. Born in Wallingford in 1724, a signer of the Declaration of Independence, he was largely responsible for bringing the colony of Georgia into the fold with the other 12 colonies,

Moses Yale Beach. Inventor of a rag-cutting machine used in the paper business for over a century, publisher of the *New York Sun*, the largest penny newspaper in the 1840s, and founder of the AP News Service.

Major Gervais Raoul Lufbery. Became the first American Ace in World War I by shooting down 17 German planes.

Robert Wallace and Samuel Simpson. Early leaders in the silverware industry.

Mary Atwater Choate. Founder of Rosemary Hall school in 1890.

Brig. Gen. Arthur Dutton. One of the Civil War "boy" generals of the 2nd West Point class of 1861.

Events

Memorial Day Parade.

Summer Concert Series. Wednesdays in July and August on the Parade Ground.

Celebrate Wallingford. First weekend in October along North & South Main Sts.

Holiday Stroll. Along Center St., first Friday in December.

The South Entrance to the 2.1 mi. Quinnipiac River Linear Trail is used for walking, jogging and biking. Robert Beaumont

Address Book

Town Sites
www.wallingfordct.gov
www.wallingfordct.myrec.com

American Silver Museum
153 South Main St.
www.wallingfordcthistory.org

Dutton Park
North Main St.

Lufbery Park
Cheshire Rd.

Paul Mellon Arts Center
333 Christian St.
203-697-2239
www.choate.edu

Quinnipiac River Linear Trail
Hall Ave.

Toyota Oakdale Theatre
95 S. Turnpike Rd.
203-265-1501
www.oakdaletheatre.net

Wallingford Historical Society
180 South Main St.
/pages/Wallingford-historicalsociety

Wharton Brook State Park
Rt. 5

[Passport Stamp / Signature & Date Here]

Waterbury

By Michael C. Dooling, Archivist at Mattatuck Museum

Waterbury, founded in 1674, was originally part of a large tract known as Mattatuck (Algonquin for "place without trees"). Eventually, Mattatuck was broken into five towns and portions of four others. Waterbury became home to an enormous brass industry starting early in the 19th century. The early manufacture of brass buttons soon led to numerous companies including Waterbury Clock, Waterbury Watch, and the "Big Three" brass companies: Scovill, Chase Brass, and American Brass.

The wealth in the city, driven by its thriving industries, led to the construction of beautiful buildings designed by famous architects and of scenic parks. Waterbury is at the crossroads of Rt. 8 and I-84 and is easily identified by a large cross on a hill overlooking the city on the former site of tourist attraction, Holy Land, USA, a miniature interpretation of the Holy Land. A number of famous people have called Waterbury home including actress Rosalind Russell, the home run king before Babe Ruth, Roger Connor, and former Commissioner of Major League Baseball, Fay Vincent, Jr.

Today, Waterbury is home to several brass and metal forming companies, two major hospitals, and three colleges: UConn, Post University, and Naugatuck Valley Community College.

Interesting Places

Mattatuck Museum Arts and History Center. In the former Masonic Temple, the museum houses an extensive collection of artwork by American artists with a concentration on those from Connecticut, a massive collection of buttons from Waterbury and around the world, and a history gallery that highlights Waterbury and the Naugatuck Valley. Open Tues.-Sat., 10 AM-5 PM, Sun., Noon-5 PM.

Palace Theater. Designed by renowned theater architect Thomas White Lamb and built in 1922, it was completely restored in 2002. The stunning interior holds 2,640 seats and is a frequent stop for touring companies of major shows and concerts.

Republican-American Building. Designed by McKim, Mead & White as Waterbury's Union Station and now home to the Republican-American newspaper. The building and clock tower were patterned after the Palazzo Pubblico and Torre del Mangia in Sienna, Italy.

Father McGivney Statue. Dedicated to the Waterburian founder of the Knights of Columbus, Father Michael J. McGivney. At the intersection of Meadow and Grand Sts.

Waterbury City Hall. Designed by Cass Gilbert, built in 1916, and completely restored in 2010. Gilbert also designed the Chase Building across the street and three smaller buildings nearby.

Waterbury Green. Originally laid out in 1843, the Green is anchored at one end by the Carrie Welton fountain with a life-size bronze statue of her horse Knight, and on the other end by an imposing Civil War monument. West Main St.

Waterbury's Churches. Waterbury's churches, many with awe-inspiring architecture include: Basilica of the Immaculate Conception, 74 West Main (on the Green); Saint John's Episcopal Church, 16 Church St. (west end of the Green); Shrine of St. Anne, 515 South Main; Our Lady of Lourdes, 309 South Main; and Holy Trinity Greek Orthodox Church, 937 Chase Parkway.

Lewis Fulton Memorial Park. Designed by the sons of Frederick Law Olmstead with two ponds, lovely walking paths, and gently rolling landscape, 70 acres.

NOTES

The Mattatuck Museum is an art and regional history museum on the Green in downtown Waterbury, that is housed in the former Masonic Temple. Michael Dooling

Greater Waterbury's Center for the Performing Arts, The Palace Theater's exquisite complex showcases a performance schedule boasting professional Broadway tours, educational programs, family entertainment and much more. Courtesy of Louis Belloisy and the Palace Theater

ADDRESS BOOK

Town Site
www.waterburyct.org

Lewis Fulton Memorial Park
Cooke St.

Mattatuck Museum Arts and History Center
144 West Main St.
203-753-0381
www.mattmuseum.org

Palace Theater
100 East Main St.
203-346-2000
www.palacetheaterct.org

Republican-American Building
389 Meadow St.

Waterbury City Hall
235 Grand St.
203-597-3444

[Passport Stamp / Signature & Date Here]

West Haven

By Jon E. Purmont, City Historian

While West Haven is one of Connecticut's oldest settlements (1648) the city is one of its youngest municipalities (1961). Among the state's smallest urban areas (10.75 sq. mi.), it is a city with a diverse population of 55,564 (2010 census) reflecting a rich mosaic of cultures, religions, and traditions.

West Haven has developed from an early farming village to a largely industrial, manufacturing economy in the 19th and 20th centuries and then to a modern 21st century economy which is largely service-based.

Today the city is home to the University of New Haven with a student body of nearly 6,000. The collegians come from many parts of the United States, Asia, Europe, the Middle East, and Africa. In addition, the former site of the Bayer Corp. has now been transformed into the Yale-West Campus which is projected to have upwards of 1,000 people studying and working which adds a new dimension to West Haven's development.

One of the city's unique and most valuable assets is its shoreline with its popular and much utilized shorefront walkway. This popular recreational area, adjacent to Long Island Sound, extends over two miles of scenic city-owned beachfront. It is a "jewel" not to be missed by visitors.

The shorefront includes accessible beaches with adequate parking, numerous restaurants, and a Conference Center nearby. Whether one fancies flying kites, swimming, bicycling, fishing or simply strolling alongside the water, there is something for everyone at West Haven's shoreline.

In June 2014 at Sea Bluff Beach (Ocean Ave.), the city became home to one of the "Where Angels Play" playgrounds constructed along the East Coast. Built to honor the children tragically killed at Sandy Hook School in Newtown, CT, the West Haven play area was named for Charlotte Bacon, one of the young victims of that tragedy. The playground on the beach is a must-stop for young children to enjoy.

Historical Sites & Museums

Like many Connecticut towns and cities, West Haven's Town Green is the most recognizable landmark in the center of the city. The First Congregational Church, which graces the Green with its impressive white steeple, has been located there since 1722 although the present structure dates to 1860. Nearby is the second oldest Connecticut Episcopal house of worship, the Church of the Holy Spirit, which traces its founding to 1726.

During the American Revolution, on July 9, 1779, the Green was the scene of a famous incident involving the local Congregational Minister and the invading British troops. Reverend Noah Williston tried to flee the church carrying important records. The British threatened to kill him but British Adjutant William Campbell stepped forward and saved his life.

Later that day, Campbell was mortally wounded by local militia. He is believed to be buried at a site on Prudden Street near the University of New Haven. It is a unique place of rest because it honors a British soldier killed on American soil. Years later West Haven re-named a major thoroughfare in his honor.

West Haven Historical Society. Houses special exhibits and archives of West Haven history.

Ward-Heitmann House Museum (c.1684). Oldest standing structure in the city.

West Haven Veterans Museum and Learning Center. Honoring veterans who fought in American Wars.

Notes

Savin Rock Museum and Learning Center. Artifacts and memorabilia of Savin Rock Amusement Park.

The city motto proudly states: Nil Desperandum!! Never Despair!!

The 1860 First Congregational Church graces the spacious West Haven Town Green, a peaceful oasis in the city. Podskoch

Charlotte Bacon's Playground at Sea Bluff Beach on Ocean Ave. honors Charlotte who was a victim of the Sandy Hook Elementary School shooting. Susan Walker

Address Book

Town Site
www.cityofwesthaven.com

Charlotte Bacon's Playground
Sea Bluff Beach
1083 Ocean Ave. #1075

Savin Rock Museum and Learning Center
6 Rock St.
203-937-6666 or 203-937-3566
www.savinrockmuseum.com

Ward-Heitmann House Museum
277 Elm St.
203-937-9823
www.wardheitmann.org

West Haven Historical Society
686 Savin Ave.
203-932-0088
www.westhavenhistory.org

West Haven Veterans Museum and Learning Center
30 Hood Terrace
203-934-1111
www.whmilmuseum.org

[Passport Stamp / Signature & Date Here]

WOLCOTT

By Florence Goodman, Wolcott Historical Society

Wolcott's early history began as a tale of two towns: Farmington in the east and Waterbury in the west. Prior to that the region was a densely wooded area that was the hunting grounds for the Tunxis Indians.

In the early 1700s settlers began to inhabit various sections of town. One of the earliest settlers, John Alcocke (Alcott), purchased 117 acres and built a house on Spindle Hill in the western section of town. As more settlers moved into these two areas, disputes over town boundaries arose; thus Bound Line Road was born. This road was the dividing line between Waterbury and Farmington so the name Farmingbury was created.

The early settlers of Farmingbury had to travel substantial distances to attend public worship meetings on the Sabbath so in 1760 and 1761 they petitioned the General Court to establish themselves as a separate and distinct ecclesiastical society. Both petitions were denied because the towns of Waterbury and Farmington needed their financial support for their ministry and schools. The Court however agreed to give Farmingbury the services of a minister, the right to operate its own schools, and an exemption from Waterbury parish taxes during the five winter months. In 1767 and 1768 they petitioned again and were denied, but finally in1770 the General Court in New Haven allowed them to become a distinct and separate parish. On November 13, 1770 at the home of Joseph Atkins they held their first meeting of the Ecclesiastical Society. At this time the Congregational parish officers were elected, a tax rate was set, and construction of a meetinghouse was agreed upon. Members of the colonial drum band helped raise the frame of the church in April 1772 and by November the first meeting was held in that church.

By the mid-1770s Farmingbury was supporting Connecticut in the American Revolution. Over the course of that war Farmingbury sent 102 militiamen between the ages of 15 to 50. With the end of the war came a resurgence of population and by the mid-1780s the parish population was 600.

In 1787 Farmingbury petitioned the General Assembly to be freed entirely from its parent towns of Waterbury and now Southington (which had been divided out of Farmington in 1779), but were denied. Petitions failed again in 1792, 1793, and 1795 because of strong opposition from Southington, but in May of 1796 the town was granted its freedom by a tie-breaking vote cast by the state's Lieut. Governor, Oliver Wolcott. To show their appreciation the town representatives voted to change the name from Farmingbury to Wolcott.

Wolcott boasts of two prominent men born and raised in the Spindle Hill section of town. First was Seth Thomas who was a well-known clockmaker born in 1785. He built his first clocks here and gave jobs to many locals who helped in the production. The second was Amos Bronson Alcott born in 1799. He was a well-known educator, philosopher, poet, and Yankee peddler who later moved to Pennsylvania where his daughter, Louisa May Alcott was born.

One of many bridges found on the 3.5-mile Mill Pond Trail. It overlooks the Woodtick Reservoir. Rob Pierpont

Notes

Interesting Places

Wolcott Historical Society Stone Schoolhouse (1825) Museum. Houses a collection of over 200 years of local history.

Historic Town Green and Historic District. Located on both Center St. (Rt. 322) and Bound Line Rd.

Peterson Park. Offers basketball, tennis, volleyball, rollerblading, a skate park, and walking trail.

Mattatuck Trail. The 35-mile trail begins at Peterson Park.

Wolcott Dog Park. Next to Peterson Park.

Mill Pond Way Walking Trail. The 3.5-mile trail in the Woodtick section of town on Wolf Hill, Munson, Nichols, and Woodtick Rds.

Woodtick Recreation Area. Beach, swimming, and pavilion.

BAW Baseball Fields.

Wolcott Sports Complex.

Farmingbury Hill Golf Course.

The stone schoolhouse was the 1821 Woodtick School located on Nichols Road. Today it is owned by the Wolcott Historical Society and serves as their museum. Florence Goodman

Address Book

Town Site
www.wolcottct.org

BAW Baseball Fields
180 Nichols Rd.

Farmingbury Hill Golf Course
141 East St. (Rt. 322)
203-879-8038
www.farmingburyhillsgolf.com

Mill Pond Way Walking Trail
www.wolcottct.org

Peterson Park / Mattatuck Trail
123 Mad River Rd.

Wolcott Historical Society Stone Schoolhouse Museum
155 Nichols Rd.
203-879-9818
www.wolcotthistory.org

Wolcott Sports Complex
473 Spindle Hill Rd.
203-879-8383
www.wolcottsoccer.com

Woodtick Recreation Area
201 Nichols Rd.

[Passport Stamp / Signature & Date Here]

Woodbridge

By Martha German, Amity & Woodbridge Historical Society

Woodbridge lies west of New Haven with a population of approx. 10,000 and an area of 19.3 sq. mi. The town is noteworthy for maintaining its rural character in close proximity to a large city.

Settlement began in the mid-1600s with Richard Sperry who aided the Regicides, Whalley and Goffe, with food and hiding places. This area was called Chestnut Hill and later enlarged into Amity Parish. The town was incorporated in 1784, and named to honor Benjamin Woodbridge, minister of the Congregational Church from 1742-1785.

Woodbridge features numerous 18th and 19th century homes including the c. 1772 Thomas Darling House, headquarters of the Amity & Woodbridge Historical Society. Thomas Darling (1720-1789) was a Yale graduate, an entrepreneur, justice of the peace, and gentleman farmer. His friends included Yale classmate Benjamin Woodbridge, Roger Sherman, Benjamin Franklin, and Yale President Ezra Stiles. The entire town center including the buildings and green are designated as a Historic District on the National Register of Historic Places.

Woodbridge's agricultural past is revealed in the many stone walls visible in second growth woods, and in the mill (grist, saw, cider, and textile) foundations and dams on every river. The town is reputed to be the original "home of the friction match." Resident Thomas Sanford sold his formula for matches to William A. Clark who invented machinery for large scale production, and established the Clark Match Factory in 1835. Residents augmented their income making matchboxes for Mr. Clark at a penny a box.

Open space preservation has long been a town priority. The Woodbridge Park Association, incorporated in 1928, is one of the earliest non-profit land trusts in Connecticut. It oversees the nearly 100-acre Alice Newton Street Memorial Park. The Woodbridge Land Trust, formed in 1964, owns over 170 acres, holds conservation easements on another 540 acres, and maintains many of the town's hiking trails. In addition, the Trust hosts one of Connecticut's seven Chestnut research groves.

The town's business district, concentrated in lower Woodbridge on the border with New Haven, includes a variety of restaurants, specialty gift shops, and markets, including the New England Brewing Co., the Yarn Barn, and the eponymous Woodbridge Running Co. This area, the West River flood plain abutting the dramatic West Rock Ridge, provided fertile soil for extensive early 20th c. market gardens. The land known as "The Flats," has yielded many Native American artifacts. A spring 2018 initiative is to create a modern, interactive history museum to showcase these artifacts and other facets of the town's past. Woodbridge was a regular stop on The Leatherman's circuit. Students peeked out the windows of South School as he trudged past to his shelter nearby. One of them remembered, "In the woods in the south part of Woodbridge is one of his caves, sheltered by a few overhanging rocks; here he slept, and kept some dishes to be used once a month, and there were two books written in some foreign tongue."

Places of Interest

Hiking Trails. Trail Maps are available at the Town Hall for Alice Newton Street Memorial Park, West

The late 1800s restored South School. Ken Hull

Notes

Rock Ridge State Park, Elderslie Preserve, Racebrook Tract, and Sperry Park.

Jewish Community Center of Greater New Haven.

Massaro Community Farm & CSA. A non-profit organic farm on 57 acres of town-owned land. Volunteers offer educational and family events.

South School. Restored one-room school overseen by the Historical Society and available for tours. It was one of five district schools in use from the 19th c. until 1929 when the "Central Grammar School" was constructed.

Thomas Darling House Museum. The Darling House is open from 2-4 PM on the 3rd Sun. of March; the 3rd Sun. of July; the 3rd Sun. of Oct. & the 1st Sun. of Dec. and by appointment. Also spring and fall "Tavern Night" Dinners; Koan Farms CSA. www.koanfarms.com.

Ace Begonias. Nursery/Retail Shop specializing in Rieger begonias, herbs, annuals, and perennials.

Blue Check Deli. Open 6 AM-5 PM; over 50 years in business.

Brookside Farm Market. Est. 1984.

Merry Mountain Farm. Seasonal family-run stand offering native and local fruits and vegetables.

Savino Vineyards. Family-owned winery and tasting room.

Woodbridge Running Company.

The Yarn Barn.

The c.1772 Thomas Darling House. Jerry Dougherty

Address Book

Town Sites
www.woodbridgect.org
www.woodbridgeparks.org

Ace Begonias
231 Seymour Rd. • 203-393-9685
www.acebegoniasct.com

Blue Check Deli
382 Amity Rd. • 203-387-3810

Brookside Farm Market
324 Amity Rd. • 203-298-0659

Jewish Community Center of Greater New Haven
360 Amity Rd. • 203-387-2522
www.jccnh.org

Massaro Community Farm & CSA
41 Ford Rd.
www.massarofarm.org

Mountain Farm
420 Amity Rd.

New England Brewing Company
75 Amity Rd. • 203-387-2222
www.newenglandbrewing.com

Savino Vineyards
128 Ford Rd. • 203-387-1573
www.savinovineyards.net

Thomas Darling House Museum
1907 Litchfield Tpke.
www.woodbridgehistory.org

Woodbridge Running Company
7 Landin St. • 203-387-8704

The Yarn Barn
1666 Litchfield Tpke. • 203-389-5117
www.theyarnbarn.com

[Passport Stamp / Signature & Date Here]

Middlesex County
CROMWELL
PORTLAND
EAST HAMPTON
MIDDLETOWN
MIDDLEFIELD
DURHAM
HADDAM
EAST HADDAM
CHESTER
KILLINGWORTH
DEEP RIVER
ESSEX
CLINTON
WESTBROOK
OLD SAYBROOK

CHAPTER 4

Middlesex County

Chester

By Cary Schuler Hull, Chester Historical Society

Day after day, visitors to the small town of Chester describe it as "charming," "picture-perfect," "idyllic," and "unique," while 4000 Chester residents simply and happily call it "home."

Ten miles from Long Island Sound, Chester is bordered on the east by the Connecticut River and on the west and northwest by the state-owned Cockaponset State Forest. You can visit by boat to one of its marinas, by ferry from Hadlyme over the Conn. River, by air to the Chester Airport, or by car from Rt. 9. But visit you must!

Settled in 1692, Chester was an active mill town until the early 20th century, thanks to the abundant water power of its streams and brooks. There is very little manufacturing today, but some of the old factory buildings have been restored and repurposed. The Brushmill By The Waterfall restaurant (www.thebrushmill.com) at the foot of Rt. 9 once manufactured carpet sweepers and brushes; a Susan Bates knitting needle factory is now the Goodspeed Opera House's Terris Theatre; and an auger mill on the Pattaconk Brook is home to the Chester Historical Society's Museum.

The center of Chester features a picturesque and historic Main Street with interesting architecture, elegant shops, art galleries, and superior restaurants. Strike up a conversation with a resident, who just might mention having been an extra in the movie, "It Happened to Jane," with Doris Day and Jack Lemmon, filmed in Chester in 1958.

Interesting Places

Cedar Lake. This 80-acre town-owned lake has a public beach with seasonal lifeguard coverage, picnic tables, grills, a pavilion, and food concession. A state-owned boat launch is at the northern end of the lake.

Chester Center. In our intimate, historic and easily walkable village center, you will find a delightful collection of shops, excellent restaurants, and galleries. It is especially vibrant on Sundays from mid-June to mid-Oct., when the Chester Sunday Market hosts local farmers and vendors and musicians, and on First Fridays, when all businesses are open till 8 PM or later with special happenings and gallery openings.

If you're in Chester between April 1 and Nov. 30, be sure to take a ride across the Conn. River on the Chester-Hadlyme Ferry. The state's quaint, second-oldest ferry offers a pleasant 10-minute ride and a beautiful view of Gillette's Castle in East Haddam. The ferry landing gives a pretty view of the river in all seasons. $6/vehicle/weekend. The dock is at the end of Ferry Road.

Chester Meeting House. Built in 1795 and restored in 1972, this cherished landmark building (National Register of Historic Places) is open for special events only, but take a peek inside the windows. It's also visible on "It Happened to Jane." Located on the town green.

Chester Museum at The Mill. The Chester Historical Society operates a museum at this 1860s mill site just steps from the center of town overlooking a waterfall and the Pattaconk Brook. Two floors in the beautifully restored building exhibit

The center of Chester at dusk with shops and restaurants aglow. Skip Hubbard

Notes

the story of Chester. In the small museum shop you can purchase a DVD of "It Happened to Jane." Open on weekends in summer or by appointment; free admission.

Cockaponset State Forest. In Connecticut's second-largest state forest, you can enjoy swimming and fishing in the Pattaconk Lake, plus hiking and cross-country skiing. Seasonal parking fee.

The Terris Theater. The Susan Bates factory (where knitting needles and crochet hooks were made beginning around 1900) became the renowned Goodspeed Opera House's second stage (and intimate theatre) in 1984. Here several productions get their start before going on to New York or across the country. Productions run May through Nov.

The Chester Historical Society operates "The Chester Museum at The Mill" in an 1860s mill overlooking a waterfall and the Pattaconk Brook. Exhibits tell the history of Chester. Skip Hubbard

Address Book

Town Site
www.chesterct.org

Cedar Lake
West Main St. (Rt. 148)

Chester Center
www.visitchesterct.com
www.chestersundaymarket.jimdo.com

Chester-Hadlyme Ferry
Ferry Rd.

Chester Meeting House
4 Liberty St.

Chester Museum at The Mill
9 West Main St.
www.chesterhistoricalsociety.org

Cockaponset State Forest
Cedar Lake Rd.
www.ct.gov/deep

The Terris Theater
33 North Main St.
860-873-8668
www.goodspeed.org

[Passport Stamp / Signature & Date Here]

Clinton

By Cathy Weiss, Clinton resident and freelance writer – www.cathyweiss.info

One day I accidentally got lost in the town of Clinton a few miles west of Madison. As I was navigating my way back to Rt. 1, I discovered a treasure trove of neighborhood streets with lovely views of rivers, marshes, and Long Island Sound that I never knew were there. I vowed to know this town better, and maybe one day live there. If you visit, I urge you to go off of the beaten path to find hidden pockets of beauty, most of which have benches or gazebos to linger.

Clinton was at first a plantation named Kenilworth in 1667. It was renamed Killingworth by the middle of the 18th century and after many changes in use the town was named after New York Governor DeWitt Clinton.

When Benjamin Franklin was Postmaster General, he traveled the road to Boston in his cushioned chaise, with gangs of men behind in carts filled with stones, which they dropped as each mile was registered on the cyclometer Franklin had attached to the chaise's wheels. One of these stones, marked "25 N.H.," was set on the south side of "Boston Post-road," in colonial Kenilworth. It can be seen, today, on East Main St. Across the street from this ancient marker is the birthplace of one of our country's greatest universities. For it is here that Yale came into existence. It was first called the Collegiate School with Reverend Pierson as its first rector. After Pierson's death in 1707, the Collegiate School was moved to New Haven and named Yale after a substantial donation by Elihu Yale, a Boston-born Merchant.

The Adam Stanton House was built in 1789, when rector Pierson's house was torn down. It rises at one end of the lot where the original Collegiate School once stood. Of interest are the many original parts of the school that are built into the currently standing Adam Stanton House pictured here.

Interesting People, Places, and Things To Do

Walk the Main Street Downtown.

Visit the many art and antique shops, talk to the friendly people as you stroll, grab some brick oven pizza. Be sure to stop into the local breakfast spot, The Coffee Break on East Main St.

Want an insider secret spot? The gazebo behind town hall offers a great place to eat your lunch with great views. Then walk it off with a short stroll to the historic Adam Stanton House. If you visit in summer, catch the farmers market or a free concert on the town green. The Clinton Art Society's Show, the CT Opera, and a huge church fair all take place the third week of August.

Meander, bicycle, and discover beaches and a great harbor area with a multitude of food choices and kayaks and paddleboards for rent. Photograph views of rivers, salt marshes, and Long Island Sound make great mementos.

Embrace your "chicness" and do what most people visit Clinton for: Premium Outlet shopping at exit 63 off I-95. When you are about to drop, relax at award-winning Chamard Vineyard farther down Rt. 81, where you can taste wines, have dinner, hear music in the barn, or roam the grounds. You will find Clinton has a variety of relaxing activities to offer.

The Adam Stanton House 1789. Cathy Weiss

Notes

One of the many beaches in Clinton for swimming, kayaking, and fishing in Long Island Sound. Cathy Weiss

Enjoy an afternoon at the 40-acre Chamard Vineyards, Farm, Winery and Bistro where you can taste their great wines and enjoy a delicious lunch or dinner. Chamard Vineyards

Address Book

Town Site
www.clintonct.org

Adam Stanton House
63 E. Main St.
860-669-2132
www.adamstantonhouse.org

Chamard Vineyard
115 Cow Hill Rd.
860-664-0299
www.chamard.com

Clinton Crossing Premium Outlets
Exit 63 off I-95
860-664-0700
www.premiumoutlets.com/outlet/clinton-crossing

Clinton Town Hall
54 E. Main St.
860-669-9333

The Coffee Break
27 E. Main St.
860-664-5066
www.coffeebreakclinton.com

[Passport Stamp / Signature & Date Here]

Cromwell

By Eliza H. LoPresti, former Cromwell resident

Cromwell is conveniently situated between Hartford and New Haven with access to the major state highways and excellent schools. It has grown to be a popular suburban bedroom community. The town includes a generous mix of businesses, industry and some agriculture.

Cromwell was incorporated and officially named in June of 1851, becoming Connecticut's 149th town. Prior to this, its 13.5 sq. mi. was part of Middletown, its neighbor to the South, and referred to as the "North Society" or more formally as "Middletown Upper Houses." The North Society of Middletown sought to incorporate on their own due to the often flooded Connecticut and Sebethe rivers, which caused a geographical inconvenience in traveling to greater Middletown and also what the citizens claimed as managerial neglect, mostly of the roads.

There was some confusion in the naming of Cromwell, with town leaders initially suggesting other names including Hamlin, North Middletown, and Upper Middletown. When the resolution incorporating the town was finalized, the name "Cromwell" appeared in it without the townspeople's knowledge. This has been attributed to Bulkely Edwards, a prominent member of the general assembly and strong admirer of Oliver Cromwell. Legend has it he filled in the name on the resolution while carrying it to the general assembly, though there are other conflicting accounts.

Due to being bordered on the east by the Connecticut River, Cromwell was once a prosperous port town. A bustling marine area existed on the banks of the river and was a major source of income until the 1850s. Many large homes built by affluent sea captains still stand in the neighborhoods in the southeast of town.

Cromwell enjoyed a century as a manufacturing hub starting in the 1840s. The most prominent business was the J. & E. Stevens Co. (1843-1950) which crafted cast iron hardware, mechanical banks and toy pistols, and eventually became one of the largest manufacturers of cast iron toys in the country. Their original factory on Nooks Hill Rd. still stands and operates today as Horton Brasses.

As manufacturing in the region died down in the first half of the twentieth century, the face of Cromwell changed once again. The town became known for its nurseries and the largest, Pierson Greenhouses (1908-1991), was one of the most prolific growers of roses in the world, earning Cromwell the nickname of Rose Town.

In the 1950s Cromwell's residential and business segments began exponential growth. Development of neighborhoods and condominium complexes brought more residents to town along with numerous retail stores, restaurants, and hotels.

Today, the Connecticut River can be enjoyed at two public parks along River Rd. Cromwell Landing and Frisbee Landing offer easily accessible peaceful river views. Frisbee Landing hosts a robust farm market on Friday evenings, June through September. The market has become a favorite event and boasts live music, food trucks, and local produce and products.

Main Street is lined with many large historical homes built by the prominent manufacturing families of the 1800s. One, the Stevens Frisbie home, now houses the informative Cromwell Historical Society.

Interesting Places

Cromwell Historical Society. In the historic Stevens Frisbie House, open Sat. and Sun. 1-4 PM.

Cromwell Farmer's Market. At Frisbee Park at River Landing, Fridays 4 AM-7 PM, June-Sept.

Notes

Cromwell Landing. Small riverfront park, water views, picnic tables, open space, fishing from rocks.

Cromwell Meadows, State Wildlife Management Area. Part of the Federal Wildlife Restoration Program, hunting, hiking, and an abundance of wildlife sightings.

River Highlands State Park. 177 acres of trail hiking with river views. Open 6 AM–6 PM year-round, located by the railroad tracks.

Watrous Park. Hiking trails, pavilion, splash pad, playground, basketball court, tennis courts, baseball fields, and skate park.

Pierson Park. Playground, walking loop, baseball and football fields and special events.

PGA Travelers Championship at the TPC River Highlands Golf Course. Private golf club open for membership or ticket holders to the PGA Travelers Championship in June of each year.

The Italianate-style Stevens Frisbie House was built (c.1853) by John Stevens, who, with his brother Elisha, founded the J. & E. Stevens Co., which manufactured hardware and toys. Eliza LoPresti

Address Book

Town Site
www.cromwellct.com

Cromwell Farmer's Market
1 River Rd.
www.cromwellfarmersmarket.org

Cromwell Historical Society
397 Main St.
www.www.cromwellhistory.org

Cromwell Landing
98 River Rd.

PGA Travelers Championship at the TPC River Highlands Golf Course
676 Main St.
www.tpc.com/riverhighlands

Pierson Park
West St.

River Highlands State Park
Field Rd.

Watrous Park
Herbert Porter Rd.

[Passport Stamp / Signature & Date Here]

Deep River

By Frank Santoro and Rhonda Forristall, curator, both of the Deep River Historical Society

The early history of Deep River is a story of men, ships, and the sea. Its yards launched 67 ships from 1794 to 1882. Sailing on the clipper ship Nightingale, one of its captains set the speed record from New York to Australia and Shanghai to London. As the Industrial Revolution washed over America's shores, its river (which is actually quite shallow) powered many mills and factories. It became the center of the manufacture of Ivory products from elephant tusks shipped from Africa. It was a stop on the Underground Railroad in the years leading up to the Civil War. During World War II, it was a center for the manufacture of the gliders which were used in the invasion of Normandy. One of its families was instrumental in the manufacture of luxury wooden yachts and later PT boats for the Navy. Its role as an industrial powerhouse gave it the name "Queen of the Valley."

For a while, however, its glitter faded with the decline of manufacturing. The acclamation "Queen of the Valley" gave way to the bumper sticker "Scruffy but Proud." But in a remarkable rebirth, Deep River has re-invented itself in what its Deputy First Selectman has referred to as the "quintessential pre-shopping mall small town." Today, it has a vibrant retail town center along with a certain Norman Rockwell, old-fashioned-white-picket fence quality. It is a place of fife and drum parades, horseshoe pitches (and horse farms), outdoor summer concerts, and a front seat on a riverfront atmosphere that has been referred to by the Nature Conservancy as one of the Western Hemisphere's "last great places" and by an international treaty (the Ramsar Convention) as a wetland of international importance.

Interesting Places

The Landing. The place of the former shipyards where today the steam train of the Valley Railroad discharges its passengers on River Rd. for a cruise along the river.

The Stone House. Home of the Deep River Historical Society where the history of the town comes alive and is home to the Ivory Bleach House which is the only one left standing in North America. Curator Hours: Tues. & Thurs. 10 AM-Noon.

Kirtland Street. Contains a parade of old sea captains' houses.

River Road. A place where magnificent estates line the bluffs along the Connecticut River.

Deep River Town Hall. A flat-iron building built in 1896 that is on

Deep River is a small town nestled between Essex and Chester along the banks of the lower Connecticut River. Rhonda Forristall

Notes

the National Historic Register. It houses the original Columbia oil painting, created by the editorial cartoonist Pulitzer Prize winner C.D. Batchelor in 1946.

Events

The Deep River Ancient Muster. DRAM, the largest fife and drum parade in the world, is held on the third Saturday of July.

Deep River Landing was the former shipyard where 67 ships were launched from 1794 to 1882. Today there is a park, a boat launch, and the Valley RR steam-engine passenger train that cruises along the Connecticut River. Rhonda Forristall

Address Book

Town Site
www.deepriverct.us

Deep River Ancient Muster
Devitt Field, Southworth St.
www.dram.fifedrum.org

Deep River Historical Society at The Stone House
245 Main St.
860-526-1449
www.deepriverhistoricalsociety.org

Deep River Town Hall
174 Main St.

[Passport Stamp / Signature & Date Here]

Durham

By Sarah Atwell, President, Durham Historical Society

Durham, originally called Coginchaug and later changed to Durham after Durham, England, is a small town of approximately 7,000 people that was settled in 1699 (inc. 1708).

The town hosts the annual Durham Fair, the largest volunteer agricultural fair in New England. The fair is held on the last full weekend of September. The fair was established in 1916 but was not held after the disastrous hurricane of 1938 or during 1942, 1943, or 1944 due to WWII. The fair expanded beyond the town green and grew from a one-day event during its early years to an event that now draws over 200,000 people to the four-day event.

Durham has a rich history and many famous residents and their families have been buried in the Old Durham Cemetery. Durham's first minister, who was also the first graduate of Yale College, is buried here as are Elias and Eunice Austin, parents of Moses Austin, whose plan of settlement led to the first Anglo-American colony in Texas. Major General James Wadsworth, whose gravestone was recently restored, lived on Main Street, was a member of the Continental Congress in 1784, Comptroller of the State, town clerk and selectman of the town at various times during his career. Durham played an active role in the Revolutionary War. Over 100 men served, oxen were sent to Valley Forge to help feed the Continental Army, and it was host to Sheldon's 2nd Regiment of Continental Light Dragoons during the winter of 1778 by permission of General Washington, who traveled through Durham twice, commemorated by the Washington Trail through the region.

Durham is also home to one of the first public libraries in the country, which was established in 1733. Early industry in town included shoe making, manufacturing, and farming. The town had three metal box manufacturing companies at one time, supplying the country with anything from first aid kits for private business and military use, to industrial cabinets, to safe deposit boxes.

Today, Durham has a beautiful historic district, a vibrant community with many social and school organizations, and open space for hiking and preservation.

Interesting Places

Durham Historical Society. Next to the Durham Town Hall, is available to visitors by appointment. The building is also known as the Center School and was used as a school from 1775-1923. Also located on the property is the Sabbath Day House and the WWII Air Spotter's Tower. The Sabbath Day House provided shelter for families who traveled from the outskirts of town for church in the early years. Several of these buildings were located on the town green in the 18th century. The Air Spotter's Tower was located on a farm in open space and was staffed by volunteers during WWII.

Old Durham Cemetery. At the corner of Main St. and Cemetery Rd.

Mill Bridge. The stone arch was built in the 1822 and uncovered during construction in 1994. It replaced a wooden structure that collapsed due to ice flow while a stagecoach was crossing, killing two passengers. It is located across Cemetery Rd. from the Old

The Old Durham Cemetery c.1700. Sarah Atwell

NOTES

Durham Cemetery.

Durham Fair. Held annually in September.

Hiking Trails. Mattabesett Trail, Field Forest Preserve Trails, Curtis Woodlands, Mount Pisgah Mountain Bike Trail, all managed by Connecticut Forest and Park Association.

The Durham Historical Society has these historic buildings (L-R): Sabbath Day House, WWII Air Spotter's Tower, and Center Schoolhouse (historical society headquarters). Sarah Atwell

ADDRESS BOOK

Town Site
www.townofdurhamct.org

Durham Historical Society
38 Town House Rd.
860-716-5497

Durham Fair
www.durhamfair.com

Old Durham Cemetery
Corner of Main St. & Cemetery Rd.

Mill Bridge
Across from the Old Durham Cemetery

HIKING & TRAILS

Mattabesett Trail
Field Forest Preserve Trails
Curtis Woodlands
Mt. Pisgah Mountain Bike Trail
www.ctwoodlands.org

[Passport Stamp / Signature & Date Here]

East Haddam

*By Wendy M. Vincent, Executive Editor, **Epic Magazines**: Exploring the people, places, history, art and culture of Connecticut*

Historic homes, rolling pastures, stone walls, an opera house, a swing bridge, and a grand castle overlooking the Connecticut River! What more could one ask for in a town? Tucked along the eastern banks of the Connecticut River, East Haddam encompasses nearly 57 sq. mi.; is located approx. halfway between New York City (2 hrs.) and Boston (1 hr.); and includes the communities of Moodus, Lake Hayward, and Hadlyme.

Originally inhabited by Native American tribes–the Wangunk, the Mohegan, and the Nehantic–the area was known as "Machimoodus," meaning the place of noises, due to a series of earthquakes. Residents still refer to unusual rumblings as "the Moodus noises." In 1662, East Haddam was purchased from the natives for 30 coats, or $100.

Industry over the years includes agriculture, timber farming, shipbuilding, manufacturing, and entertainment. By 1700, there were thirty permanent homesteads. By the 1800s, there were over 15 operating mills, and the population had grown to 3,000. In the 1800s, America's oldest continuously performing drum corps, the Moodus Drum and Fife Corps, was formed by Hezekiah Percival and in 1877, the Goodspeed Opera House opened. The early 1900s saw the growth of the resort areas of Bashan Lake, Lake Hayward, and Moodus Reservoir.

Today, East Haddam is home to upwards of 9,000 residents and offers an opportunity to explore the history, art, and scenic beauty of a rural New England town. In the fall, check out the "Thunder in the Valley" Drum and Fife Muster. During the summer, "Music on the River" brings musical groups to the Green along the river with views of the bridge.

Interesting Places

The Goodspeed Opera House. The birthplace of original productions like Annie and Man of La Mancha.

Nathan Hale School House. Hale taught in this one-room schoolhouse during 1773. It is behind St. Stephen's Episcopal Church, and is owned by the Connecticut Society of the Sons of the American Revolution.

Oldest Bell. Hanging in the bell tower at St. Stephen's at 31 Main Street is what is believed to be the oldest bell in America. Cast for a Spanish monastery in 1815 the bell arrived here in 1834 as ballast on a ship. For information, visit www.ststeves.org.

Gillette Castle State Park. Includes the castle-like home of William Gillette, an actor famous for his portrayal of Sherlock Holmes. Features a visitor center with gift shop, a grille, views of the Connecticut River, trails, and picnicking. During the summer, the East Haddam Stage Co. offers free outdoor live theater performances. Mr. and Mrs. Gillette can sometimes be seen inside the castle entertaining visitors.

Venture Smith Grave. In the First Church of Christ Congregational Cemetery is the grave of Venture Smith (1729-1805), an African slave who purchased his freedom. Venture Smith Day is celebrated annually in the fall.

East Haddam Historical Society

The 1913 Swing Bridge over the Connecticut River and the 1876 Goodspeed Opera House. Cassandra Day

NOTES

and Museum. For history on East Haddam head to the museum featuring exhibits including the Moodus Drum and Fife Corps, the Moodus Mills, and artists Langdon Kihn and Heinz Warneke.

Not One, but Two Libraries. The Rathbun Free Memorial Library (1935) and The East Haddam Free Public Library (1888).

Devil's Hopyard State Park. Mystery surrounds this 1,000-acre state park that features waterfalls, trails, grills, picnicking, fishing, and camping.

Ray of Light Farm. A rescue and therapy center that offers pony rides, a tack store, and rescue animals.

Rivers, Lakes, and Parks. Enjoy hiking, boating, fishing, and outdoor activities at any number of lakes and parks including Eightmile River, Salmon River, Bashan Lake, Moodus Reservoir, Lake Hayward, Machimoodus State Park, and Sunrise State Park.

Don't forget to stop in and support local businesses, our unique stores, farm stands, antique dealers, wineries, coffee shops, and restaurants.

Gillette Castle, the home of famed actor Sherlock Holmes, is a living museum open to the public.
Lydia Roloff

ADDRESS BOOK

Town Site
www.easthaddam.org

Devil's Hopyard State Park
366 Hopyard Rd.
www.ct.gov/deep

East Haddam Free Public Library
18 Plains Rd., Moodus
www.easthaddamlibrarysystem.org

East Haddam Historical Society and Museum
264 Town St.
www.easthaddamhistory.org

East Haddam Stage Co.
www.ehsco.org

Gillette Castle State Park
67 River Rd., Hadlyme
www.ct.gov/deep

Goodspeed Opera House
6 Main St.
860-873-8668
www.goodspeed.org

Nathan Hale School House
31 Main St.
860-873-3399

Rathbun Free Memorial Library
36 Main St., East Haddam

Ray of Light Farm
232 Town St.
www.rayoflightfarm.org

Venture Smith Grave
499 Town St.

[Passport Stamp / Signature & Date Here]

East Hampton

By Kira Roloff and Marty Podskoch, Members Chatham Historical Society and Dean Markham, Member Joseph N. Goff House Museum

East Hampton, a town in Middlesex Co., includes two villages: Middle Haddam and Cobalt. It is approximately 10 miles east of Middletown with a population of 12,959 (2010).

The area, inhabited by the Wangunk Indians, was called Pocotopaug, a Pequot word meaning "lake with pierced islands." A Wangunk legend said that Princess Namoenee jumped to her death at Markham's Cove, a willing sacrifice to appease the Great God Hobomoko and bring an end to the many drownings the Wangunk tribe had suffered. The legend goes that there were no more drownings.

In 1739, settlers from Eastham and Chatham on Cape Cod purchased lots from Middletown proprietors who were granted ownership in East Middletown and the Three Mile Division. Led by Ralph Smith, several families settled on their new holdings at Hog Hill in the Middle Haddam section of town. In 1746 the community was named Easthampton parish. Middletown petitioned the General Assembly to create a new township called Conway which was incorporated as Chatham in 1767 as Connecticut's 71st town. In 1841 the area now encompassing Portland became a separate township. In 1915, the residents renamed the town East Hampton after the original name of Easthampton.

William Barton in 1808 established a bell-making factory making cow bells, sleigh bells, church bells, and other types. Apprentices of Barton learned the trade and started their own businesses. In 1832, brothers Abner and William Bevin, started their company (Bevin Brothers) later joined by their brothers Chauncey and Philo, and is the only remaining bell manufacturer. Over 40 companies produced millions of bells sold world-wide. Other notable bell producers were Starr Bros. Bell Co., The N. N. Hill Brass Co. and Gong Bell. No wonder East Hampton is called "Belltown USA."

The village of Cobalt got its name when cobalt was discovered in 1762 and mined but ore separation problems ended this industry by 1859. Middle Haddam on the Connecticut River, was a thriving shipbuilding center that launched many of the famous Clipper Ships in the late 18th and early 19th century. One builder, Thomas Child, constructed 237 ships.

In the late 19th and early 20th century, summer tourists were drawn to Lake Pocotopaug's waterfront cottages, casinos, and hotels. Many traveled from the cities on the Air Line Railroad.

Witch hazel, used as an astringent and as a base in cosmetics and patent medicines, was produced commercially since the late 19th century by American Distilling, the world's largest producer. Visit www.americandistilling.com.

Interesting Places

Chatham Historical Society Museum. Preserving town history in two buildings featuring toys, bells, clothing, furniture, etc. Also has the restored 1840 Chestnut Hill Schoolhouse.

Hurd State Park. Features hiking, picnicking, and kayaking.

The Air Line Trail travels through East Hampton and is used year round by thousands of walkers, bikers, runners, and skiers. Podskoch

Notes

Joseph N. Goff House Museum. Provides a wide variety of cultural and enrichment programs to celebrate the town's heritage.

Pumpkin Town USA. A seasonal attraction at Paul's & Sandy's Too garden center has a town full of pumpkin people and seasonal treats.

Comstock Covered Bridge (1873). Connects East Hampton with Colchester. One of 3 surviving Conn. covered bridges in the Salmon River State Forest that features fishing, picnicking, and hiking. Two miles west of the junction of Rt. 149 & Rt. 16.

Old Home Day Celebration. Annual event 1st weekend after 4th of July with largest parade in Middlesex Co. Entertainment, food, carnival rides, and crafts.

Air Line State Trail. Features hiking, biking, and cross-country skiing on old Air Line Railroad right-of-way. Named because it followed a path as "if a line had been drawn through the air" between New Haven & Boston. The trail connects East Hampton with Thompson.

Middle Haddam Public Library. Housed in a historic building. Provides a wide variety of materials and programs.

Nelson's Family Campground. Has a pool, playground, recreation room, Wi-Fi, etc.

Notable People

Joel West Smith (1837-1924). Invented the first typewriter for Braille. He is buried in Lake View Cemetery.

East Hampton Chatham Historical Society Museum and 1840 Chestnut Hill Schoolhouse on Bevin Blvd. Cheryl Gioielli

William A. O'Neill (1930-2007). 84th Governor of Connecticut, 1980-1991, lifelong resident of East Hampton.

Address Book

Town Site
www.easthamptonct.gov

Air Line State Trail
www.ct.gov/deep

Chatham Historical Society Museum
6 Bevin Blvd.
www.chathamhistoricalct.org

Comstock Covered Bridge
www.coveredbridgesite.com

Hurd State Park
Off Rt. 151 on Hurd Park Rd.
www.ct.gov/deep

Joseph N. Goff House Museum
2 Barton Hill Rd.
www.goffhouseehct.blogspot.com

Lakeside Bar & Grill
81 N. Main St.
860-467-6891
www.lakesidebar-grill.com

Middle Haddam Public Library
2 Knowles Rd., Middle Haddam
860-267-9093
www.middlehaddamlibrary.com

Nelson's Family Campground
71 Mott Hill Rd.
www.nelsonscampground.com

Pumpkin Town USA
93 E. High St.
www.pumpkintown.com

Sweet Jeans Café
13 N. Main St.
860-467-6334
/SweetJeansCafe

[Passport Stamp / Signature & Date Here]

Essex

*By Zachary Lamothe, author of **Connecticut Lore and More Connecticut Lore***

Essex has been lauded as the "Best small town in America." Although it's quaint, Essex's charm is only the outer layer of this multifaceted municipality. It was a center of the shipbuilding industry in the 18th and 19th centuries and was attacked by the British during the War of 1812. Twenty-eight American ships were burned as the British sailed up the Connecticut River in a surprise attack. A parade commemorates this event in May. The first American submarine, the Turtle, was constructed in Essex for use in the American Revolution.

The Nehantic Indians were the first people to live in the Essex area. It was known as Potopaug Point, a name from the area's indigenous peoples. The Saybrook Colony was settled in 1635 with its inclusion as part of Connecticut five years later. In 1648 the Potopaug Quarter was established to include the towns of Essex, Deep River and Chester. The area that we refer to as Essex remained the Potapoug Quarter of Saybrook until 1854 when the state legislature split off Essex Village to become the Town of Essex. Centerbrook (including the present day Ivoryton) was added five years later. Ivoryton is justly named because the village was the site of two of America's largest ivory products manufacturers.

Essex Village is centered around Main, Ferry, and Pratt streets. Its prime shopping district is on Main Street featuring a jumble of businesses such as art galleries, a toy store, and restaurants as well as stately 18th century homes. The end of Main Street leads to a cul-de-sac adjacent to the Connecticut River.

Interesting Places

Connecticut River Museum. Learn about the history and environmental features of New England's main river. Also on site is a replica of the Turtle submarine. The museum is located at the end of Main Street's cul-de-sac in a former steamboat warehouse. Schedule: Columbus Day to Memorial Day, Tues-Sun. 10 AM-5 PM. Memorial Day to Columbus Day, 7 days/week: 10 AM-5 PM.

Essex Public Library. A great place for children and adults. Books, computers, Wi-Fi, genealogy research, and much more.

Griswold Inn. "The Gris" has been a crowd pleaser since 1776. Essex's dining and lodging mainstay features live music most nights in the taproom. Make sure to stop by for the Jovial Crew, sea chanteys featuring Connecticut's own Cliff Haslam on Monday nights for a raucous good time.

Essex Steam Train and Riverboat. Ride the rails in an historic steam train from Essex to Deep River to take in the natural splendor of the lower Connecticut River Valley. The riverboat Becky Thatcher awaits passengers from the train on an adjoining Connecticut River cruise up to the East Haddam bridge.

Ivoryton Playhouse. There is no better venue for live theater than the historical Ivoryton Playhouse. Legendary actors such as Katharine Hepburn and Marlon Brando have all graced this stage and the professional actors put on well-known plays and musicals from March to December.

Winter Wildlife and Eagle Cruises. Connecticut River Expeditions runs a series of cruises on the river

After visiting the many shops in town, visitors enjoy a stroll down Main St. to the Connecticut River Museum (L) and the town dock. Zachary Lamothe

Notes

throughout the year, but one that is truly unique is the eagle cruise. The eagles call this area home during the months of February and March and cruises occur on the weekends. The boat departs from the Essex River Museum.

You'll feel like you've stepped back in time when you board the old-fashioned Essex Steam Train and take in the marvelous scenery of the Connecticut River Valley. Jerry Dougherty

The 1776 Griswold Inn incorporates many artifacts from its past in its décor, including paintings of Clipper ships and steamboats and a collection of historic guns. Zachary Lamothe

Address Book

Town Site
www.essexct.gov

Connecticut River Museum
67 Main St.
860-767-8269
www.ctrivermuseum.org

Essex Public Library
33 West Ave.
860-767-1560
www.youressexlibrary.org

Essex Steam Train and Riverboat
1 Railroad Ave.
860-767-0103
www.essexstreamtrain.com

Griswold Inn
36 Main St.
860-767-1776
www.griswoldinn.com

Ivoryton Playhouse
103 Main St., Ivoryton
860-767-7318
www.ivorytonplayhouse.org

Winter Wildlife and Eagle Cruises
860-662-0577
www.ctriverquest.com

[Passport Stamp / Signature & Date Here]

Haddam

By Elizabeth Malloy, Haddam Historical Society

Haddam, which is located in the lower Connecticut River Valley in Middlesex Co., is a vibrant community with a rich heritage, and over 8,000 acres of recreational open space. The town is comprised of distinct villages including Haddam, Higganum, Hidden Lake, and Tylerville and has the unique distinction of being the only town in the state of Connecticut that is bisected by the Connecticut River. It has residents living on both sides. Haddam Neck, on the east side of the river, has no bridge or direct connection to the main part of town. Haddam is primarily a residential community with an excellent school system and a population of 8,346.

The earliest residents of Haddam were members of Wangunk tribe of Native Americans who hunted, fished and grew corn, beans and tobacco, and had relatively peaceful relationships with neighboring tribes.

In 1662 the Connecticut Colony purchased from the Wangunks the land the English called "Plantation at Thirty Mile Island" for 30 coats. In 1668 the town was formally established and named Haddam after the English village of Much Hadham. The early residents of Haddam were farmers who grew rye, corn, and grass and raised cattle. The river played an essential role in the town's existence for the first 200 years, providing transportation and income. Shipyards were built along both sides of the river, and many of the brooks and streams provided waterpower for small mills and factories.

During the Revolutionary War, Haddam was a provision town and supplied the Continental Army with fish, beef, and pork. Haddam men served in the local militia and participated in privateering, the state sanctioned practice of capturing enemy ships.

In the early 19th century, as Haddam's farmland became depleted, many residents emigrated west, although trade and industry, including shipbuilding, fishing and quarrying did expand. In 1785 Middlesex County was formed, and Haddam was designated a half shire town, sharing county responsibilities with adjoining Middletown. The municipalities were required to build a court house and jail, and shared court responsibilities for over 100 years. The court system moved out of Haddam in the 1880s, but the jail remained active until the early 1970s.

In 1802 the Middlesex Turnpike opened through town and served as the main overland route between Hartford and the shoreline. The Connecticut Valley Railroad was built in 1871, and Haddam boasted five stations from Goodspeed's to Higganum.

Large scale industry came to Higganum in the early 19th century including Higganum Manufacturing (later Clark Cutaway Harrow), which produced farming implements, and D. & H. Scovil Hoe Co. which manufactured planters' hoes. These industries brought many immigrants to the community including Swedes, Irish, and Italians. By the mid-20th century, most industry had moved or had been scaled back, and Haddam became a primarily suburban residential community. One exception was the construction of the Connecticut Yankee Atomic

This historic marker lists the 28 proprietors of Haddam who in May 1662 purchased 104 sq. mi for 30 coats (worth around $100) from four Native American chiefs, two queens, and others. Elizabeth Malloy

Notes

Power Plant in Haddam Neck in 1968 which produced more than 110 billion kilowatt hours before closing in 1996.

Interesting Places

Thankful Arnold House Museum/ Haddam Historical Society.

Shad Museum.

Veteran's Museum.

Brainerd Memorial Library.

Cockaponset State Forest.

Haddam Meadows State Park.

Eagle Landing State Park.

Higganum Reservoir State Park. Just off Rt. 154, Higganum

Brainerd Quarry Preserve.

Haddam Neck Fair. Labor Day Weekend.

The Thankful Arnold House, which dates from the late 18th century, is distinguished by its gambrel roof with an unusual bell-shaped profile. Built in three stages between 1794 and 1810, it provides a glimpse of the life of the Widow Thankful Arnold in the late 1820s shortly after her husband's untimely death. It is a museum of the Haddam Historical Society. Elizabeth Malloy

Address Book

Town Site
www.haddam.org

Brainerd Memorial Library
920 Saybrook Rd.
www.brainerdlibrary.lioninc.org

Brainerd Quarry Preserve
Injun Hollow Rd., Haddam Neck
www.middlesexlandtrust.org

Eagle Landing State Park
14 Little Meadow Rd.

Haddam Neck Fair
15 Quarry Hill Rd., Haddam Neck
www.haddamneckfair.com

Shad Museum
212 Saybrook Rd.
www.haddamshadmuseum.com

Thankful Arnold House Museum
14 Hayden Hill Rd
www.haddamhistory.org

Veteran's Museum
7 Candlewood Hill Rd.
www.haddam.org/veterans

[Passport Stamp / Signature & Date Here]

Killingworth

By Thomas L. Lentz, Municipal Historian

Killingworth, located in Middlesex Co., originally included the Town of Clinton to the south. Killingworth was first settled in 1663 as the plantation of "Homonoscitt" (Hammonasset). On May 9, 1667, the General Court of the Colony of Connecticut ordered that "ye towne of Homonoscit shal for ye future be named Kenilworth." This date is traditionally used for the founding of Killingworth. The descendants of many of the original settlers began moving to the northern part of the town after 1700. In 1735, the General Assembly passed an act dividing the town into two Ecclesiastical societies. In 1838, an act of the legislature split Killingworth into two towns with the northern society retaining the name Killingworth and the southern society becoming Clinton.

The majority of Killingworth residents were farmers although many mills were built on streams and rivers. Population reached a peak in the first part of the 19th century but then declined as residents moved westward to better farming land. At the end of the 19th century, immigrants from Europe replaced many of the old families who were departing. Population reached a low point of 482 in 1930 but began to increase in the 1950s. Population continued to increase greatly with new residential development but has slowed in recent years. Population in 2020 was 6,174.

The nature of the town today is characterized by low-density residential use, forested lands, agricultural lands, open spaces, parks, and historical features. The major highways are Rt. 81 running from Clinton to Haddam and Rt. 80 running from Madison to Deep River. There is a Commercial District along parts of Rts. 80 and 81. Killingworth is a member of Regional School District 17 that includes the town of Haddam. Houses of worship are the Killingworth Congregational Church, Emmanuel Episcopal Church, St. Lawrence Roman Catholic Church, and the Living Rock Church. Emergency services are provided by the Killingworth Volunteer Fire Department, the Killingworth Ambulance Assn., and a Resident State Trooper.

The Parmelee House at the Parmelee Farm on Route 81 was built by Horace and Eunice Parmelee in 1847. Thomas L. Lentz

Interesting Places

Chatfield Hollow State Park. Offers hiking trails, a swimming beach, trout fishing, mountain biking, rock climbing, and picnicking areas. The Indian caves were used as winter shelters by the Hammonasset. The Civilian Conservation Corps laid the ground work for a future state park by building roads, trails, dam, nature museum, swimming area, and picnic areas in the 1930s.

Parmelee Farm. A 132-acre complex owned by the town that includes a farmhouse, stone barn, pavilion, and a one-room schoolhouse. Events at the farm include concerts, farm markets, tag

The Federal style Killingworth Congregational Church on Rt. 81 was completed in 1820. Thomas L. Lentz

Notes

sales, scouting projects, educational experiences, benefit programs, community gardens, and many other community activities. There is an extensive trail system developed by the Killingworth Land Conservation Trust.

The Congregational Church in Killingworth. This Federal-style meetinghouse was completed in 1820 and is on the State Register of Historic Places. The Parsonage (1866) and Old Town Hall (1881) are nearby.

Emmanuel Episcopal Church. Known as "The Little Church in the Wilderness," began construction in 1803 and is on the National Register of Historic Places.

Killingworth Library. Loans books and multimedia, provides displays and exhibits, has book sales, and offers lectures on a variety of topics.

Killingworth Historical Society. Located in the 1847 Parmelee House at the Parmelee Farm. It owns the Union District schoolhouse built in 1800 on Roast Meat Hill Rd. and the Black Rock schoolhouse on Recycle Way.

Chatfield Hollow State Park was built by the Civilian Conservation Corps in the mid-1930s. The CCC constructed a large dam creating a Schreeder Pond and built Oak Lodge under the white pine trees that is used as a nature museum. Podskoch

Address Book

Town Site
www.townofkillingworth.com

Chatfield Hollow State Park
381 Rt. 80

The Congregational Church in Killingworth
273 Rt. 81

Emmanuel Episcopal Church
50 Emanuel Church Rd.

Parmelee Farm
265 Rt. 81
www.parmeleefarm.org

Killingworth Historical Society
www.killingworthhistorical.org

Killingworth Library
301 Rt. 81
860-663-2000
www.killingworthlibrary.org

[Passport Stamp / Signature & Date Here]

Middlefield

By Jessica Lobner, Director, Levi E. Coe Library

Only 12 sq. mi., 4 mi. long and 3 mi. wide, Middlefield was a district of the town of Middletown until 1866. Originally, people from Middletown came to Middlefield for one reason: farming.

Middlefield's first settler is believed to be Benjamin Miller, a rugged 'Paul Bunyan-type' who, two centuries after his death, was mentioned in a 1938 Boston Globe article. Ripley's Believe It or Not claimed that Miller called for his neighbors to help him haul a bear he killed and that he was heard from eight miles away and therefore declared it "The Loudest Shout in History."

Another one of the founding fathers was John Lyman, who helped to establish the oldest and richest operating family farm in Connecticut, Lyman Orchards. Originally, the Lymans grew mostly peaches but after a few devastating late freezes, they switched to apples because it is a heartier crop. It is also rumored that the Lyman Homestead was a stop on the Underground Railroad.

In the 19th century, Middlefield was considered unsurpassed in industrial ingenuity in New England because of the way the residents used Middlefield's water sources to create a myriad of things in a number of factories: nails, pistols, pewter, bone buttons and even washing machines, to name a few, and at one point, Middlefield was the largest producer of sheep and wool in the entire country.

Middlefield was home to a number of inventors as well. William Lyman invented a gun sight that was very popular with hunters and the Powder Ridge Ski Park was home to the world's first snowmaking machine.

Interesting Places

Lyman Orchards. It is Connecticut's destination for family fun with pick your own fruits, locally sourced foods, and handmade pies in the Apple Barrel market, and golf at the three award-winning courses and driving range.

Powder Ridge Park. Your "go to" place for year-round adventure sports in Connecticut featuring skiing, snowboarding, tubing, synthetic snow (365 days a year!), and mountain biking for all ages. The Ridge is also host to cultural events, sports competitions, and music and beer festivals.

Wadsworth Falls State Park. Enjoy hiking or biking on varied trails or spend some time enjoying the beautiful falls.

Old North Burying Ground. Served as the final resting place for many of Middlefield's earliest settlers. It was laid out in 1737 and was used regularly until a new burial ground was established in 1828. Beyond its role as a cemetery, the Old North Burying Ground depicts family life in early Middlefield. Family members were buried together, and tombstones often indicate the family bonds. Stillborn children were buried in marked graves alongside adults killed in farming accidents. The graves of enslaved Africans were unmarked, although they were recorded in the community's written histories. For more information, call the Middlefield Historical Society.

Powder Ridge Resort features skiing, snowboarding, tubing, and mountain biking. Enjoy the fire at The Ridge Restaurant & Tavern that is open year-round. Powder Ridge

Notes

Historic Levi E. Coe Library. Born in Middlefield in 1828, Levi E. Coe later settled in nearby Meriden, where he became president of the Meriden Savings Bank and also served as a judge. He built and donated the library that bears his name in his hometown and the Richardsonian Romanesque-style library was dedicated in 1893. The building was expanded in 1974 to connect to the neighboring Library Hall, the former St. Paul's Episcopal Church that the library had acquired in 1920. In 2021, Levi E. Coe library became the first library in the state of Connecticut to have a walking labyrinth installed on the premises. A labyrinth is a single path from the outer edge that winds, in a circuitous way, to the center. Labyrinths are used worldwide as a way to quiet the mind, calm anxieties, reduce stress and encourage meditation. All are welcome to visit during daylight hours.

Blackbird Tavern. While roaming around Middlefield, one can make a pit stop at the Blackbird Tavern, a comfy outpost that offers pub basics like wings and steaks, plus various beers in a convivial setting. .

Levi E. Coe Library has been serving the community since 1893. It provides information, books, ebooks, programs, online databases, and research. Bill Konefal

Address Book

Town Site
www.middlefieldct.org

Blackbird Tavern
6 Way Rd.
860-349-3860
www.blackbirdtavern.com

Historic Levi E. Coe Library
414 Main St.
860-349-3857
www.leviecoe.lioninc.org

Lyman Orchards
3 Lyman Rd.
860-349-1793
www.lymanorchards.com

Middlefield Historical Society
405 Main St.
860-349-0665

Powder Ridge Park
99 Powder Hill Rd.
866-860-0208
www.powderridgepark.com

Wadsworth Falls State Park
721 Wadsworth St. on Rt. 157

[Passport Stamp / Signature & Date Here]

Middletown

By Carolyn Youngblood Laban, historian, artist, and former resident of Middletown

Middletown, originally known as Mattabeseck by the Native Americans, is located just above "The Narrows" on the Connecticut River. It lies halfway between Long Island Sound and Connecticut's first settlement in Windsor, hence the name of "Middletown" (founded in 1653).

Because the river's water was too shallow for sea-going vessels to travel north of Middletown, it became the last stop for Sea Traders from The West Indies and countries wishing to trade with the colonists. It became the home for ship builders who built mansions along the shores of Middletown. By the mid-1700s this small town first settled by approx. 15 English settlers became known as the wealthiest and most populated Connecticut city and the most important seaport between Boston and New York.

The rich soils of Middletown proved to be good farming land. It also bore a lead mine that produced ammunition for the patriots during the Revolutionary War (1775-1783). George Washington is said to have visited Middletown to speak with his friend General Comfort Sage.

Middletown's productivity continued to excel even after the shipping business declined in the early 1800s. By 1870 there were 130 manufacturing companies. Immigrants began moving into Middletown to work in factories producing marine hardware, textile products, machinery, and tools.

Prior to the 1800s the population of Middletown was primarily English and African American. At the turn of the century, the Irish, Germans, Swedish, Jewish, Poles, and Italians moved in and created a richly diverse combination of cultures. Today Middletown's diversity of cultures is reflected in its wide variety of restaurants on the beautiful banks of the Connecticut River.

Main Street is one of the widest Main Streets in New England which proves to be perfect for annual festivities such as Fourth of July fireworks on the River, an Annual Motorcycle meet and an antique car show. Check with Middletown Events calendar online.

Wesleyan University is located blocks from downtown so if you come for a visit you can spend your days walking around Wesleyan Campus and Main Street where you will find entertainment, food, history, education, and a choice of religious houses. There are five different churches within a walk down Main Street.

Interesting Places

Freedom Trail.

Wadsworth Mansion at Long Hill (1911).

Wadsworth Park. Swimming, picnicking, mountain biking, and hiking trail.

Connecticut Trees of Honor Memorial. For a peaceful walk, Located within Middletown's Veteran Memorial Park.

Greater Middletown Military Museum. At Veterans Memorial Park.

Kid City Children's Museum. A truly unique "must-do" experience for small and big children alike.

Main Street in Middletown has a variety of great restaurants ranging from Italian, Thai, Indian, Mexican, and Vegetarian. Podskoch

Notes

Wesleyan R. J. Julia Bookstore. The 13,000-sq. foot store features a variety of over 18,000 books, café, and Wesleyan books and apparel.

Inn at Middletown. Elegant hotel in a former colonial-style armory with a New England tavern and an indoor heated pool.

O'Rourke's Diner. This Landmark diner (since 1941) serves creative American classics and Irish dishes for breakfast and lunch. Featured in *Yankee Magazine* as one of the top diners in New England.

Restaurants

Café 56. Serves breakfast and lunch, foods and culinary traditions from different countries, continents, and ethnic backgrounds.

Celtic Cavern. An underground gastropub with live music.

Herd on Main. Featuring fresh, locally sourced creations.

First and Last Tavern. Italian cuisine.

Eli Cannons Bar. Serves pub fare and micro brews. Over 35 rotational beers on tap from local breweries. In the summertime, they have a "beach" out back!

Coyote Blue. Mexican food.

Mattabesett Canoe Club. Features seafood and American food.

You'll be delighted as you wander the aisles of Amato's Toy and Hobby. It's packed with over 30,000 unique toys, hobby supplies, model trains in all gauges, science project supplies, Boy Scout & Girl Scout uniforms and much more. Podskoch

Address Book

Town Site
www.middletownct.gov

Amato's Toy and Hobby
395 Main St. • 860-347-1893
www.amatosmiddletown.com

Inn at Middletown
70 Main St. • 860-854-6300
www.innatmiddletown.com

Kid City Children's Museum
119 Washington St. • 860-347-0495
www.kidcitymuseum.com

Greater Middletown Military Museum
200 Walnut Grove Rd.
www.gmvmm.com

Wadsworth Park
721 Wadsworth St.

Wesleyan R.J. Julia Bookstore
413 Main St.
www.gmvmm.com

FOOD

Café 56
102 Court St.
www.cafe56ct.com

Celtic Cavern
45 Melilli Plaza • 860-343-2954
www.celticcavern.com

Coyote Blue
1960 Saybrook Rd. • 860-345-2403
www.coyoteblue.com

Eli Cannon's
695 Main St. • 860-347-3547
www.elicannons.com

First and Last Tavern
220 Main St. • 860-347-2220
www.firstandlastmiddletown.com

Herd
200 Main St. • 860-346-4373
www.herdonmain.com

Mattabesett Canoe Club
80 Harbor Dr. • 860-347-9999
www.canoeclubmiddletown.com

Mikado Japanese
3 Melilli Plaza • 860-346-6655
www.mikadoct.com

O'Rourke's Diner
728 Main St. • 860-346-6101
www.orourkesmiddletown.com

Tibetan Kitchen
574 Main St. • 860-343-3073
www.tibetankitchen.us

[Passport Stamp / Signature & Date Here]

Old Saybrook

By Old Saybrook Historical Society & Old Saybrook Chamber of Commerce

To get a quick idea of Old Saybrook's natural beauty, significant history and friendly people join us on a quick tour as we 'depart' from the 1850s railroad station and the nearby 1787 Upper Cemetery to head south on Main St.

Here at the corner is sea captain Ambrose Whittlesey's House, now part of Saybrook Country Barn.

This wide four-lane street is lined with small shops, many of which are former homes and each with its own history.

Two "re-purposed" buildings border the town green, a former elementary school is now the Town Hall, and the old Town Hall is now the Katharine Hepburn Cultural Arts Center.

On the corner of Main Street and the Old Boston Post Road is the Humphrey Pratt Tavern, site of the town's first post office in 1795 and early stage stop for travelers. Here, too, the Marquis de Lafayette spent the night when he toured the country in 1824.

Nearby is the pharmacy where Miss Anna James, Connecticut's first African-American female pharmacist, prepared and dispensed prescriptions and friendly advice to all in need.

Across the street is the Congregational Church whose early 18th Century members wrote the Saybrook Platform which still provides guidance for governing Congregational churches today.

Here too is the 1767 Gen. William Hart House, Old Saybrook's most prominent historic figure and the home of the Old Saybrook Historical Society.

Farther south Main becomes College Street and a detour to North Cove will reveal homes of merchants and ship captains who traded in the West Indies and became privateers during the American Revolution.

The old taverns have become luxurious homes and the old wharfs are now the sites of private docks.

Back on College Street you'll see the "ancient burial ground" and the final resting place of Lady Fenwick, a hardy pioneer who hunted and maintained a garden in the first fort.

Adjacent to the cemetery is the Yale Boulder marking the location where the noted institution began in 1701.

At the Saybrook Fort Memorial Park one finds a statue of Lion Gardiner, engineer and soldier, who built the fort and laid out a town.

This is a good place to read the historic markers and imagine the lives of the Algonquin and Nehantic Indians who lived here, the first Dutch traders who explored here in 1623 and named the area Kievets Hoeck, and the later conflict between the English settlers and the Pequot Indians.

Remains of the railroad can be seen and traveling across South Cove on the causeway brings into view the "cottages" of Fenwick with its golf course and two 19th Century lighthouses.

Statue of Lion Gardiner at Saybrook Point. He built a fort to protect settlers from both the Dutch colonists and Native Americans. He also designed the layout of the town. Old Saybrook Historical Society

Notes

Follow the shoreline for a few miles to two town beaches and you will reach the Post Road and the Bushnell House and Farm, the fifth oldest house in the state.

Head north and you will reach The Preserve, a 1,000-acre coastal forest with its many trails.

Head east toward the Connecticut River and you might find where David Bushnell built and tested the "Turtle," his first underwater craft in 1776.

Here, too, is the old electric power house that propelled trolleys from New Haven to New London and nearby is the John Whittlesey House, home of the first ferry man who began in 1662 transporting passengers and animals across the river.

Interesting Places

The Katharine Hepburn Cultural Arts Center (1911). "The Kate," located in an historic theatre/town hall and listed on the National Register of Historic Places. The center includes a 250-seat theatre that presents work in music, theater, opera, dance, comedy, film, and a variety of children's programming.

Historic Walking Tour. Self-guided tour from the railroad station to the "millstone" highlighting 36 historic landmarks. Map is available at the Old Saybrook Chamber of Commerce office and website.

Harvey's Beach. Open year-round, offers bathhouses, showers, snack bar, and lifeguards during summer.

Saybrook Point Resort & Marina. At the mouth of the Connecticut River, provides convenient access to Long Island Sound, and offers world-class amenities.

Gen. William Hart House (1767). Contains an exhibit gallery and notable artifacts of local and state importance, and heritage garden. Includes the Frank Stevenson Archives, a library, geneology records and historic resources for Old Saybrook and area towns. Open Tuesday and Thursday mornings and by appointment. For further information visit: www.saybrookhistory.com.

Bike the Old Saybrook Loop. A 10-mile scenic circle of Old Saybrook.

Address Book

Town Site
www.oldsaybrookct.gov

Gen. William Hart House
350 Main St.
860-395-1635
www.saybrookhistory.org

Harvey's Beach
Great Hammock Rd. (Rt. 154)

Katharine Hepburn Cultural Arts Center: The Kate
300 Main St.
860-510-0473
www.thekate.org

Old Saybrook Chamber of Commerce
1 Main St.
860-388-3266
www.oldsaybrookchamber.com

Saybrook Point Resort & Marina
2 Bridge St.
860-395-2000
www.saybrook.com

[Passport Stamp / Signature & Date Here]

Portland

*By Bob McDougall, author of **Images of America: Portland**, Museum Director of the PHS's Ruth Callander House Museum of Portland History and former Municipal Historian*

The area near the center of the State in the Connecticut River Valley, was inhabited by Wangunk Indians, whose name translated means "Big Bend," the geographic characteristic that makes it easy to locate Portland on a map, just look for the largest bend in the river.

Europeans settlers were granted the land on the east side of the river in 1652, later known as the East Parish of Middletown (1714-1767), as Chatham (1767-1841), and finally incorporated as Portland in 1841, becoming Connecticut's 140th town, and the 11th town, of an eventual 15, in Middlesex Co. The town celebrated its 175th Anniversary in 2016.

The first permanent settler, James Stancliff, an English stonecutter, built his home here about 1690.

Portland became famous for its brownstone, which was quarried for over 200 years. It was used in the construction of public buildings and mansions still to be seen in major coastal cities, most notably in New York City and Boston.

Portland has a rich history, rooted in natural resources and human ingenuity. Its resources include the river, stone, arable land, and forests that enabled commerce in quarrying, shipbuilding, and tobacco growing. Ingenuity was evident in inventions such as E. I. Bell's Connecticut Steam Brownstone, which revolutionized the building industry by pre-shaping and cutting stone before shipping it to building sites.

Once a land of employment opportunities it attracted immigrants over the years to meet the demand for labor. In 1840s Irish, 1860s Swedish, 1890s Russian/Polish, and 1910s Italians. Today most residents are employed out of town.

Today Portland is identified with the Arrigoni Bridge (1938) which connects it to Middletown across the Connecticut River. Known for its three 18-hole golf courses, several marinas, and the Brownstone Exploration and Discovery Park located in the National Historic Landmark Portland Brownstone Quarries, Portland also has numerous hiking trails in Meshomasic State Forest and along the Airline Rail Trail. There is also the Helen Carlson Wildlife Sanctuary which includes the historic cranberry bog, and the Riverfront Park which hosts a free concert series each summer.

Notable People

Sylvester Gildersleeve. Established Gildersleeve's Shipyard, which built over 350 ships from 1838-1932.

Oscar Hedstrom (1871-1960). Co-founder Indian Motorcycle Manufacturing Company. He retired in 1911 to live on the banks of the Connecticut River in Portland.

Thomas Pickering. Invented a governor in which revolving balls acted against curved flat springs; the result was his 1861 "Pickering Governor" that improved the steam engine.

John H. Sage (1847-1925). Co-author of *Birds of Connecticut* (1913), secretary of the American Ornithologists' Union 1889-1917.

Elizabeth Jarvis Colt. The widow and heir of firearms manufacturer Samuel Colt, founder of Colt's Manufacturing Co.

Interesting Places

Meshomasic Forest (1903). The first State Forest in Connecticut and in New England, and 2nd in U.S. Site

The Ruth Callander House Museum of Portland History. Bob McDougall

Notes

of 2 Civilian Conservation Corps camps in 1930s. Over 9,000 acres today in Portland, East Hampton, Glastonbury, Marlborough, and Hebron. Features hiking, letter-boxing, and hunting.

Brownstone Exploration and Discovery Park. Adventure center for rock climbing, swimming, zip lining, hiking, cliff jumping and more in an old brownstone quarry.

Ruth Callander House Museum of Portland History. Ruth, a former member of the Portland Historical Society (PHS), donated her home to the society to be used as a museum to preserve the history of Portland.

St. Clement's Castle & Marina. Originally built by Howard Taylor for his family in 1898. It was restored in 1990s and used for weddings and other events.

Town Hall. Repurposed the 1889 Central School.

Town Events: Chocolate Festival (Feb.), Town-Wide Tag Sale (May, Sat. of Mother's Day Weekend), Memorial Day Parade, Strawberry Picking, Summer Concerts at Riverfront Park, Portland Agricultural Fair (Oct.), Halloween on Main St., Festival of Wreaths, and Light Parade.

Address Book

Town Site
www.portlandct.org

Brownstone Exploration and Discovery Park
161 Brownstone Ave.
www.brownstonepark.com

Ruth Callander House Museum of Portland History
492 Main St.
www.portlandhistsoc.org

St. Clement's Castle & Marina
21931 Portland-Cobalt Rd.
www.saintclementscastle.com

Town Hall
33 E. Main St. • 860-342-6743

Cemeteries

Center Cemetery 55 Fairway Dr.
St. Mary's Cem. 261 Marlborough St.
Swedish Cemetery 184 William St.
Trinity Church Cemetery 345 Main St.

Food

Burger Heaven
870 Portland-Cobalt Rd.
www.burgerheavenct.com

Compagna
151 Marlborough St. • 860-398-5411
www.campagnact.com

Zip lines at Brownstone Exploration and Discovery Park. Brownstone Exploration and Discovery Park

Concentric Brewing
91 Main St. • 860-398-5411
www.concentricbrewing.com

Eggs Up Grill
1462 Portland-Cobalt Rd.
860-342-4968
www.eggsuprestaurant.com

Fabian's Pizza
279 Main St. • 860-342-1516

Farrell's
245 Marlborough St. • 860-342-1516
www.farrellsrestaurant.com

Melilli's Café & Grill
264 Main St. • 860-342-4035
www.melillicafeandgrill.com

Portland Ale House
188 Main St. • 860-807-3930
www.portlandalehouse.com

Primavera Pizzeria
222 Main St. • 860-342-5222

Sarah's On Main
246 Main St. • 860-788-3035

Tommy's Pizza Palace
330 Marlborough St. • 860-342-2450
www.tommyspizzaportland.com

Top Dog Hot Dog Wagon
Rt. 66 • 510-843-7250

Winchester Café
1374 Portland-Cobalt Rd.
860-342-0224
www.winchestercafe.com

[Passport Stamp / Signature & Date Here]

WESTBROOK

By Marcy Fuller, President, Westbrook Historical Society

Westbrook is a small town with beautiful beaches located along a four mile stretch of Long Island Sound a few miles west of the mouth of the Connecticut River. It was first settled in 1648 as the west portion of Saybrook. In 1726 it became a parish and in 1840 was incorporated as the separate town of Westbrook. The early settlers were farmers, fisherman, ice harvesters, and sea captains. Our most famous sea captain was Joseph Spencer who commanded the "Davy Crockett". It was launched in Mystic in 1853 and was a very successful clipper ship. The "Old Leatherman" used a cave in Westbrook as one of his stops along his circuitous route. David Bushnell, the inventor of the submarine "Turtle" was born in Westbrook in 1742. A replica of the Turtle can be viewed in the town hall. The multitude of Indian artifacts found in the area testify that this was once an ideal refuge where Indians camped.

The historic and picturesque Boston Post Road (Rt. 1) runs through the center of town. Paralleling Rt. 1 is Interstate 95 where the Connecticut State Police Troop F is located. Just off exit 65 from I-95 you will find; the Westbrook train station where you can catch a train to Boston or New York, the Shoreline Medical Center that offers 24/7 emergency care, cancer treatment and diagnostic outpatient services, an outlet mall, and a movie theater. The Valley Shore YMCA is a short drive from the center of town. Westbrook is home to Water's Edge Resort and Spa, a beautiful beachfront banquet facility with restaurant, accommodations, spa and exclusive shops.

The late actor and comedian Art Carney called Westbrook home for many years. It is also the location of Oxford Academy, a private, young men's boarding school known for its 'one on one' instruction.

On the 4th Saturday of August since 1960, Fife and Drum Corps from all over the East Coast gather for the Westbrook Muster in the center of town. The parade and musical presentation feature songs and uniforms of the American Revolution and Civil War with a very festive atmosphere.

Westbrook is the boating capital of Connecticut and Pilots Point Marina is nestled along the coast at the confluence of the Menunketesuck and Patchogue Rivers.

The town's largest manufacturer is the Lee Company, which specializes in miniature precision fluid control components for aerospace and other highly specialized instrumentation.

INTERESTING PLACES

Stewart B. McKinney National Wildlife Refuge Salt Meadow Unit. Located along the Atlantic Flyway and provides resting, feeding, and nesting habitat for over 280 species of migratory birds. There you can enjoy the many walking paths and marsh overlooks and two historic homes.

Westbrook Historical Society. Located on the town green in what was the original public library built in 1904. It is open Wednesday mornings and Saturdays during the summer.

Westbrook Hunt Club. A full-service hunter/jumper facility offering training, boarding, and riding lesson programs. WHC hosts a full schedule of horse shows.

The Lee Company's Museum of Early Engineering Technology is open by appointment only.

Notes

The Westbrook Historical Society is in the former 1904 town library building at 1196 Boston Post Rd. (Rt. 1). Marcy Fuller

The 950-acre Stewart B. McKinney National Wildlife Refuge is composed of 10 separate units that span 70 mi. of Connecticut coastline. Its headquarters is at the Salt Meadow Unit in Westbrook. Marcy Fuller

Address Book

Town Site
www.westbrookct.us

Lee Company's Museum of Early Engineering Technology
121 S. Main St.
www.microhydraulics.com

Stewart B. McKinney National Wildlife Refuge Salt Meadow Unit
733 Old Clinton Rd.
860-399-2513
www.fws.gov

Water's Edge Resort and Spa
1525 Boston Post Rd.
860-399-5901

Westbrook Historical Society
1196 Boston Post Rd.
860-399-7473

Westbrook Hunt Club
319 Pond Meadow Rd.
www.westbrookhuntclub.com

[Passport Stamp / Signature & Date Here]

Hartford County
HARTLAND
GRANBY
SUFFIELD
ENFIELD
EAST GRANBY
WINDSOR LOCKS
EAST WINDSOR
CANTON
SIMSBURY
WINDSOR
BLOOMFIELD
SOUTH WINDSOR
AVON
BURLINGTON
WEST HARTFORD
HARTFORD
EAST HARTFORD
MANCHESTER
FARMINGTON
WETHERSFIELD
GLASTONBURY
BRISTOL
PLAINVILLE
NEW BRITAIN
NEWINGTON
ROCKY HILL
MARLBOROUGH
SOUTHINGTON
BERLIN

CHAPTER 5

HARTFORD COUNTY

Avon

By Terri Wilson, President, Avon Historical Society and Nora O. Howard, Avon Town Historian

Avon is in the Farmington Valley just ten miles west of Hartford. It's population in 2021 was about 18,800, with 7,300 households. Avon was originally called Northington, and had 160 residents in 1754 when the first meeting house was built. On May 5, 1830, after petitioning the Connecticut General Assembly, Northington was incorporated into a "distinct town, by the name of Avon." The Farmington Canal was completed in 1835, linking Avon to New Haven and Northampton, Mass. Passengers, produce, and freight could more easily make the journey from the Connecticut Valley to other regions, creating more opportunities and economic growth. Immigrants from Europe in the early 1900s provided a talented work force for the Climax Fuse Factory (later named Ensign-Bickford). Skilled immigrants were instrumental in building Avon Old Farms School. Avon's excellent educational system of today started in seven one-room schoolhouses located around the town in the 19th century.

Avon's past is present. The town converted the former Ensign-Bickford Co. fuse factory buildings into offices and artist's workshops. In the landscape are reminders of the Farmington Canal, the railroad, and the old Albany Turnpike (Rt. 44). The Avon Historical Society operates the restored 1865 Pine Grove School House (listed on the National Register of Historic Places), the 1823 School House No. 3. In 1996, the Town of Avon and the Gildo T. Consolini Post 3272, Veterans of Foreign Wars, dedicated the Avon Veterans Memorial on the Town Green. Its history is preserved, maintained and collected by the Avon Historical Society and the Avon Free Public Library's Marian Hunter History Room.

Interesting Places

Farmington Canal Heritage Trail. An 80-mile trail running from New Haven to Northampton, Mass. and paved for walkers, bikers and roller bladers. It is also part of the East Coast Greenway from Florida to Maine.

Pine Grove School House (1865). Open on Sun. 2-4 PM during the summer months.

West Avon Congregational Church 1818 and Avon Congregational Church 1819 have many events all year long open to the public.

Avon Old Farms School. The 860-acre boys' boarding school was designed and built in 1927 by the country's first woman architect, Theodate Pope Riddle, whose home, Hillstead, in Farmington is open to the public as a museum.

Marian Hunter History Room. The Avon Free Public Library is open to genealogists, researchers, and others during regular business hours. In addition, the Avon Historical Society has rotating exhibits outside the room in the History Corner.

First Company Governor's Horse Guards (1778). The oldest active continuously mounted Calvary Unit in the U.S. The public is invited on Thurs. evening 7:30-10 PM for their weekly training.

Farmington Valley Arts Center. One can see local artists work on paintings and jewelry and look at the many gallery and gift shops.

Countryside Park. A 17.5-acre park with two ponds, picnic area, and trails.

The 1865 Pine Grove School House has been restored by the Avon Historical Society. It is open to the public during the summer. Nora O. Howard

Notes

The Avon Free Public Library is the home of the Marian Hunter History Room that is helpful for doing genealogy research. The Avon Historical Society has rotating exhibits on local history topics. Nora O. Howard

Address Book

Town Site
www.avonct.gov

Avon Congregational Church
6 West Main St.

Avon Historical Society
www.avonhistoricalsociety.org

Avon Old Farms School
500 Old Farms Rd.

Countryside Park
335 Huckleberry Rd.

Farmington Valley Arts Center
25 Arts Center Ln.
860-678-1867
www.artsfvac.org

First Company Governor's Horse Guards
280 Arch Rd.
www.ctfirsthorseguard.org

Marian Hunter History Room
281 Country Club Rd.

Pine Grove School House
3 Harris Rd.

West Avon Congregational Church
280 Country Club Rd.

[Passport Stamp / Signature & Date Here]

Berlin

By Lorraine Stub and Sallie Caliandri, Berlin Historical Society

The Town of Berlin lies at the geographic center of Connecticut and includes the boroughs of Kensington and East Berlin. Its first inhabitants were the Wangunks who lived along the flood plain of the fertile Mattabessett River. In 1659 Richard Beckley of New Haven purchased 300 acres from Chief Taramaugus and settled in Western Wethersfield, later designated Beckley Quarter. Decades later Richard Seymour led a group of families from Farmington to settle in The Great Swamp area along what is now Christian Lane. They built a fort and after years of walking back and forth to church in Farmington, they established their own society. The first minister, Rev. William Burnham, was ordained in 1712 and the first meeting house was completed. The society also included the southern part of New Britain. New Britain formed its own society in 1754. In 1774, the "Kensington Parish" split again and two meeting houses were built. The Kensington Meeting House at 312 Percival Ave. remains a church. The Worthington Meeting House at 723 Worthington Ridge over time was a church, town hall, school, and town offices. It awaits its next use as a museum and cultural center.

Berlin was incorporated in 1785 from parts of Farmington, Middletown, and Wethersfield. Small parts of Wallingford were added approx. 10 years later. New Britain was a part of the town until 1850.

One of the first industries to flourish in Berlin was the tin industry. In 1740 Irish immigrants, Edward and William Pattison began making the first household tinware in this country. As the number of tinsmiths grew in Berlin, marketing of tinware and other goods expanded by hiring young salesmen to travel up and down the East Coast via horse and wagon. The Yankee Peddler became the iconic symbol of Berlin. Peck-Stowe-Wilcox in East Berlin were the first toolmakers for the tin industry. Their business evolved into a thriving iron and steel industry with Berlin Iron Bridge designing and fabricating lenticular truss bridges throughout the country. Berlin stepped into the dawn of the industrial revolution when Simeon North developed a milling machine to produce the first interchangeable parts for flint-lock pistols used in the War of 1812.

While laying the first railroad tracks in Berlin, workers discovered clay deposits ideal for manufacturing brick. Berlin had many brickyards, turning out 90,000 bricks per day. The industry attracted waves of Italian immigrants, and helped build factory buildings in New Britain as this area was becoming the machine-tool center of the country. Evidence of the brickyards remains in the numerous clay pit ponds throughout town.

Many know Berlin only for the Berlin Turnpike, once the main thoroughfare through the heart of Connecticut. Diners, motels, drive-ins, restaurants, and gas stations line the road. It is said that the turnpike was the inspiration for the movie "American Graffiti," and it is still common to see antique muscle cars on display on Friday nights.

Places of Interest

Berlin Historical Society Museum. In the former 1901 Peck Library

Berlin Historical Society (BHS), in the former Peck Library, exhibits include brick manufacturing, tin-making, and gun production that showcase the development of Berlin. BHS

Notes

building. Open April thru Dec. on Sat. 1-4, or by appointment, except holiday weekends.

Berlin's Historic District. Worthington Ridge from Mill St. (Rt. 372) south to the Berlin Turnpike. Download the walking tour guide at www.town.berlin.ct.us.

First Civil War Monument. Erected in 1863 next to the 1774 Kensington Congregational Church green on Percival Ave. The monument was designed by noted landscape artist Nelson Augustus Moore.

The oldest Civil War Monument in the U.S. was erected in 1863 after six Kensington soldiers were killed in 1862. It is at the corner of Percival Ave. and Sheldon St. in Kensington. Jerry Dougherty

Berlin's Open Space hiking trails. Berlin has preserved hundreds of acres of former farm and orchard lands providing an outstanding network of hiking trails connecting to the state blue trail system.

Lions Club Berlin Fair. Held the third weekend of Sept. for three days on Beckley Rd. This agricultural fair's roots go back to a church Harvest Festival in 1882 that became the State Agricultural Fair held in Berlin until 1918 and revived by the Lions Club in 1949.

Veterans Memorial Park. Green space with walking paths and story boards telling the history of each military conflict experienced by our country. It is across from Stop and Shop in Berlin.

Silver Lake. For boating and fishing.

Address Book

Town Sites
www.berlinct.gov
www.town.berlin.ct.us

Berlin Historical Society Museum
305 Main St., Kensington
860-828-5114
www.berlincthistorical.org

First Civil War Monument
Percival Ave.

Lions Club Berlin Fair
430 Beckley Rd., East Berlin
www.ctberlinfair.com

Silver Lake
282 Norton Ln.
www.ct.gov/deep

Veterans Memorial Park
Veterans Way

[Passport Stamp / Signature & Date Here]

BLOOMFIELD

By Dick Pierce, former President, Wintonbury Historical Society

Bloomfield (2010 pop. c. 20,000) shares a short border on its south side with Hartford and another at the north with the Farmington River. On its east lies Windsor, and on its west lies Simsbury. Connecticut Routes 185, 187 and 189 stretch south to north, and Routes 218, 178, and 305 go east to west.

Originally part of Windsor, the Bloomfield area was settled in 1642 by Edward Messenger, who wanted more land for farming. By 1734, Windsor settlers in Messenger's area had increased in such numbers that 27 of them successfully petitioned the legislature for permission to hold their own winter church services from November to March, which was granted for two years. They were so pleased with the opportunity that two years later those same Windsor settlers joined with other worshippers from Farmington and Simsbury to successfully petition the Windsor Church for authorization to establish the parish of Wintonbury with year-round services and its own minister. Eventually, in 1835, a petition for the status of a town was granted. At the time, this new town of "Bloomfield" was all farmland with a few small industries.

Trolley service was extended from Hartford into Bloomfield along Blue Hills Ave. as far as Mt. St. Benedict cemetery in the mid-1890s, presenting the opportunity for development in the southeast section of Bloomfield, with convenient connections to Hartford.

Post-World War II Bloomfield witnessed a mass exodus from the central city and the introduction of major employers in Bloomfield's new industrial parks. This trend and the "open" nature of Bloomfield, both with respect to space and new arrivals, saw an unprecedented period of residential expansion. New employers, new home construction and new families resulted in a school population growing from 1,000 in 1950 to 3,500 in 1960 and to almost 5,000 in 1970.

As the number of minority students grew, it became apparent that a pattern of de facto school segregation was developing. With the support of the Town Council, the Board of Education, and citizen groups, a plan was drawn up to construct a central middle school to house all pupils in grades 5 through 7. The completion of this plan was a major step in integrating Bloomfield schools and was cited in the town's All-America City award in 1971. Since then, Bloomfield citizens have built a successful multiracial town by working together in government, education, neighborhoods, and volunteer organizations.

INTERESTING PLACES

Tumblebrook Country Club. Private course.

Gillette Ridge Golf Club. Public course.

Wintonbury Hills Golf Course. Municipally-owned.

Prosser Public Library. Intersection of Rts. 178 and 189.

McMahon Wintonbury Branch Library on Blue Hills Ave. (Rt.187).

The 1796 Old Farm School is the oldest public building in Bloomfield. It was used as a school until 1922. The Wintonbury Historical Society maintains it as a museum. Jerry Dougherty

Notes

Wintonbury Historical Society. Maintains a museum and keeps the adjacent Old Farm School (1796) open Sunday afternoons May through October.

4-H Auerfarm. Preserves some of the town's agricultural heritage and is open to visitors.

Hiking

Penwood State Park. Nearly 800 acres donated by industrialist Curtis H. Veeder who wished that his beloved hilltop, "be kept in a natural state so that those who love nature may enjoy this property as I have enjoyed it." Its extensive trail system is maintained by the Connecticut Forest and Park Association. Facilities include bathrooms, picnic shelter, and tables. No fee.

Metacomet Trail. Accessible in Penwood State Park, and on the nearby Heublein Tower Trail, both off Rt. 185 near the Simsbury town line.

A bridge leading to Penwood Ledge that is part of a trail system in the approx. 800-acre Penwood State Park. The trails are maintained by the Connecticut Forest and Park Association. Dennis Hubbs

Address Book

Town Site
www.bloomfieldct.gov

4-H Auerfarm
www.auerfarm.org

Gillette Ridge Golf Club
1360 Hall Blvd.
860-726-1430
www.giletteridgegolf.com

McMahon Wintonbury Branch Library
Blue Hills Ave. (Rt.187)
www.prosserlibrary.info

Penwood State Park
560 Simsbury Rd.
www.ct.gov/deep

Prosser Public Library
Intersection of Rts. 178 & 189
www.prosserlibrary.info

Tumblebrook Country Club
376 Simsbury Rd.
860-242-4600
www.tumblebrookcc.com

Wintonbury Hills Golf Course
206 Terry Plains Rd.
860-242-1401
www.wintonburyhillsgolf.com

Wintonbury Historical Society
153 School St. (Rt. 178)
860-243-1531
www.bloomfieldcthistory.org

[Passport Stamp / Signature & Date Here]

Bristol

By Teresa Goulden, Supervisor of Branch Services, F.N. Manross Memorial Library, Forestville

The City of Bristol is in the southwest corner of Hartford County, in central Connecticut, approx. 20 miles from Hartford. Best known, today, as the home of ESPN, Bristol was originally an agricultural village. The first permanent settler, in 1728, was Ebenezer Barns in the West Woods section of Farmington (Bristol's mother city). During the time of the French and Indian Wars, West Woods came to be called New Cambridge, and in 1785 it became the Town of Bristol. Shortly after, in 1790, Gideon Roberts founded the clock-making industry for which Bristol became famous and which led to the related manufacture of brass, bearings, and springs. By the time Bristol incorporated as a city in 1911, it had long been a thriving manufacturing center. Many who became wealthy from this industriousness built stately homes, still to be admired, in the area known as Federal Hill.

Interesting Places

American Clock & Watch Museum. One of the largest displays of American clocks and watches, the museum is housed in an 1801 Federal-style home with a sundial garden. Open seasonally and by appointment. Admission fee.

Bristol Historical Society. Houses both the Bristol Sports Hall of Fame and the Memorial Military Museum. Open Wed. & Sat. 10 AM-2 PM.

Bristol Public Library and F. N. Manross Memorial Library.

Family-owned farms. All on Chippens Hill, with store or farm stand. Robert's Orchard, Minor's Farm, and Green Acres Farm.

Harry C. Barnes Memorial Nature Center. Situated on 68 acres with hiking trails, the center features interactive exhibits and activities; an extensive collection of reptiles and amphibians; and live birds of prey. Open Thurs. thru Sat., 10 AM-4 PM; Sun. Noon-4 PM. Free admission. (Donations encouraged) Trails are open every day, year-around from dawn to dusk.

Hoppers Birge Pond Nature Preserve. Hiking and walking trails on 200 acres featuring Native American trails, glacial land formations (kettles, eskers, and drumlins), and roads from Colonial times. Take Rt. 69 north from Rt. 6; then go left on Cypress St. to parking area.

Imagine Nation Children's Museum. Three floors of twelve interactive museum studios. Each studio is a related collection of exhibits focused around a common theme that invites self-guided investigation and hands-on learning. Hours vary by season. Admission is $10.00 per visitor.

Lake Compounce Theme Park. The oldest, continuously-operating amusement park in North America, with origins dating back to 1846. Open during summer season, with off-season special attractions. Admission fee.

New England Carousel Museum. Dedicated to the "preservation of operating carousels and carousel memorabilia," it is also home to the Museum of Fire History. Open Wed. thru Sat. 10 AM-5 PM; Sun. Noon-5 PM. Admission fee.

Rockwell Park. Beautiful and historic, the park was given to

Children flock to the Imagine Nation Children's Museum with its three floors of interactive activities and even a small restaurant for a snack or ice cream. Teresa Goulden

NOTES

the city by Albert and Nettie Rockwell in 1911. Includes regular and toddler playgrounds; splash pad; outdoor swimming pool (Admission fee); sports courts; picnic areas; trails; free skate park; and free summer concert series.

Veterans Memorial Boulevard Park. A 25-acre park stretching from Main St. to Downs St. along Memorial Boulevard, which was dedicated on Armistice Day in 1921. A walking path with mile markers takes visitors past lovely plantings, a fountain, benches, and the monuments and memorials honoring Bristol's veterans.

At the American Clock and Watch Museum, visitors learn about the clock making industry in Connecticut where it once was the "clock capital" of the U.S. It has the largest display of American clocks and watches–over 5,500 timepieces! Teresa Goulden

ADDRESS BOOK

Town Sites
www.bristolct.gov
www.bristolallheart.com
www.ci.bristol.ct.us
www.bristolrec.com

American Clock & Watch Museum
100 Maple St. • 860-583-6070
www.clockandwatchmuseum.org

Bristol Historical Society
98 Summer St. • 860-583-6309
www.bristolhistoricalsociety.org

Bristol Sports Hall of Fame
98 Summer St. • 860-583-6309
www.bshof.org

Bristol Public Library
5 High St. • 860-584-7787
www.bristollib.com

F. N. Manross Memorial Library
260 Central St. • 860-584-7790
www.bristollib.com/manross

Green Acres Farm
1924 Perkins St. • 860-583-5700

Harry C. Barnes Memorial Nature Center
175 Shrub Rd. • 860-583-1234
www.elcct.org

Imagine Nation Children's Museum
1 Pleasant St. • 860-314-1400
www.imaginenation.org

Lake Compounce Theme Park
186 Enterprise Dr. • 860-583-3300
www.lakecompounce.com

Memorial Military Museum
98 Summer St. • 860-582-1537

Minor's Farm
409 Hill St. • 860-589-0861

New England Carousel Museum
95 Riverside Ave. • 860-585-5411
www.thecarouselmuseum.org

Robert's Orchard
125 Hill St. • 860-582-5314

Rockwell Park
238 Jacobs St. • 860-584-6160
www.bristolrec.com

Veterans Memorial Boulevard Park
111 N. Main St.

Burlington

By Jackie Guy Shadford & Beth Salsedo, Burlington Historical Society

Burlington is a scenic hill town of natural beauty on the western edge of Hartford County. Defined by its natural environment of forests and watercourses, almost half of the land in the town is owned by three public water supply companies and the State of Connecticut. It is home to the Sessions Woods Wildlife Management Area and the State Fish Hatchery.

Located 20 miles west of Hartford, Burlington borders the Farmington River to the east and the foot of the Berkshire Mountains to the west. The earliest inhabits were the Tunxis Indians, a peaceful tribe, whose central village was located in Farmington. The forest and rocky hills of Burlington was their hunting ground. They welcomed the early settlers in hopes that they would protect them from two neighboring war-like tribes: the Mohawks on the west and the Pequots to the east.

The Tunxis Tribe signed a deed transferring title of the area known as the Tunxis Plantation to the white settlers in 1640. Five years later the name was changed to Farmington. Burlington was part of the northern reserved lands of Farmington named "West Woods." In 1785, it was part of "New Cambridge," which included the town of Bristol. In 1806, it was incorporated as the town of Burlington.

For many years the West Woods was unchartered and undeveloped with only a few foot paths and trails. In 1721 the Farmington proprietors divided the area into tiers and lots. Even with the land divided and apportioned to landowners development remained slow. This was due primarily to the rugged terrain. In 1774 an independent Ecclesiastical Society was established, as residents found it difficult to travel to the central village of Farmington for Sunday worship, town meetings, schooling of children, or for supplies.

Settlement increased after the Revolutionary War. Most of the early settlers were farmers who had another trade, such as blacksmiths, clockmakers, and tinsmiths. They manufactured wagons, carriages, window sashes and other wooden objects. When the railroads came to Bristol many industries relocated there. Wood and water were the town's resources and agriculture has remained important throughout the 20th century.

Early stagecoach lines ran through the Farmington Valley. Burlington was on the direct route of the Hartford and Litchfield Stage Line. The Elton Tavern on the green was a station where the horses were changed. The 1810 registered historic building is home to the Burlington Historical Society and used as a house museum and meeting place for the town. Each September, "Tavern Day" includes a community celebration and country fair.

Interesting Places

Hiking & Walking Trails. A paved section of Rails to Trails along the Farmington River connects the villages of Collinsville and Unionville. Burlington has over 110 miles of hiking on 25 different trail combinations.

Nassahegon State Forest. Offers hunting, hiking, mountain biking (on approved official mountain biking trails), and bird watching. It is crossed by the Blue-Blazed Trails system.

The Elton Tavern (1810) on the Town Green is operated as a museum by the Burlington Historical Society. It was originally a stagecoach stop and tavern. Jackie Guy Shadford

Notes

Sessions Woods Wildlife Management Area. A 700-acre tract managed for wildlife habitat. CT DEEP Facilities include an education center with an exhibit area and a large meeting room. Located on Rt. 69 approx. 3 miles south of Rt. 4 in Burlington. The Center is open Mon. thru Fri., 8:30 AM-4 PM (except holidays). Trails open from sunrise to sunset.

Burlington State Fish Hatchery (1923). Operated by CT DEEP in Nassahegon State Forest. Facility includes a building for egg incubation, fish pools and ponds, and a short nature trail. Raises brown trout and rainbow trout that are distributed into state lakes, ponds, rivers and streams with public access. Free admission. Open daily 8 AM-3:30 PM. Tours are self-guided or by reservation.

Elton Tavern (1810). Burlington Historical Society's headquarters and collections house museum. Originally a private home used as a stagecoach stop and tavern. Located on the Burlington Green. Open to the public by chance or by arrangement.

Inside the Burlington State Fish Hatchery at 34 Belden Rd. where fish eggs incubate and are hatched. When the fish reach 3" they are moved to intermediate tanks.
Jerry Dougherty

Address Book

Town Site
www.burlingtonct.us

BurlingtonLand Trust
www.burlingtonlandtrust.org

Burlington State Fish Hatchery
34 Belden Rd.
860-673-2340
www.ct.gov/deep

Elton Tavern
Burlington Historical Society
781 George Washington Tpke.
www.burlington-history.org

Nassahegon State Forest
273 Punch Brook Rd.

Sessions Woods Wildlife Management Area
341 Milford St.
www.ct.gov/deep

[Passport Stamp / Signature & Date Here]

Canton

By David Leff (1955-2022), Poet Laureate, Deputy Town Historian of Canton

Canton's landscape is rugged and hilly with ledge frequently close to the surface. The lower Cherry Brook Valley and the area around the brook's confluence with the Farmington River are an exception, having a margin of arable land. Native Americans lived for thousands of years in the thickly forested landscape, and U.S. Rt. 44, today's principal artery through town, approximately follows a major Indian path.

Canton was originally part of Simsbury and the first white settlers arrived in 1737. Organized settlement began in what is now Canton Center where a Congregational church was established in 1750. Canton Village (once called Suffrage) was also an early settlement. The Town of Canton was created by the General Assembly in 1806 upon petition of residents. Some say the name was a nod to the busy China trade of the day, others due to the town's beauty resembling a Swiss Canton.

In the early days Canton was typical of upland communities, dominated by subsistence agriculture with blacksmith's shops and small mills, including those that ground grain and sawed timber. In 1826, Samuel Collins, his brother and cousin, all in their twenties, bought land and water rights along the Farmington River in what was then called South Canton. Here they established the world's first factory for the production of axes with the innovative idea of selling them pre-sharpened.

Eventually the concern would be the world's largest maker of edge tools and the community would become known as Collinsville. Hundreds of axe, machete, and knife patterns were manufactured as well as plows, shovels, picks, adzes, hammers, wrenches, and other tools. The company achieved worldwide fame and its products became especially well known in South and Central America. The population grew rapidly from the middle of the nineteenth to the middle of the twentieth century drawing immigrants from French Canada, Scandinavia, and western and eastern Europe. The Collinsville plant closed in 1966 and tools bearing the Collins name are now made outside the country.

Today Canton consists of four villages, each with its distinctive personality: Canton, Canton Center, North Canton, and Collinsville. The commercial heart of town, which began in Canton Center, migrated to Canton Village, and then moved to Collinsville, is now back in Canton Village along the U.S. Rt. 44 corridor. Town Hall remains in Collinsville.

Interesting Places

Canton Historical Museum. Operated by the Canton Historical Society has a large array of Collins Co. tools, Victoriana, Indian artifacts, and much more.

Roaring Brook Nature Center. Contains a hub of information about the outdoors and a center of environmental activity with exhibits, animals, and trails.

Historic Districts include Collinsville and Canton Center.

Canton Land Conservation Trust. Maintains trails on over 2,000 acres of land and sponsors outdoor programs.

Farmington River Trail. A paved path that follows an old railroad bed. A portion runs from Collinsville to Canton Village, including a dramatic crossing of the Farmington River on a steel truss bridge. www.traillink.com

Memorial Day Parade. Held in Collinsville, it is a delightfully old-fashioned event that includes veterans, Scouts and fire trucks in the line of march, as well as a touching ceremony at the Village Cemetery in Collinsville.

Notes

Collinsville Halloween Parade. The Saturday before Halloween, it draws thousands of people in costume to a village ghoulishly decorated in the holiday spirit and includes a costume contest.

Christmas in Collinsville. Held in early December it includes a champagne walk, a charity craft fair, horse-drawn wagon rides, visits from Santa, and more.

Collinsville Hot. A July village and river celebration with live music, outdoor yoga, a kids "Chill Zone," outdoor artisan market and local business expo, food, and a sizzling fire performance.

The Collins Co. factory in Collinsville produced axes, plows, shovels, picks, adzes, hammers, wrenches, and other tools.
David Leff

Address Book

Town Site
www.townofcantonct.org
www.mainstreetcanton.org

Canton Historical Museum
11 Front St., Collinsville
860-693-2793
www.cantonmuseum.org

Canton Land Conservation Trust
11 Front St., Collinsville
860-693-2793
www.cantonlandtrust.org

Roaring Brook Nature Center
70 Gracey Rd.
860-693-0263
www.roaringbrook.org

Events

Christmas in Collinsville

Collinsville Hot
Main St., Collinsville
/CollinsvilleHot

Halloween Parade
Main St., Collinsville
www.collinsvillehalloween.com

Memorial Day Parade

[Passport Stamp / Signature & Date Here]

East Granby

By William & Ruth Westervelt, East Granby Historical Society

East Granby (2010 pop. 5,148) is 17 miles NW of Hartford and in Hartford Co.

When traveling up the Farmington River from Windsor in about 1643, there was no way that John Griffin could know that he would be the first settler in what would be part of Simsbury, then part of Granby, and then in 1858, the Town of East Granby. As a resident of Windsor, he was exploring its northern regions for suitable forest land for harvesting pitch.

Our town was one of the last six towns to be established by the General Assembly of Connecticut.

It was originally established as "The Turkey Hills Ecclesiastical Society," as most early settlements were founded around church authorship.

Early colonists were mainly farmers, as were most of the early settlers in Connecticut, but many had tradesmen skills to supplement income. James Moor, a local farmer, planted many acres of mulberry trees to feed silk worms for the production of silk. His brick house still resides on North Main Street.

Although few signs of early transportation are now evident, there was both a railroad and part of the Farmington canal in town.

For more East Granby history, consult *"East Granby: The Evolution of a Connecticut Town"*, by Betty Guinan and Mary Jane Springman, *"Barns of East Granby"*, by Harold Holly and Betty Guinan, as well as numerous documents by Albert Carlos Bates.

Interesting Places

Bradley International Airport. On East Granby's eastern border, it is a major transportation center.

New England Air Museum. A wonderful place to visit and has an extensive collection of aircraft, engines and exhibits, with activities for enthusiasts of all ages.

Golf courses. Copper Hill and Airways invite players of all levels.

U.S. National Kayak Qualifying Races. Held at Farmington River Gorge. Spring event with transportation from the Town Hall. The event occurs at the end of Tunxis Ave. Times available on the Town website.

Old Newgate Prison. Tories, thieves, debtors once resided here in an abandoned copper mine. It has recently been partially restored. Across the road is the Viets Tavern, used by many stagecoach riders in the early days.

East Granby Historical Society Barn. Has a refurbished 1857 Concord Coach. Open 2nd and 4th Sunday of the month, 2-4 PM, until Oct. or by appointment.

East Granby Farms. An extensive park once a very active farm operated by the Viets family's horse and cattle operation. Part of the marketing of their farm involved driving cattle across what is now Bradley Field to the train station at Windsor Locks.

Metacomet Trail. Running along a traprock ridge from south to north through the entire town. On this trail are newly restored headstones of victims of small pox. The memorial represents whole families that were wiped out in the 18th century. Access points at Rt. 20 & Newgate Rd. intersection, and at Hatchet Hill Rd.

The Old Newgate Prison. East Granby Historical Society

Notes

Granby Railroad Station. Built c.1853, it is on Rt. 189 on "rails-to-trails" (a bike and multi-use trail from New Haven to Northampton MA) Trail access at Granby Station, Rt. 20 near East Granby/Granby line, and Copper Hill Rd.

Cowles Park. Approx. 4 miles of great hiking trails and an extensive network of mountain bike trails. Parking area off Rt.187.

Notable Person

Walter Wick (1953-). Author of the prolific *I Spy* and *Can You See What I See?* children's book series.

A 1857 Concord Coach and the East Granby Historical Society Barn Museum.
Tami Zawistowski

Address Book

Town Site
www.eastgranbyct.org

Airways
1070 S. Grand St., West Suffield
860-668-4973
www.airwaysgolf.com

Bradley International Airport (BDL)
Schoephoester Rd., Windsor Locks
860-292-2000
www.bradleyairport.com

Copper Hill
20 Copper Hill Rd.
860-653-6191
www.copperhillgolf.com

East Granby Farms
85 N. Main St.
www.eastgranbyct.org

East Granby Historical Society Barn
85 N. Main St.
www.eastgranby.com

New England Air Museum
36 Perimeter Rd., Bradley Field
www.neam.org

Old Newgate Prison
Newgate Rd.
www.eastgranby.com

[Passport Stamp / Signature & Date Here]

East Hartford

By Craig Johnson, President, Historical Society of East Hartford

The town of East Hartford, located across the Connecticut River from Hartford, was incorporated in 1783. The land was purchased in 1640 from the Podunk Indians, a branch of the Algonquins. Called the Three Mile Lands, the early proprietors of the purchase divided the land into lots, settled and farmed. The first sawmill and other mills were at the falls of the Hockanum River in the now Burnside section of town. In 1672 Hartford's eastern bounds were extended by another five miles on land that was later destined to become the town of Manchester.

During colonial times, the river that divided Hartford was a challenge to those residents living on the east side. They had to ferry across the dangerous river to attend church and to conduct matters of business. At the start of the 18th century, after much petitioning, the east side of Hartford was allowed its own congregational church and meeting house. In 1712, the first cemetery on the east side was started. Petitioning to establish a separate town charter began in 1726 but was not successful until the end of the Revolutionary War.

Toward the end of the war, the French army, under the command of General Comte de Rochambeau, encamped his 5,000 troops here on his way to join George Washington's army in upstate NY to begin the last major offensive– the campaign at Yorktown, VA. Much of the gunpowder used by Washington's army came from the Pitkin powder mills along the Hockanum. For most of the 19th century, East Hartford was agricultural with the predominate crop being tobacco. The first bridge across the Connecticut River was built in 1810. In 1849, the railroad came through town and paper mills began to flourish.

East Hartford gave its share of volunteers in the American Civil War and in 1868 a monument was erected in Center Cemetery, honoring those who made the ultimate sacrifice. Around the start of the 20th century, the town looked far more suburban than rural with new public buildings, utilities, schools and transportation. The first major manufacturing was started in 1929 when Pratt & Whitney Aircraft moved its headquarters to East Hartford. Tremendous growth in town population followed during the Second World War and postwar years.

Interesting Places

The former airport located at Pratt & Whitney called Rentschler Field is one of East Hartford's prime areas of development. University of Connecticut Husky Football is now played at Pratt & Whitney Stadium, close to where Cabela's has its store.

The town has some beautiful parks, the most scenic is Great River Park along the banks of the Connecticut River where band concerts are held during the summer. The Connecticut River shore is home of the campus of Goodwin College, an accredited nonprofit offering career-focused programs.

The Hockanum River Linear Park Association has miles of scenic hiking trails through town.

1868 Civil War monument in Center Cemetery. Craig Johnson

Notes

The Historical Society of East Hartford, Inc. opens its museum buildings for free tours during the summer months. These are the 1761 Makens Bemont House (also called the Huguenot House), the 1821 one-room Goodwin Schoolhouse and the 1850 Burnham Blacksmith Shop.

The Historical Society of East Hartford buildings (L-R): Goodwin Schoolhouse, Makens Bemont House ("Huguenot House"), and Burnham Blacksmith Shop. Craig Johnson

Address Book

Town Site
www.easthartfordct.gov

Cabela's
475 East Hartford Blvd.
860-290-6200

Center Cemetery
944 Main St.

East Hartford Public Library
840 Main St.
860-290-4329

The Historical Society of East Hartford, Inc.
307 Burnside Ave.
860-528-0716
www.hseh.org

Hockanum River Linear Park Association
www.hockanumriverwa.org

Pratt & Whiney Stadium at Rentschler Field
615 Silver Ln.
860-610-4700
www.rentschlerfield.com

[Passport Stamp / Signature & Date Here]

East Windsor

By Gary Mazzone, East Windsor resident

In the 1600s, East Windsor was populated by the Podunk, Namerick, and Scanticoke Indians. It is located in north central Connecticut midway between Hartford and Springfield, MA. Interstate 91 runs through the town.

The Town of East Windsor was originally part of Windsor. In 1648, John Bissell started a ferry service from Windsor to the east side of the Connecticut River. Windsor residents had decided to graze their cattle in the large meadows there. It wasn't until about 1675 when residents permanently began to live in East Windsor.

In 1768, the Connecticut Legislature incorporated East Windsor as a separate town, which comprised the towns of Ellington and South Windsor. Present-day East Windsor is 26.8 sq. mi. in area and includes five villages, Warehouse Point, Broad Brook, Windsorville, Scantic, and Melrose. The town had a population of 11,162 in the 2010 census.

Notable residents of East Windsor include theologian Timothy Edwards, and John Fitch, who was one of the inventors of the steamship. Fitch was most famous for operating the first steamboat service in the United States.

During the 20th century, East Windsor was one of the largest tobacco producing towns in the state. Tobacco is still grown here with the Dingess and Markowski farms being prominent producers of broadleaf tobacco in the Connecticut River Valley. East Windsor has become a suburb of Hartford, yet maintains its agrarian roots.

Interesting Places

The Connecticut Trolley Museum. One of the largest trolley museums in New England, it is located one mile east of I-91. Take exit 45 onto Rt. 140 east. The museum is one mile on the right.

The Connecticut Fire Museum. Located on the same grounds as the Trolley Museum. Days of operation: Weekends in April, May, Sept., and Oct., and daily June 3-Aug. 31 with holiday hours in Nov. and Dec. Call for daily hours.

Scantic River State Park. Lies partially in East Windsor. There is trout fishing and the river is navigable via canoe for several miles through woods and farmland with access points on Melrose Rd., Church St., Sabonis Landing on Scantic Rd., and Osborn's bridge at Omelia and Woolam Rds.

East Windsor Historical Museum. It is open on Sat. 9 AM-Noon and by appointment.

Skylark Airport. A privately owned, public access airport, has a 3,250 runway, and maintains a flight school.

The Southern Auto Auction. A wholesale, dealer-only, car auction operating since 1947. It is one of the largest auto auctions in the nation and is the largest employer in East Windsor. Auctions are held every Wednesday. Dealers must be registered to enter the auction.

The East Windsor Historical Society (EWHS) Museum in the 1817 East Windsor Academy. It was built by a stock company in 1817 to provide higher education, primarily for local boys. The lower floor was equipped as a school with college students, mostly from Yale, as teachers. Jerry Dougherty

Notes

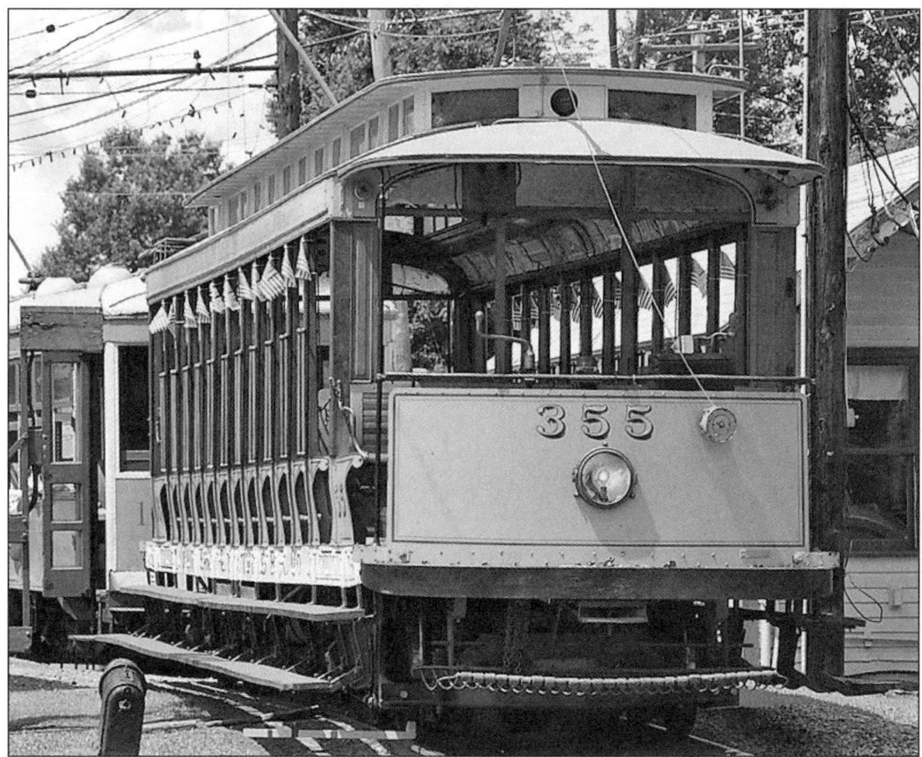

The 1902 Fair Haven and Westville Railroad #355 trolley is one of over 70 pieces of rail equipment dating back to 1869 at the Connecticut Trolley Museum. There are historic passenger and freight trolley cars, interurban cars, elevated railway cars, passenger and freight railroad cars, service cars, locomotives, and a variety of other equipment from railways around Connecticut. Connecticut Trolley Museum

Address Book

Town Site
www.eastwindsor-ct.gov

Connecticut Fire Museum
58 North Rd. #9606
860-627-6540
www.thefiremuseum.org

Connecticut Trolley Museum
58 North Rd. #9606
860-627-6540
www.ct-trolley.org

East Windsor Historical Museum
115 Scantic Rd. (Rt. 191)
www.eastwindsorhistory.wordpress.com

Skylark Airport
54 Wells Rd.
860-623-8085

Southern Auto Auction
161 S Main St.
860-292-7500
www.saa.com

[Passport Stamp / Signature & Date Here]

Enfield

By Michael Miller, Enfield Historical Society

Enfield's first European settlers arrived in 1679 from Salem, Mass. and by the end of 1680 about 25 families had settled in the area. In 1683, the Town of Enfield was incorporated as part of Massachusetts Bay Colony, the result of a 1642 surveyor's error. A 1695 survey corrected the error, but it wasn't until 1750 that Enfield seceded from Massachusetts and became part of Connecticut Colony.

Enfield attracted important religious leaders. In the mid-1700s the religious revival known as the "Great Awakening" took place. On July 8, 1741, Jonathan Edwards of Northampton, Mass. preached one of the most intense "fire and brimstone" sermons of all times, "Sinners in the Hands of an Angry God," at Enfield's second meeting house. In 1781, Mother Ann Lee, leader of the new religious group called the Shaking Quakers by their detractors, arrived in Enfield for the first of three visits. Despite sometimes violent opposition, she attracted dedicated followers who founded the Enfield Shaker community. The Connecticut community grew to 250 members and encompassed 3,000 acres before closing in 1917 as a result of changing social and economic conditions.

Villages with names like Wallop and Scitico sprang up within Enfield's 60 square miles as citizens began farming the more fertile areas of the town, or built factories along the brooks and rivers that provided power for industry. Orrin Thompson established the first carpet mill on Freshwater (Asnuntuck) Brook in 1828. The carpet industry quickly expanded, as did the village of Thompsonville that grew around it. The carpet mills employed thousands by the early 1900s, but economic factors led to a gradual decline in the industry, until the last mill closed in 1971. In 1835 Allen Loomis built a gunpowder mill on a stream in Scitico. Colonel Augustus Hazard joined Loomis's company in 1837 and quickly became the driving force behind Enfield's gunpowder industry. The village around his mills was named Hazardville in his honor. At its peak the Hazard Powder Company covered hundreds of acres and produced tons of black powder each day. After decades of declining demand, operations ceased on Jan. 14, 1913, following a major explosion that destroyed much of the plant.

Interesting Places

The Old Town Hall. Opened on Jan. 1, 1775 and served the community as the third meetinghouse of the First Ecclesiastical Society. In 1776 Enfield's Minutemen were attending services in the building when Captain Abbey used his famous drum to announce the outbreak of war at Concord and Lexington. Today it is a museum operated by the Enfield Historical Society. Open Sundays May through October, and year-round by appointment. Free admission.

Martha A. Parsons House Museum. Home of Connecticut Women's Hall of Fame inductee Martha Parsons. Features original George Washington Memorial wallpaper which was printed in Boston in 1800 following his 1799 death. Open Sundays, May through October, and year-round by appointment. Free admission.

Wallop School Museum. Open one Sunday per month, June thru Sept., 2-4:30 PM, and by appointment.

The 1800 Wallop School operated in Enfield for 147 years and is now a museum. Michael Miller

Notes

Free admission. One-room school built in 1800 and operated until 1947.

Scantic River State Park. Birding, fishing, and hiking.

Kings Island Boat Launch. Access to the beautiful Connecticut River and Kings Island. Boating, fishing, and bird watching, especially bald eagles in winter.

The Old Town Hall Museum houses a large and varied collection from dinosaur tracks to farming, the Shakers, the carpet and gunpowder industries, and much more. Michael Miller

Address Book

Town Site
www.enfield-ct.gov

Kings Island Boat Launch
49 Parsons Rd.

Martha A. Parsons House Museum
1387 Enfield St.
860-745-6064
www.enfieldhistoricalsociety.org

The Old Town Hall
1294 Enfield St.
860-745-1729
www.enfieldhistoricalsociety.org

Scantic River State Park
2010 S. Dust House Rd. and 640 Hazard Ave.
www.ct.gov/deep

Wallop School Museum
250 Abbe Rd.
860-745-1729
www.enfieldhistoricalsociety.org

[Passport Stamp / Signature & Date Here]

Farmington

By Rose Ponte, Farmington resident

The first Amerindians here had made the bend in the Farmington River a meeting and trading spot; their descendants, the peaceful Tunxis tribe, welcomed the English in 1640. Renamed in 1645 for the occupation of its inhabitants, Farming-ton then included the modern towns of Avon, Burlington, Bristol, Plainville, New Britain, Berlin, and Southington. In 1700, the population was 700 and by 1774 it reached 6,000. This explosive growth led to the settlement of the seven outlying parishes plus emigration to Vermont and the Western Reserve. During the Revolution Rochambeau's French troops bivouacked here twice. The economic prosperity of 1785-1800 led to the construction of many fine homes by architect Judah Woodruff.

The Industrial Revolution led to the construction of the Farmington Canal and the industrial growth of Unionville. The Canal opened in 1828 to ferry manufactured goods to New Haven's port, but it was never a commercial success and closed in 1848. In Unionville a waterpower system at the drop in the river furnished power to a nuts & bolts factory, several paper mills, and small shops producing hardware, cutlery, wood screws, muskets, hooks & eyes, and flutes. Late in his life, Lambert Hitchcock made furniture here; and the Hart shop produced pikes sold to John Brown, who later used them at Harpers Ferry. A strong abolitionist town, in 1841 Farmington became involved in the Amistad case when the rebellious Mendi blacks, freed by the Supreme Court, came here to live for nine months. Led by Cinque, 35 men and 3 young girls stayed until money was raised for their passage home to Africa. In 1843 Sarah Porter founded her Farmington Female Seminary; this serious academic school prospered and is now Miss Porters School.

Geographically, the separation of Avon and Plainville reduced the town to its current size, 28.7 square miles. The coming of the trolley in 1893 started the transition of Farmington into a suburb of Hartford, and the automobile accelerated that change. Since 1950, the town's population has ballooned from 3,500 to over 26,000 bringing to town Westfarms Mall, UConn Health Center, Tunxis Community College, several corporate headquarters, and spawning new non-profit groups like Winding Trails, the Historical Society, the Unionville Museum, and the Land Trust. Farmington and Unionville villages preserve much of our architectural past. There are 14 houses all or part of which date from the 1600s and another 51 houses from the 1700s. In addition, over 30% of our land is preserved as open space. (Note: Farmington Historian Betty Coykendall's History of Farmington has been condensed because of limited space.)

Interesting Places

Hill-Stead Museum. A National Historic Landmark on a 152-acre estate; complete with a 1901 Colonial Revival house and landmark Impressionist art. It offers tours and an array of programs.

Stanley-Whitman House (1720). Historic house museum with historic gardens, an educational building, many colonial programs and on the National Register of Historic Places.

Unionville Museum. Features thematic exhibits; a gem of a former small Carnegie Library, on the National Register of Historic Places.

Farmington Historical Society. Featuring exhibits, lectures, events, and tours of the Freedom Trail's Underground Railroad and Amistad sites.

Lewis-Walpole Library of Yale University. Research center for 18th-century studies and an essential resource for the study of Horace Walpole and Strawberry

NOTES

Hill. Its collections include important holdings of 18th-century British prints, drawings, manuscripts, rare books, paintings, and decorative arts. Open only to scholars, by appointment.

Barney Library (1917-1918). Originally a perfect example of a Doric "temple with wings."

Extensive System of Trails. Information and maps, GPS coordinates, and parking.

Historic walks. Includes Farmington's freedom trail throughout Farmington.

Suburban Park. Historic landmark in the center of Unionville; containing 20.5 acres of open space with 2 miles of hilly walking trails, containing five circular "kettles" formed during the glacial age and the remnants of an "electrical" amusement park.

Farmington and Pequabuck Rivers. Provide a habitat for wildlife and many aesthetic and recreational opportunities including canoeing, fishing, kayaking, and swimming, with three handicapped accessible trails to the Farmington River Fishing Piers.

Westwoods Golf Course. Designed by Geoffrey S. Cornish, it is an 18-hole, 4,407-yard, par-61 country setting golf course.

Hill-Stead Museum, on 152 acres in Farmington, houses impressionist masterpieces, historic gardens, and women's history. The Drawing Room (pictured here) showcases works by Monet, Manet, and Degas, to name a few. Rose Ponte

ADDRESS BOOK

Town Site
www.farmington-ct.org

Barney Library
75 Main St.
860-673-6791
www.farmingtonlibraries.org

Farmington Historical Society
138 Main St.
www.fhs-ct.org

Hill-Stead Museum
860-677-4787
35 Mountain Rd.
www.hillstead.org

Lewis-Walpole Library at Yale University
154 Main St.
860-677-2140
www.walpole.library.yale.edu

Stanley-Whitman House
37 High St.
www.stanleywhitman.org

Unionville Museum
15 School St., Unionville
860-673-2231
www.unionvillemuseum.org

Westwoods Golf Course
14 Westwoods Dr.
860-675-2548

[Passport Stamp / Signature & Date Here]

Glastonbury

By Khara Dodds, former Glastonbury Director of Planning and Land Use

Having a land area of 52.5 sq. mi. in central Connecticut the Town of Glastonbury is the state's 11th largest town. Glastonbury offers the coveted balance of thriving business, local attractions, and recreational parks & open spaces. It's a community that is rich with culture, attractions, and thriving businesses. As one of the state's oldest municipalities, Glastonbury is dedicated to preserving the historic sites, parks, and riverfront property while investing in new development that will contribute to the town's prosperity.

A town that grew up along the banks of the Connecticut River, Glastonbury was formally founded in 1693 with settlers first arriving in 1636. The town was named after Glastonbury in Somerset England. Settlement began with the tribes of the Connecticut River Indians, known as the Wongunks. Fertile Connecticut River meadows attracted increased settlement in the mid-1600s, with the first house built around 1649. Glastonbury's agricultural heritage remains an important component of the town's overall cultural and economic makeup.

Shipbuilding was important through the 1870s, with over 250 major sailing vessels built, and supplies exported to as far as the West Indies. Roaring Brook and Salmon Brook supported the Hartford Manufacturing Co., the Hopewell Woolen Mill, and the Glastonbury Knitting Co. at Addison.

Glastonbury is home to the oldest continuously operating ferry in the U.S. that runs between South Glastonbury and Rocky Hill dating back as far as 1655. The town is also believed to be the first commercial soap manufacturing business in the world called the J.B. Williams Soap Factory. In the early 1840s, this company was formed by J.B. Williams and his brother William Stuart Williams. The remaining parts of the soap factory complex still stand and have been converted into the Soap Factory Condominiums.

People of Interest

John Howard Hale. Known as "Peach King Hale" he developed a peach that could withstand New England winters and was disease resistant. He was also one of the founding fathers of Storrs Agricultural College, now the University of Connecticut.

Saglio Brothers. Formed the company, Arbor Acres, and were among the first to use genetic engineering in chicken production. By 1958, Arbor Acres had gone world-wide: 50% of all chickens consumed in the world were from Arbor Acres.

Smith Sisters. Five sisters were abolitionists and supporters of the Women's Suffrage Movement that stimulated change in Connecticut and the nation.

Gideon Welles. Secretary of the Navy under Abraham Lincoln and Andrew Johnson, and Father of the Modern Navy.

Interesting Places

Cotton Hollow Preserve.
Great Pond Preserve.
Shoddy Mill Preserve.
J.B. Williams Park.
Center Green.
Glastonbury Ferry/Ferry Landing.
Blackledge Falls.
Buckingham Park.

The Riverfront. Includes Glastonbury Boathouse, Riverfront Community Center, Riverfront Park, and boat launch.

An aerial shot of Riverfront Park & Boathouse. Paul Coco

Notes

Civil War Memorial. On Hubbard Green.

Museum on the Green. Home of the Glastonbury Historical Society.

The Old Cider Mill. Oldest continually running cider mill in the country.

Welles-Shipman-Ward House.

Kimberly Mansion. Once home to Abby and Julia Evelina Smith, political activists involved in causes including abolitionism and women's suffrage. National Landmark.

The Micah House and Chapel at the Thomas Hale Homestead.

Popular Events

Summer Music Festival. Annual concert series held in the summer months at Riverfront Park.

Apple Harvest Festival. Annual festival held in the Fall in Riverfront Park. October.

Visit Glastonbury's farms! Glastonbury's farms offer a variety of locally grown and prepared consumer goods including Pick-Your-Own produce, Christmas trees, homemade ice cream, cut flowers, honey, cider, and more!

Address Book

Town Site
www.glastonburyct.gov

Blackledge Falls
3874 Hebron Ave.

Buckingham Park
1285 Manchester Rd.

Center Green 2340 Main St.

Civil War Memorial 18 Hubbard St.

Cotton Hollow Preserve
493 Hopewell Rd.

Glastonbury Ferry/Ferry Landing
300 Ferry Ln., Rocky Hill

The Museum on the Green is housed in the first Town Hall built in Glastonbury c.1840. It served for 100 years and is now the home of the Glastonbury Historical Society. Ken Leslie

The Glastonbury Farmers Market Coalition, Inc. operates a Farmers Market on Wednesdays, June thru October, 4-7 PM, rain or shine. Children's activities and local produce are available.

Historical Society of Glastonbury & Museum on the Green
1944 Main St. • 860-633-6890
www.hsgct.org

Great Pond Preserve
451 Great Pond Rd.

J.B. Williams Park 719 Niepsic Rd.

Kimberly Mansion 1625 Main St.

Old Cider Mill
1287 Main St. • 860-778-4460

The Riverfront 300 Welles St.

Thomas Hale Homestead
2183 Main St.

Shoddy Mill Preserve
111 Shoddy Mill Rd.

Welles-Shipman-Ward House
972 Main St., South Glastonbury

Shopping

Eric Town Square 124 Hebron Ave.

Somerset Square 140 Glastonbury Blvd.

Events

Apple Harvest Festival
Riverfront Park (300 Welles St.)

Glastonbury Farmers Market
Hubbard Green (Main & Hubbard Sts.)

Summer Music Festival
Riverfront Park (300 Welles St.)

[Passport Stamp / Signature & Date Here]

Granby

By Lisa Fiedler, resident and author of many novels for children and young adults

The town of Granby, approx. 26 miles northwest of Hartford, is in Hartford Co. In 2010 the population was 11,282. The town includes West Granby and North Granby. This rural town is in the foothills of the Litchfield Hills of the Berkshires. From the 1890s to the 1920s a large number of Swedish immigrants came to live in Granby.

Located at the distinctive 'notch' (part of Southwick, MA that jogs down into CT) on the Connecticut-Massachusetts border, Granby was originally part of the adjacent town of Simsbury. It was founded in 1660 and incorporated in 1786. Extensive rural and woodsy areas, along with a lengthy stretch of the Salmon Brook River, likely contribute to the black bear population in this small town, where residents are rarely surprised to see these handsome animals wandering through their yards. Examples of the natural breathtaking beauty of Granby include the waterfall in Enders State Forest, and the Dewey-Granby Oak, an approx. 500-year-old white oak, one of the oldest trees in New England, boasting branches that reach beyond 70 feet from a trunk that is 27 feet in circumference. The town of Granby is known for its many farms, especially Holcomb Farm, and at one time some of the best tobacco came from this area.

Places of Interest

McLean Game Refuge. Former Conn. Governor and U.S. Senator donated 4,400-acre preserve to Granby and Simsbury. It is a beautiful place to enjoy the majesty of the outdoors, and possibly interact with the local wildlife as well. From Simsbury travel north on Rt. 10/202. The Game Refuge is on your left, approx. one mile south of Granby Center. www.mcleangamerefuge.org

Salmon Brook Historical Society. Maintains the Abijah Rowe house (c.1732), the Weed-Enders house (1792), the Cooley School (1870), and the Colton-Hayes Tobacco Barn & Museum (c.1914), with many exhibits of 18th and 19th century life.

Holcomb Farm. A working enterprise since the early 1700s, it boasts 367 acres of land, as well as a number of handsomely appointed indoor spaces for classes, meetings, and private gatherings.

Enders State Forest. It is in the towns of Granby and Barkhamsted. In 1970 it was established with a 1,500-acre parcel of woodlands donated to the state by the children of John and Harriet Enders. Features: hiking hunting, birding, picnicking, and letterboxing. Rt. 212 Barkhamsted Rd., Granby. www.ct.gov/deep

Dewey-Granby Oak. One of the oldest trees in New England. The property where the tree is was purchased in 1997 by the Granby Land Trust which maintains the ancient oak tree.

Two Libraries. The heart of the town and source of information, books, videos, activities, and programs. Granby Public Library, and Frederick H. Cossitt Library, a Queen Anne style building, designed by Jasper Daniel Sibley and built in 1890.

The 1890 Frederick H. Cossitt Library in North Granby. Lisa Fiedler

Notes

The Dewey-Granby Oak is one of the oldest trees in New England. Its trunk is 27 ft. in circumference with 70 ft. long branches. Lisa Fiedler

Address Book

Town Site
www.granby-ct.gov

Dewey-Granby Oak
67-79 Day St.

Frederick H. Cossitt Library
388 North Granby Rd., North Granby

Granby Public Library
15 North Granby Rd.
860-844-5275

Holcomb Farm
11 Simsbury Rd., West Granby
www.holcombfarm.org

Salmon Brook Historical Society
208 Salmon Brook St.
860-653-9713
www.salmonbrookhistorical.org

[Passport Stamp / Signature & Date Here]

Hartford

By Michael McGarry, City Councilman, 1993-1999

Hartford was first settled by the Dutch who established a trading fort "House of the Good Hope" in 1633 at the confluence of the little river (Park, now underground) and the long river (the Connecticut). Beaver pelts, wampum and supplies were traded with Indian tribes from what is today's Connecticut, Western Massachusetts and points West. In 1635, English settlers under Rev. Thomas Hooker took residence, built public buildings, and divided land into farms and roadways.

After a series of incidents, mainly over use of land, the English settlers took possession of the fort in 1653, ending Dutch influence forever except for street names in the "Coltsville" area. Hartford soon gained fame with "The Fundamental Orders, 1638-1639" based on the proposition that "The Foundation of Authority is laid in the free consent of the people". Considered "The First Written Constitution known to history that created a government and it marked the beginning of American Democracy". Connecticut is known as the Constitution State to this day.

After the Pequot Wars, 1638, the population of Central Connecticut grew with Hartford emerging as the center of manufacturing, finance, trade and politics. Notables in history include Samuel and Elizabeth Colt, Francis Pratt, and Amos Whitney (today's United Technologies) and the actress, Katherine Hepburn who called Hartford home. J.P. Morgan, once America's richest man, left his mark in the city with a donation of land for City Hall.

Hartford now is a city of about 125,000 and is the state capital. It has a Mayor/Council form of government with a revitalized downtown and about a dozen commercial strips crisscrossing 16 neighborhoods. Its cultural diversity includes European, Hispanic, African, and Asian populations constantly infusing new life to the city.

Points of Interest

Ancient Burying Ground. Oldest historic site in Hartford, and the only one surviving from the 1600s.

Artists Collective. Provides greater Hartford area youth year-round professional training in dance, music, drama, visual and martial arts.

Bushnell Center for the Performing Arts.

Coltsville. Once owned by the Colt family, includes Colt dome (on firearms factory), worker housing, Church of the Good Shepherd, Colt Park itself, and "Potsdam Village" built for Willow Furniture makers. Now in process of becoming a National Park. Tours during warm weather start at Colt Monument (entrance to Colt Park). Call ahead.

Connecticut Convention Center.

Connecticut Historical Society. Museum, library, research and educational center. Est. 1825. Official statewide historical society and one of the oldest historical societies in the country.

Connecticut Science Center. A nine-story, 40,000 sq. ft. center contains interactive exhibits consisting of videos, audios, visuals, tactile components, programs, & live demonstrations.

Front Street District. Features dining, dancing, and many forms of entertainment.

The Capitol. Public Tours Mon.-Fri.

Governor's Residence. Elegant Colonial Revival 1909 home. Residence to state governors since 1945. Hour-long guided tours for groups only.

Harriet Beecher Stowe Center. Home of Harriet Beecher Stowe, author of Uncle Tom's Cabin. Stowe's 5,000 sq. ft. cottage-style house is adjacent to the Mark Twain House and open to the public.

Hartford Stage. Tony-award winning dramas, classics, musicals,

Notes

Shakespeare, new plays and shows.

Hartford Yard Goats. Double-A minor league baseball team at Dunkin' Donuts Park.

Mark Twain House & Museum. Samuel Langhorne Clemens home from 1874-1891. Museum contains permanent exhibition on Twain's life and work and rotating exhibition hall. Daily tours 9:30 AM-5:30 PM.

Real Art Ways. Features movies and art exhibits. Open 2-9 PM daily.

Riverfront/Riverside Park. Features rowing docks, a boat launch, volleyball, cricket and playgrounds, plus our challenge course, Riverfront trails, sculptures, fishing, and athletic fields.

TheaterWorks. Contemporary theater produces plays and musicals.

Wadsworth Atheneum (1842). Oldest continuously-operating public art museum in U.S. featuring world famous artists.

XL Center. Multi-purpose arena and convention center features sports, music, etc.

Address Book

Town Site
www.hartfordct.gov

Ancient Burying Ground
60 Gold St. • 860-724-5234
www.theancientburyingground.com

Artists Collective
1200 Albany Ave. • 860-527-3205
www.artistscollective.org

Bushnell Center
166 Capitol St. • 860-987-6000
www.bushnell.org

The Capitol
210 Capitol Ave. • 860-240-0222
www.ctconventions.com

Colt Park
130 Wethersfield Ave. • 413-271-3980

Connecticut Convention Center
100 Columbus Blvd. • 860-249-6000
www.ctconventions.com

Connecticut Historical Society
1 Elizabeth St. • 860-236-5621
www.chs.org

Connecticut Science Center
250 Columbus Blvd. • 860-SCIENCE
www.ctsciencecenter.org

The Corning Fountain (1899) in Bushnell Park was presented by John J. Corning (Corning Glass Works of New York) to Hartford as a tribute to his father, John Benton Corning (1811-1896), a Hartford businessman who operated a gristmill on the site. The Capitol building is in the background. Andy Hart-Hartford News

Dunkin' Donuts Park
1214 Main St. • 860-246-GOAT
www.yardgoatsbaseball.com

Front Street District
860-527-0100
www.frontstreetdistrict.com

Governor's Residence
990 Prospect Ave. • 860-524-7355

Hartford Stage
50 Church St. • 860-527-5151
www.hartfordstage.org

Harriet Beecher Stowe Center
73 Forest St. • 860-522-9258 x317
www.harrietbeecherstowe.org

Mark Twain House & Museum
351 Farmington Ave. • 860-247-0998
www.marktwainhouse.org

Real Art Ways
56 Arbor St. • 860-232-1006
www.realartways.org

Riverside Park
5o Columbus Blvd.
www.riverfront.org

TheaterWorks
233 Pearl St. • 860-527-7837
www.theaterworkshartford.org

Wadsworth Atheneum
600 Main St. • 860-278-2670
www.thewadsworth.org

XL Center
1 Civic Center Plaza • 800-745-3000
www.xlcenter.com

[Passport Stamp / Signature & Date Here]

Hartland

By Joanne Groth, President, Hartland Historical Society

Abutting the Massachusetts border in Hartford County, Hartland sits atop the scenic hills of northwestern Connecticut. It is blessed with natural beauty, abundant laurel in spring, lush green in summer, riotous color in fall, and a white blanket in winter. Wildlife abounds from moose and bear to bobcats and turkeys. Glacial impact left a "hollow" between the town's East and West mountains that once was inhabited but now holds Hartford's water supply. Part of a land settlement of "western lands" in 1733, it became Hart (Ford) Land, and the name was shortened to Hartland. Incorporated in 1761, it became Connecticut's 69th town. Population is about 2,500 (2017).

Hartland residents were productive early with a calico factory in 1836 (one of the first in the United States) and paper production in 1874. There were also wagon shops, tanneries, gristmills and sawmills, carding mills (intermixes fibers producing a continuous web) fulling mills (a step in making woolen cloth that cleaned the wool eliminating oils, dirt, and impurities, making it thicker), and clothing mills, ironworks, blacksmith shops, piano framing, doll making, and even a mica mine and ski slope. Cider mills and distilleries flourished until Prohibition. Tobacco, grains, vegetables, and dairy farms prevailed.

With both Methodist and Congregational church history, today there are two Congregational churches: The First (1768) and Second (1780) Congregational. There is also the Bethany Lutheran Brethren (1941) Church. The two main cemeteries are the East Hartland, run by the Hartland Cemetery Association, and the West Hartland, which the town oversees. There are also a few family lots.

In 1820 ten small school districts were located around town and a few of the buildings remain as homes today. Today the school (1949) is in one building on the East side enrolling about 200 students from Pre-K to Grade 8. High school students can choose Granby Memorial, Northwest Regional 7, or Oliver Wolcott School.

Notable Citizens

Thomas S. Giddings II, the first permanent settler (1754).

Simon Baxter, driving force to incorporate town in 1761 and a noted Loyalist in the Revolution.

Titus Hayes Sr., ground corn for the Continental Army. His gristmill stone is in the East Hartland cemetery.

Consider Tiffany, whose handwritten journal is in the Library of Congress, tells of Nathan Hale's capture during the American Revolution.

Asher Benjamin II, architect and author of "The Country Builder's Assistant" (1797), influenced the look of cities and towns throughout New England, including Hartford's Old State House staircase, Deerfield Academy, and Beacon Hill in Boston.

Uriel Holmes, a prominent landowner and agent for the Connecticut Land Company that handled the property sales to "Western Reserve" Ohio in 1800s.

David Gaines (1891-1940), author of notes on old houses,

A portion of the Coach Stop Restaurant was the first house built in 1764 on the East Hartland Town Green. Sandy Lisella

Notes

vital statistics, the East Hartland Cemetery, and various families.

Stanley Ransom (1897-1975), founder of the Hartland Historical Society, author of History of Hartland (1961), and the driving force for our town library.

Places Of Interest

Gaylord House Museum (1845). Headquarters the Hartland Historical Society's collection of artifacts and records. Open on the first Sun. of the month from May-Oct. from 2-4 PM or by appointment.

Camp Alice Merritt. First permanent Hartford Council Girl Scout camp. Opened in 1925, it was sold to the town in 1992. A residents-only site for hiking, swimming, and other activities.

The 1845 Gaylord House Museum in West Hartland is operated and maintained by the Hartland Historical Society. Joanne Groth

Coach Stop Restaurant. Built by Uriel Holmes (1764), it was the first house on the town green in East Hartland. It is the only restaurant in Hartland.

Barkhamsted Reservoir and Saville Dam (1930-1940). The Metropolitan District Commission (MDC) built the Saville Dam in neighboring Barkhamsted that impounded the Farmington River East Branch for nearly 8 miles (13 km) extending into Hartland. A Rt. 20 roadside lookout on the west side offers views of the flooded hollow.

Tunxis State Forest. Offers scenic hikes by waterfalls with trail information available online.

Town Events

Memorial Day Parade (May)

Firemen's Carnival (July/August)

Historical Society Blueberry Picnic (August) and Santa Breakfast (December).

Hartland Land Trust Speaker Series. Dates and times vary yearly. See www.hartlandlandtrust.org.

Address Book

Town Site
www.hartlandct.org

Camp Alice Merritt
Rt. 20, East Hartland

Coach Stop Restaurant
6 Hartland Blvd., East Hartland
860-413-3545

Gaylord House Museum
Rt. 20, West Hartland
860-379-1610
www.hartlandhistoricalsociety.com

Hartland Land Trust
www.hartlandlandtrust.com

Tunxis State Forest
www.ct.gov/deep

[Passport Stamp / Signature & Date Here]

Manchester

By Joe Camposeo, retired City of Manchester Clerk

The history of Manchester began in the early 1600s when colonists found opportunities to prosper and to build a community. Like many other Connecticut locations, much of the land was used for farming. Initially, this area, as well as other tracts east of the Connecticut River, became known as Orford Parish.

It was during the Orford Parish era that its waterways, terrain, and roads led to the emergence of manufacturing in what is now Manchester. Most notably, the Bigelow, the Hop Brook, and the Hockanum rivers were excellent sources of power and improved delivery of products from prime locations and tollways. From this, new opportunities were spawned to build schools, houses, commercial enterprises, and churches. In 1823, Orford Parish became the town of Manchester.

Manchester was now at the start of the "enhanced age of manufacturing." Many changes followed. There were local governing officials and town meetings to promote education, commerce, and lifestyle, even more than in prior years. Perhaps the most significant development was the emergence of raw silk manufacturing by the sons of George and Timothy Cheney in 1835. In the eyes of many, Manchester was the "silk capital of the world." From their beginnings with a small mill on the Hop Brook to their recognition as a large, premier manufacturer of silk, the Cheney Brothers had a major impact on the growth of Manchester. They created jobs, built schools, and places for people to live; they created roads and railways, and much more.

It was during this era that Manchester's population tripled in size. Many other manufacturers were also partners to Manchester's success. The Hilliardville Mill was the first to successfully produce cotton in Connecticut. Pitkin Glass Works made glass bottles. Other local companies produced paper, wool and gun- powder. Notable names included Case Brothers, and Bunce paper mills; Lydall and Foulds, maker of tools and needles; and Carlysle Johnson, invented the friction clutch in 1884. All contributed significantly to a changing, dynamic town.

From its beginning, Manchester, the "Silk City" has been a special place to live and to enjoy. Despite all that was to change as Manchester grew, business owners and community leaders were driven to keep Manchester special. It is the common thread that links those that sought prosperity here in the 1600s to the nearly 60,000 people living and working here today. This is where THE PAST MEETS THE FUTURE!

Places of Interest

Cheney Historic District. A vast array of manufacturing buildings, mansions, and sites that once were the world's largest manufacturer of silk.

Cheney Hall (1867). Famous speakers and entertainers have graced the stage. Currently the home for the "Little Theatre of Manchester."

Fire Museum. Display of antique fire trucks and equipment.

Manchester Historical Society History Center and the Old Manchester Museum

Keeney School. One-room school from 1700.

Pitkin Glass Works. The remains of the Pitkin Glass Works building

One of the many events held on Manchester's Main St. is the "Crusin' on Main" that draws thousands of old-car enthusiasts. Don Janelle

Notes

is at the intersection of Parker and Porter Streets. Artifacts and samples of the glass can be found at the Old Museum on Cedar Street.

Union Village. Home of the first dynamo power manufactures in the country. On the Hockanum River. www.livingplaces.com

Case Mountain Park. Famous waterfalls and several trails leading to a vista of Manchester.

Parks for Recreation. Over 2,500 acres including Center Park, Charter Oak Park, Center Springs Park, Northwest Park, and Wickham Park.

Cheney Clock Tower Mill is part of the Cheney Brothers Historic District. Dick Jenkins

Lutz Children's Museum. Great place to learn about science and nature. Also the home of Chuckles the ground hog who predicts winter's end each year on Ground Hog Day.

Popular Events

Manchester Road Race. Every Thanksgiving Day as many as 14,000 runners participate in this nearly five-mile run through the streets of Manchester. Since its beginning, the race has attracted world renowned runners.

Cruisin' on Main. Yearly, Main Street is lined with several thousand classic cars.

Did You Know?

1. *Money Magazine* named Manchester the "Best Place to Live in Connecticut" in Jan. 2018.

2. The fountain pen was invented by Frank Holland of Manchester in 1881. He later sold the rights to the Parker Company.

3. At different times, Katherine Hepburn and James Cagney enjoyed the famous Shady Glen dairy restaurant while visiting.

Address Book

Town Sites
www.manchesterct.gov
www.downtownmanchester.org

Case Mountain Park
200 Case Mtn. Rd.

Cheney Hall
177 Hartford Rd.
www.cheneyhall.org

Fire Museum
230 Pine St.
www.thefiremuseum.org

Keeney School
106 Hartford Rd.
www.manchesterhistory.org

Lutz Children's Museum
247 S. Main St.
www.lutzmuseum.org

Manchester Historical Society
175 Pine St.
www.manchesterhistory.org

Old Manchester Museum
126 Cedar St.
860-647-9983

Pitkin Glass Works
Intersection of Parker & Porter Sts.
www.pitkinglassworks.org

Events

Manchester Road Race
www.manchesterroadrace.com

Cruisin' on Main
903 Main St.

[Passport Stamp / Signature & Date Here]

Marlborough

By Violet Schwarzmann, Director, Marlborough Senior Center

Marlborough is in Hartford Co. bounded on the west by East Hampton, by Glastonbury on the north, Hebron on the east, and Colchester on the south. Its population in 2010 was 6,404.

On May15, 1736, 14 subscribers from the towns of Glastonbury, Colchester, and Hebron petitioned the General Assembly for winter privileges. They were not fully established as the Society of Marlborough until 1747. In 1803 Marlborough was incorporated as a town with land taken from the three towns. Town vital records begin 1803. Barbour collection records cover 1803-1852.

During Colonial times the heart of what is now Marlborough was the crossroads of two well-traveled routes known as Hockanum Path and Monhege Trail and travelers used this route to go from Hartford to New London. Today's Rt. 66 was a cart path that took farmers and their crops to Middletown for transport on the Connecticut River. Travelers found this crossroads to be an ideal place for rest, refreshment, and change of horses at Sadlers' Ordinary and at Marlborough Tavern, which was also the residence of Mary Hall, an educator, who became the first woman lawyer to practice at the bar of Connecticut.

The Colonial General Assembly in 1747 designated this area an Ecclesiastical Society and named it Marlborough. In 1803 the Assembly incorporated Marlborough as a "district town" deriving its lands from Colchester, Hebron, and Glastonbury.

Sadlers' Ordinary, built about 1653 near Lake Terramuggus, entertained travelers on the Path to Monhege between the Thames and Connecticut Rivers. The first schoolhouse here was built in 1760, a time when farms and sawmills flourished.

Marlborough Tavern opened its doors late in the Colonial period. Local industry, chiefly in textiles, was spurred by the New London Turnpike during the 19th century, but vanished with the burning of the last mill in 1907.

In 1964, a new highway was opened, setting Marlborough on another course for change. With two exits in Marlborough, Rt. 2 paved the way for the town to be discovered once again. Young families working in Hartford were captivated by Marlborough's quiet beauty and simple life. During the years that followed, Marlborough experienced another boom. Neighborhoods and developments sprang up, and the town saw a return of businesses, restaurants, and shops. At present Marlborough is mainly a residential community.

Interesting Places

Richmond Memorial Library. Provides access to information from a wide range of sources in a variety of formats.

Blish Memorial Park. On Lake Terramuggus it features swimming, boating, and a playscape.

Marlborough Arts Center. Open to visitors to enjoy the crafts of artisans. It holds community events and live music.

Sadler's Restaurant. Patio or fireside dining. Features seafood specials, comfort food, creative salads, and more.

The Marlborough Art Center at 45 N. Main Street holds fine art exhibits, community programs, and music events. Violet Schwarzmann

Notes

Shops at the Marlborough Barn. A blend of antiques and collectibles together with works by Connecticut artisans, with more than 40 vendors.

Farm at Carter Hill. A unique farm experience: a general store, outdoor eatery, bed and breakfast, ice cream and outdoor pavilion and a variety of farm animals.

Château Le Gari. Picturesque vineyard & winery offering tastings, special events and weddings.

Marlborough Tavern. Built sometime around 1740, the house is older than the United States itself. President Andrew Jackson even once stopped in.

Notable People

Chris Cillizza. CNN journalist. Born 1976.

A.J. Pollock. Major League Baseball player with the Arizona Diamondbacks; attended RHAM High School in Hebron. Born 1987.

Gretchen Ulion. Ice hockey gold medalist in 1998 Winter Olympics. Born 1972.

Sadler's Restaurant, named after the early colonial tavern Sadler's Ordinary is at 61 N. Main St. It is a great place for lunch or dinner and offers fireside or patio dining. There is also great shopping next door at the Old Country Barn stores and Ranunculus flower shop. Podskoch

Address Book

Town Site
www.marlboroughct.net

Blish Memorial Park
32 Park Rd.

Château Le Gari
303 S. Main St.
860-467-6296
www.chateaulegari.com

Farm at Carter Hill
6 E. Hampton Rd. (Rt. 66)
860-906-7866
www.thefarmatcarterhill.com

Jessica's Garden & Lobster Shack
198 E. Hampton Rd. (Rt. 66)
860-295-1685
www.jessicasgarden.net

Marlborough Arts Center
231 N. Main St.
860-295-9389
www.marlborougharts.org

Marlborough Tavern
3 E. Hampton Rd.
860-365-5942
www.marlboroughtavernct.com

Marlborough Town Hall
26 Main St.

Richmond Memorial Library
15 School Dr.
www.richmondlibrary.info

Sadler's Restaurant
61 N. Main St.
860-295-0006
www.eatatsadlers.com

Shops at the Marlborough Barn
45 N. Main St.

[Passport Stamp / Signature & Date Here]

New Britain

By Terry Crescimanno, New Britain resident & retired librarian

New Britain, known as the "Hardware City," is in Hartford Co., approx. 9 miles southwest of Hartford. Its first settlers arrived in 1687, and it became a separate parish of Farmington in 1754 known as the New Britain Society. Colonel Isaac Lee, a founding member, chose the name of New Britain, in honor of the country of Great Britain.

New Britain was incorporated as a town on June 18, 1850. Though it was only 13.2 sq. mi. it was steadily growing as an industrial community, and on Jan. 13, 1871, the city of New Britain was incorporated.

Through the 19th and 20th centuries New Britain was first called the "Hardware Capital of the World." Alvin and Seth North, along with H.C. Whipple started a company in 1812 to make hooks and eyes from plated wire. The business evolved into North & Judd with the addition of Lorin F. Judd in 1863. Other early industrialists included Frederick Stanley, who with his brother William began the Stanley Works in 1852 manufacturing bolts, doorknobs, handles, and other hardware items. Philip and Frank Corbin produced locks as early as 1851, while H.E. Russell and Cornelius Erwin formed Russell & Erwin during the same period. The two companies would eventually merge into the American Hardware Corp. in 1902. Fafnir Bearing Co. was incorporated in 1911.

The factories of New Britain employed generations of European immigrants, first from Ireland, Germany, and Sweden, then later Italy and Poland. Later the two largest demographic groups were Polish-Americans at 19.9% and Italian-Americans at 12.9%.

New Britain has a proud sports legacy ranging from Walter Camp, born in 1859 and known as the "Father of American Football," to George Springer, the 2017 World Series MVP for the Houston Astros. Did you know that the basketball technique of dribbling was first used at the New Britain YMCA?

Looking to a more energy-efficient future, New Britain is linked to Hartford by CTfastrak, Connecticut's first dedicated bus-only rapid transit system.

Interesting Places

New Britain Museum of American Art (1903). First museum in the U.S. dedicated to American art. Its collection dates from 1739 and has grown to more than 8,300 items.

New Britain Industrial Museum. Collects, preserves, and exhibits items representing more than 200 years of invention and innovation.

New Britain Youth Museum. Over 12,000 items related to regional and cultural history and the natural sciences. A fun, interactive space that offers programs on culture and arts for children and young adults. (Also operates Hungerford Park Nature Center).

Hungerford Park Nature Center. Maintains 27 acres of guided woodland. Home to many domestic animals and native wild birds. There is a farmyard, indoor exhibits, walking trails, and a picnic and play area.

New Britain YMCA. Gym, pool, exercise, etc.

The New Britain Stadium, home of the N.B. Bees of the Atlantic League of Professional Baseball. Terry Crescimanno

Notes

New Britain Bees. Members of the Futures Collegiate Baseball League. Family-friendly entertainment.

Walnut Hill Park. Designed by noted landscape architect Frederic Law Olmsted, and listed on the National Register of Historic Places, the park is home to a rose garden, playgrounds, ballfields, and a walking/cycling circuit. The Darius Miller Shell hosts a summer music festival series.

Central Connecticut State University (1849). Connecticut's oldest publicly funded university and a great resource for cultural and athletic events. www.ccsu.edu.

New Britain Symphony.

Hole in the Wall Theater. Basic philosophy: "Theater should be available to everyone, regardless of one's ability to pay."

New Britain Repertory.

Notable Person

Abe Ribicoff (1910-98). U.S. Congressman, Conn. Governor, and JFK's Secretary of Health and Education.

The New Britain Museum of American Art (1903) is the first institution dedicated solely to acquiring American art. Terry Crescimanno

Address Book

Town Site
www.newbritainct.gov

Hole in the Wall Theater
116 Main St.
860-229-3049
www.hitw.org

Hungerford Park Nature Center
191 Farmington Ave., Kensington
www.newbritainyouthmuseum.org

New Britain Industrial Museum
185 W. Main St.
860-832-8654
www.nbindustrial.org

New Britain Museum of American Art
56 Lexington St.
860-229-0257
www.nbmaa.org

New Britain Repertory
23 Norden St.
www.connecticuttheatrecompany.org

New Britain Stadium
230 John Karbonic Way
www.nbbees.com

New Britain Symphony
114 W. Main St.
www.newbritainsymphony.org

New Britain YMCA
50 High St.
www.nbbymca.org

New Britain Youth Museum
30 S. High St.
860-225-3020
www.newbritainyouthmuseum.org

Walnut Hill Park
184 W. Main St.

[Passport Stamp / Signature & Date Here]

NEWINGTON

By Newington Historical Society & Trust

Newington is located south of Hartford in central Connecticut adjacent to New Britain, Wethersfield, and Berlin.

Newington's first settlers were from Wethersfield. About 1665 the original Wethersfield colonists bought a parcel of land from Native Americans, which now comprises Wethersfield, Glastonbury, Newington, Rocky Hill, and a part of Berlin.

In 1677 Wethersfield granted four men the right to build a sawmill on the pond (Mill Pond) near the grazing lands west of Cedar Mountain, making use of the natural waterfall to manufacture pipe (barrel) staves. This is where Newington began. This first industry lasted about 100 years until the wood in Pipe Staves Swamp dwindled, which ended production.

In 1708 the Newington settlers petitioned Wethersfield for a separate parish. Two years later the Wethersfield Town Meeting allowed them the right to worship by themselves from December through March because of the difficulties in traveling across the mountain from Newington to Wethersfield. In 1712 they successfully petitioned to be a separate parish and have their own minister.

Travel between Newington and its parent community remained a difficult task through the 18th century. and until the establishment of the Hartford-New Haven Turnpike around 1800, no direct route to Hartford existed. Thus, Newington continued to grow in relative isolation, forming the strong family and community bonds that are still evident today.

In 1871 Newington became one of the last towns to be incorporated.

INTERESTING PLACES

The Berlin Turnpike is the busiest retail and restaurant area in town with many chain and big-box operations. However, the center of Newington centered around the United Church of Christ Congregational Church at 1075 Main St. offers many locally owned eateries and boutique shops with a more leisurely pace. The Chamber of Commerce office located at 1046 Main St. can offer many ideas for exploring this strong family community

Mill Pond Park. The Waterfall, which claims to be the smallest natural waterfall in the country, is the centerpiece of the official town seal. The park is well-used for outdoor activities for adults and children. A popular walking path circles the historic mill pond.

Churchill Park. An area for recreation and picnics has a walking path connecting it to the fields at Clem Lemire Sports Complex off New Britain Ave.

Newington Historical Society & Trust (NHS&T) maintains two historic houses. The Kellogg-Eddy House is the official town museum. The Enoch Kelsey House is noted for trompe l'oeil wall paintings and weaving looms. Admission by appointment can be arranged by contacting the NHS&T. Many 18th and 19th century homes dot the landscape throughout the town, including the Deming-Young Farm.

Lucy Robbins Welles Library. Next to the Town Hall, it is beloved by

The c.1799 Enoch Kelsey House at 1702 Main St. has been restored by the Newington Historical Society and made into a museum. NHS&T

Notes

the townspeople and has many popular programs and an extensive collection of books and media.

American Radio Relay League. Visitors are welcome at the national organization for amateur radio operators (W1AW). Mon. thru Fri. 9 AM-Noon and 1-4 PM.

Mill Pond Falls, under Mill Pond and inside Mill Pond Park, has a wooden footbridge that spans the top of the falls. An observation area is in front of the falls. Jerry Dougherty

Address Book

Town Site
www.newingtonct.gov

American Radio Relay League
225 Main St.
860-594-0297
www.arrl.org

Churchill Park
1991 Main St.

Deming-Young Farm Foundation
282 Church St.
860-666-1016

Enoch Kelsey House
1702 Main St.
860-666-7118

Kellogg-Eddy House
679 Willard Ave.
860-666-7118

Lucy Robbins Welles Library
100 Garfield St.
860-665-8700

Mill Pond Park
123 Garfield St.

Newington Historical Society & Trust
679 Willard Ave.
860-666-7118
www.newingtonhistoricalsociety.org

[Passport Stamp / Signature & Date Here]

PLAINVILLE

By Gert LaCombe and Nancy Eberhardt of the Plainville Historical Society

The small but mighty town of Plainville obtained its name in 1831 when the Federal Government opened the first post office. Before that time we were called the Great Plain of Farmington, home to the Tunxis Indians who resided in the area and created the first trails, one of which is known today as the Blue Trail.

In 1869 we separated from Farmington to become a town in the heart of the Farmington River Valley. The town covers approx. nine-square miles and became known as the "Crossroads of Connecticut" when the Farmington Canal was put into service in 1828.

Manufacturing has been a major factor in the business and industrial development of our town from the earliest farmers, tinsmiths, and clock shops, to the building of a huge textile mill called the Plainville Manufacturing Co. Built in the 1850s it provided employment to 10% of the town's population until the 1920s and was a big employer of women which made a definite impact on the lifestyle of the families. During the war eras 1899-1940s Trumbull Electric was one of the town's biggest employers and remained so until it was purchased by General Electric in 1918.

From its infancy Plainville has been a pathway for travel through the valley from all directions beginning with the early construction of the Hartford New Haven Turnpike, now known as Rt. 10, and forward to today's I-72 & I-84. We are conveniently located to serve surrounding areas with the recent acquisition of the Robertson Airport and now are able to reach out to the world.

INTERESTING PLACES

Plainville Historic Center. The site was built in 1890 as Plainville's first Town Hall. It has eight display rooms which include the Tunxis, Farmington Canal, Barn, Mill, Victorian Kitchen, and Victorian Parlor, Genealogy & Research, and Children's rooms. Office hours are Mon. and Wed. 9-12 noon year-round. There is also the Hepworth Gallery in the old Town Court Room. Summer Display hours on Sat. 12:30-3:30 from June 1 to Nov. 1. Docent and group tours by appointment year-round.

Plainville Campgrounds. A religious revival of the 1800s brought Methodists by train to a campground area in the northwest section of town on Camp St. Worshipers came each summer to hold meetings at the Tabernacle surrounded by small Victorian homes that were built by area churches and individuals. The buildings have been restored and serve as summer and year round homes.

Old East Street Burying Ground. Located on Rt.10 where lie the soldiers of the Revolutionary War and the French and Indian Wars. Contact Historic Center for entrance.

Charles H. Norton Park. It was gifted to the town by the Norton and Hoerle Families. It hosts a Balloon Festival every August. It also has a restored portion of the old Farmington Canal. On Norton Park Rd. off South Washington St.

Tomasso Nature Park. It was given to the town by the Tomasso brothers to be kept as a nature preserve located off Rt.177 on Granger Lane.

Paderewski Park on Cook St. and Memorial Park on Whiting St. in Plainville Center.

The Plainville Historic Center, in the former 1890 Town Hall, is operated by the Plainville Historical Society. Gert LaCombe

Notes

Robertson Airport. It was founded by Stan Robertson in the 1940s on the property where Nels Nelson made his first flight in 1911 making it Connecticut's oldest airport. Operated by Interstate Aviation.

Historic Homes of Plainville. Can be found traveling up Broad St. to Red Stone Hill and along East St., Rt. 10 where a few lovely homes remain.

Congregational Church of Plainville. Founded in 1837 by the Farmington Church members living in Plainville.

Broad St. School. An early elementary school now known as the Ann Torrant Senior Housing.

Famous People

Governor John Trumbull. Governor in the early 20s.

Charles Norton. Inventor/ Industrialist.

Anna Granniss. International Poet.

Alfred Hepworth. (1876-1962) paintings displayed in many U.S. galleries.

Lyman Homer. "Black Governor" (Note: in Colonial times, enslaved and free Black Americans elected their own leader).

Doris Disney. Prolific mystery writer.

In 2008 volunteers constructed the Petit Memorial Gazebo in memory of Jennifer Hawke-Petit (Jenna) and her two daughters Michael Rose Petit (KK) Haley Elizabeth Petit (Haze). The gazebo is on the banks of the restored Farmington Canal at Norton Park. Gert LaCombe

Address Book

Town Site
www.plainvillect.com

Charles H. Norton Park
1-15 Norton Park Rd.

Congregational Church of Plainville
130 W. Main St.
www.uccplainville.org

Memorial Park
Whiting St.

Old East Street Burying Ground
Rt. 10

Paderewski Park
93 Cook St.

Plainville Campgrounds
320 Camp St.
www.plainvillecampgrounds.org

Plainville Historic Center
29 Pierce St.
860-747-6577

Robertson Airport
62 Johnson Ave.
860-747-5519

Tomasso Nature Park
Granger Ln., off Rt.177

Witch's Dungeon Classic Movie Museum
103 E. Main St.
860-583-8306
www.preservehollywood.org

[Passport Stamp / Signature & Date Here]

Rocky Hill

By Leslie Kerz, Rocky Hill Historical Society

Hill, in Hartford Co., lies west of the Connecticut River. Originally the land of the Wangunk tribe, Europeans began to settle in the area in c. 1630 as part of Wethersfield which became Stepney Parish in 1722. In 1843, Stepney Parish attained separate town status as Rocky Hill, so named for a ridge that rises on the northeast section. This area is now Quarry State Park, acquired under the Connecticut Recreation and Natural Heritage Trust Program. Rocky Hill's location on the Connecticut River made it a natural port for Wethersfield and an early center for shipbuilding, agriculture, and trade. The Rocky Hill-Glastonbury Ferry, which began operations in 1655, is the country's oldest continuously operating ferry service.

The Connecticut River and its maritime trade have always figured prominently in Rocky Hill's history. Floods that occurred around 1700 changed the river course and made Wethersfield unsuitable as a river port. Rocky Hill became the head of navigation for large vessels. The Ferry Park area was a busy shipyard from the 1750s through the mid-19th century and one of the chief ports of the region. Trade was extensive with the West Indies, and privateers sailed from Stepney Parish during the Revolutionary War and the War of 1812. Many old-time sea captains' houses are still standing.

The Great Meadows, 1000 acres along the Connecticut River, has been farmed since the 11th century. The Morgan State archeological site, located in The Great Meadows, is an 11th-14th century Native American village site, excavated in the early 1980s. The site's excellent preservation led to tens of thousands of recovered artifacts.

The Connecticut Valley Railroad began in 1870, and many residents started commuting to Hartford and Middletown for work and school. A traprock quarry, which provided work for immigrants, many from Italy, opened in 1898. It closed in 1957. In 1964 the Lone Pine Archeological site was discovered in the quarry yielding artifacts dated back to 6,300 BCE.

By the late 20th century Rocky Hill had become a bedroom community for many people working in Hartford, as well as a place for businesses and industry. Rocky Hill maintains its heritage with dedicated open space/parks, a new riverfront redevelopment project, and seven working farms.

Places of Interest

Dinosaur State Park. A National Landmark. Hundreds of dinosaur footprints were discovered in 1966 and are now on display in the park building along with related exhibits.

Rocky Hill-Glastonbury Ferry. Today, a diesel tug and barge, is operated from June through October. Drivers, pedestrians, and bicyclists can enjoy a peaceful short ride across the river and avoid a 13-mile detour to Glastonbury over the Putnam Bridge. Located on Ferry Landing Rt. 160.

Academy Hall Museum. Home of the Rocky Hill Historical Society (RHHS), it displays a wealth of artifacts, photos, books, and files, including The Morgan Site (11th-14th century Native American village site on the Connecticut River). The museum is of particular interest. It was built in 1803 as a

The Rocky Hill-Glastonbury Ferry, started in 1655, is the oldest continuously running ferry service in the U. S. Originally a raft, today it is a three-car barge propelled by a towboat. Leslie Kerz

Notes

school for navigation and higher mathematics and was financed in part by public funds and private subscriptions.

Dividend Pond Park. The Dividend Pond Trails and Archaeological District is made up of 68 acres with 3 miles of marked trails along Dividend Brook. In the 18th and 19th centuries, this was a booming industrial area. There are ten archaeological sites. Old Forge Rd.

Quarry Park. A state-owned, town-managed park that was once a traprock quarry. It is made up of 84 acres with commanding views of Hartford, Glastonbury, and the Connecticut River. The park offers passive and active recreational opportunities to the public such as hiking and bird watching. Old Main St. opposite Marshall Rd.

The 1803 Academy Hall Museum was built as a school for higher math and navigation. It is now the home of the Rocky Hill Historical Society that has displays of artifacts (some dating back to 6,300 BCE), photographs, period rooms; changing exhibits on local and state history; and a library. RHHS

Address Book

Town Site
www.rockyhillct.gov

Academy Hall Museum
785 Old Main St.
860-563-6704
www.rhhistory.org

Dinosaur State Park
400 West St.
860-529-5816
www.dinosaurstatepark.org

Dividend Pond Park and Archaeological District
Dividend and Old Forge Rds.

Quarry Park
34A Old Main St.

[Passport Stamp / Signature & Date Here]

Simsbury

By Sarah Nielsen, Simsbury Main Street Partnership Inc.

Simsbury has been ranked in the Top Ten Best Places to Live by CNN Money Magazine, and it's also one of the best places to visit. From strolling and shopping along our picturesque main street to exploring our 75 miles of biking and walking trails, great things are always happening in town. Our Simsbury Meadows Performing Arts Center is proud to be the summer home of the Hartford Symphony Orchestra, whose outdoor concerts attract thousands each season. The Performing Arts Center also hosts acts as diverse as Willy Nelson, Tedeschi Trucks Band, and Harry Connick, Jr.

Our 235-acre Simsbury Farms town recreation complex includes 4 swimming pools, an 18-hole golf course, tennis courts, a covered skating rink, and one outdoors rink. Our town calendar is packed with community and cultural events.

Simsbury was Connecticut's 21st town, incorporated in May of 1670. Guests can hike to the top of our 165-foot Heublein Tower in Talcott Mountain State Park and view some of the best fall foliage in New England or spend quiet moments in Great Pond State Forest, Penwood and Stratton Brook State Parks or McLean Game Refuge, as close to a third of our land is designated open space. Visitors often stop to picnic under the Pinchot Sycamore Tree (Rt. 185 Hartford Rd.), the largest tree in Connecticut, named after Simsbury's native son Gifford Pinchot. Foodies adore our farm-to-table restaurants with renowned chefs Tyler Anderson (Millwrights) and Chris Prosperi (Metro Bis), while families have many delicious and fun options for even the most discriminating palates.

For couples looking to tie-the-knot, Simsbury is a top destination. Whether it's an elaborate affair at our numerous facilities such as The Riverview or the Simsbury Inn, or a more intimate affair along our Old Drake Hill Flower Bridge, these make memories to treasure. And while standing on the bridge, be sure to look for kayaks and canoes along the Farmington River.

Simsbury has been a farming community through most of its history, and guests can still enjoy these amenities today. Rosedale Farms & Vineyard is on the CT Wine Trail tour, while Tulmeadow Farm Store offers farm fresh ice cream in addition to their local honey and fresh produce. And what adventure would be complete without a visit to the petting zoo at Flamig Farm or an equestrian event at Folly Farm!

Simsbury is the only town in Connecticut to make the National Trust for Historic Preservation's Dozen Distinctive Destinations list. Be careful visiting Simsbury, because before you know it, you'll want to call it home!

Places of Interest

Simsbury Historical Society. More than one dozen structures, gardens, library, significant regional artifacts and important period and thematic collections.

Flamig Farm. Visit animals, farm store, or have a party.

Folly Farm. Equestrian and events facility.

Heublein Tower in Talcott Mountain State Park. Rt. 185 to Summit Ridge Dr.

A picnic under the 200-300 year-old Pinchot Sycamore tree. It was named for conservationist and Connecticut-born Gifford Pinchot. Ray Padron

Notes

Old Drake Hill Flower Bridge. 1 Old Bridge Rd.

Rosedale Farms & Vineyards.

Simsbury Farms Golf Course.

Simsbury Meadows Performing Arts Center.

Tulmeadow Farm Store.

Onion Mountain State Park. Three miles of trails.

Massacoe State Forest. Two separate blocks of woodland totaling 370 acres. The largest block, Great Pond (Great Pond Rd.), is home to the town's biggest standing water body. Features fishing, birdwatching, and hiking. The other block is Stratton Brook State Park. Built by the Civilian Conservation Corps in the 1930s. Features swimming, fishing, picnicking, hiking, ice skating, and a walking & bike path.

Town Parks.
www.simsbury-ct.gov

Simsbury Bike Trails.
www.simsbury.bike/maps-routes

A bicyclist on the single lane 1892 Drake Hill Flower Bridge that was replaced by another bridge nearby in 1992. The bridge was restored in 1992 for pedestrians & bicycles and has 62 flower boxes, 32 hanging baskets, and Cottage Gardens. Ray Padron

Address Book

Town Sites
www.simsbury-ct.gov
www.townofsimsbury.com
www.simsburyevents.com
www.shopsimsbury.com

Flamig Farm
7 Shingle Mill Rd. • 860-658-5070
www.flamigfarm.com

Folly Farm
75 Hartford Rd. • 860-658-9943
www.follyfarm.us

Heublein Tower
1 Summit Dr.
www.friendsofheubleintower.org

Massacoe State Forest
149 Farms Village Rd. (Rt. 309)

Onion Mountain State Park
71 W. Mountain Rd., West Simsbury

Rosedale Farms & Vineyards
25 E. Weatogue St. • 860-651-3926
www.rosedale1920.coms

Simsbury Farms Golf Course
100 Old Farms Rd. • 860-658-6246
www.simsburyfarms.com

Simsbury Historical Society
800 Hopemeadow St.
www.simsburyhistory.org

Simsbury Meadows Performing Arts Center
22 Iron Horse Blvd.
www.simsburymeadowsmusic.com

Tulmeadow Farm Store
225 Farms Village Rd.
www.tulmeadowfarmstore.com

[Passport Stamp / Signature & Date Here]

Southington

By Phil Wooding, Town Historian and member of Southington Historical Society

Although Southington was formally established as a town separate from Farmington in 1779, its roots go back to a much earlier time. Samuel Woodruff moved from Farmington to the area then known as "Panthorne." The settlement grew, prospered, and came to be known as "South Farmington" and then later, "Southington."

A meeting house, independent of the Farmington parish, was first constructed here in 1726 and was used until 1757. Its location on the site of the present Oak Hill Cemetery is commemorated by the First Meeting House stone and plaque.

Southington became a thriving community with the construction of dwellings, taverns, and stores. Industry flourished rapidly. In 1767, Atwater's gristmill was established and by 1790, Southington had a button factory, sawmills, a brass foundry, and potash works. In addition, the first machines to make carriage bolts were developed in Southington.

Important town visitors during the Revolutionary War include Washington, Lafayette, and Count Rochambeau.

Southington today is a growing community, once described as "A Microcosm of America." The town is located in Hartford Co., within 20 miles of Hartford and 9 miles of Waterbury, and includes the sections of Plantsville, Milldale, and Marion. The town is 36.8 sq. mi., ranking it 40th out of 169 Connecticut towns and its population is approx. 43,000. Today Southington is a modern residential, commercial, and industrial community proud of its history.

Interesting Places

The Barnes Museum (1836). Beautiful 17-room fully furnished home has personal belongings of three generations of the Bradley and Barnes families in the Southington Center Historic District. The museum collection includes family diaries and photographs chronicling every aspect of daily life. Tours Mon. thru Wed. and Fri. 1-5 PM, Thurs. 1-7 PM. Sat. only, 1st & last from the last weekend of Sept. thru the last weekend of June, 1-5 PM.

Southington Historical Society Museum. Housed in the town's first formal library, built in 1902. Has displays of artifacts of the town's history such as military, industrial, farming, business, and sports memorabilia. Call 860-621-4811 for days open or to schedule tours. (Corner of Main St. Rt. 10 & Meriden Ave. Rt. 120)

Milldale Depot (1892). The last railroad depot standing in Southington, which at one time had four separate stops on the New Haven & Northampton Railroad "Canal Line". It handled passengers and freight and is located along the Farmington Canal Greenway Rail Trail. The depot features photos, artifacts, information on local industry, the Farmington Canal, and the railroad and trolley systems in the area. Open weekends from Memorial Day to Labor Day, 9 AM-4 PM.

Linear Trail. Is part of the Farmington Canal Heritage Trail. The paved trail runs approx. 4 miles from the Cheshire/Southington town line north to Lazy Lane in

The Southington Historical Society Museum, aka the Historical Arts Building, is in the former 1902 town library. Jerry Dougherty

NOTES

Southington.

Oak Hill Cemetery (1733). The first meeting house was constructed here in 1726 and was in use until 1757. Corner of Queen St., Rt. 10 & Flanders St.

Southington Drive-In Theater. One of only three remaining outdoor theaters in the state and owned by the town of Southington. It opened in 1955 and closed in 2002. Now it screens classic family movies on a limited schedule during summer months.

Crescent Lake. The 56-acre lake provides boating, canoeing, fishing, kayaking, picnicking, and sailing. There are also 223 acres and approx. 6.5 miles of hiking trails. Open daily, 7 AM–8 PM.

Apple Harvest Festival. Held over two weekends each autumn since 1968. There is a variety of live music, entertainment, food, contests, crafts, children's activities, and carnival rides.

Lake Compounce (1846). A 332-acres amusement and water park located in Southington and Bristol. The oldest continuously operating amusement park in the U. S., and home to the 14th oldest wooden roller coaster in the world. Open May-Dec., with 44 rides, 5 roller coasters, and 13 water rides.

The historic 1836 Barnes Mansion at 85 North Main St. in the heart of Southington embodies Southington's rich history. Take a tour and you are transported to an era when ladies wore high-button shoes and elegant lace dresses and men donned top hats for social occasions. Barnes Mansion

ADDRESS BOOK

Town Site
www.southington.org

Apple Hrvest Festival
www.southingtonahf.com

The Barnes Museum
85 North Main St.
860-628-5426
www.thebarnesmuseum.weebly.com

Crescent Lake
403 Shuttle Meadow Rd.

Milldale Depot
447 Canal St.
www.southington.org/traindepot

Oak Hill Cemetery
95 Flanders St.

Lake Compounce
www.lakecompounce.com

Southington Drive-In Theater
995 Meriden-Waterbury Tpke.
www.southingtondrive-in.org

Southington Historical Society Museum
239 Main St.
www.southingtonhistory.org

[Passport Stamp / Signature & Date Here]

South Windsor

*By Maria Carvalho, South Windsor resident and author of **Hamster in Space!** and various published short stories*

Located ten miles northeast of Hartford, South Windsor offers a unique combination of historical neighborhoods alongside thriving commercial and industrial districts. Its outdoor recreational areas, plentiful shopping and dining options, and highly-regarded school system make it popular with both residents and visitors alike. The town's notable natives include theologian Jonathan Edwards, steamboat inventor John Fitch, and clockmaker Eli Terry.

South Windsor's roots stretch back to 1636, when the Plymouth Company purchased a large area of land from the Podunk Indians. Subsequently named "Windsor" by its English settlers, the land was bisected by the Connecticut River.

Initially, the new inhabitants made their homes only on the west side of the river, while the east side was used for farming. The settlers' need to constantly traverse the waterway led to the development of John Bissell's ferry service, which began operating in 1641. This ferry service ran until 1917, making it the longest-running ferry in the country.

Windsor's families eventually began building homes on the east side of the river, and this area became the town of East Windsor in 1768. South Windsor then separated from East Windsor in 1845.

The town flourished as a wealthy farming community in the 18th and 19th centuries, and many elegant homes were constructed on the lush farmland. South Windsor's riverport also made it an active trading center, with flax and tobacco its main exports.

The heart of the town was Main Street, which served as a key thoroughfare for stagecoaches traveling between Hartford and Springfield; the numerous taverns and inns along this road made it popular with travelers who stopped to rest and get fresh horses. One such traveler was John Adams. After riding down Main Street in 1771, he recorded in his diary: "I have spent this morning in riding through Paradise; my eyes never beheld so fine a country."

Now called 'old' Main Street by residents, this scenic road is the core of an area referred to as the East Windsor Hill Historic District. A ride down old Main Street offers a fascinating look back into South Windsor's rich history: many of its homes date to the 1700s and 1800s, and showcase an array of distinctive architecture, including Georgian, Colonial, Federal, and Greek Revival styles. Farmland is still abundant and there are a number of historic buildings along the street, including a still-operational Post Office that is one of the nation's oldest.

Interesting Places

Major Michael Donnelly Land Preserve. 115-acre nature preserve with hiking trails running through woods and fields.

Nevers Road Park. Family-friendly park with trails and athletic fields, a "Bark Park" for dogs, and a Boundless Playground for children of all physical abilities.

Wood Memorial Library and Museum. 1920s-era library that hosts cultural events and features exhibits such as Indian artifacts and antique furniture.

The Promenade Shops at Evergreen Walk. Large outdoor mall with a wide variety of stores and restaurants.

Nomad's Adventure Quest. Family entertainment center includes ziplines, rock climbing walls, laser-tag, and glow-in-the-dark mini-golf.

Notes

The South Windsor Post Office, at 1865 Main St., is located in a 1727 building that sold dry goods and groceries. It is one of the nation's oldest continually operating post office. It received the first Government post rider in 1783. Jerry Dougherty

The 1920s era Wood Memorial Library and Museum is a vibrant cultural center where music, history, art, and nature come alive. It features exhibits such as Indian artifacts, antique furniture, and an annual Gingerbread House Festival. Jessica Vogelgesang

Address Book

Town Site
www.southwindsor.org

Major Michael Donnelly Land Preserve
1165 Sullivan Ave.

Nevers Road Park
Corner of Sand Hill and Nevers Rds.

Nomad's Adventure Quest
100 Bidwell Rd.
860-290-1177
www.nomadsadventurequest.com

The Promenade Shops at Evergreen Walk
501 Evergreen Way
www.thepromenadeshopsatevergreenwalk.com

Wood Memorial Library & Museum
783 Main St.
860-289-1783
www.woodmemoriallibrary.org

[Passport Stamp / Signature & Date Here]

Suffield

By Mary Anne Zak, historian and Suffield resident

At the southern border of the Massachusetts Bay Colony, Southfield joined Westfield and Northfield as outposts of colonial Springfield in 1660. The first syllable of 'Southfield' was pronounced like the first syllable of 'southern' and the name eventually became 'Suffield.' Suffield became part of the Connecticut colony in 1749 when boundary negotiations realigned maps.

Mid-17th century trapper-brothers named Harmon harvested the area's dense wilderness. They regularly sent hundreds of pounds of mink and beaver pelts to England through early fur trader William Pynchon, to whom King Charles granted the charter for the Massachusetts Bay Colony. Early settlers avoided Southfield's dense wilderness until Pynchon's son John built the first sawmill at Stony Brook.

King Philip, a Wampanoag chief known as Metacomet, led four native American tribes in resisting British colonization. They burned Southfield in 1675. Settlers had buried their valuables and evacuated to short-lived safety in Springfield's stockade. But Springfield was burned October 5, 1675.

John Pynchon reported to his son in England: "All my mills, both corn and saw-mills are burnt down, those at home, and in other places, and four of those houses and barns with them, belongeth to me also. So that God hath laid me low."

God was central to 17th century Puritans dedicated to the scriptures and to Oliver Cromwell's goal of reforming the Anglican and Roman Churches and cleansing them of Catholicism. Their Puritan community became the First Church of Christ, the only legal religious organization in Connecticut until 1818. After King Philip's War, Pynchon built the first home in Southfield in 1677.

Pynchon and his followers steadily acquired land, possessions, wealth, and influence. They remained English for 100 years while growing away from English monarchial government and learning self-government.

Success in agriculture generated success in banking and insurance while the growing community produced many mills, skills, talents, and enterprises. New homes and structures saluted succeeding historic and architectural periods. Suffield became one of Connecticut's most beautiful and prosperous towns.

Interesting Places

Main Street Rt. 75. Designated a State Scenic Highway for 4.3 miles through the center of town. Stately homes and large shade trees line this beautiful stretch of roadway. An ideal walk in May.

King House Museum. Historic home shows the graciousness of the 18th century with interesting architecture and treasures from the Suffield Historical Society. Wed. & Sat. 1-4 PM, May-Sept.

Phelps/Hatheway House (1760s). It is set off from the street by an ornate fence and magnificent gardens maintained by the garden club. Open for afternoon tours every day from May 15 to Oct. 15.

Suffield Academy (1833). A private co-educational preparatory school on a beautiful campus that has boarding and day students.

Kent Memorial Library. Offering a wealth of books, movies, exciting

Dr. Alexander King, a physician, farmer, politician, and deacon of the Congregational church, built his home in 1764 on South Main Street in Suffield. It is now a museum operated by the Suffield Historical Society. Cormac Sullivan

Notes

and instructional events, and more!

Metacomet Trail. A blue-blazed Connecticut Forest & Parks Assoc. Trail traverses the summit of West Suffield Mountain from the south. The north end follows the west and north boundaries of Sunrise Park through Suffield Land Conservatory property to the junction of Phelps Rd. and Mountain Rd.

Sunrise Park. Open daily 8 AM to dusk for Suffield residents and their guests (town stickers required): boating, fishing, swimming, picnicking, playground, hiking trails, summer day camp, horseshoes, ice-fishing, and crosscountry skiing are all available.

Windsor Locks Canal State Park Trail. Historic 4.5-mile trail from Windsor Locks to Suffield, was once used during the 1800s by horses and mules to tow boats along the canal. Seasonal.

Jesse F. Smith Memorial Forest. Open for public picnicking, camping with a permit, horseback riding, and crosscountry skiing. Closes at dusk.

Lewis Farm Bird Sanctuary. Managed by the Hartford Audubon Society. It has hiking trails throughout the sanctuary. Open Sunrise-Dark.

Stony Brook Park. A 70-acre park open to public for hiking, fishing, picnicking, crosscountry skiing, and camping with a permit. Closes at dusk.

The Phelps-Hatheway House & Garden, was built on South Main St. in 1761. It has been a museum since 1972. It provides visitors a window into a wide variety of 18th century home construction methods. Cormac Sullivan

Address Book

Town Site
www.suffieldct.gov

Emmanuel Episcopal Church
50 Emanuel Church Rd.

Kent Memorial Library
50 N. Main St.
860-668-3896
www.suffield-library.org

King House Museum
232 S. Main St.
www.suffieldhistoricalsociety.org

Lewis Farm Bird Sanctuary
Located off Hill St.
www.suffieldrec.com

Phelps/Hatheway House
860-247-8996
www.ctlandmarks.org/phelps-hatheway

Stony Brook Park
175 Mountain Rd.

Sunrise Park
2075 Mountain Rd., West Suffield

Windsor Locks Canal State Park Trail
Canal Rd.

[Passport Stamp / Signature & Date Here]

West Hartford

By Joyce Petrella, West Hartford resident

Once considered merely the West Division of Hartford, West Hartford has grown into a dynamic town known for its blending of historic charm and contemporary living.

Prior to its incorporation in 1854 as a distinct town, West Hartford was already placed prominently in history. Before the arrival of the Europeans, the Wampanoag, Pequot, Tunxis, and other Algonquin tribes, had been enjoying this location west of the Connecticut River. In 1636, Reverend Thomas Hooker, a Puritan leader from the original settlers in Massachusetts settled the Hartford area and expanded westward. Thomas and his wife, Sarah Whitman Hooker, made their home in West Hartford. Built between 1715 and 1720, the house can still be found on 1237 New Britain Ave. and is listed on the National Register of Historic Places. The home was a site of great activity during the Revolutionary War.

The Hooker's slave, Bristow, who bought his freedom in 1775, continued to live on the Hooker homestead and is the only known African American person buried in the West Hartford Old Center Cemetery. The cemetery is located on North Main Street in the center of West Hartford.

West Hartford's most prominent native son is undoubtedly Noah Webster, the author of the colonies' first American Dictionary of the English Language. Webster's dictionary was influential in defining the American lexicon and spelling as distinct from the British. His Grammatical Institute of the English Language or "Blue-Backed Speller" so named for its recognizable bright blue cover, became a tool for teachers in the newly founded United States. His birthplace is the home of the West Hartford Historical Society where you can take tours of this well-preserved 18th century house and museum.

Today, West Hartford brings a new meaning to "Blue Back" with its latest development of a retail hub in the center of town. Rich with restaurants for every palate, shopping boutiques and a broad offerings of entertainment options, Blue Back Square has become a popular gathering place.

Interesting Places

For naturalists, West Hartford boasts two reservoirs with over 3000 acres of paths through scenic woodlands. There are miles of paved and gravel roads for joggers, cyclists, and walkers as well as areas for picnicking. Many areas are wheelchair accessible. Elizabeth Park, on the boundary between the West Hartford line and the City of Hartford, is known for its expansive lawns and seasonal gardens. Opened in 1897, it has America's oldest public rose garden, which explodes with color every June. The Pond House Café serves an eclectic menu with views of the park's lily pond.

The Governor's Residence is located close to Elizabeth Park on 990 Prospect Ave. Built in 1909, the mansion has been the family residence of Connecticut's Governors since 1945. The home is open only for tour groups but well worth a drive-by as it is an excellent example of Georgian Revival architecture of the early 20th century and listed on the National Register of Historic Places.

Families with young children will find hands-on fun and learning at The Children's Museum in the center of West Hartford. They will be greeted by Conny the Whale, a 60-foot life-sized replica of a sperm whale. Children can climb inside Conny before entering the Museum where they will find the museum's zoo, learn about dinosaurs that once lived in the Connecticut area as well as taking in an educational show at

Notes

the planetarium. West Hartford offers variety of experiences for all interests and tastes.

West Hartford Reservoirs and Reservoir 6. 3,000 acres of some of the most beautiful woodlands and trails. www.themdc.org.

The birthplace of Noah Webster, author of the first American dictionary, is the home of the West Hartford Historical Society where you can take tours of this well-preserved 18th century house and museum. Joyce Petrella

Address Book

Town Site
www.westhartfordct.gov

Blue Back Square
65 Memorial Rd.
860-882-0678
www.bluebacksquare.com

The Children's Museum
950 Trout Brook Dr.
860-231-2824
www.thechildrensmuseumct.org

Elizabeth Park
1561 Asylum Ave.
www.elizabethparkct.org

The Governor's Residence
990 Prospect Ave.

Noah Webster House
227 S. Main St.
860-521-5362
www.noahwebsterhouse.org

The Pond House Café
1555 Asylum Ave.
860-231-8823
www.pondhousecafe.com

Sarah Whitman Hooker Homestead
1237 New Britain Ave.
860-785-9549
www.sarahwhitmanhooker.org

[Passport Stamp / Signature & Date Here]

Wethersfield

By Amy Northrop Wittorff, Executive Director, Wethersfield Historical Society

The origins of Wethersfield, Connecticut's "most ancient town," can be traced back to 1634 when ten adventurers from Watertown in the Massachusetts Bay Colony began to settle on the meadows of the Connecticut River. In 1649, Wethersfield built and launched the first vessel of the colony's West Indies trade. Locally built vessels traded in ports all along the Atlantic Rim, most notably in trade for the distinctive Wethersfield Red Onion. Wethersfield acquired wealth and influence through this trade through the 18th century.

The town's citizens were leaders in the Revolutionary War. Comte de Rochambeau and George Washington met in Wethersfield and planned the campaign that resulted in the victory at Yorktown. The town sent 193 of its men off to the Civil War.

With the decline of the red onion trade in the early 19th century, Wethersfield developed a strong industry in commercial seed growing and maintained its identity as a small agricultural community. Its location on the trolley and rail lines made Wethersfield one of Hartford's first residential suburbs. The Connecticut State Prison was located on Wethersfield's cove from 1826-1963. It was considered a model of early 19th century prison reform when it was built. By the time it closed in 1963 it was plagued by riots and overcrowding. The bucolic Cove Park now occupies the land where the prison once stood.

Wethersfield embraced historic preservation as early as the 1920s, and today, the Connecticut meadows are preserved, as are the houses in Connecticut's largest historic district encompassing two sq. mi. The Historic District of Old Wethersfield has nearly 200 buildings that were erected before 1850. Many other significant historic sites reside throughout the town.

Interesting Places

Begin your Wethersfield visit at the town's visitor center, the Keeney Memorial Cultural Center and the Wethersfield Museum, operated by the Wethersfield Historical Society. Parking and admission are free, and local museums and businesses are within easy walking distance. The society offers research assistance at its Old Academy Library down the street at 150 Main St. The society's Hurlbut-Dunham House and Cove Warehouse Maritime Museum are open weekends Memorial Day-Columbus Day. The Keeney Center is open year-round, Tues. thru Sat. 10 AM-4 PM and Sun. 1-4 PM. All museums are free.

While at the Keeney Center, pick up a free map of the Wethersfield Heritage Walk, a 3-mile self-guided tour consisting of 22 interpretive markers that highlight points of historical significance throughout Old Wethersfield.

Visit the Webb-Deane-Stevens Museum across the street from the Keeney Center to see four impeccably restored 18th and 19th century houses and a Colonial Revival garden. Open May 1 thru Oct. 31, 1-4 PM, except Tuesdays, 10 AM-4 PM. Open weekends only April and Nov.

First Church of Christ is at the corner of Main and Marsh Streets. Built in 1765, it was known as the

The Keeney Memorial Cultural Center, visitor center for the Town of Wethersfield and home to the Wethersfield Historical Society. Wethersfield Historical Society

NOTES

"church that onions built" since parishioners paid their building tax in ropes of red onions, the town's cash crop at the time. Behind the First Church is the Ancient Burying Ground. Wethersfield Historical Society has a searchable database of burials on its website at wethersfieldhistory.org.

Continue along Marsh St. to Broad St. and stroll on the expansive Broad Street Green, bordered by historic homes and Anderson Farms' seasonal farm stand.

Back on Main Street visit the Old Wethersfield Country Store, the Heirloom Market at Comstock-Ferre, Wethersfield Antiques and Heart of the Country. In fine weather enjoy outdoor dining at several restaurants along Main Street including Lucky Lou's in the historic 1783 Deming-Standish House. Don't forget ice cream at the Main Street Creamery!

The Webb-Deane-Stevens Museum features three 18th century houses on their original sites in the center of Old Wethersfield. (L-R) the 1769 Silas Deane House, the 1789 Isaac Stevens House, and the 1752 Joseph Webb House. Charles Lyle

Wethersfield Academy for the Arts presents workshops, classes and special events.

The Great Meadows Conservation Trust hosts a variety of walking tours, hikes and canoe tours throughout the year. Visit www.gmct.org.

Old Wethersfield hosts a variety of community events throughout the year, including Wethersfield Heritage Weekend on Memorial Day weekend, free outdoor concerts at the Keeney Center on Tuesday evenings in July; "Scarecrows on Main," the Cornfest, Old Wethersfield Craft Fair, Coveside Carnival and the historical society's Old Wethersfield Lantern Light Tours in the fall. The Holidays on Main Street Fair wraps up the year on the first Thursday evening in December.

ADDRESS BOOK

Town Sites
www.wethersfieldct.gov
www.historicwethersfield.org
www.thegreatelm.com

Circa Antiques & Collectibles
422 Main St. • 860-436-5122
www.circaonmain.com

First Church of Christ
Main St. / Marsh St.

Heart of the Country
169 Main St. • 860-257-0366
www.heartofthecountryonline.com

Heirloom Market at Comstock Ferre
263 Main St. • 860-257-2790

Lucky Lou's
222 Main St. • 860-257-0700
www.luckylousbarandgrill.com

Main Street Creamery
271 Main St. • 860-529-0509
www.mainstreetcreamery.com

Memorial Cultural Center
200 Main St.
www.wethersfieldhistory.org

Old Wethersfield Country Store
221 Main St. • 860-436-3782
www.owcsct.com

Webb Deane Stevens Museum
211 Main St. • 860-529-0612
www.webb-deane-stevens.org

Wethersfield Academy for the Arts
431 Hartford Ave. • 860-436-9857
www.wethersfieldarts.org

Wethersfield Historical Society
www.wethersfieldhistory.org

[Passport Stamp / Signature & Date Here]

WINDSOR

By Christine Ermenc, retired Executive Director, Windsor Historical Society and Victoria MacGregor, First Town Downtown

Windsor, Connecticut's oldest English settlement has evolved from a remote frontier outpost established in 1633 on lands occupied by Poquonock, Podunk, Sicaog, and Tunxis indigenous peoples to a diverse, suburban community. Today, the town of Windsor encompasses thirty square miles of fertile land at the juncture of the Connecticut and Farmington Rivers. In the 17th century, its boundaries stretched from Litchfield to Tolland. Over the years, 21 separate "daughter" towns have formed from Windsor, as well as five smaller village centers within town limits: Windsor Center, Poquonock, Rainbow, Hayden Station, and Wilson.

In its earliest years, Windsor was agricultural, with trade becoming a growing part of the town's economy by the 18th century. Abundant clay deposits in Windsor soils supported the development of close to forty flourishing brickyards by the 1830s. In 1889, Edward Terry proved that electricity could be transmitted eleven miles from the Rainbow Power Station to the Hartford Electric Co. power station, showing scientists across the country that electric transmission of long distances was viable for commercial use. The first shade-grown tobacco produced in this country was grown under cheesecloth tents in the village of Poquonock in 1900. The tents blocked direct sunlight and increased humidity, approximating growing conditions of the plants' native Sumatra.

By the early 20th century, increasing numbers of Windsor residents were commuting into Hartford workplaces by streetcar, and its agricultural products found ready markets in the capitol city. But by mid-century, agriculture was waning and fields were left vacant. The town saw an opportunity to attract urban industries along the eastern seaboard hampered from expansion by dense and costly urban land. Windsor's location near two interstate highways and Bradley International Airport has led to the development of a thriving business and industrial district. At the same time, Windsor takes pride in its historic neighborhoods, and its lovely river walks and parks.

INTERESTING PLACES

Windsor Historical Society (WHS). Founded in 1921 with free exhibits on history of Windsor featuring objects from 1633 settlement of Windsor to present. In-house research library open to public including thousands of historic town photos, documents, family records, etc. Walking distance to historic Strong-Howard & Chaffee houses available to tour. Open Wed.-Sat. 11 AM-4 PM. Adults $8, Seniors $6 for house tours and library.

Vintage Radio & Communications Museum of Connecticut. Exhibits on the evolution of radio, telephone, and computer from the 1800s to the 1970s. On-site recreation of a 1940s recording studio. Open Thurs.-Fri. 10 AM-3 PM, Sat. 10 AM-5 PM, Sun. 1-4 PM. Adults $10, Seniors $7.

Northwest Park & Nature Preserve. 473-acre park opened in 1972. Tobacco farmland converted into forests and fields with a nature center, animal barn, picnic area, and 12 miles of hiking trails. Home to the Connecticut Valley Tobacco

Windsor Historical Society's museum & library at 96 Palisado Ave., Windsor. WHS

Notes

Museum. Open to the public from dawn to dusk.

Luddy/Taylor Connecticut Valley Tobacco Museum. Preserving and teaching the history of cigar-tobacco agriculture in Connecticut. Features a tobacco curing barn with exhibits of early and modern equipment and a year-round facility holding archives of photos, writings, documents, etc. Located within Northwest Park & Nature Preserve. Open Wed.-Fri. Noon-4 PM, Sat. 10 AM-4 PM.

Oliver Ellsworth Homestead. Tour home of Oliver Ellsworth, successful CT political figure and one of five men who drafted the Constitution. Complete with furnishings owned by the Ellsworth family. Past guests include Presidents George Washington & John Adams. Open Fri.-Sat. Noon-4 PM. Adults $5.

The 1867 Farmington River Railroad Bridge is just west of Palisado Ave. and north of Pleasant St. It is a perfect example of a stone arch railroad bridge. Melanie Oliveira

Address Book

Town Site
www.townofwindsorct.com

Luddy/Taylor Connecticut Valley Tobacco Museum
135 Lang Rd.
860-285-1888
www.tobaccohistsoc.org

Northwest Park & Nature Preserve
145 Lang Rd.
860-285-1886
www.northwestpark.org

Oliver Ellsworth Homestead
778 Palisado Ave.
860-593-2127
www.ellsworthhomesteaddar.org

Vintage Radio & Communications Museum of Connecticut
115 Pierson Ln.
860-683-2903
www.vrcmct.org

Windsor Historical Society
96 Palisado Ave.
860-688-3813
www.windsorhistoricalsociety.org

[Passport Stamp / Signature & Date Here]

Windsor Locks

By Karen Giannelli, Kimberly Pease and Rose Horan, Windsor Locks Historical Society

Windsor Locks (pop. 12,498 in the 2010 census) is a town of just under 9 and 1/2 sq. mi. on the Connecticut River halfway between Hartford and Springfield, MA.

Pine Meadow (later Windsor Locks) was a part of the original Ancient Windsor settlement. In 1663 Henry Denslow became the first English settler of Pine Meadow. The early English settlers were later joined by Irish immigrants, followed by the French in the 1880s, Italians in 1896, and Polish immigrants at the end of the 19th century. Each group became an integral part of the formation of Windsor Locks.

The first industries of the town included sawmills and gristmills, followed by wool carding, and later paper production. The Dexter Corp. was founded in 1767 and made paper. It remained the oldest corporation on the New York Stock Exchange until it was sold in 2000. In 1857 the town's other paper manufacturer, Persse and Brooks, was rumored to be the largest paper mill in the world.

In May 1827 the construction of the Windsor Locks and Canal began to help move goods north on the Connecticut River, bypassing the rapids. It was a difficult and strenuous project made possible by 400 Irish workers. On Nov. 11, 1829 the canal was finished. In 1833 Pine Meadow changed its name to Windsor Locks, after the newly constructed locks. Windsor Locks was incorporated as a town in 1854.

In the 20th century, Windsor Locks survived massive flooding in 1936 and in the Hurricane of 1938. The dawn of World War II led to the construction of a military airfield which became Bradley International Airport in 1957. During the war the Army Air Force operated a USO Club at the corner of Spring and West Sts. At the end of the war the building was offered for sale for $1.00 and was purchased by Rensselaer Polytechnic Institute and moved to Troy, NY, where it is now the RPI Playhouse. Other notable events include the World Championship of Windsor Lock's 1965 Little League team and the inauguration in the same year of Windsor Locks' daughter, Ella Grasso, as the 83d Governor of Conn., the first female governor in the U.S.

Windsor Locks is justifiably proud of its rich history. We welcome you to explore this history throughout this site.

www.windsorlockshistoricalsociety.org

Places of Interest

The New England Air Museum. An aerospace museum located at Bradley International Airport. It consists of three display hangars and has additional storage-only hangars and a collection of vintage and specialty aircraft.

Windsor Locks Canal State Park Trail. A public recreation area that parallels the Connecticut River for 4.5 mi. between Suffield and Windsor Locks. The old tow path is paved and offers spectacular views of the river and an abundance of wildlife.

The Canal State Park. A refuge area for the American Bald Eagle that nest along the river.

Windsor Locks Historic Train Station. Under renovation.

The 1861 Noden-Reed Barn houses exhibits on farming life, antique sleighs, carriages, farming tools, and horse stalls. James Roche

Notes

Noden-Reed Farm. On land (90 acres) originally purchased by Samuel Denslow in 1759. The farm's last owner, Gladys Reed, bequeathed the remaining 22 acres, the house, and the 1867 brick barn to the town. The house, barn and garage/greenhouse are managed by the Windsor Locks Historical Society with support from the town. This property is the home of the first decorated Christmas tree in New England. The property is also part of the town's park system.

Memorial Hall (1890). It was the quarters for the J.H. Converse Post, No. 67, Grand Army of the Republic, and has served over the years as a center for memorial activities for those who served in all wars. Presently the American Legion occupies the building and gives tours on Sundays. At the corner of Elm St. (Rt. 140) and Main St. (Rt. 159).

The lock at the north end of the Windsor Locks Canal that ended in the late 1840s.
www.traillink.com

Address Book

Town Site
www.windsorlocksct.org

Canal State Park
Canal Rd., Suffield
www.ct.gov/deep

New England Air Museum
36 Perimeter Rd.
860-623-3305
www.neam.org

Noden-Reed Farm
58 West St.
www.windsorlocksct.org

Windsor Locks Historic Train Station
225 Main St.
800-872-7245
www.wltrain.org

[Passport Stamp / Signature & Date Here]

New London County
LEBANON
FRANKLIN
SPRAGUE
LISBON
GRISWOLD
VOLUNTOWN
COLCHESTER
BOZRAH
NORWICH
PRESTON
SALEM
NORTH STONINGTON
MONTVILLE
LEDYARD
LYME
WATERFORD
STONINGTON
EAST LYME
NEW LONDON
GROTON
OLD LYME

CHAPTER 6

NEW LONDON COUNTY

Bozrah

*By Zachary Lamothe, author of **Connecticut Lore and More Connecticut Lore***

The land which would become the Town of Bozrah was originally settled as part of the Nine Mile Square that Uncas, the Sachem of the Mohegan tribe, sold to the English colonists in 1659. This land would eventually be named Norwich. In 1786, the segment called Bozrah was the 86th town admitted into Connecticut. Bozrah is in New London County, NW of Norwich.

While many towns use monikers rooted in either the language of its indigenous peoples or its English settlers, the name Bozrah comes from the Hebrew word for "sheepfold." The Bible mentions the town of Bozrah in current-day Jordan. Legend has it that a judge inquired about the brightly colored garments of a juror and quipped: "Who is this that cometh from Edom, with dyed garments from Bozrah?"

Bozrah's early identity was primarily agrarian, and it still is today. Throughout its history though, Bozrah had pockets of industry grow alongside its pastureland in the villages of Fitchville, Leffingwell, and Bozrahville, which is now Gilman. The Yantic River, Gardner Brook, and Pease Brook supplied the power for the mills.

Fitchville, Bozrah's main village, has the town's only school, town hall, and post office. It was once the site of the Fitchville Mfg. Co. which was purchased by the Palmer Brothers as a quilt manufacturer (1886). Along with the factory, a mill town emerged, including row houses, a dam, a church, and a town hall. Unfortunately, the once stately factory complex fell victim to a series of fires from 1969 to 1972 that destroyed the property.

Today's Bozrah is a sleepy country town with its share of worthwhile places to visit and interesting history to uncover.

Interesting Places

Hopemead State Park. This small, little-known state park is located on Cottage Rd. The main path leads from the road to the banks of Gardner Lake. With a few viewsheds of the lake, guests can launch a canoe, swim, or explore its 60 acres.

Bozrah Farmers Market. This is one of the premier markets in the nation. It features fresh produce and poultry, along with baked goods, dairy farm products, and confections. It is dog-friendly and has musical entertainment. Open on Fridays from July to October, 4-7 PM, the market is located at 45 Bozrah St. at the Maples Farm Park. The park's hiking trails are open year-round.

Bozrah Rural Cemetery. Here are the graves of Jane Maria Johnson and her killer, William Irving. In Victorian Bozrah this daughter of a prominent doctor was not allowed to be in love with an immigrant handyman. Knowing their love could never be, Irving murdered Johnson and soon after, committed suicide. Legend says he is buried standing on his head. His stone details the grisly murder.

Odetah Camping Resort. A well-manicured campground situated on the shore of Fitchville Pond. Enjoy fishing, swimming, and seasonal activities at this family favorite. Odetah also includes a challenging miniature golf course, Knolls and Holes.

The 1742 Bozrah Rural Cemetery where the graves of Jane Maria Johnson and her killer, William Irving are. Jerry Dougherty

Notes

The Bozrah Town Hall (c.1832) was originally owned by mill owner Asa Fitch. It was used as a silk farm plant and then as a recreation center for mill workers. It was acquired by the town in 1949. Zachary Lamothe

Address Book

Town Site
www.townofbozrah.org

Bozrah Farmers Market
45 Bozrah St.
www.bozrahfarmersmarket.org

Bozrah Rural Cemetery
Schwartz Rd.

Hopemead State Park
17-25 Cottage Rd.

Odetah Camping Resort
38 Bozrah St. Extension
800-448-1193
www.odetah.com

[Passport Stamp / Signature & Date Here]

Colchester

By Sheila Tortorigi, Collections Chair, Colchester Historical Society

Colchester is a beautiful inland town situated in New London County, in eastern Connecticut. It is ten miles east of the Connecticut River and twenty miles north of Long Island Sound. The villages of Westchester and North Westchester are within Colchester. The land is generally fertile, gravelly loam, with some places that are rough and stony.

The Town of Colchester was founded in 1698 just north of the present town green. A group of men from Wethersfield obtained authority from the Colony in Hartford to start a new plantation called Jeremy's Farm. One of these men, Nathaniel Foote, purchased land from Uncas, the Sachem of the Mohegan. It is said that Foote traded a few trinkets to the Indians for the land. Foote's grandfather had emigrated from Colchester, England and the English settlers wanted to establish the vision of that town, here in Colchester.

Like many towns in New England, life was centered around farming and the church parish. By 1756 Colchester was one of the most thriving rural towns in the Colony. There were several gristmills and sawmills. Bacon Academy, a higher learning institute, was built in 1802. Many wealthy families sent their children to this fine school. Many graduates went on to important accomplishments and leadership positions. The industrial heyday in Colchester brought many businesses, such as the Hayward Rubber Co. With the industrial growth came the demand for labor and resulted in further population growth.

By 1900 farming had diminished, and factories had closed or burned down. Jewish immigrants began settling in Colchester, seeking a pleasant place to live. Farming families took in Jewish immigrants as boarders to supplement their income. The area quickly became the "Catskills of Connecticut," where tourists came from the cities to relax. The tourist industry boomed throughout the 1930s.

Colchester's Motto is "Where tradition meets tomorrow." The history of Colchester's past is respected while embracing the challenges of changing with the future.

Interesting Places

Colchester History Museum. Housed in the old "Rev. Ballard Homestead," the museum offers two floors of temporary and permanent exhibits featuring the history of Colchester.

Nathan Liverant and Son Antiques & Fine Art. Located in a former Baptist meeting house.

Harry's Place. An open air drive in began in 1925 by Ruby Cohen. Open Mar. thru Oct. it serves up hotdogs, hamburgers and fried seafood.

Recreation Complex. Includes playgrounds for young and older children, a skate park, a splash park, a walking path, picnic and tennis facilities, and several sports fields.

Chanticlair Golf Course. A public 9-hole golf course.

Lions Club Skating Pond. Offers skating in winter.

Ruby & Elizabeth Cohen Woodlands. A 206-acre wooded open space including 2 ponds, a marsh viewing area, streams, hiking trails, a butterfly-pollinator garden, and the Colchester Story Walk

Harry's place has been a favorite tourist attraction for over 90 years.
Harry's Place

NOTES

that provides an opportunity for visitors to walk and read a book to youngsters focused on nature or wildlife.

Air Line Trail State Park. Stretches across eastern Connecticut. This linear trail dates from the 1870s, and today draws walkers, hikers, horseback riders, and bikers. In Colchester there are several access areas including a large parking and information center on Bull Hill Rd. Trail map at www.ct.gov/deep.

Day Pond State Park. A public recreation area covering 180 acres in Westchester. Visitors to the park will find the stone foundations from the colonial era when water from the pond powered the nearby sawmill. Now stocked with trout, Day Pond is an attractive area for fishermen and swimmers. Follow Rt. 149 and turn onto Day Pond Rd.

Salmon River State Forest. Enjoy a day of fishing and a picnic along the Salmon River and visit Comstock Covered Bridge. On Rt. 16 at the East Hampton-Colchester line.

Discover Colchester Walks. The Colchester Land Trust conducts hikes in various locations through town. Visit their website for dates and location.

Craigin Memorial Library. The original neo-classic 1905 building was expanded in 2002. It is a public library and technology center.

Colchester History Museum. Sheila Tortorigi

ADDRESS BOOK

Town Site
www.colchesterct.gov

Chanticlair Golf Course
288 Old Hebron Rd.
www.chanticlair.com

Colchester Community Theatre
www.colchestercommunitytheatre.com

Colchester History Museum
24 Linwood Ave.
www.colchesterhistory.org

Colchester Land Trust
www.colchesterlandtrust.org

Craigin Memorial Library
8 Linwood Ave.
860-537-5752

Day Pond State Park
Rt. 149

Harry's Place
104 Broadway St.
860-537-2410
www.harrysplaceburgers.com

Lions Club Skating Pond
292 Halls Hill Rd.

Nathan Liverant and Son Antiques & Fine Art
168 South Main St.
www.liverantantiques.com

Recreation Complex
215 Old Hebron Rd.

Ruby & Elizabeth Cohen Woodlands
96 McDonald Rd.

[Passport Stamp / Signature & Date Here]

East Lyme

By Elizabeth Hall Kuchta, East Lyme Town Historian

Along Long Island Sound and Niantic Bay is the Town of East Lyme. It was first settled in the mid-1600s. In 1719 it became the Second or East Society of Lyme and incorporated as a town in 1839. East Lyme has two villages, Flanders in the northern part and Niantic along the coast. The town covers 34.8 sq. mi. and rises from sea level to almost 500 feet in the north. Interstate 95 passes through the northern part of town and runs almost parallel with the Boston Post Road (Rt. 1).

The Nehantic Indians were the first inhabitants of the area dating back over 5,000 years. They spent the summer along the shore and in winter moved to longhouses in the hills. The tribe was split with the arrival of the Pequots around 1600 with some moving to Rhode Island to live with the Narragansetts. Later with the arrival of the Mohegans, many married into that group. In 1880 the tribe was declared extinct, though there are still many who have descended from the Nehantics.

The northern section of town along the Boston Post Road was first to be developed. Farms were set up and streams were dammed for sawmills and gristmills. Later several mills for fulling wool, making cotton rope, and wicking and wood turning were established. The area was named Flanders in honor of the woolen industry in Flanders, Belgium.

In the early 1800s shipyards were set up along the Niantic River and by the 1840s there was a fleet of over 40 schooners and sloops sailing to "George's Banks." The many lakes in town were iced and the ice blocks taken to a wharf on the bay to be shipped to the New York fish market. There is an abundance of granite in the hills and by 1815 the first quarry was started. These quarries sent stone to be used in many buildings and monuments along the east coast.

In 1851 the railroad was constructed along the shoreline and people began to settle that part of town which came to be called Niantic. Travelers on the trains noticed the area and began building summer homes on the land jutting into the Sound. These areas of town continue to have many summer-only residences.

Interesting Places

There are many attractions which bring people to visit our town. Both areas have many shops and fine restaurants. Marinas, boat launches, and charter fishing boats are located along the river. There are three historic houses which are open to the public. Memorial Day-Labor Day.

Thomas Lee House (1660). One of the oldest wood frame homes in Connecticut in its primitive state.

Samuel Smith Farmstead (1685). Outstanding example of a simple colonial-era farmstead.

Thomas Avery House (1845), Brookside Farm Museum. Greek Revival home and grounds showcasing family and agricultural life 1840 to mid-20th century.

Book Barn. Has four separate stores with over 500,000 books. Open every day from 9 AM-9 PM.

Children's Museum of Southeastern CT. A great place for kids to have fun and learn. Tues.-Sat. 9:30 AM-4:30 PM. Sun. Noon-4:30 PM.

The 1660 Thomas Lee House is operated by the Niantic Historical Society. Elizabeth Hall

Notes

Niantic Bay Boardwalk. A 1.3-mile boardwalk along Niantic Bay that is a favorite spot for walking and viewing the Sound. Entrance at Cini Memorial Park, Rt. 156 just before the Niantic River Bridge, Niantic.

Oswegatchie Hills Nature Preserve. Contains 457 acres with 7 miles of trails. Three miles pass through an abandoned pink granite quarry. The Preserve overlooks the environmentally fragile Niantic River to the east. It was officially opened in 2007.

Nehantic State Forest. In the towns of East Lyme, Salem, and Lyme. Activities include hunting, hiking, fishing and picnics.

Rocky Neck State Park. Offers swimming, hiking, and camping. 3 miles west of Niantic. (Exit 72 from I-95).

Niantic River. A great place to kayak.

Randi White has been operating the Book Barn for over 30 years in Niantic where he has four stores and many outside book shelves and small buildings with books neatly organized according to topics. Podskoch

Address Book

Town Sites
www.eltownhall.com
www.discovereastlyme.com

Book Barn
41 W. Main St., Niantic
607-739-5715
www.bookbarnniantic.com

Brookside Farm Museum
33 Society Rd.
860-739-0761

Children's Museum of Southeastern Connecticut
409 Main St., Niantic
860-691-1111
www.childrensmuseumsect.org

Oswegatchie Hills Nature Preserve
www.oswhills.org

Rocky Neck State Park
244 W. Main St., Niantic

Samuel Smith Farmstead
82 Plants Dam Rd.
www.samuelsmithfarmstead.org

Thomas Lee House
Giant's Neck Rd. & Rt. 156, Niantic
860-739-6070
www.eastlymehistoricalsociety.org

[Passport Stamp / Signature & Date Here]

Franklin

By Zachary Lamothe, author of ***Connecticut Lore*** *and* ***More Connecticut Lore***

In 1659 the land that would eventually be known as the town of Franklin was purchased from Mohegan Sachem, Uncas, by colonists from Old Saybrook as part of the Nine Mile Square which would become the towns of Norwich, Bozrah, Franklin, Sprague, and Lisbon. The first white settler to come to Franklin was John Ayer, in 1663. His descendants still live in town. Franklin was known as the West Farms section of Norwich. In 1716, West Farms was granted its own Ecclesiastical Society with its first Congregational Church built two years later. The church became the focal point of this small agrarian community, and it continues to be prominent in Franklin today. The Ecclesiastical Society governed the town until 1945. The town was incorporated as Franklin, named for Benjamin Franklin, in 1786.

Throughout its settled history, Franklin has maintained its rural identity with much of the town being used as farmland. Along with its pastoral setting, Franklin also has vast swaths of woodland, some accessible to the public in parks that include Ayer's Gap and the Franklin Wildlife Management Area. Stone walls that meander through the dense forest acknowledge how nature has reclaimed this once deforested countryside.

Since the nearby towns of Norwich and Willimantic (part of Windham) grew into centers of commerce and industry, Franklin was mostly known for the highway, Rt. 32, cutting through it, the shortest route between the two urban centers. Franklin's terrain is punctuated by its sloping hillsides; the town is comprised of seven hills.

Interesting Places

Blue Slope Farm and Country Museum. This working farm welcomes visitors and includes a museum with a collection of tools and farm equipment that were used in colonial America, as well as barnyard animals and seasonal hay and sleigh rides.

Ashbel Woodward House Museum (1835). A Greek Revival home dedicated to Franklin's heritage.

Ayer's Gap/Bailey's Ravine. A serene setting for a wooded hike up a steep hillside that offers the visitor views of waterfalls, dramatic cliffs, and fine panoramas of the adjacent countryside. The trail can be accessed at 291 Pond Rd. (Rt. 207).

Modesto's. Some say Norwich's best restaurant is actually in Franklin! Modesto's specializes in Italian and Mexican cuisine. It is a comfortable, but classy, establishment with unforgettable dishes that make this dining locale worthy of repeated visits.

The Victorian House. An antique store whose wares are spread throughout the rooms of an old Victorian abode. From furniture to comic books and vinyl records, this second-hand institution is always a treat to rummage through..

Hop-Bee Honey. When locally made honey is combined with hops, which are traditionally used for brewing beer, the result is hop-bee honey. Made here in Franklin and sold in area shops, the honey

The 1718 Congregational Church in Franklin. Zachary Lamothe

Notes

pairs perfectly with savory foods and cheese plates.

Notable Person

Lafayette Foster. (1806-1880) Born in Franklin, he was a teacher, a lawyer a politician, and a judge. He was a US Senator (1855-1867) and President pro tempore of the Senate (1865-1867). After the assassination of President Lincoln in 1865 Foster was next in line to be President.

The Blue Slope Country Museum Inc. is dedicated to preserving farming & country-life artifacts on a 380-acre 4th-generation New England dairy farm. Zachary Lamothe

Address Book

Town Site
www.franklinct.com

Ashbel Woodward House Museum
387 Rt. 32, North Franklin

Blue Slope Farm and Country Museum
138 Blue Hill Rd.
860-460-9877
www.blueslope.com

Hop-Bee Honey
34 Audette Rd., North Franklin
/BeeKeeperChris

Modesto's Restaurant
10 Rt. 32, North Franklin
860-887-7755
www.modestosrestaurant.org

The Victorian House
7 Baltic Rd. (corner Rt. 32)

[Passport Stamp / Signature & Date Here]

Griswold

By Betsy Foy and Mary Rose Deveau, members of Griswold Historical Society

The Town of Griswold, incorporated in 1815, was named after Governor Roger Griswold. Jewett City was incorporated as a borough of Griswold in 1895. Griswold also contains the villages of Pachaug, Glasgo, Hopeville, Rixtown, and Doaneville.

In the early days the Pachaug and Quinbaug rivers enticed the Mohegan and Pequot tribes to establish fishing grounds. In the mid-1600s the abundant waterways attracted settlers into the town which at that time was the northern part of Preston. Cornmills and sawmills were built as well as textiles industries. In 1771 Eliezer Jewett opened several mills and an irrigation plant. His success led to the area being called Jewett City. In 1809 John and Lafayette Tibbits started the Jewett City Cotton Mfg. Co. However, the company struggled and was sold to Samuel Slater and his brother, John. The mill name was changed to the Slater Co. The following year John Slater, along with his son John Fox Slater, introduced many mechanical improvements. At this time, Hopeville was developing into a thriving industrial town with mills, houses, and a church. In 1711 Stephen Gates opened the first gristmill and later added a sawmill. In 1818 Elizah Abel added a woolen mill in the area. John Slater realized the potential of Hopeville and purchased three established mills. He also constructed a new satinette fabric (cotton-wool combination) mill. He named this new mill, the "Hope Mill," as he was hopeful the new fabric would be accepted. Soon the village, pond, and eventually the state park, all had the name Hopeville derived from Slater's inspiration.

Many fires developed in the Hopeville region from the late 1880s to the early 1900s and slowly most of the buildings and mills were destroyed. Hopeville State Park is approx. ½ mile from the site of the lost village of Hopeville. In the 1930s the Civilian Conservation Corps constructed the state park. The CCC also rehabilitated the Avery house that was built in 1771. Records show one early inhabitant of the house was Captain J. Avery (c.1854). It is on the National Register of Historic Places. The house is presently known as the Hopeville Pond Park House. In 1806 Glasgo Village was named for Isaac Glasko (1776-1861), a man of mixed Native American and African American heritage. He harnessed the water power and established a blacksmith shop producing farm and carpentry tools. Glasko specialized in whaling implements. He was awarded several patents on harpoons, spades, and mining knives and was well-known in the ports of New England. Being a wealthy man, he took the opportunity to send his daughter, Eliza, to the Prudence Crandall School for Negro Girls in Canterbury (now a historic house museum).

The Jewett City Savings Bank, built in 1930, has recently been renovated and upgraded to a modern, open-concept financial institution. A recent beautification project has made Jewett City's Main Street a picture of bright lights and country charm. Jewett City's retail area has many amenities: a hardware store, restaurants, historic churches, banks, and quaint shops.

Places of Interest

Hopeville Pond State Park. 554-acre park; 80 sites for seasonal camping, swimming, biking, hiking (Nehantic Trail), fishing, and ballfield.

The beautiful Griswold Veterans Memorial Park was built on the site of the former Ashland Mill complex, which was destroyed by fire in March 1995. Betsy Foy

Notes

Address Book

Town Site
www.griswold-ct.org

Griswold Historical Society Museum
26 Main St., Jewett City
www.thelastgreenvalley.org

Hopeville Pond State Park
929 Hopeville Rd.
www.ct.gov/deep

Slater Memorial Library
26 Main St., Jewett City
860-376-0024

Slater Memorial Library. Romanesque Revival building constructed in 1884 with funds from John Fox Slater. In 1930 it doubled in size with an addition of the Fanning Annex, funded by a local businessman (and financial genius) David Hale Fanning.

Griswold Historical Society (GHS) Museum. Located on the second floor of the Slater Memorial Library. Items illustrate life in New England during the 18th and 19th centuries, highlighting many Griswold historical events. Exhibits are themed around a farmer's workshop, a kitchen, school, and children's playthings. Open seasonally from Mar.-Nov.

Ashland Mill Bridge and Veterans Memorial Park. The bridge (1886) was originally a lenticular pony-truss bridge serving the millyard of the Ashland Cotton Co. The Ashland Mill was destroyed by fire in 1995 and the bridge was replaced in 1999. Veterans Memorial Park (1999) was built on the site of the former Ashland Mill Complex. The park has a cannon, gazebo, a short track for walking, and a beautiful waterfall on Ashland Pond.

Hopeville Pond was formed by impounding the Pachaug River. The area was a major fishing ground for the Mohegans. At low water the stone weirs, constructed by the Indians at angles from the river banks, are visible. Today the area is a state park. DEEP

[Passport Stamp / Signature & Date Here]

Groton

By Judy Kelmelis, Reference Librarian, Groton Public Library

Nestled between the Thames and Mystic rivers in SE Connecticut the Town of Groton was originally part of New London. John Winthrop Jr., son of the governor of Massachusetts, was instrumental in its formation and named the new town after his birthplace in England. It was incorporated in 1705. Early attempts at farming were defeated by the rocky soil.

In 1723 the people turned to shipbuilding for trading among the colonies and the Caribbean. The village of Mystic was the busiest part of the town. In Groton 32 vessels were built from 1784 to 1800. After the Revolutionary War, Groton re-established its commercial activities. Shipbuilders began to build ships again. Groton built 28 more ships from 1800 to 1807.

General Benedict Arnold, a Norwich native, sailed into Groton and on Sept. 6, 1781 started the Battle of Groton Heights at Fort Griswold against Lt. Col. William Ledyard and his small militia. Colonel Ledyard and over 100 soldiers perished in the battle and the massacre was a notorious tragedy in state history. A monument was erected on the battlefield in 1830 from native Groton stone and Fort Griswold became a state park in 1902.

After the War of 1812 Groton sailors turned to harvesting seals and then whales. After the discovery of gold in California in 1849 faster ships were needed to travel with supplies and miners. The result was the building of clipper ships in Groton.

Morton Freeman Plant, a local financier and philanthropist, built Branford House as his summer home in 1902 at Avery Point. It was designed by his wife and built by Robert W. Gibson at a cost of three million dollars. The estate was used for agriculture through the 1930s and then passed to the U.S. Coast Guard. Today, UConn's Avery Point campus is located there.

While the whaling industry brought much work to Groton, ship manufacturing evolved. During WWI, the Groton Iron Works Co. built cargo ships for the U.S. Shipping Board. The first submarine was built in Groton in 1929. The launch of the Cuttlefish, the first submarine to have a welded hull was also the first contract with the U.S. Navy in 1933.

By 1942, the U.S. Navy and General Dynamics Electric Boat Co. purchased the land for the construction of submarines. On Jan. 21, 1954 the USS Nautilus, the world's first nuclear submarine, was launched.

There is rich history and interesting places to explore in Groton. Its 45.3 sq. mi. contains three state parks, six museums, and a golf course.

Interesting Places

Haley Farm State Park. A public recreation area that preserves Colonial-era farmland as open space. The park's 267-acres are connected to the Bluff Point State Park (Depot Rd.) by way of a pedestrian bridge over railroad tracks. Park activities include bicycling and walking. Directions: Rt. 215 south to Brook St. to the 1st right to Haley Farm Lane.

Fort Griswold State Park. A former American defensive fortification

The Branford House, originally a 31-room mansion that rivaled those in Newport, cost three million dollars in 1903. Today it is part of the UConn campus at Avery Point and is rented for weddings. Groton Public Library collection

Notes

named after Deputy Governor Matthew Griswold.

U.S. Navy Submarine Force and Museum. Managed exclusively by the Naval History & Heritage Command division of the U.S. Navy, a repository for many special submarine items of national significance, including the USS Nautilus (SSN-571).

Avery-Copp House. Built c.1800 on the banks of the Thames River. The house passed from generation to generation of the same family, and is a wonderful time capsule of local history.

Branford House Museum. On UConn Avery Point Campus.

Shennecossett Golf Course. An 18-hole municipal course.

Take a free inside tour of the Nautilus, the first U.S. atomic submarine. There is also free admission to the adjacent Submarine Force Library and Museum, a great place to learn about the history of submarines in the U.S.
Jerry Dougherty

Address Book

Town Site
www.groton-ct.gov

Avery-Copp House
154 Thames St.
860-445-1637
www.averycopphouse.org

Branford House Museum
1084 Shennecossett Rd.
860-405-9000
www.averypoint.uconn.edu

Fort Griswold State Park
Park Ave. & Monument St.
860-449-6877
www.fortgriswold.org

Shennecossett Golf Course
93 Plant St.
860-448-1867
/ShennyGolf

Sift Bake Shop
5 Water St., Mystic
860-245-0541
www.siftbakeshopmystic.com

U.S. Navy Submarine Force and Museum
1 Crystal Lake Rd.
800-343-0079
www.ussnautilus.org

[Passport Stamp / Signature & Date Here]

Lebanon

By Grace Preli, (future) Town Historian!

Lebanon is in eastern Connecticut directly south of Willimantic and northwest of Norwich.

Lebanon is a step back in time. The town surrounds the famed mile-long green, the longest in the country and the only one still used for agricultural purposes. The town center isn't one of bustling commerce, instead it is a single blinking traffic light, a slow moving tractor laden with hay bales, and friends and neighbors calling out "hello's" as they meet for an evening walk. The farmland and open fields pay homage to a rich agricultural community while the homes and environs evoke Lebanon's storied Revolutionary beginnings. It is a place with a slower pace.

The town, named after the country Lebanon for the large cedar forests, was originally known by the Mohegan people as Poquechaneed. Lebanon was incorporated after several grants and purchases by, among others, Maj. John Mason and Reverend James Fitch in 1700. Lebanon earned its nickname "The Heartbeat of the Revolution" for its important part in the Revolutionary War. Jonathan Trumbull, one of George Washington's chief quartermasters, ran Connecticut's war effort from the War Office on the Green. His son-in-law William Williams was one of the signers of the Declaration of Independence. Trumbull's three sons were instrumental in the wartime efforts: Joseph was a colonel in the army, Johnathan Jr. was a secretary to George Washington, and John was Washington's personal aide.

The Revolutionary past can be seen in many of the homes which still surround the green. The Historical Society Museum and Visitor's Center on Trumbull Highway is an excellent place to start. Many of the historic homes have been preserved and are open for visitors throughout the year. Information can be found online at either the Museum or Town Hall website.

There are over 100 farms in Lebanon and 14 of them are among the 70 farms preserved with the CT Farmland Trust. To learn about or support the town's farmers visit the weekly (Saturdays, June-October) Farmers Market (at the Lebanon Town Hall, 579 Exeter Rd.) or one of the many road side farm-stands, including West Green Farm, Bluebird Hill Farm, and Sweet Acre Farm. Take a yoga class on the Green during summer months, or attend one of the many events for youngsters and adults alike at the new library located at 580 Exeter Rd.

Annual events include the Dance Fest, a picnic-celebration around the Fourth of July, and a monthly concert on the third Wednesday evening of each summer month. The earliest agricultural fair of the season is held in Lebanon the second weekend of August and the Antiques Show and Book Sale are held the last Saturday of September on the Green. The Christmas Tree lighting, the first Sunday of December, is another great time to feel the spirit of the town.

The beauty of Lebanon is best felt while walking or biking down dirt roads, around the Green or through one of the trail systems. There are 7.5 miles of the Airline Trail in the west part of town and eight miles of mountain biking trails in Moween State Park on the shores of Red Cedar Lake. Swimming isn't allowed in any of the lakes but Lake Williams or Savin Pond are great places to launch a kayak or indulge in an afternoon picnic. For a real treat, visit one of the favorite local sunset spots: on Bogg Lane, near the

The Lebanon Historical Society Museum, Beaumont House (L) and Visitors Center (R) on the Green in the center of town is where visitors can explore Connecticut's Revolutionary past and the town's history. It features hands-on room, exhibits, genealogy library, and gift shop. Grace Preli

Notes

intersection with Chappell Road, or off Rt. 289 on Village Hill Road, looking west over the corn fields.

Interesting Places

There are many historical homes surrounding the green that are open seasonally to visitors. They include the Governor Jonathan Trumbull House, birthplace of John Trumbull, "America's Patriot Artist" now owned and maintained by the CT Daughters of the American Revolution. The Wadsworth Stable, located next to the Jonathan Trumbull House was moved to Lebanon from Hartford in 1954. Jeremiah Wadsworth was a close friend of the Trumbull's and served as commissary general of the Continental Army and also helped supply the French troops, who camped on the green during the Revolutionary War.

Dr. William Beaumont, considered the "Father of Gastric Physiology" published a book in 1833 describing digestion. His home is now a museum, exhibiting 19th century medical instruments and a recreated doctor's examining room. It is on the Lebanon Historical Society campus. Grace Preli

The War Office on the Green, the center of defense and provisions and the meeting place of the Council of Safety during the Revolutionary War, is owned by the Sons of the American Revolution. It is here that more than 500 meetings of the Council took place. Meetings were attended by leaders such as George Washington, General Henry Knox, General Rochambeau the French commander, and the Marquis de Lafayette.

The Jonathan Trumbull Jr. House, located on the other side of the Green was home to General George Washington's secretary during the Revolutionary War and the place where George Washington himself spent the night of March 4, 1781. It is maintained and owned by the Town of Lebanon and is open for visitors in the summer months.

The Dr. William Beaumont House is located behind the Lebanon Historical Society Museum. Dr. William Beaumont is considered the "Father of Gastric Physiology" and his book, "Experiments and Observations on the Gastric Juice and the Physiology of Digestion" published in 1833, is still used today.

Address Book

Town Sites
www.lebanonct.gov
www.lebanontownhall.org

Dr. William Beaumont House
856 Trumbull Hwy. (Rt. 87)
860-642-6579

The Green Market
199 West Town St.
860-468-0323

Gov. Jonathan Trumbull House and Wadsworth Stable
169 West Town St.
860-642-7558
www.govtrumbullhousedar.org

Jonathan Trumbull Jr. House Museum
780 Trumbull Hwy. (Rt. 87)
860-642-6100

Kalamatos Family Pizza
385 Beaumont Hwy.
860-423-1211

Lebanon Historical Society Museum and Visitor's Center
856 Trumbull Hwy. (Rt. 87)
860-642-6579
www.historyoflebanon.org

Lebanon Green Vineyards
589 Exeter Rd.
860-222-4644
lebanongreenvineyards.wordpress.com

The Log Cabin Restaurant
383 Trumbull Hwy. (Rt. 87)
860-456-7663
www.logcabinct.com

The War Office on the Green
149 West Town St.
860-334-2858
www.connecticutsar.org

[Passport Stamp / Signature & Date Here]

Ledyard

By Kit Foster, President, Ledyard Historical Society

The Town of Ledyard was created on June 1, 1836. Originally part of its southern neighbor Groton, its citizens had created a separate Ecclesiastical Society in 1727, citing "extreme difficulties" in attending church because of a "lack of horses" and distance from the meeting house. Rather than becoming "North Groton" at the full separation, they memorialized Col. William Ledyard, martyred as he led a 150-man brigade protecting Fort Griswold against British forces led by Norwich native Benedict Arnold on Sept. 6, 1781.

A meeting house had been constructed at the geographic center of the new 40-square-mile Society. Settlements had sprung up on the western boundary, the shores of the Thames River, where a trading post was established at Allyn's Point. In 1740 Ralph Stoddard and John Hurlbutt were chartered to operate a ferry to Montville. The surrounding community took its name, Gales Ferry, from a subsequent ferryman. As a portal to the wider world, the village attracted residents involved with whaling and ocean shipping.

In June 1813, Commodore Stephen Decatur, blockaded by British warships, retreated with his small squadron to New London Harbor. He sailed the ships up the Thames to Gales Ferry, where he off-loaded armaments and established fortifications on Allyn's Mountain. Over the following winter he remained in town, teaching navigation before escaping to New York over land. Today the hill is locally known as "Mount Decatur."

Since 1878, Gales Ferry has been home to the Harvard-Yale Regatta, the country's oldest intercollegiate athletic event. Both universities established boat houses and training camps for oarsmen and the event continues today, one weekend each spring on a unique four-mile course on the Thames.

Seafaring aside, the major livelihood remained agriculture. As road transportation improved, local farming became less important. Dow Chemical Co. opened a plant at Allyn's Point in 1952. Rapid expansion of submarine construction at Groton and increased staffing at the adjacent Naval Submarine Base saw Ledyard's population rise dramatically in the 1960s, accompanied by several housing developments.

Today, Ledyard is home to 15,000 people, with four elementary schools, a middle school and a high school. Town government is a mayor-council system, which succeeded the traditional Board of Selectmen in 1971. The Dow operations have greatly downsized, even as massive development of Native American resort casinos, both in Ledyard and neighboring Montville, have transformed the regional economy and workforce.

Interesting Places

Nathan Lester House (1793) and Farm Tool Museum. Operated by the Historic District Commission and Ledyard Historical Society. Open Memorial Day to Labor Day, from 2-4 PM on Tues. and Thurs and 1-4:30 PM on Sat. and Sun.

Ledyard Oak. Once the second largest oak tree in the state, it succumbed to gypsy moth defoliation in the 1960s but still takes pride of place on the Town Seal. A new oak was planted next to the site of the original. Located

The 1793 Nathan Lester House and Farm is the home of the Tool Museum housing a collection of artifacts belonging to the Ledyard Historical Society. Kit Foster

Notes

at the Lester House property.

Up-Down Sawmill. Unique water-powered sawmill that operates in spring and fall during sufficient water flow. There is also a working blacksmith shop at the site. Open Sat. 1-4 PM from April to May and Oct. to Nov.

Pequot Museum & Research Center. It interprets the Mashantucket Pequot Native American history. Open Wed-Sat. 9 AM-5 PM. In November open Tues.-Sat. from 9 AM-5 PM. It is adjacent to the tribe's Foxwoods Resort Casino, renowned for gaming, entertainment, shopping and dining.

The historic water-powered Ledyard Up-Down Sawmill is on Lee's Brook. It was restored in the 1970s and staffed by volunteers. Sawing demonstrations are on Saturday afternoons in the spring and fall. Kit Foster

Address Book

Town Site
www.ledyardct.org

Foxwoods Resort Casino
350 Trolley Line Blvd.
860-312-3000
www.foxwoods.com

Ledyard Oak
153 Vinegar Hill Rd., Gales Ferry

Ledyard Up-Down Sawmill
172 Iron St. (Rt. 214)
www.ledyardsawmill.org

Nathan Lester House
153 Vinegar Hill Rd., Gales Ferry
860-464-2040
www.ledyardhistory.org

Pequot Museum & Research Center
110 Pequot Tr., Mashantucket
800-411-9671
www.pequotmuseum.org

[Passport Stamp / Signature & Date Here]

Lisbon

By Kenneth E. Mahler, Lisbon Historical Society

The Town of Lisbon was formed from Norwich and incorporated in 1786. It is a 16.26 sq. mi. rural historic community (pop. 4,356 2020 census) in New London Co. Lisbon is approx. 7 miles northeast of downtown Norwich and sits at the crotch of the Quinebaug and Shetucket Rivers in a National Heritage Corridor known as "The Last Green Valley." Lisbon is bordered to the north by Canterbury, to the west by Sprague, and to the east by Jewett City and Griswold.

Jabez and Joseph Perkins bought land in a section of Norwich (c. late 1600s) and named it Newent after their town in England. They were merchants whose ships sailed to Europe, and the town got its name from the port of Lisbon, Portugal where the Perkins brothers traded. The first settlers were 16 people who arrived in Newent in 1716.

By the 1800s, Lisbon's economic base included agriculture as well as wool and silk factories. In 1837, the Norwich-Worcester Railroad cut a tunnel through a hilly section of town along the Quinebaug River. It is the oldest fully active U.S. railroad tunnel.

Lisbon's recreation and historic sites, bucolic setting, shopping and dining offer visitors opportunities to explore, shop, or just relax and enjoy.

Notable Person

Ebenezer Tracy. A Revolutionary War craftsman known for making Windsor chairs that are prized by collectors and museums.

Interesting Places

Scenic Road Rt. 169. In 1991, Congress designated 32.10 mi. of road as scenic. It begins at the Norwich line, travels through Lisbon, and ends at the Massachusetts border. This "scenic road" is well known for its spectacular year-round views.

Andrew Clark House (1740). On the National Register of Historic Places.

Anshei Israel Synagogue (1936). The synagogue's 15 founding families were immigrants from Russia and Poland who lived in Lisbon and nearby towns. More immigrants from eastern Europe joined the congregation at the beginning of World War II. The synagogue was abandoned in the late 1980s, and in 1999 was donated to the town. It is leased and maintained by the Lisbon Historical Society, and is on the National Register of Historic Places.

Lathrop-Mathewson-Ross House (1761). On the National Register of Historic Places. Ross Hill Rd.

John Bishop House Museum (1810). The Federalist-style house is on the state register, and was part of a much larger piece of farm property. It was taken over by the town in the mid-1980s. It is restored and is leased and maintained by the Lisbon Historical Society. Open for tours June till late Sept. 10 AM-2 PM.

John Palmer House. A restored Cape Cod, colonial farmhouse. Former home of John Palmer, a preacher and a "Separatist" leader of the "Great Awakening" period.

The Captain Burnham Tavern (c.1760). This stagecoach tavern had 127 acres on the Norwich-Woodstock turnpike of old, served until the late 1830s when the introduction of the railroad caused it to be used as a farm. Then the Town of Lisbon purchased it and continues to lease it for farming. The tavern building is undergoing restoration, and has been nominated as a candidate for the National Register.

Taft Tunnel (1837). Oldest active railroad tunnel in America. It serves the main line of the Providence and Worcester Railroad from Worcester to New London and west.

Notes

Newent Congregational Church (1723).

Boat Launch. A public access launch to the Shetucket River for boating and fishing.

Lisbon Meadows Park. Has 59 acres. Includes baseball and soccer fields, a tennis court, walking trails, and accommodations for picnics and small gatherings.

Shopping Malls. Lisbon Landing and Crossing at Lisbon are both on River Rd. (Rt. 12).

Places To Eat. Panera Bread, Just Breakfast and Things, Green Onion Lisbon Pizza.

The John Bishop House Museum (1810) is maintained by the Lisbon Historical Society. Ken Mahler

Address Book

Town Site
www.lisbonct.com

Andrew Clark House
45 Ross Hill Rd.

Anshei Israel Synagogue
142 Newent Rd.

The Captain Burnham Tavern
223 N. Burnham Hwy.

Green Onion Lisbon Pizza
10 River Rd. (Rt. 12)
860-376-3817
www.greenonionlisbon.com

John Bishop House Museum
11 S. Burnham Hwy.
www.lisbonct.com

John Palmer House
291 N. Burnham Hwy

Just Breakfast and Things
13 River Rd.
860-376-4040
/JustBreakfastAndThings

Lisbon Historical Society
www.lisbonhistoricalct.org

Lisbon Meadows Park
39 S. Burnham Hwy.

Newent Congregational Church
12 S. Burnham Hwy.

Panera Bread
160 River Rd.
860-376-9100

[Passport Stamp / Signature & Date Here]

Lyme

By Douglas Nielson, local historian

Lyme is noted for its rural character, and for preserving its agricultural heritage and open space; about half of the town is protected open space. Lyme's land trust recently celebrated its 50th year.

What is now the town of Lyme was originally the Third (or North) Society of the town now known as Old Lyme, which was settled in the mid-seventeenth century, mostly by families from Saybrook Colony. As the settlers spread out, they started settling in Bill Hill, Brockway Ferry, Ely's Ferry, the Sterling City area, Reed's Landing (now the village of Hamburg), Hadlyme (where the ferry still runs), and Joshuatown, an area that was ceded to settlers by Joshua, also known as Attawanhood, who was a son of Uncas, the Mohegan sachem.

The ferries crossing the Connecticut River aided in commerce and communication, and farming, logging, shipbuilding, and milling also provided livelihoods. Early water-powered mills were mostly sawmills, but in the late eighteenth century other types of mills were built, such as gristmills for grinding grain, and fulling and carding mills for processing textiles. Many mills remained active, in one capacity or another, into the 1940s. Sterling City, now a quiet residential area, was a particularly busy manufacturing center.

In 1855, Lyme separated from its southern portion, which became known as Old Lyme.

Many historic buildings can be found in Lyme, and many picturesque old houses can be seen on the back roads. There are almost 50 pre-Revolutionary houses, and over 100 built by 1850. Lyme's churches include: Grassy Hill Congregational Church, built in 1812; Lyme Congregational Church in Hamburg, built in 1814; and the former Baptist Church (1862), which now houses Lyme's town offices.

Places to Visit

Nehantic State Forest. Beautiful park includes two large lakes, each with a boat launch, picnic areas, and miles of trails. Rt. 156, just south of Hamburg.

The Lyme Town Hall, in the former Baptist Church, is at 480 Hamburg Rd. (Rt. 156). Jerry Dougherty

The Chester-Hadlyme ferry leaving the Chester dock on its way to Hadlyme. This seasonal ferry has been crossing the Connecticut River since 1769. It is the second oldest continuously operating ferry service in the state and is a state historical landmark. Lydia Roloff

Notes

Lyme Land Conservation Trust. Now in its 50th year, the Land Trust maintains trails in many different habitats throughout town.

Lyme Town Hall. In the historic former Baptist Church, paintings by local American Impressionists and other artists can be found here.

Hadlyme Ferry Historic District. Historic district contains several houses dating from 1820 and before.Don't miss an opportunity to ride the ferry across the Connecticut River, with views of Gillette Castle.

H. L. Reynolds Store. Known locally as "Jane's Store," this general store and landmark has been in business at this location since the mid-1800s.

In 1905 Luther Brockway started a small country market in the heart of Hadlyme not far from the ferry. In 2013 it was restored and opened as the Country Market, serving signature sandwiches, salads, soups, croissants, cookies, and coffee.
Kira Roloff

Address Book

Town Site
www.townlyme.org

The Country Market
1 Ferry Rd., Hadlyme
860-526-3188
www.hadlymecountrymarket.com

Hadlyme Ferry Historic District
Ferry Rd., Hadlyme

H. L. Reynolds Store
264 Hamburg Rd. (Rt. 156), Hamburg
860-434-2494

Lyme Land Conservation Trust
www.lymelandtrust.org

Lyme Town Hall
Rt. 156

[Passport Stamp / Signature & Date Here]

MONTVILLE

By Greg Wismar, Heritage Villager and Montville Mayor Ronald K. McDaniel

Located halfway between New York and Boston, Montville sits on tribal lands in the northeastern corner of the township. The site of the Mohegan Sun Casino, Montville is a place well worth visiting in its own right.

Although Native Americans had long been present in the coastal area of Connecticut, the Mohegans arrived just a short while before the first English colonists came to the area. Associated with the Pequot group, the Mohegans had been living in what is now upstate New York. They settled into an agricultural existence along the banks of the Thames River under the leadership of their Sachems, most notably the leader Uncas. Perhaps because they also were relative newcomers, the Mohegans were welcoming to the initial English colonists as they arrived. Forging an alliance with the new white settlers proved to be ultimately beneficial to the Mohegan people. In 1645, Narragansett warriors from what is now Rhode Island came west and surrounded the Mohegan village of Shantok, attempting to starve the villagers into submission. Under cover of night, Uncas sent an emissary to the English settlement at Saybrook requesting aid. His call was answered and English assistance arrived. Commemorating that event is a stone monument in the Shantok Village of Uncas by the river which has a plaque stating: "Here stood the fort of Uncas, Sachem of the Mohegans and friend of the English. Here in 1645 when besieged by the Narragansetts he was relieved by the bravery of Lieut. Thomas Leffingwell."

New bonds of friendship had been forged that set a distinctive pattern in the area that continues to the present. The Native American presence is perhaps more prominent in Montville than it is in any other Connecticut community. It is rather ironic, then, that the name of the town is from the French for "hill house" rather than perpetuating an historic Indian term, as is done in Naugatuck. About 60 years before the time of the chartering in 1786, the North Parish of New London, what became Montville, was served by a charismatic clergyman by the name of James Hillhouse. Although he was deposed from his pastorate for a number of controversial reasons in the 1730s, there were many people who remained loyal to Hillhouse. Some speculate that partisans in the State Assembly loyal to him paid him this tribute.

Montville is the sum of its parts and more. Within the borders of the Town of Montville are the distinctive communities of Palmerton, Oakdale, Mohegan, Chesterfield, and Uncasville. Each has its own personality and is worth a visit.

INTERESTING PLACES

Mohegan Sun. Casino and top entertainment, dining, premier shopping, luxury hotel, spa, pool, and golf.

Raymond Library.

Tantaquidgeon Museum. Moheghan artifacts displayed.

Nature's Art Village. Includes: Dinosaur Place. A 60-acre outdoor park complete with prehistoric nature trails with 40 life-sized

NASKART is a multilevel indoor Go-Kart Racing and Trampoline Park in Oakdale. NASKART

Notes

dinosaurs. Discovery Depot. One can dig for gems and pan for "gold." There are shops offering unique gifts from around the world and a museum, The Past Antiques Market and Museum. Displays on technology from steam engines to search engines and it documents our industrial revolution. Also, the Copper Creek Miniature Golf Course.

NASKART. Country's largest multilevel indoor electric racetrack and trampoline.

Wide World of Indoor Sports.

Gardner State Park. Boat launch.

The Tantaquidgeon Musuem is the oldest Native American-owned and operated museum in America. John Tantaquidgeon and his children Gladys and Harold built it in 1931. Ronald K. McDaniel

Address Book

Town Site
www.townofmontville.org

Mohegan Sun
1 Mohegan Sun Blvd., Uncasville
888-226-7711
www.mohegansun.com

NASKART
1 Satchatello Industrial Dr., Oakdale
860-444-7700
www.naskartracing.com

Nature's Art Village
1650 Hartford-New London Tpke.
860-443-4367
www.naturesartvillage.com

Raymond Library
832 Raymond Hill Rd., Oakdale
860-848-9943
www.raymondlibrary.weebly.com

Tantaquidgeon Museum
1819 Norwich-New London Tpke.
860-235-8057

Wide World of Indoor Sports
2 Satchatello Industrial Dr., Oakdale
www.wideworldofindoorsports.com

FOOD

Big Belly Kelly's
262 CT-163 • 860-326-5633

Brown Derby Lounge
158 Norwich-New London Tpke.
860-848-3407

Chen's Restaurant
1031 Norwich-New London Tpke.
860-848-8838

David's Place
1647 CT-85 • 860-442-7120
www.davidplacect.com

Friendly Pizza
321 Norwich-New London Tpke.
860-848-0338

Golden Palace Chinese
2173 Norwich-New London Tpke.
860-848-1246
www.goldenpalace-ct.com

Great Wall Chinese
1242 Old Colchester Rd., Oakdale
860-859-0533
www.greatwalloakdale.com

Herb's Country Deli
1105 Norwich-New London Tpke.
860-848-1936
www.herbsdelicountrystore.com

Longshots Sports Café
2020 Norwich-New London Tpke.
860-892-8811
www.longshotssportscafe.com

Moravela's Pizza
712 CT-163 • 860-367-0330
www.moravelaspizzact.com

Nino's Pizzeria
1031 Norwich-New London Tpke.
860-848-2020

Oakdale Pizza
1242 Old Colchester Rd., Oakdale
860-859-1666

Oriental Bar and Grill
867 Norwich-New London Tpke.
860-892-8081

Uncasville Diner
884 Norwich-New London Tpke.
860-848-7932
www.uncasvillediner.com

[Passport Stamp / Signature & Date Here]

New London

By Stephen McCue, retired Social Studies teacher and native of New London

Historic, picturesque, and charming aptly describe this small city on the banks of the Thames River where it meets Long Island Sound. The municipality, founded about 1646, lays claim to a harbor deep enough to handle large ocean-going ships, yet also sustains a large pleasure fleet of sail and power vessels. The U.S. Coast Guard Academy is located here, and directly across the Thames, the U.S. Navy has berthed much of its Atlantic submarine force. The state pier also services freighters from numerous lands.

Originally called Pequot Harbor after the Pequot Indians who dominated the area, Puritan settlers, renamed the city New London. The town quickly grew into a prosperous port, where much of Connecticut's needs were imported. During the American Revolution, the city was home to numerous 'privateers' who successfully raided British shipping. The English took note of this activity, and near the end of the Revolution, the town received a serious setback, when it was destroyed by the traitor Benedict Arnold who had joined the British Army. The town quickly recovered and became a bustling enterprise once again. A Colonial era (1784) courthouse, which still stands at the head of the city's main thoroughfare, was built just three years after the disaster occurred.

There are several other surviving buildings of note in the city, too. The Hempstead House, where legend has it that several British Officers had lunch while the town burned, is open to the public today. The stone Huguenot House, which shares the same property as the Hempstead structure, is also available for tours. The elegant home of Nathaniel Shaw (built in 1756 by Capt. Nathaniel Shaw) is located a short walk from the other two surviving homes.

The Whaling industry fired the prosperity of the city in the mid-eighteenth century and the impressive Whale Oil Row in the downtown area, with its classic Greek columns, gives proof to the fortunes made during that time. There are numerous other interesting sites and a number of good restaurants in the downtown area. Many other buildings are worth noting , should a visitor decide to take the Segway walking tour of the city's center. There are 30 plaques placed along the tour citing each location's historic importance.

Today the city is a transportation center where rail, road, and marine travelers meet. Ferries depart to Block Island, Long Island, and Fishers Island and trains stop frequently while traversing the main Boston to Washington corridor.

Interesting Places

Coast Guard Academy. Tours of the campus are held most Mondays and Fridays at 1 PM in Waesche Hall. You must be logged in to register. The Coast Guard Museum tours are also available. Formal reviews of cadets in their military dress are held outdoors on certain Fridays at 4 PM in fall and spring (weather permitting) and feature precision marching, riflery, music, flags, and occasional honorary guests. Call Public Affairs for specific dates. Coast Guard Band concerts schedule at www.uscg.mil.

Connecticut College. Their Arboretum (750 acres) and

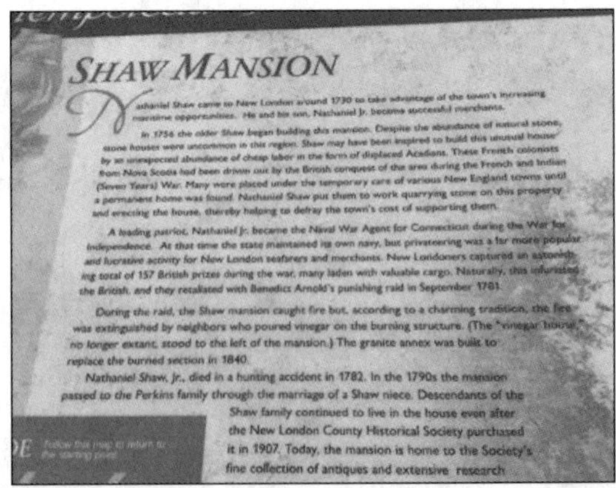

Founded in 1870 the New London County Historical Society is housed in the historic 1756 Shaw Mansion near the corner of Bank and Tilley Streets in New London. Steve McCue

Notes

Botanical Garden Open sunrise to sunset.

Mitchell College. Founded in 1938 this small private liberal arts college on the Thames River.

New London County Historical Society. In Shaw Mansion. Tours: Wed.-Fri. 1-4 PM, Sat. 10 AM-4 PM, from Mid-May to Mid-October.

Ocean Beach Park. 1/2-mile boardwalk along a pristine beach plus an Olympic-size swimming pool, amusement rides, water slide, and other attractions.

Fort Trumbull State Park. A civil war era fort with a fine museum.

Ye Antientist Burial Ground. Early settlers are buried here.

Waterfront Park. Scenic walk along the city's riverfront and access to city's docking facilities.

The Old Customs House. Several interesting exhibits. Winter Thurs.-Sun. 1-5 PM. Apr.-Dec. Wed.-Sun. 1-5 PM.

Nathan Hale Schoolhouse. Purportedly the last location where Nathan Hale taught before his tragic hanging as a spy by the British.

Monte Cristo Cottage. Boyhood home of Eugene O'Neill, Nobel Prize winning playwright. Several of his plays were set in the cottage.

New London is the home of the U.S. Coast Guard Academy. There are tours and activities available to the public. Consult website for schedule. Wikipedia.com

Address Book

Town Site
www.newlondonct.org

Coast Guard Academy
15 Mohegan Ave. • 860-444-8270
www.cga.edu

Connecticut College
270 Mohegan Ave.
www.conncoll.edu

Fort Trumbull State Park
90 Walbach St.
www.ct.gov/deep

Ocean Beach Park
90 Neptune Ave.

The Hempstead House
11 Hempstead St.

Monte Cristo Cottage
325 Pequot Ave. • 860-443-5378
www.theoneill.org

Nathan Hale Schoolhouse
19 Atlantic St.

New London County Historical Society
11 Blinman St.
www.nlhistory.org

Ocean Beach Park
90 Neptune Ave.

The Old Customs House
150 Bank St. • 860-447-2501
www.nlmaratimesociety.org

Waterfront Park
1 Waterfront Park, Downtown

Ye Antientist Burial Ground
1 Bulkeley Pl.

[Passport Stamp / Signature & Date Here]

North Stonington

By Robin Rice, North Stonington Historical Society and Amy Kennedy, Director of Wheeler Library

North Stonington is in New London County in the southeastern corner of the state, adjacent to the Rhode Island border. In 2010 its population was 5,297.

North Stonington is a town of natural beauty with hills, farmland, and unique village districts accented by iconic stone walls. Defining the southeastern corner of Connecticut, the town covers 54 sq. mi., making it one of the largest.

North Stonington's earliest history is entwined with that of Stonington, which was settled by the English in 1649 and whose progeny spread inland to populate the stony land to the north. By 1717 a "North Society" of Stonington's Congregationalist community was established, and in 1807 the town was incorporated as North Stonington, despite the society's request to name it Jefferson. Just prior, when religious fervor of the "Great Awakening" swept through the mid-1700s, North Stonington became a bastion of the Baptist denomination. Today, a "Greek Revival style" Congregational Church (1846) and early Baptist churches remain.

Clarks Falls, Laurel Glen and, notably, Milltown, the town village center, are just a few districts that thrived during the late 1700s and 1800s. Utilizing the power of town rivers, locals established sawmills, gristmills, and fulling mills, along with tanneries, iron works, cabinet making shops, and dye houses during the town's industrial heyday. North Stonington mainly relied on cottage industries such as woolen goods, carpets, and silk for its economy until the Civil War, after which the area became primarily agricultural. For years, the town was known for raising turkeys, and at Thanksgiving, a local storekeeper shipped many a bird to Washington to grace the President's table. In Milltown 18th and 19th century buildings comprise most of the 58 town sites on the National Registry of Historic Places. Today, dairy farming is a principal industry.

Interesting Places

Wheeler School and Library. An association library that was originally constructed to serve as the town's secondary school and library. With a front entrance flanked by two marble lions, the building, and especially its beautiful top floor, is worth a stop.

Hewitt Farm. 104 acres includes forests, fields, wetlands, and streams. More than a mile of hiking trails, including the town's Bicentennial Trail. I-95 to Exit 92 and take a left on Rt. 2 through the traffic circle for several miles. Look for the preserve entrance on the right at Hewitt Rd.

Stephen Main Homestead (1781). Headquarters for the North Stonington Historical Society. Also the home of the A. Morgan Stewart Memorial Library.

Jonathan Edwards Winery. A picturesque setting for weddings and events, and some of the best wine in New England.

Hikes

Lantern Hill. Elevation 491', it is known for the fantastic views of the surrounding greenery of North Stonington. From Norwich take Rt. 2 down to Foxwoods Blvd., then turn onto Wintechog Hill Rd. Parking on the right.

North Stonington Village Center and Town Hall. William Ricker

Notes

Narragansett Trail. A 16-mi. Blue Blazed trail traveling through Ledyard, Voluntown and North Stonington and going to the CT/RI border. Maintained by Connecticut Forest & Park Assoc.

Kayak & Canoe

Spalding Pond. A reservoir near Rt. 216 and Clarks Falls Rd.

Lake of Isles. An 88-acre lake at the end of Lake of Isles Rd.

Wyassup Lake.

Billings Lake.

Constructed in 1900 of Westerly R.I. granite, the Wheeler School and Library was a secondary school (1900-1945). It has been a public library from 1908-present. William Ricker

Address Book

Town Site
www.northstoningtonct.gov

Avalonia Land Conservancy
www.avalonialandconservancy.org

Billings Lake
100 Billings Lake Rd.

Hewitt Farm
Rt. 2 & Hewitt Rd.

Jonathan Edwards Winery
74 Chester Main Rd.
860-215-3725
www.jedwardswinery.com

Lake of Isles
1 Clubhouse Dr.
www.lakeofisles.com

North Stonington Land Alliance
www.nslandalliance.org

Spalding Pond
Rt. 216 & Clarks Falls Rd.

Stephen Main Homestead
1 Wyassup Rd.

Wheeler School and Library
101 Main St.
860-535-0383
www.wheelerlibrary.org

Wyassup Lake
145 Wyassup Lake Rd.

[Passport Stamp / Signature & Date Here]

Norwich

By Tom Callinan, Connecticut's first "Official State Troubadour" and resident of Norwich

Dubbed 'The Rose of New England' in the mid-1800s, Norwich is located in southeastern Connecticut at the confluence of three rivers: the Shetucket, Yantic, and Thames, on land that had been known as Mohegan Country since the early 1630s. In the mid-1640s, English colonists from Old Saybrook supported Mohegan Sachem, Uncas, in conflicts with the neighboring Pequot and Narragannsett tribes. In 1659, after those hostilities had subsided, Sachem Uncas granted a '9-mile Square' to those English colonists. Norwichtown, situated around a triangular green at the base of Meetinghouse Rocks, was the original hub of that which evolved into the City of Norwich.

Tom Callinan has written over 25 songs about Norwich that reveal the history of the town from its origins to the present-day. On the facing page, you'll find the lyrics to one of them: "Where Three Rivers Come Together [Norwich Through The Centuries]."

Places to Visit

City Hall (1870-1873). Beautiful large red brick building on the National Register of Historic Places.

Slater Museum. A historic building and art museum on the grounds of the Norwich Free Academy.

Mohegan Park. Features fishing, meeting space, picnic tables, playscape, running and walking track, swimming, and Rose Garden.

Ponemah Mill. A massive former textile mill along the Shetucket River converted to lofts.

Leffingwell House Museum (c.1675). One of the finest restored examples of New England Colonial architecture. Open to the public on Saturdays from April to October, 11 AM-4 PM.

Benedict Arnold (1683-1761). Born a British subject in Norwich, he fought for the Continental Army and later defected to the British Army. There is a commemorative plaque located on Arnold Place just past Backus Hospital going east on Rt. 2.

Norwich Heritage and Regional Visitors Center. Open Wednesday thru Sunday, 10 AM-4 PM from the end of May to the end of October.

Greater Norwich Area Chamber of Commerce. Tom Callinan

Slater Memorial Museum. Tom Callinan

Notes

Where Three Rivers Come Together [Norwich Through The Centuries]

By Tom Callinan

Norwich was founded in 1659,
By settlers from Old Saybrook,
who numbered 69.
Settlement was mainly
around the pie-shaped Green,
And a wharf was made at Yantic Cove,
where Mohegans oft had been.
By 1694 the landing
moved down by the Thames.
Where ships could be off-loaded,
and the cityscape had changed.
Two east/west roads headed
in-and-out of town:
Washington Street and Broadway,
from the port to Norwichtown.

*Where three rivers come together: Shetucket,
Yantic, Thames, You'll find "The Rose Of
New England," and Norwich is her name.*

Ships that sailed from England
brought the Norwich merchants goods,
Until the hated Stamp Act
reduced the likelihood
That imports would be desired
since ingenuity,
Combined with raw materials,
made for self-sufficiency.

And in the Revolution,
Norwich sent its sons
To fight the redcoats of the King
with General Washington.
The patriots who served
are named upon a plaque,
By the gate to the ancient graveyard,
off the beaten track.

*Where three rivers come together: Shetucket,
Yantic, Thames, You'll find "The Rose Of
New England," and Norwich is her name.*

A century of prosperity
was brought about by steam
That was tempered by the Civil War,
two-thirds in-between.
After that Ponemah was
the largest mill in all the land.
Trains and boats were coming in and out
for some life sure was grand.
Everyone from everywhere
made her grow beyond compare,
From armaments and silverware,
to whaling guns and Windsor-chairs.
The home of abolitionists,
and folks from many lands and hues
Norwich was multi-cultural
before that term was used.

*Where three rivers come together: Shetucket,
Yantic, Thames, You'll find "The Rose Of
New England," and Norwich is her name.*

The 20th century started fine,
but halfway through, declined,
For some, the sun had set,
the "Rose" was wilting on the vine.
But its architecture showed,
with treasures built to last,
That hope should not be lost;
her best days hadn't passed.
Today the "Rose" is on the rise,
attracting tourists' eyes.
Three rivers still converge there,
and that's where still she lies.
Bridging now with yesteryear,
Mohegan Park is there today.
Some will come for just a weekend
some like me decide to stay.

*Where three rivers come together: Shetucket,
Yantic, Thames, You'll find "The Rose Of
New England," and Norwich is her name.*

Address Book

Town Site
www.norwichct.org

City Hall
100 Broadway St.

Greater Norwich Area Chamber of Commerce
187 Main St.
860-887-1647
www.norwichchamber.com

Leffingwell House Museum
348 Washington St.
www.leffingwellhousemuseum.org

Mohegan Park
Mohegan Park Rd.

Norwich Heritage & Regional Visitors Center
69 East Town St., Norwichtown
860-886-1776

Norwich Historical Society
307 Main St.
860-886-1776
www.norwichhistoricalsociety.org

Ponemah Mill
607 Norwich Ave., Taftville

Slater Museum
108 Crescent St.
860-887-2506
www.slatermuseum.org

[Passport Stamp / Signature & Date Here]

Old Lyme

By Douglas Nielson, local Lyme historian

Old Lyme is on the shore of the Long Island Sound, just east of the Connecticut River. The permanent population is about 8,000, expanding by several thousand in the summer. It also includes the villages of Laysville, Black Hall, South Lyme, and Soundview.

Old Lyme was originally settled by people from Saybrook Colony across the river. In 1665, it separated from Saybrook, and two years later took the name "Lyme," after Lyme Regis in Dorset, England, where many of the settlers came from. The town eventually grew to include the present-day towns of Lyme and Old Lyme, most of East Lyme and part of Salem. When the other towns eventually established themselves as separate legal entities, the town took the name "Old Lyme" to indicate that it was settled earlier than the other Lymes. Early industries included farming, fishing, logging, milling, and shipbuilding. It was also a center of commerce, thanks in part to the Boston Post Road, surveyed by Benjamin Franklin, which runs through the center of town. This route is now designated as U.S. Route 1.

With the greater mobility provided by steamboats and railways in the late 1800s, Old Lyme became a popular summer vacation spot and noted art colony, the first in the U.S. to adopt Impressionism. Many well-known painters, such as Willard Metcalf and Childe Hassam, lived in town at least temporarily, often at Miss Florence's boardinghouse, now the Florence Griswold Museum.

Places to Visit

Ferry Landing State Park. The boardwalk goes under the railroad drawbridge and out into the marshes right at the mouth of the Connecticut River. Great for picnics, fishing and bird watching.

Florence Griswold Museum. This wonderful art collection began in 1899 when Florence Griswold's boardinghouse first attracted artists who wanted to paint the area en plein air. Be sure to visit the house (built 1817) and the gallery, as well as William Chadwick's studio.

Lyme Academy College of Fine Arts. Four-year accredited college offering BFA degrees. Gallery in the John Sill House (built 1817) open to the public during exhibits.

Lyme Art Association. The Association incorporated in 1914 and took up residence in this charming building in 1921. Regular exhibits by association members.

Old Lyme Cemetery. Also known as Duck River Cemetery; the oldest grave dates to 1676. Veteran's graves from the French and Indian War and the American Revolution.

Old Lyme Historic District. Runs along Lyme Street (U.S. Route 1) from Sill Lane in the north to the South Green at the corner of McCurdy Road. It includes 75 properties, such as the McCurdy House (1754), which once hosted both Washington and Lafayette, and the Peck Tavern (1680), with eight buildings older than 1800, and 50 built before 1900. This was the commercial center of Old Lyme before a new shopping area was built along Halls Road; several small shops can still be found here. Other notable buildings are: Old Lyme Congregational Church

Florence Griswold Museum, an art museum at the home of Florence Griswold (1850-1937), was the center of the Old Lyme Art Colony, the early center of development of American Impressionism. Doug Nielson

Notes

(1909), Old Lyme Baptist Church (1843), Old Lyme Inn (c.1856), Capt. Samuel Mather House (c.1790), and the Bee and Thistle Inn (1756).

Phoebe Noyes Griffin Library. Original building dates to 1897. Several American Impressionist paintings are displayed here.

Old Lyme Land Trust Trails. The Land Trust maintains 70 properties in various parts of town, with parking, and hiking trails.

Boat launch areas. CT DEEP maintains several boat launches in town. Many, such as Great Neck and Watch Rock, are great places to picnic or just sit and look at the water. See www.lisrc.uconn.edu.

Peck Tavern, a historic tavern (now a private residence) at 1 Sill Lane, may date to the 17th century. It is one of the town's oldest buildings and was an important local meeting place in the 18th century. Douglas Nielson

Address Book

Town Site
www.oldlyme-ct.gov

Ferry Landing State Park
398 Ferry Rd.
www.lisrc.uconn.edu

Florence Griswold Museum
96 Lyme St.
860-434-5542
www.florencegriswoldmuseum.org

Lyme Academy College of Fine Arts
84 Lyme St.
860-434-5232
www.lymeacademy.edu

Lyme Art Association
90 Lyme St.
860-434-7802
www.lymeartassociation.org

Old Lyme Cemetery
3 Bittersweet Ln.

Old Lyme Land Trust
www.oldlymelandtrust.org

Phoebe Noyes Griffin Library
2 Library Ln.
860-434-1684
www.oldlyme.lioninc.org

[Passport Stamp / Signature & Date Here]

PRESTON

By Linda Christensen, Preston Historical Society

The Town of Preston is in New London Co. in the southeastern region of Connecticut. This semi-rural town is 31.3 square miles in area. Commercial activity is centered on a few small retail centers along the major roads and there is very little industry. Topographically, the area is primarily the result of glacial action during the last ice age. Small streams in Preston drain into the Thames River or its tributaries, the Shetucket and Quinebaug, with freshwater fish in its streams. Second growth woods cover much of the town and Poquetanuck Cove is rich in shellfish.

At the time of early exploration, the Pequot tribe controlled much of Eastern Conn., though the major centers of native population were outside Preston, a small number continued to live in the area into the 20th century. In the mid-1600s, one of the first settlers was Jonathan Brewster who acquired land from Uncas at the mouth of Poquetanuck Cove on the Thames, later called Brewster's Neck. Originally part of the Nine Miles Square which was Norwich, in 1686, 19 people petitioned the General Court for the incorporation of a new town, which was granted in 1687. On March 17, 1687, Owaneco, son of Uncas, deeded the area of the new town to the English inhabitants. Preston received its name from the English home of the Park family, early settlers. Most of the settlers were English colonists who migrated from already established towns. Town government had much the same form as today, with officers first called townsmen and later selectmen, and a town clerk.

Long Society, a separate area along the eastern edge of Norwich across the Thames, Shetucket and Quinebaug established a new Congregational Society and in 1786 was transferred to Preston with town meetings being held at the Long Society Meetinghouse, the Town House. Meetings were later transferred across the street to the former district school which functioned as the Town Hall until 1974.

In 1786, the village of Poquetanuck became part of the town. This area developed around industrial activities influenced by the Episcopal Church centered on the two brooks that flow into the head of Poquetanuck Cove. Gristmills, ironworks, and some shipbuilding were found in this area.

Though older established families were moving, there was an influx of Europeans willing to farm. Italians, Poles, and many notable Jewish farmers came into the area. Agriculture was the primary economic activity, though Poquetanuck village played an early role with a port facility. Preston, well-suited for the grazing of livestock and with a good supply of timber, prospered especially with the nearby markets of Norwich and New London.

The major industrial base in the 19th century was the woolen industry with the Cooktown and Hall mills. A birch mill was another activity which used local resources. In 1904, the Norwich State Hospital was established on a large tract of land along the Thames. Though it was a self-contained facility, staff and personnel were often local residents. It closed in 1996. The town presently finds itself between two major casinos, Foxwoods, in Ledyard, and Mohegan Sun, in Uncasville. The heavy pressures of

The c.1819 Long Society Meetinghouse was used both as a church and for civic functions, the reason for its plain, not overtly religious appearance. Linda Christensen

Notes

traffic and services has weighed on the town. The loss of forest and farmland has continued to change the character of the town.

Interesting Places

Long Society Meetinghouse and Cemetery. With an 18th century Broadside meetinghouse. Owned by the Preston Historical Society and used for meetings, exhibits, weddings.

Robbins Blacksmith Shop. An 1874 chestnut building still used for educational purposes and tours.

Preston City Congregational Church. Originally built in 1693 was the original town Meetinghouse.

Revolutionary War Memorial. Honors the Preston Soldiers of the Revolutionary War

Roseledge Country Inn. A 1720 country home, surrounded by early stone walls.

Captain Grant's Bed and Breakfast. A National Historic 1754 Inn, in a 1687 village.

Amos Lake. A 113-acre lake featuring boating, swimming, camping, and fishing. Boat launch at 158 Rt. 164.

Two Wineries: Dalice Elizabeth Winery and Preston Ridge Winery.

Preston Ridge Vineyard is situated on 60 bucolic acres just 15 miles from Long Island Sound at 100 Miller Rd. Enjoy a glass of wine and enjoy the breathtaking views of the countryside for more than 20 miles. Preston Ridge Vineyard

Address Book

Town Site
www.preston-ct.gov

Captain Grant's Bed and Breakfast
109 Rt. 2A
860-887-7589
www.captaingrants.com

Dalice Elizabeth Winery
6 Amos Rd.
860-889-9463
www.daliceelizabeth.com

Long Society Meetinghouse and Cemetery
Long Society Rd.
860-887-5828
/PrestonHistoricalSocietyCT

Preston City Congregational Church
321 Rt. 164
www.prestoncitycongregational.org

Preston Ridge Winery
100 Miller Rd.
860-383-4278
www.prestonridgevineyard.com

Revolutionary War Memorial
Rt. 165 & Old Shetucket Tpke.
/PrestonRevolutionaryMemorial

Robbins Blacksmith Shop
Old Shetucket Tpke.

Roseledge Country Inn
418 Rt. 164
860-892-4739
/Roseledge

[Passport Stamp / Signature & Date Here]

Salem

By William Schultz, Salem Historical Society

Between 1664 and 1699, all of the favorite hunting grounds of the Mohegans (known as Paugwonk) were in the hands of the settlers. This was completed when Uncas, before his death, deeded the west side of Gardner Lake to Major Mason, his friend and Mohegan protector. This deed included a house which once stood across from the Gardner Lake Firehouse. The Town has had several names: New Salem, Salem Parish, Society of Salem, and Paugwonk. A small area around Gardner Lake is called Paugwonk today. In 1725, the people petitioned the Connecticut General Court to form the largest plantation (approx. 9,000 acres) in Salem. It was owned by Colonel William Browne, a loyalist who fled to England in March 1776. The land was sold off by the General Court of Connecticut.

Historic Places and Notable People

Music Vale Seminary. Founded by Oramel Whittlesey in 1825, it was the first school to issue degrees in Connecticut. Students came from as far away as Nova Scotia with enrollment reaching 100 students a year. Whittlesey also manufactured pianos with the factory located on the site of the current Salem Firehouse. With the onset of the Civil War, enrollment plunged. The seminary had burned down to the ground but was rebuilt. In 1867 Whittlesey died and the school was not rebuilt when it burned down a second time. Today only a modest sign near Route 85 states rather unobtrusively, "Site of Music Vale Seminary: First Music Normal School, 1835-1876."

Fairy Lake Farm. The first electrified farm in the United States. Frederick Rawolle was an engineer and held the patent on a system to fracture oil wells which made him a millionaire retiring at age 32. Rawolle settled in Salem and acquired 2,000 acres from Mountain Lake (Horse Pond), all the way to the Salem Four Corners by 1924. The farm was located in Paugwonk and Fairy Lake. Rawolle designed a hydroelectric system to run the farm. The project came to a halt with the Stock Market Crash of 1929.

Bela Lyon Pratt, Sculptor. One of the most prominent sculptors of his time. Pratt is best known for his works of Nathan Hale and John Winthrop. After the close of Music Vale Seminary in 1876, Pratt purchased the land as a vacation retreat. A red barn is the only structure left.

Hiram Bingham III. An explorer sponsored by Yale University who discovered Machu Picchu in Peru in 1911. The artifacts discovered in 1911 were recently returned by Yale to Peru in an agreement with the Peruvian government.

Hiram Bingham IV. Vice consul in France at the outbreak of World War II and saved thousands of Jews. "Harry" Bingham was honored by Israel in 2011 and a U.S. Postal Stamp was issued in his honor in 2006.

Interesting Places

Several houses are listed on the national Register of Historic Places: the Woodbridge Farm, Ebenezer Tiffany House, and the Abel Fish House. Also on the Registry is the Town Green which has not changed much since 1840. In 1980 the area around the Salem Green was designated a Historic

The Salem Historical Society Museum (SHS) building was originally built in 1740 in Norwich as the Christ Episcopal Church. It was moved in 1831 by the Episcopal Society of Salem. As membership declined the town purchased it and in 1971 leased it to the SHS. Elbert Burr

Notes

District and enrolled on the National Registry.

Salem Historical Society Museum. Items displayed are farm equipment, local art, and artifacts from Music Vale Seminary.

The Olde Ransom and Farm Carriage Museum. 19th and 20th century wagons and carriages are displayed; some are one of a kind.

Salem Land Trust. Salem Land Trust has provided protection to 20% of land in Salem with eight beautiful preserves and nature walks.

The Red House Cultural Arts Center. Original fine art and handmade gifts by local artists and artisans. Hands-on classes offered by many of the same local artisans.

Salem Valley Farms Ice Cream. Seasonal, window-serve operation since 1988 whipping up homemade ice cream in many original flavors.

Fox Farm Brewery. Beautifully transformed dairy barn brews a variety of beers on tap.

Salem 5K Road Race. Memorial Day Parade and Strawberry Shortcake Festival. Salem Apple Festival held the last weekend in October on the Town Green features everything apple: apple pies to apple fritters to hot dogs with apple sauerkraut. Salem Annual School Book Sale. The last weekend in October.

Dave Wordell driving the "Blue Bird" to the Salem Historical Society Museum. The coach is a replica that carried students of Music Vale Seminary to the Norwich & New London railroad stations. Antique Carriage and Sleigh Museum

Address Book

Town Site
www.salemct.gov

Salem Historical Society Museum
3240 Hartford Rd.
860-859-3873
/SalemHistoricalSociety

The Olde Ransom Farm
509 New London Rd.
860-859-5336
www.ransomfarm.com

The Red House Cultural Arts Center
22 Darling Rd.
860-608-6526
www.salemredhouse.com

Salem Land Trust
www.salemlandtrust.org

Salem Valley Farms Ice Cream
20 Darling Rd.
www.salemvalleyfarmsicecream.com

Fox Farm Brewery
62 Music Vale Rd.
www.foxfarmbeer.com

Events

Memorial Day Parade
Salem Annual School Book Sale
Salem Apple Festival
Salem 5K Road Race
Strawberry Shortcake Festival

[Passport Stamp / Signature & Date Here]

SPRAGUE

By Glenn Alan Cheney, Sprague resident and writer www.cheneybooks.com

Sprague, in eastern Connecticut at the northern end of New London Co., had a population of 2,984 in 2010. It is bordered by Norwich, Franklin, Scotland, Canterbury, and Lisbon. State highways 97 and 207 run through it and meet at the center of town.

The territory was first a tribal area, then a religious area of Congregational churches, then an entrepreneurial area created for corporate purposes, and most recently a residential area owned and operated by some 3,000 citizens and a handful of businesses.

Sprague is composed of three loosely defined villages. Baltic is considered the center of town. Versailles is at the southern end and Hanover on the eastern side. The town was incorporated in 1861 to accommodate a major cotton mill being constructed on the Shetucket River at Baltic. Land for the new town was taken from Franklin, on the west side of the river, and Lisbon, to the east.

Baltic was essentially built as a mill town, with the mill on one side of the Shetucket, the workers' houses on the other. It is one of few villages in New England that retains most of its original architecture and general appearance. The mill burned in 1999. St. Mary Church and Holy Family Academy are the most impressive buildings in town. Until a few decades ago, Baltic was populated almost entirely by mill workers, the majority of whom were French Canadians.

Hanover is the oldest settlement in Sprague, originally formed as an Ecclesiastical Society founded on Hanover Congregational Church, which still stands. It was a quiet little village in the 18th century and is again in the 21 centuries, but in the time between it was a busy industrial town. In the early 1800s, the Little River powered a silk mill near Potash Hill Rd., a sawmill, a gristmill, and a woolen mill, the latter owned by Pratt Allen, a descendant of Revolutionary hero Ethan Allen. The Allen Woolen Mill closed in 1895 during the second Grover Cleveland administration. It remained closed until 1899, when a Scottish immigrant bought it. His name was Angus Park. He renamed it Airlie Mill. The mill operated until 1975, when it burned.

Versailles formed around the Versailles woolen mill on the Shetucket. Its name somehow evolved to the spelling of the famous palace in France but the pronunciation is the same as the woolen mill. The village identity today centers around a small post office and Versailles Methodist Church.

INTERESTING PLACES

Sprague Historical Museum. On the upper floor of the gristmill, which is on Main St. across from Town Hall.

Shetucket River. A popular place to fish for trout, salmon, etc. Parking is available at the junction of Rts. 97 and 207. A ramp to the water allows access for those in wheelchairs. The town offers to give people and small boats a lift to a spot upstream on the Shetucket on Saturday when the Scotland Dam releases water. The Little River in

The Sprague Historical Museum is on the third floor of the 155-year old Grist Mill at 76 Main St., Baltic. Glenn Alan Cheney

NOTES

Hanover is a beautiful stream rich in trout.

Sprague Land Preserve. A forested area of a few hundred acres bordered by the Shetucket River. It has many trails and is often enjoyed by horse riders.

The town is especially beautiful during fall foliage. The scenery along country roads rivals that of Vermont.

See www.ctsprague.org for more information about the town.

Sprague village on the Shetucket River, showing where the 1899 Baltic Mills Co. (cotton mill) and the dam used to be. Glenn Alan Cheney

ADDRESS BOOK

Town Site
www.ctsprague.org

Sprague Historical Museum
76 Main St., Baltic
860-822-6867
www.ctsprague.org

Sprague Land Preserve
Holton Rd., North Franklin

[Passport Stamp / Signature & Date Here]

Stonington

By Zachary Lamothe, author of ***Connecticut Lore*** *and* ***More Connecticut Lore*** *and Fred Burdick, Stonington Historian*

Stonington's history has been shaped by being situated on Long Island Sound. It comes with a storied past of a Native American legacy, a maritime heritage, and its part in two wars against the British. The land which is Stonington was originally inhabited by the Pequot tribes Pawcatuck and Mistack. The first European settlers arrived in 1649, with a trading post on Pawcatuck River set up soon after. In 1658, the area of Stonington, called Southerton, became part of Massachusetts but it reverted back to Connecticut four years later. It was first known as Mistick with a name change to Stonington in 1666. Stonington's boundary is marked by the Pawcatuck River, which straddles the Connecticut border with Rhode Island, and the Mystic River, which separates it from Groton. The Town of North Stonington was officially incorporated in 1807, although it had been the northern parish of Stonington since 1724. Stonington is divided into villages including the Stonington Borough, Pawcatuck, Lords Point, Wequetequock, Mystic, and Old Mystic. The last two are both in Stonington and Groton.

Stonington's character is defined by its access to the Atlantic Ocean, especially in reference to the presence of the British Navy in its harbor during the American Revolution in 1775 or during the War of 1812. In August of 1814 the British sent demands for the surrender of the town. They bombarded Stonington with canon fire, but instead of surrender, a small group of citizens banded together to fight off the enemy. Although shelled, the town remained without traumatic damage or lives lost. Industries such as seal hunting, whaling, and fishing became vital to the Stonington's economy. It welcomed a large influx of Portuguese immigrants who settled in Pawcatuck, as well as Stonington Borough, with many becoming fishermen. Also, its tourist industry is centered on its waterside location.

Interesting Places

Mystic Seaport. This living-history museum is the finest of its kind in the country. Its exhibits focus on New England's maritime past and feature an array of seasonal activities, including the annual Sea Music Festival in June.

Mystic Aquarium. The most heralded aquarium in New England houses an array of marine life including beluga whales, penguins, and sea lions.

Downtown Mystic. The quaint New England seaside community welcomes visitors with a smorgasbord of restaurants and shops.

Olde Mistick Village. This outdoor shopping center is set in a 1700s New England village and even includes a working waterwheel, a church, as well as a 21st century movie theater. Look for the annual Cabin Fever Festival and Chowder Cook Off each February.

Stonington Historical Society. Founded in 1895, it consists of the Capt. Nathaniel B. Palmer House Museum, a National Historic Landmark, the Old Lighthouse Museum at Stonington Point, and the Richard W. Woolworth Library and research center.

Denison Homestead Museum. Built in 1717 by a grandson of Captain George Denison, who settled in Stonington in 1654, also called Pequotsepos Manor. Listed on the National Register of Historic Places. Operated by the Denison Society.

Stonington Borough. Another enclave of restaurants, shopping, and galleries in a seaside setting. Make sure to visit the Old Lighthouse Museum at the end of Water Street.

Wequetequock Burial Ground.

Notes

Founded in 1650, called the Founders Cemetery, as four of the founders of Stonington are buried within its walls: William Chesebrough, Thomas Stanton, Thomas Minor, and Walter Palmer, as are many of their descendants.

Beer'd Brewing Company. When first opened in 2012, Beer'd was the smallest in the state. Five years later it had made its mark on the regional beer scene with such well-regarded libations as their Hobbit Juice and Frank & Berry Double IPAs.

A vintage photo of the 1840 Stonington lighthouse and possibly the keeper and his family. The building became the first museum lighthouse in the nation after the Stonington Historical Society bought it from the federal government in 1925. The museum is now in the seven-room keeper's house. Fred Burdick Collection

Address Book

Town Site
www.stonington-ct.org

Beer'd Brewing Company
22 Bayview Ave. (in the Velvet Mill)
860-213-9307
www.beerdbrewing.com

Denison Homestead Museum
120 Pequotepos Rd.
www.denisonhomestead.org

Mystic Aquarium
55 Coogan Blvd., Mystic
860-572-5955
www.mysticaquarium.org

Mystic Seaport
75 Greenmanville Ave., Mystic
www.mysticseaport.org

Olde Mistick Village
27 Coogan Blvd., Mystic
www.oldemistickvillage.com

Stonington Historical Society
40 Palmer St.
www.stoningtonhistory.org

Wequetequock Burial Ground
Palmer Neck Rd.

[Passport Stamp / Signature & Date Here]

Voluntown

By Emily Allard, Director, Voluntown Public Library

Voluntown is located in the northeast corner of New London Co. on the R.I. border. It is conveniently accessible from I-95 and I-395, Rt. 2 and scenic Rt. 49.

In 1700, a six-mile square tract was granted to King Philip's War Volunteers who were given lots to build homesteads. It was from this act that "Volunteer Town" or Voluntown, received its name. It was incorporated in 1721. Farming was the chief occupation and abundant water encouraged textile mill industry as early as 1711.

Today about 70% of Voluntown contains the Pachaug State Forest, the largest in Connecticut, with more than 27,000 acres. The word "Pachaug" is derived from the Native American term meaning bend or turn in the river. Pachaug-Great Meadow Swamp, considered one of the finest and most extensive Atlantic white cedar swamps in Connecticut, is a National Natural Landmark. Old cellar holes and miles of stone "fences" in the woods give evidence that the land was once farmed or pastured. Nearly every brook has old mill sites and dams.

LEGENDS AND STORIES

Studio Farm. In 1914, a New York stage actor bought a house and land on Pendleton Hill Road. Stories have been told of actors such as Douglas Fairbanks and Mary Pickford starring in cowboy movies filmed in and around Voluntown. However, none of his films are found in any film libraries, although many local people recalled being in his films.

Strong Man. Elmer Bitgood was hailed as one of the strongest men in the world. He would regularly lift platforms of boulders and "steers on hoof." His homemade stone barbells are now the property of the Historical Society and are secured on a local farm.

HAUNTINGS

Mrs. Gorton, on Bailey Pond Road, threatened death to anyone who stole her lilacs. A 15-year-old boy took this as a challenge, stealing some. Months later he disappeared while fishing on a pond. Even after her house rotted away to nothing more than a stone foundation, people report glimpsing an old woman grooming her lilacs.

In 1654 a child named Maud died of diphtheria and was buried in the woods near Hell Hollow Road. Locals say Maud's mother was a witch who placed a protective curse on the child's grave. If people near the vicinity of the grave mention her name, a curse is placed on them.

Hell Hollow Road got its name from the legend of an Indian woman said to have been killed by British soldiers in the 1600s. Her ghost haunts Hell Hollow and her plaintive wailing can sometimes be heard. Local hunters have told of hearing strange noises there.

Along Hell Hollow Road are EVPs (electronic voice phenomena), orbs, cold spots and strange lights, which many enjoy seeking with modern equipment.

Stop at the library to read about more hauntings.

INTERESTING PLACES

Pachaug State Forest. Recreational activities include camping, hiking, (including wheelchair accessible

The Voluntown Public Library at 107 Main St. is a great friendly place for books, information, and programs. You can also get your CT 169 Club book signed or stamped here. Jerry Dougherty

Notes

Rhododendron Sanctuary Trail), bicycling, off-road motorcycling, snowmobiling, horseback riding, fishing (wheelchair access), hunting, and boating.

Lavender Hill Alpaca Farm. Visit with alpacas and shop local products. Open Sat. & Sun. 10 AM-4 PM.

Wylie School (1856-1939). Used as a meeting space and museum. Junction of Ekonk Hill and Wylie School Rds.

Voluntown Historical Mural. Painted by elementary children; located next to the town hall.

Voluntown Peace Trust. An educational, resource, and support center dedicated to non-violent social change and sustainable living.

Tamarack Lodge. Once an abandoned wagon wheel forge, the Tamarack Lodge began as a rustic resort in 1947. Newly opened in 2017, it offers family dining, live music, a banquet hall, and cabin rentals.

On Saturday, September 21, 2019 a Civilian Conservation Corps Worker Statue was dedicated at the Pachaug State Forest in Voluntown to honor those who worked in the Voluntown camp. They built roads & trails, dams & campgrounds, and planted thousands of trees during the Great Depression (1933-1942). Two CCC boys, Mike Caruso (L) and Harold Ohler (R) are standing with the local senator and Sharon Viadella. Viadella

Address Book

Town Site
www.voluntown.gov

Lavender Hill Alpaca Farm
411 Beach Pond Rd.
860-917-5154
www.lavenderhillfarmalpacas.com

Tamarack Lodge
21 Ten Rod Rd.
860-376-0224
www.tamaracklodgect.com

Voluntown Historical Mural
115 Main St.

Voluntown Peace Trust
539 Beach Pond Rd.
www.voluntownpeacetrust.org

[Passport Stamp / Signature & Date Here]

Waterford

By Robert M. Nye, Municipal Historian

For most of the period before European settlement, the Nehanticks occupied what is now Waterford. The early settlers of Pequot, formally named New London in 1658, laid out their house lots with their farm lots surrounding the town which included present-day Waterford. Formerly the "West Farms" of New London, Waterford never established a town center. Only Jordan Village and Quaker Hill resemble anything like a village center. Objecting to New London taxes and desirous of establishing a community around the Baptist Church, Waterford was incorporated as a separate town in 1801.

Farming and fishing occupied the lives of most Waterford citizens. Gristmills and sawmills were an important part of the local economy as were fulling, woolen, oil, and paper mills. By the 1890s, an increasing number of the old farms turned to truck and dairy farming.

Waterford's only major industry was quarrying. The largest and most productive of the commercial quarries was at Millstone Point (site of the nuclear power station since 1967). Many landmarks of national significance, including the base of the Statue of Liberty, are of Millstone granite. Beginning mid-19th century, immigrants came in turn from Ireland, Sweden, Finland, England, Scotland, and Italy to work in the quarries adding diversity to the native-born population.

Wealthy summer residents found the Waterford shoreline to their liking as early as the 1820s. Most notable is the former estate of Edward S. and Mary Stillman Harkness. The Oswegatchie Colony at Pine Neck on the Niantic River was a seasonal enclave of the wealthy for much of the first third of the 20th century. Riverhead, Pleasure Beach, and Mago Point were popular summer retreats for a growing middle class.

The face of rural Waterford began to change dramatically after 1900 when "trolley car subdivisions" first appeared in Quaker Hill and shortly thereafter along the Boston Post Road. Waterford was well on its way to becoming a suburb. In the 1970s Waterford became a major retail shopping destination with the development of Crystal Mall and more recently, Waterford Commons.

Places of Interest

Harkness Memorial State Park. Former Harkness Estate including the 1907 Eolia mansion on more than 200 acres on Long Island Sound. Listed in the National Register of Historic Places.

Seaside State Park. Formerly the Seaside Sanatorium, the first institution designed for heliotropic treatment of children suffering from tuberculosis. Designed by acclaimed architect Cass Gilbert. 36 acres on Long Island Sound. Listed in the National Register of Historic Places.

Eugene O'Neill Memorial Theater Center. Former Walnut Grove Farm, estate of Edward Hammond. Home to the National Playwrights Conference, National Music Theater Conference, National Puppetry Conference, Caberet & Performance Conference, National

Waterford Beach Park has a quarter-mile long sandy beach that provides one of the best intact dune systems in the state. Ann Nye

Notes

Theater Institute, & National Critics Institute. Listed in the National Register of Historic Places.

Waterford Beach Park. Adjacent to the O'Neill Theater. Natural beach, outstanding view of Long Island Sound, extensive tidal marsh.

Connecticut College Arboretum. 300-acre arboretum and botanical gardens on the college campus and in the towns of New London and Waterford.

Waterford Historical Society. Historic buildings on the Jordan Park Green. Listed in the National Register of Historic Places. By appointment only.

Waterford Speed Bowl.

The elegant 1907 Eolia summer mansion of the Harkness family set on 230 seaside acres of sweeping lawns, stately trees, and spectacular gardens in the Harkness Memorial State Park. Ann Nye

Address Book

Town Site
www.waterfordct.org

Connecticut College Arboretum
270 Mohegan Ave., New London
www.conncoll.edu/thearboretum

Eugene O'Neill Memorial Theater Center
305 Great Neck Rd.
www.theoneill.org

Harkness Memorial State Park
275 Great Neck Rd.
www.ct.gov/deep/harkness

Seaside State Park
36 Shore Rd.
www.waterfordct.org/recreation-parks

Waterford Beach Park
305 Great Neck Rd.
www.waterfordct.org/recreation-parks

Waterford Historical Society
65 Rope Ferry Rd.
www.waterfordhistoricalsociety.org

Waterford Speed Bowl
1080 Hartford Tpke. (Rt. 85)
www.speedbowlct.com

[Passport Stamp / Signature & Date Here]

SOMERS
STAFFORD
UNION
ELLINGTON
TOLLAND
WILLINGTON
VERNON
COVENTRY
MANSFIELD
BOLTON
ANDOVER
COLUMBIA
HEBRON
Tolland County

CHAPTER 7

Tolland County

ANDOVER

By Donald Carso, Andover resident

Andover is a small town, about 16 sq. mi., in east central Connecticut. It is bordered by the towns of Bolton, Hebron, Columbia, and Coventry. The Hop River runs through it and flows into the Willimantic River on its way to Long Island Sound. The river's name derives from the Old English term for a narrow valley.

The earliest residents of Andover were the Nipmuck and Pequot Native American tribes. In 1635, the English joined with Uncas, Chief of the Mohegans, to annihilate the Pequots and give their eastern region to the Mohegans. Subsequently, this agreement was violated and the towns east of the Connecticut River were settled. Families moved into the Andover area around 1710. Some of their original small houses still exist with later homes much larger as the area prospered. Farming, dairy, herds of sheep and horses were the usual commerce with the horses being sent to the West Indies. Forest products such as lumber, cordwood, and charcoal along with maple syrup were, also, important. In 1793, a toll road was created from Hartford to Providence, RI. This road, now Rt. 6, made it much easier to get products to major markets.

Andover's contribution to the Revolutionary War, was volunteers for the Washington's army. By 1780, the British were concentrated in New York City. General Rochambeau landed with his army in Newport. Called to meet with General Washington in Wethersfield, he galloped through Andover on his way to the meeting. The Kingsbury family in Andover offered him a cool drink on his way. General Washington, also, followed this route to meet with the French in Newport. Later, in 1781 Rochambeau brought his army through Andover on the old Rt. 6 which he described as "a pretty little valley where several brooks flow into the (Hop) river." Then, after victory in New York, part of his army spent a frigid winter in tents near The First Congregational Church off old Rt. 6.

Andover was incorporated as a town in 1848 with 500 residents. In 1849 the Hartford, Providence & Fishkill completed the Hartford to Willimantic via Andover track. It was very important to the town's economy.

In 1873 the Air Line rail from Boston to New Haven, also known as the New Haven, Middletown and Willimantic RR ran through Andover in the late 19th Century; nicknamed Air Line Rail because its route was as the crow flies. The railroad made transportation easier and faster. Today the Airline Rail Trail, following the old tracks allows biking, hiking, and horseback riding from East Hampton to Willimantic to Andover, and on to Bolton and Vernon now that a scenic covered bridge spans Rt. 316. At all times of the year, this is a beautiful trail as it travels by swamps, rivers, and over bridges that were once tall railroad trestles with views for tens of miles. www.andoverconnecticut.homestead.com

Two lakes are found in Andover: Bishops Swamp, also known as Jurovaty Pond, and Andover Lake which was created in 1927 by damming a stream and flooding farmland. Andover Lake is one of the cleanest lakes in Connecticut. No motors of any kind are allowed and almost all the houses surrounding the lake are year-around homes.

The 1927 Andover Public Library is at the corner of Long Hill Rd. and Rt. 6. Podskoch

Notes

Address Book

Town Site
www.andoverconnecticut.org

Andover Historical Society Museum
17 School Rd.
www.andoverconnecticut.homestead.com

Andover Public Library
355 Rt. 6
860-742-7428
www.andoverconnecticut.org

Channel 3 Kids Camp
73 Times Farm Rd.
www.channel3kidscamp.org

Interesting Places

Andover Historical Society Museum. It has over 100 enlarged and enhanced photographs, maps, documents, and paintings of Andover from past years. It also contains a huge mural painted by local artists showing major events in Andover's history from the 1600 on. Another area has antiques and other articles that will help people understand the life style of past generations.

First Congregational Church (1825). On Rt. 6 and the corner of Long Hill Road.

Andover Public Library (1927). A thriving part of the community that hosts a variety of events including book discussion for adults and storytime for children.

Channel 3 Kids Camp. Provides year-around recreational and educational programs to children and teens from New England.

Andover Historical Society Museum was the former Town Hall. It is at the intersection of Rts. 6 and 316, next to the Veterans Memorial and the Andover Covered Bridge. Jerry Dougherty

[Passport Stamp / Signature & Date Here]

Bolton

By Hans DePold, retired Bolton Historian and Elizabeth C. Waters, CCTC, Town Clerk of Bolton

The town of Bolton in Tolland Co. is approx. 15 miles east of Hartford. Bolton has an area of 14.7 sq. mi. and is primarily a residential community with an economy mostly of small businesses. In the 2010 census the population was 4,986. The town got its name because many settlers came from Bolton, Lancashire, England.

In the year of 1673, the land now Bolton, belonged to the Mohegan tribe lead by the wise and noble Sachem Uncas. But soon Puritans arrived filled with passion for virtue, knowledge, and teaching. Bolton was then born at the crossroads of the two pre-historic Native American trails that met in what is now called Bolton Notch. The most famous trail is known as "Ye Olde Connecticut Path," the route that Connecticut's first traders and settlers took from the Bay Colony to settle Connecticut in 1636. The Puritans founded Bolton in 1720 and state records show that Bolton had a formal school system no later than 1731.

The inland colonial route through Bolton was safe from any British naval surprise attack. That made the "Ye Olde Connecticut Path" the first choice for marching the Continental and the French armies from Boston and Providence down to finally defeat the British at Yorktown, Virginia in 1781. They often camped in Bolton. Washington and Rochambeau, stayed at the Bolton Heritage Farm House several times. In 2012 that road was designated the Washington-Rochambeau Revolutionary Route National Historic Trail.

Agriculture was the main economy of the town. Farmers grew wheat, hay, corn, oats, rye and flax for linen. They raised cattle, horses, and sheep for export. Other products were pork, beef, butter, cheese, cider, and cider brandy.

Some of the early industries were a gristmill, hat manufacturers, cigar makers, and distilleries. The quarry industry in Bolton sent flags of stone to Baltimore, Washington, New Orleans, and Philadelphia as early as 1820.

Today Bolton remains a small rural town with many farms that is proud of its excellent school system.

Interesting Places

Bolton Green Historic District. It extends east about 500 yards from the green along Bolton Center Rd. The most prominent building is the Bolton Congregational Church, a Greek Revival structure built in 1818 with a truncated box-spire. Other structures are the Brick Tavern, the site of Bolton's first post office, the town hall, the Tuthill residence, and the Bolton Heritage Farm.

Bolton Center Cemetery. Some historic tombstones. Hebron Rd.

Bolton Heritage Farm. Site of Washington & Rochambeau encampments during the Revolutionary War. The Bolton interpretive panel is on the Town Green (Bolton Center Rd.) across from the Town Hall.

Bolton Ice Palace. Ice skating rink, parties and events.

Bolton Lake (Lower). Kayaking, non-motorized boats. Rt. 44.

Bolton Notch State Park. Hiking trails.

In 1725 Bolton residents built Heritage Farm for Reverend Thomas White. It was visited by Washington, Hamilton, and Rochambeau in 1780. Podskoch

Notes

Charter Oak Greenway and Hop River Trail. A Linear Park that connects various trails along the east coast. The Hartford to Bolton section of the East Coast Greenway is referred to as the Charter Oak Greenway & Hop River Trail. The Bolton section is expected to be completed in December 2018.

Fish Family Farm Creamery. Ice cream and fresh dairy products from their Jersey cows, and seasonal events.

Freja Park. Hiking and walking trails.

Owner Don Fish with his granddaughter Livi (R), and friend Sage enjoying homemade ice cream at the Fish Family Farm Creamery. Sandra Levesque

Gay City State Park. Hiking, picnicking, fishing, and swimming. Park is in Bolton and Hebron.

Herrick Memorial Park & Walking Trail. Hall rental facility, swing set, and walking trails.

Hop River Trail. Rail trail used for walking & biking.

Indian Notch. Beach seasonal only.

Munson's Chocolates. Local chocolatier offering a variety of confections.

Quarryville Cemetery. Oldest cemetery in Town with historic tombstones.

Rose Trail. Walking/hiking trail (1.5 mi.) with access to it from Bolton Heritage Farm.

Veterans Memorial. Dedicated to Bolton's Veterans that served in WWII, Korea, Vietnam, Kuwait and Afghanistan/Iraq. Bolton Center Rd./Hebron Rd. Town Green.

Address Book

Town Site
www.town.boltonct.org

Bolton Heritage Farm
266 Bolton Center Rd.

Bolton Ice Palace
145 Hop River Rd.
(860) 646-7851
www.boltonicepalace.com

Bolton Notch State Park
Rts. 6 & 44

Fish Family Farm Creamery
20 Dimock Ln.
860-646-9745
Facebook.com/fishfamilyfarmcreamery

Freja Park
Access from Morancey Rd.

Gay City State Park
386 North St., Hebron

Herrick Memorial Park & Walking Trail
29 Hebron Rd.

Hop River Trail
Steeles Crossing Rd.

Indian Notch
Rt. 44

Munson's Chocolates
174 Hop River Rd.
860-649-4332
www.munsonschocolates.com

Quarryville Cemetery
Boston Tpke.

[Passport Stamp / Signature & Date Here]

Columbia

*By Ingrid Wood, Town Historian and co-author of **Images of America: Columbia**, Arcadia Press (2013)*

Columbia, in Tolland Co. was incorporated in 1804. It is divided by three state highways, Rts. 6, 66, and 87, connecting to Hartford, Middletown, Norwich, Providence, and Boston. The town's population was 5,500 in the 2010 census Columbia is predominantly a residential and agricultural community.

Settled in 1699 by Thomas Buckingham of Old Saybrook, and Proprietors Josiah Dewey and William Clarke of Northampton, MA, this 22 sq. mi. area was conveyed in a treaty with the Mohegan Sachem Uncas. These former hunting and fishing grounds bounded by streams, swamps, and glaciated terrain, were the colonial frontier of Lebanon in the very late 1600s. Today's state parks still preserve a glimpse of this; including Hop River Trail and the Air Line Rail Trail; as well as Mono Pond. Joshua's Land Trust, a private organization, has conserved and maintains hiking trails at Utley Hill Preserve, Potter Meadow, and the Goldberg Parcel near the Hop River.

Lebanon Crank or the North Society was known for Eleazar Wheelock's revivalist preaching, the Great Awakening. His "Latin School" of 1743 had been re-invented by 1755 as Moor's Indian Charity School. Dartmouth College, founded in 1769, attributes its origins to this school, sited on Columbia's municipal campus, part of Columbia Green Historic District, accessible from Rt. 87.

18th and early 19th century water-powered mills once dotted Columbia's streams. These gave impetus to the town's center, now Columbia Green Historic District, and to the creation of Columbia Lake reservoir. Two 19th century railroads conveyed manufactured goods (lumber, shingles, hats, and baskets), dairy products, and produce to nearby cities. Graded rail beds of the Hop River Trail SP (part of the East Coast Greenway) and Air Line Rail Trail SP are an easy amble, enjoyed by hikers, cyclists, and bird watchers alike.

Interesting Places

Columbia Green Historic District. The Indian Charity School (c.1755) is open on special holidays, and by appointment.

Former Landmark Inn (c.1740). Now private, at Rts. 87 and 66 was an 18th century tavern and mail coach stop.

Washington-Rochambeau Revolutionary Route National Historic Trail. Marker commemorates Continental and French Army Revolutionary War troop movements in 1781. Lebanon Crank's 18th century history is included at Lebanon Historical Society Museum in nearby Lebanon. Old Yard Burying Ground (est. 1721). Reflects Puritan gravestone craftsmanship and poetic epitaphs.

Hop River State Park Trail. Former railroad line is now a 20.2-mile trail.

Air Line State Park Rail Trail. A former railroad line Stretching across eastern Connecticut from Thompson to East Hampton.

Mono Pond State Park. Fishing. Take Rt. 66 SE onto Hunt Rd., launch is on the right.

Joshua's Land Trust Properties in Columbia. Goldberg Parcel: 3.6 acres of wildlife habitat. NE corner of intersection Rts. 6 and 66. Utley Hill Preserve: 2+ miles of

Moor's Indian Charity School (1755). Ingrid Wood

Notes

trail pass by dams and old mill sites before connecting to the Town of Columbia Recreational Area. Near Erdoni Rd. Potter Meadow: 34 acres within the floodplain of Willimantic and Ten Mile rivers. Excellent wildlife habitat and birding.

Sponsored Events

Regional traditional 4th of July Parade. Co-sponsored by the Town of Columbia and the Columbia Lions Club.

Annual Winter Holiday Gazebo Lighting and choral step sing. Co-sponsored by the Town of Columbia Volunteer Fire Department and the Columbia Lions Club.

Saxton B. Little Free Library sponsored programs for adults and children. Quarterly book sale at the Chapel on the Green organized by the Friends of the Saxton B. Little Library.

Columbia Historical Society. Periodic exhibits, tours of Moor's Indian Charity School and Native American medicinal garden known as the Occom Garden.

Town of Columbia Recreation Department. Seasonal Rec Park athletic courts and ball fields offer youth and adult recreation.

Last Green Valley Walktober & Spring Outdoors. For seasonal outdoor guided tours and special activities in Columbia, visit www.thelastgreenvalley.org and search 'Walktober'.

Selected Day-trip Amenities

Heartstone Farm and Winery. Locally grown fine wines and a tasting room. Summer and fall weekend entertainment featuring local folk musicians.

Columbia Congregational Church community breakfast. All you can eat community breakfast, every second Saturday from 8-11 AM.

Various seasonal farmstands, including East Willow Farm and Cloverleigh Farm, offer locally grown organic foods.

Address Book

Town Site
www.columbiact.org

Columbia Historical Society
www.columbia-history.org

Columbia Congregational Church
325 Rt. 87 • 860-228-9306

Cloverleigh Farm
468 Rt. 87
www.cloverleighfarm.com

East Willow Farm
402 Rt. 66

Heartstone Winery
468 Rt. 87 • 860-933-1605
www.heartstonewinery.com

Indian Charity School
860-228-0110

Saxton B. Little Free Library
319 Rt. 87 • 860-228-0350
www.columbiactlibrary.org

FOOD

Lee's Stir Fry
187 Rt. 66 East, C • 860-228-8818

Motta's Pastry and Bake Shop
244 Rt. 6 • 860-228-1226
www.mottasbakery.com

The Main Moose
94 Rt. 66 East • 860-337-0113
www.themainmoose.com

Thunderbird Café
234 Rt. 6 (Columbia Ford Kia)
www.columbiathunderbirdcafe.com

HIKING & TRAILS

Joshua's Trust Properites:
www.joshuastrust.org
- **Goldberg Parcel** Rts. 6 & 66
- **Utley Hill Preserve** Near Erdoni Rd.
- **Potter Meadow** 98 Commerce Dr.

Hop River State Park Trail
Columbia Ave. & Rt. 66

Mono Pond State Park
Near 120 Hunt Rd.

Washington-Rochambeau Revolutionary Rte. Nat'l Historic Trail
Near St. Columba Church on Rt. 87

[Passport Stamp / Signature & Date Here]

Coventry

By Bill Jobbagy, Coventry Historical Society

Twenty-miles east of Hartford at the gateway to the "Quiet Corner" lies the town of Coventry. The land was known to the Mohegans as "Wongumbaug" or "crooked pond" for the curved shape of the 380-acre glacial lake in the center of town. The town was set off in 1706 to be divided by deed holders from the legatees of Joshua, third son of the Mohegan sachem, Uncas. The town was named in 1711 from the city of Coventry, England, and incorporated the following year.

During the 18th century the town was mostly a self-sufficient agrarian society centered around the Second Church on the Boston Turnpike and the First Church on the Windham Turnpike (now Main St.). The town is best known as the birthplace of America's young Revolutionary war hero Nathan Hale, who was hung as a spy by the British in 1776.

Coventry was the birthplace of Lorenzo Dow (1777-1834), the revivalist preacher who traveled through this country and the United Kingdom. He was called "crazy" for his methods of luring crowds to his camp meetings, and his biographer called his preachings "a joy to believers and a lash to all others."

More than 100 men from the town responded to the Lexington Alarm in 1775 and Coventry provided substantial amounts of clothing, cider, and pork for the Continental Army. Jeremiah Ripley kept a military provisioning depot on Ripley Hill Rd. The population of Coventry in 1790 was 2,130, remaining at that level until 1880 then accelerating after WWII to about 12,800 today.

From the early 1800s until the Great Depression, south Coventry Village was a hub of manufacturing activity starting with water-powered mills on the Mill Brook which was fed by the reservoir of Lake Wangumbaug. Fifteen mill sites were located on the 2-mile course of the brook. At their peak in 1870, mill businesses comprised more than 50 buildings and employed more than 400 people making, among other things, wool carding machinery, handmade paper, silk, cotton shirting, wool flannel and cassimere, iron forgings, percussion caps, rimfire ammunition, woolen hats, windmills, wagons, paper boxes, printing labels, fiberboard, lumber, cider vinegar, wool shoddy, fish lines.

To this day, South Coventry Village retains its authenticity, interrupted by two small, modern-day commercial retail buildings.

In 1813 the Coventry Glass Works was opened on the corner of Rt. 44 and North River Rd. It produced pocket bottles, medicine containers, and collectible whiskey flasks decorated with railroad scenes and busts of George Washington, Andrew Jackson, and Lafayette. The Connecticut Museum of Glass now stands on the site.

Adelma Grenier Simmons (1903-1996) developed herbal gardening into a popular hobby, showcasing her Caprilands Farm at 534 Silver St. By the 1950s, hundreds attended her lectures, read her books, and dined at her farmhouse restaurant where meals included unique herbal tastings and edible flowers. The farm is no longer in operation.

Following the Great Depression, the town held fast to its rural and

Nathan Hale Homestead (1776). Jerry Dougherty

Notes

farming heritage with many active farms and historical neighborhoods while growing quickly as a suburban community with significant development around Lake Wangumbaug and Eagleville Lake.

Interesting Places

Hale Homestead & Strong-Porter House. Home of the Coventry Historical Society.

Coventry Regional Farmers Market. At Hale Homestead, nationally recognized farmers market. Sun., June-Oct.

Coventry Village. Newly renovated Main St. with unique shops and restaurants in a pedestrian-friendly environment.

Connecticut Vietnam Veteran's Memorial.

Cassidy Hill Vineyard.

Twin Hills Country Club. Bread & Milk St. with the Skungamaug River Golf Course on Folly Lane.

Patriot's Park & Beach. Lake Wangumbaug.

Connecticut Vietnam Veteran's Memorial dedicated in May of 2008 to honor the 612 state residents who died during the Vietnam War. Bill Jobbagy

Address Book

Town Site
www.coventryct.org

Bidwell Tavern
1260 Main St.
860-742-6978
www.thebidwelltavern.com

Cassidy Hill Vineyard
454 Cassidy Hill Rd.
860-498-1126
www.cassidyhillvineyard.com

Coventry Glass Works
Rt. 44 / North River Rd.
www.glassmuseum.org

Coventry Regional Farmers Market
www.coventryfarmersmarket.org

Coventry Village
Main St.

CT Vietnam Veteran's Memorial
Lake St.

Hale Homestead & Strong-Porter House
2299 & 2382 South St.
www.ctlandmarks.org
www.ctcoventryhistoricalsociety.org

Patriot's Park & Beach
Lake St., Lake Wangumbaug

Twin Hills Country Club
199 Bread & Milk St., Rt. 31
860-742-9705
www.twinhillscountryclub.com

[Passport Stamp / Signature & Date Here]

Ellington

By Susan Phillips, Hall Memorial Library and Lynn Fahy, Ellington Historical Society

Ellington is a rural community of 35.5 sq. mi. on the edge of the Connecticut River valley in north central Connecticut. Nestled between Hartford and Massachusetts in Tolland County, the landscape encompasses lush farmland and rolling hills, rising to the forested and mountainous Eastern Uplands.

Ellington was first inhabited by Native Americans of the Nipmuck tribe. A large community was located on the north shore of the lake they called Wabbaquassett, now known as Crystal Lake. Settled as part of Windsor in the early 1730s and known as "The Great Marsh," the town was incorporated as Ellington in 1786. The lush land brought many farmers, and the rivers spawned many small mills. The Halladay Standard windmill, the first commercially successful windmill in North America, was invented in 1854 in Ellington by Daniel Halladay. Using wind energy to pump well water, it made the settlement of the American West possible. Immigrants from Switzerland came to the area to work in the mills and then became the first farmers from the Apostolic Christian Church in America. Their descendants currently run the largest dairy farm in New England right here in Ellington. The Ellington School, a private school established by John Hall, and his son Edward's Family School for Boys attracted students from around the state and the world in the 1800s. Edward's brother, Francis, who was a leading business pioneer in Japan when that country opened its borders to the west in the 1860s, built the Hall Memorial Library in 1903 as a gift to the town in memory of his father and brother. An outstanding example of Neo-Classical Revival architecture, it is the jewel in the crown of the Ellington Center Historic District.

In recent years, some of the vast areas of farmland have been developed and the town has grown, but Ellington retains its rural charm. Come visit us!

Interesting Places

Nellie McKnight Ellington Historical Society Museum is housed in the Nellie McKnight Federalist-style home on Main St. and features exhibits of the history of Ellington and the rural life-style of 19th century.

Ellington Center Historic District. Named to the National Register of Historic Places in 1990, many fine architectural examples from 18th century Colonial to late-19th- and early-20th century Colonial Revival line the streets surrounding the picturesque green, including the beautiful Hall Memorial Library.

Oakridge Dairy LLC. The largest dairy farm in New England has recently been transformed into a state-of-the-art facility with a 350,000 sq. ft. free-range barn housing 3,000 cows and a rotary milking parlor that can milk 72 at a time in 10-minute sessions. Tours available.

Ellington Farmers Market. A year-around market featuring a wide variety of products that are grown, harvested, produced, or handcrafted in Ellington and the state. There is a theme each week, with music, entertainment, and educational activities. Held on Sat., from May thru Oct., 9 AM-Noon in Arbor Park, and during the winter months at the YMCA from 2-4 PM.

The Hall Memorial Library in Ellington. Susan Phillips

Notes

Johnny Appleseed's Farm. Ride the wagons into the orchard to pick your own peaches, apples, and pumpkins. The retail stands offer a fine selection of locally grown fresh fruits and vegetables as well as other native produce and frozen pies, breads, fresh apple cider, and mums in many colors.

Hiking Trails. For a leisurely walk, there are rails-to-trails sections bordering the meandering Hockanum River. For more adventure, try the Blue Blazed trails in the Shenipsit State Forest climbing to Soapstone Mountain.

Events

Winterfest. Held the first Sat. in Dec., this holiday-season kickoff event takes place on the town green and in surrounding buildings. Music, crafts, food, and of course an appearance by Santa and friends, topped off with a night parade featuring floats and fire trucks decorated with lights.

Ellington Fire Department Carnival. A classic small-town carnival held on the second weekend in Sept. with food, rides, and fun.

Mini-Golf at the Library. Fun for the whole family during the bleak days of winter. The Hall Memorial Library is transformed into an 18+ hole indoor mini-golf course for the first Sat. in Feb. Food available.

Nellie McKnight Museum is owned and operated by the Ellington Historical Society. Susan Phillips

Address Book

Town Site
www.ellington-ct.gov

Ellington Center Historic District
Main & Maple Sts.

Ellington Farmers Market
Arbor Park, 33 Main St. (summer)
YMCA, 11 Pinney St. (winter)
www.ellingtonfarmersmarket.com

Hall Memorial Library
93 Main St.
860-870-3160
www.library.ellington-ct.gov

Johnny Appleseed's Farm
860-875-1000
www.johnnyappleseedfarmct.com

Nellie McKnight Ellington Historical Society Museum
70 Main St.
860-872-0121
www.ellingtonhistsoc.org

Oak Ridge Dairy
33 Jobs Hill Rd.
860-875-2858
www.oakridgedairy.com

EVENTS

Winterfest
Town Green • 860-870-3160

Ellington Fire Department Carnival
Brookside Park, Rt.140

Mini-Golf at the Library
93 Main St. • 860-870-3160

[Passport Stamp / Signature & Date Here]

HEBRON

By Kevin J. Tulimieri, Hebron resident, researcher, historical writer & early American historian

Located at important cross roads of modern day Rt. 85 and Rt. 66, the colonial settlement of Hebron began during the transformational times surrounding the conflict known as King Phillip's War. Erupting in 1675 between the English colonists and several native communities, the conflict changed the face of New England. A few local tribes allied with the English, including the Mohegans under their Sachem, Uncas, and his sons, Attawanhood and Owaneco. In 1676, Attawanhood, issued a Will granting his English friends and fellow soldiers thousands of acres of land described as "laying on both sides of the Ungoshot river", today known as the Blackledge River. The gift was confirmed by the General Court in 1687 and the first home lots were laid out in 1702. These early settlers are associated with the story of Prophet's Rock, the oldest of all of Hebron's landmarks. According to local legend, as the men of the village were out exploring, the women became concerned and ventured out to find them. The serenade of the frightened women attracted their husbands, who wandered towards the sound until they were reunited. The settlement continued to grow and was officially incorporated as Connecticut's 41st town in 1708.

The Revolutionary War again found Hebron at a crossroads of ideas. Rev. Samuel Peters was a staunch Loyalist and was confronted twice by the Sons of Liberty in 1774. He was barely saved from tar and feathers and soon after fled Hebron for England. In 1776, his abandoned home was confiscated and converted to public property. Peters' slaves, Cesar Peters, his wife, Lowis, and their children, were at the center of a dramatic rescue. In September 1787, six armed men arrived at the Peters' house and claimed possession of Cesar and his family as payment of Peter's debt. The family was to be taken to Norwich, shipped to South Carolina and sold to the highest bidder. A group of Hebron residents quickly devised a plan to charge Cesar Peters with theft of clothing and an arrest warrant was issued. The Hebron constable caught up with the group just outside of Norwich and took Cesar Peters and his family into custody. They were returned to Hebron and greeted with a large celebration. Finally, in 1789, a petition was granted by the General Assembly and Cesar Peters and his family were emancipated.

One of the more recent, but nonetheless historic, buildings in Hebron is the World War II era Aircraft Warning Service Freeman Observation Post #52. The building originally stood on top of Post Hill, now Skyline Farm. The post was in full use from November 1942 until October 1943. Each passing airplane was recorded and reported to a central station in Boston. The building was recently restored and is now on the property of Hebron Town Hall. It is a rare surviving civilian observation post out of the 14,000 that saw service.

No matter where you look in Hebron, history is waiting at every crossroad. From the natural beauty to historic buildings and events, Hebron has something special around every corner.

INTERESTING PLACES

Prophet's Rock. From Main St. (Rt. 66), turn south on Burrows

The towns of Hebron and Columbia collaborated in building an observation post, Freeman #52 on Lucius Robinson's land on Post Hill (now Skyline Farm on Rt. 66) in Columbia. It was used from 11-2-42 to 10-13-43 to spot enemy planes. Kevin Tulimer

Notes

Hill Rd. and go approx. 1.5 miles. Prophet's Rock is on the west side of Burrows Hill Rd.

Peters' House. Home of Rev. Samuel Peters and his former slaves, Cesar and Lowis Peters and their 10 children. Cesar and Lowis Peters Archaeological Site. It is listed on the Connecticut Freedom Trail at: www.ctfreedomtrail.org.

Old Town Hall/Hebron Historical Society.

World War II Civilian Aircraft Observation Post #52. Hebron Town Hall property.

Burrows Hill Schoolhouse. Established about 1730 and now owned by the Hebron Historical Society. At corner of Burrows Hill Rd. and School House Rd.

Grayville Falls Town Park. Off Grayville Rd. near the intersection with Reidy Hill Rd.

Grist Mill Trails. Off Chestnut Hill Rd.

Gay City State Park. Hiking, swimming, picnicking, and fishing. Off West St. (Rt. 85)

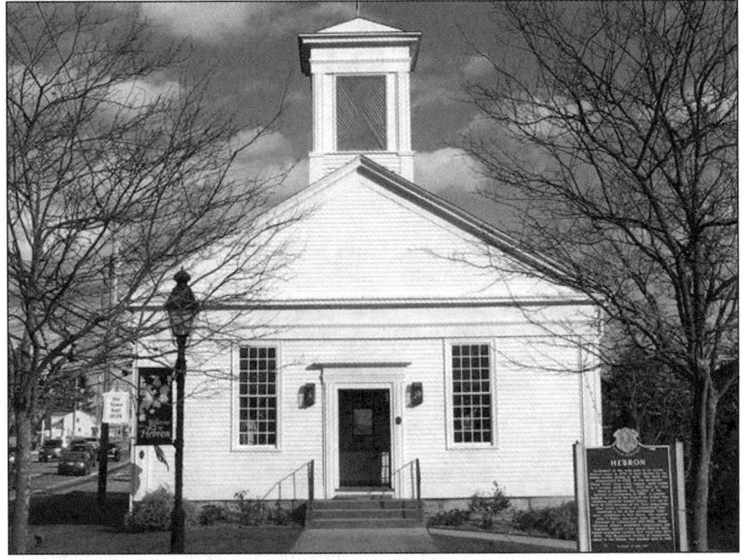

The Old Town House was built in 1838 as a Methodist meeting house. When the church broke up, the town bought it in 1863, lowered it to one story, and used it as the town hall until 1950. It was used by civic groups until 1971 when the Hebron Historical Society became the owners and use it as a museum. Kevin Tulimer

Address Book

Town Site
www.hebronct.com

Burrows Hill Schoolhouse
Burrows Hill & School House Rds.

Connecticut Freedom Trail
www.ctfreedomtrail.org

Gay City State Park
435 North St.
www.ct.gov

Grist Mill Trails
Chestnut Hill Rd.

Hebron Historical Society
22 Main St.
www.hebronhistoricalsociety.org

Old Town Hall
26 Main St.

Peters' House
150 East St.

Prophet's Rock
Burrows Hill Rd.

World War II Civilian Aircraft Observation Post #52
15 Gilead St.

[Passport Stamp / Signature & Date Here]

MANSFIELD

By Shu Qian, Mansfield resident, and Teaching & Learning Librarian, Worcester State University Library

Mansfield is a diverse and fast-growing town 8 miles north of Willimantic in Tolland Co. It encompasses the peaceful Mansfield Hollow Lake as well as Storrs, the home of the University of Connecticut. Here you can enjoy not only the beauty of nature, but also the taste of history and culture.

The Town of Mansfield was incorporated in 1720. In 1810 the country's first silk mill was built here. Then Mansfield led the country in silk production along with the neighboring town of Willimantic, which transformed the local economy from agriculture to industry. But the textile industry's heyday ended in the mid-1800s. Instead the new industry, education, became the new excitement in Mansfield after the Storrs Agricultural School was founded in 1881, now known as University of Connecticut, Storrs.

With the fast growth of the university campus, the population in Mansfield dramatically increased from 1,827 in 1900 to 26,543 in 2010. Today Mansfield has become the cultural center in the east of the state with its unique traditions and programs. The Storrs Center is the new 'pearl' of the town bringing a downtown experience to the residents and the visitors as well.

INTERESTING PLACES

Mansfield Hollow State Park. Offers boating, kayaking, fishing, biking, hiking, and picnicking.

The Storrs Center. Food, drink, outdoor concert, shopping and more.

UConn Dairy Bar & Horsebarn Hill. Delicious college-made ice cream, hiking, kiting, visiting farm animals.

UConn Sports. Check out schedules of your favorite Huskie sports team and buy tickets. www.uconnhuskies.com

Jorgensen Center for the Performing Arts. Enjoy world-class shows and performances.

Connecticut Repertory Theatre. Run by UConn Department of Dramatic Arts.

Connecticut State Museum of Natural History. Storrs.

Ballard Institute and Museum of Puppetry. Storrs.

William Benton Museum of Art.

Adventure Park at Storrs. Enjoy climbing and zip lines.

Mansfield Drive-In Theater. Movie schedule.

Mansfield Drive-In Marketplace. Eastern Connecticut's largest Flea Market. Open Every Sunday, 8 AM–3 PM indoors and outdoors, rain or shine.

Kira and Lydia Roloff, Marty's granddaughters, enjoying milk shakes at UConn Dairy Bar on Horsebarn Hill Rd. The delicious ice cream is made by the college students. Podskoch

NOTES

Just across the street from the UConn Campus in Storrs is Dog Lane in Storrs Center. It has many fine restaurants, shops, and Barnes & Noble at the UConn bookstore. Shu Qian

ADDRESS BOOK

Town Site
www.mansfieldct.gov

Adventure Park at Storrs
2007 Storrs Rd., Storrs
www.storrsadventurepark.com

Ballard Institute & Museum of Puppetry
1 Royce Circle, Ste. 101B, Storrs
www.bimp.uconn.edu

Connecticut Repertory Theatre
820 Bolton Rd. #1127, Storrs
www.crt.uconn.edu

Connecticut State Museum of Natural History
75 N. Eagleville Rd., Storrs
860-486-4460
www.mnh.uconn.edu

Jorgensen Center for the Performing Arts
2132 Hillside Rd. Unit 3104
www.jorgensen.uconn.edu

Mansfield Drive-In Theater
228 Stafford Rd.
www.mansfielddrivein.com

Mansfield Hollow State Park
151 Bassetts Bridge Rd.
www.ct.gov

The Storrs Center
1 Dog Ln., Storrs
www.storrscenter.com

UConn Dairy Bar & Horsebarn Hill
3636 Horsebarn Hill Rd. Ext., Storrs
www.dining.uconn.edu

William Benton Museum of Art.
245 Glenbrook Rd., Storrs
www.benton.uconn.edu

[Passport Stamp / Signature & Date Here]

SOMERS

By Melissa Savilonis, resident of neighboring town

The Town of Somers is in north central Conn. only 9 miles from Springfield, Mass. It was established in 1734. In the 17th century, Somers was initially a part of Massachusetts' Agawam Plantation (which became Springfield, MA in 1641); in 1682, the Enfield Parish (which included Enfield and Somers) broke off from the Springfield region. Somers was originally named East Enfield and had its first settler arrive in 1706.

Today it is a small farming and milling community. There are many attractions within its borders.

INTERESTING PLACES

Shallowbrook Equestrian Center (1962). It has year-around horse shows, lessons, indoor rink, and a polo field.

Shenipsit State Forest and Soapstone Mountain. Hiking, nature walks, running, beautiful sunrises and sunsets, and the plethora of Connecticut wildlife. Gulf Rd.

Sonny's Place. Offers family activities: mini-golf, rock-climbing, go-carts, batting cages, fine dining, ice cream. A favorite throughout the community!

Copper House Tavern. This is the best place for celebrating special occasions. Formerly the Somers Inn, renamed in 2014.

Cedar Knob Golf Course. A scenic 18-hole public course.

Pleasant View Farm. The 600-acre farm specializes in raising quality feed for horses and other classes of livestock. A Town-Wide Tag Sale is held here on the last Sunday of the month.

Four Town Fair. Usually held after the third weekend in September, it is one of the oldest fairs in the country. The 4-H Fair is also held here. Farm animals (cows, pigs, hogs, sheep, rabbits, chickens, and horses) are displayed near the tractor pull and various local bands perform.

Scantic River. A great fishing spot I visited with my dad while growing up! It has a gazebo to sit in and watch the sun come up over the water while listening to the sounds of nature or children at the playground next door. Off Rt. 190, just past All Saints Church. 25 School St. (Rt. 190) in Somersville.

Ye Olde Blacksmith Shop. Offering small furniture, puzzles, books, tools, household items, and home-baked goods. Open Saturdays 9 AM-3 PM. May, June, Sept., and Oct.

Bond 124. An Italian restaurant with a quiet woodsy view.

EM Framing. Offers beautiful homemade gifts and picture framing.

Joanna's. A converted bowling alley turned bar.

Annual Chili Cook-Off sponsored by the Somers Volunteer Fire Dept. Visit www.chilict.com.

The Old Mill Inn B&B.

Clear Mountain Alpacas B&B.

Somers Library located in the school complex.

Irish Bend Orchard.

Scantic Valley Farm.

The Keeney Mill dam forms the Mill Pond on the Scantic River in Somersville. The flatwater is great for kayaking, canoeing, and fishing. Melissa Savilonis

Notes

Pell Family Farm.

Shadow Valley Farms. There is nothing better than picking your own fruits and vegetables.

Somers is the place to check out. You may just end up staying!

Address Book

Town Site
www.somersct.gov

Cedar Knob Golf Course
446 Billings Rd. (Rt. 83)
860-749-3550
www.cedarknobgolfcourse.com

Clear Mountain Alpacas B&B
45 Pioneer Hts.
860-749-2510
www.clearmountainalpacas.com

Copper House Tavern
585 Main St.
860-265-7535
www.copperhousetaverncct.com

EM Framing
111 Main St.
860-749-4863

Four Town Fairgrounds
56 Egypt Rd.
www.fourtownfair.com

Irish Bend Orchard
90 Pioneer Hts.
www.irishbendorchard.com

Joanna's
145 Main St. (Rt. 190)
860-749-6002
www.joannasbanquets.com

The Old Mill Inn B&B
63 Maple St., Somersville
www.theoldmillinbnb.com

Pell Family Farm
92 Kibbe Grove Rd.
www.pell-farms.com

Pleasant View Farm
452 South Rd.
www.pleasantviewfarmsinc.com

Scantic Valley Farm
327 9th District Rd.
www.scanticvalleyfarm.com

Shadow Valley Farms
111 Stafford Rd.
860-749-4795

Shallowbrook Equestrian Center
247 Hall Hill Rd.
www.shallowbrook.com

Somer's Library
2 Vision Blvd.
www.somerspubliclibrary.org

Sonny's Place
349 Main St.
www.sonnysplace.com

Ye Olde Blacksmith Shop
22 Maple St., Somersville
www.somersvilleucc.org

Sonny's Place is a fun place to take the family and enjoy these activities: Go Karts, batting cages, Zipline laser tag, or miniature golf. Refreshments are available. Sonny's Place

[Passport Stamp / Signature & Date Here]

Stafford

By John Crowley, Stafford Historian

Stafford is in Tolland County in northeastern Connecticut with a population of 12,192 in 2010. It consists of the downtown area of Stafford Springs and villages of Stafford Hollow, Crystal Lake, Ellithorpe, Hydeville, Village Hill, Orcuttsville, Staffordville, and West Stafford.

Stafford was incorporated in 1719 with grants of 200 acres each given to 12 men. Stafford was initially a farming community.

The Nipmuck Indians told their new neighbors of the medical benefits of the springs in what became the center of town. The Springs of Stafford became famous for health benefits and many people came to partake of the spring waters. One famous guest was John Adams, our second President. In 1802 a hotel was built next to the Springs to house guests. The main stage line between Hartford and Boston came through Stafford. This helped in spreading the reputation of the spring waters.

Industry first came to Stafford in the form of furnaces built to take advantage of the several sources of iron ore in town. The first furnace was built in 1734. Stafford furnaces made the first stoves in Connecticut. Stafford also produced cannons and cannon balls to support America's efforts in the Revolutionary War.

In the 1830s industry came to Stafford in the form of woolen and cotton mills. From 1837 to 1841 four woolen mills were built along the waterways of Stafford. The textile industry flourished. Stafford's woolen and cotton industries have survived the years and one woolen mill survives today.

Stafford got a boost in 1850 when the railroad came through. It provided an inexpensive way to bring in raw products and ship finished goods for Stafford's many mills.

West Stafford was the home to several machine shops in the mid- to late-1800s. West Stafford is the home of the birth of the lathe and drill chuck which dramatically changed the machining industry. It was invented by Simon Fairman.

Today, with its lakes, streams, farmlands, and Shenipsit State Forest, Stafford retains its rural character.

Interesting Places

Stafford Historical Society. Served as the Stafford Public library for over 100 years. Built in 1885 as an office for Julius Converse, owner of the Mineral Springs Manufacturing Co. The museum has two floors of exhibits of Stafford photographs and memorabilia.

Stafford Library. Serving community with information, programs, and activities.

Stafford Speedway. A NASCAR sanctioned racetrack. Races are run every Friday night from spring through fall.

Stafford Hollow. A village that was the town center during the 18th and 19th centuries, before the growth of the village of Stafford Springs. The homes and buildings, including the original Town Hall and Stafford Memorial Hall, are on the National Historic Register. At junction of Rt. 19 and Rt. 319.

The Stafford Historical Society is in the 1885 building that was previously the town library, the probate judge's office, the offices of the Converse Woolen Co., and the bottling house of the Stafford Mineral Waters Co. Jerry Dougherty

Notes

Shenipset State Forest. Contains 11 parcels spread over 7,000 acres in Stafford, Somers, and Ellington. Soapstone Mt. Features hiking, mountain biking, cross-country skiing, picnicking, snowmobiling, hunting, and letterboxing. Entrance at 360 Gulf Rd., 1 mile south of Rt. 190 in Somers.

Civilian Conservation Corps Museum. The museum is in Camp Conner Administration Building. The camp was est. on June 4, 1935. The boys worked in the Shenipsit and Nipmuck State Forest where they planted trees, fought spread of gypsy moths, built roads, fought fires, and built state parks. The museum is in the Administration Building and has many photos, artifacts, and history of the camps in Conn. and camps out West where many Conn. boys worked. The CCC was established by President Roosevelt to provide work for unemployed young men, 18-25, during the Depression.

Nipmuck State Forest. 9,000 acres surround Bigelow Hollow State Park in the town of Union and include parcels in Stafford, Ashford, and other towns. Features hiking, fishing, picnicking, snowmobiling, and camping.

The Connecticut Civilian Conservation Corps Museum at 166 Chestnut Hill Rd. (Rt. 190) has CCC memorabilia and photos on display in the old Camp Connors Administration building. It is open on Sundays from Memorial Day to Labor Day weekends from Noon-3 PM. *Podskoch*

Address Book

Town Site
www.staffordct.org

Connecticut Civilian Conservation Corps Museum
166 Chestnut Hill Rd.
860-684-3013

Shenipset State Forest
360 Gulf Rd.

Stafford Historical Society
5 Spring St.
860-684-7978

Stafford Hollow
Rt. 19 & 319

Stafford Library
10 Levinthal Run
860-684-2852
www.staffordlibrary.org

Stafford Speedway
55 West St.
860-684-2783
www.staffordmotorspeedway.com

[Passport Stamp / Signature & Date Here]

TOLLAND

By Kate Farrish, Tolland Historical Society

The rural, hilly town of Tolland, settled before 1715, covers 41 square miles in north-central Connecticut 20 miles northeast of Hartford.

Originally part of Windsor, it was settled by residents whose growing families needed homesteads and moved east to land that had been purchased from the Native Americans.

The General Assembly granted the settlers a charter on May 12, 1715. The town was named after an English town in Somerset and was incorporated as Connecticut's 49th town in May 1722.

Tolland was designated as the county seat in 1785, leading residents to build a courthouse and a jail through town subscription. By early 1822, the courthouse and jail sat at the terminus of five busy turnpikes.

The Tolland Green Historic District was placed on the National Register of Historic Places in June 1997. The district features more than 50 homes and historic buildings surrounding a green with street lights designed to match those installed in the 1920s. The oldest homes, dating to the middle and late 18th century, exhibit the typical features of Colonial Connecticut architecture, including a broadside-to-the-road orientation and clapboard exteriors. Other homes have an Italianate influence or were built in the Federal, Greek Revival or Victorian styles.

The district also includes the Greek Revival-style United Congregational Church of Tolland, built in 1838, and the eclectic-style Methodist Church, which was built in 1880. The former Ratcliffe Hicks Memorial School, built in 1908, now houses the town offices and a recently expanded Tolland Public Library. The fully restored old town hall, built in 1879, is now home to the Arts of Tolland.

In the 2010 census, the population of Tolland was 15,052. Once sustained by farming, the town has retained much of its rural character and is now known for its historic green as well as the hundreds of acres of open space and hiking areas that it has preserved.

INTERESTING PLACES

Daniel Benton Homestead. Six generations of the Benton family lived in this 1720 homestead, continuously for 210 years. The cellar, with a large cooking fireplace, was used to house Hessian prisoners for 18 months during the Revolutionary War. It was opened as a museum by the Tolland Historical Society in 1970. Open Sunday afternoons from May to Oct.

Old Tolland County Jail (1856) and Museum. Tolland Historical Society operates this stone jail museum used by the state until 1968. Features the attached 1863 jailer's home, where displays of furniture and artifacts depict Tolland life and industry in the late 19th and early 20th centuries. Also there is a shed where woodworking, farm and outdoor work are depicted, with many artifacts from the same period. Some former inmates have visited the jail and told stories of life at the old "Hollyhock Hotel."

Old Tolland County Court House (1822) Museum. It was used until 1890 and considered one of the

The Tolland Historical Society operates the 1856 Old Tolland County Jail as a museum at 52 Tolland Green. Perne R. Maynard

Notes

oldest civic buildings in the state. The second floor, with a cove ceiling and a beautiful Palladian window, features a fully restored courtroom and exhibits relating to the growth of the town and the history of the building. Also operated by Tolland Historical Society. Open Sunday afternoons May-October.

Hicks-Stearns Museum. Built in the 1700s, it served as an inn. It was occupied by the Hicks family from 1845-1970. It was then home to Ratcliffe Hicks, a lawyer and industrialist who left money in his will to create an agricultural school, still located at the nearby University of Connecticut. It features family heirlooms and treasures from three generations of the Hicks family. Open May-December.

Crandall Park. Active and passive recreation area, includes, 3.8 miles of wooded hiking trails, and 380 acres of undeveloped land.

The 1822 Old Tolland County Court House has a restored courtroom with exhibits. It is one of three museums on the historic Tolland Green. Perne R. Maynard

Arts of Tolland Center. Established in the restored old Town Hall in 1997. Built in 1879, the building served as town hall until 1985. The group was founded in 1973 to supplement fine arts programming in the Tolland school system. It hosts a range of artistic and cultural experiences, including photo and art exhibits and a popular holiday Art Mart each December.

Address Book

Town Site
www.tollandct.gov

Arts of Tolland Center
22 Tolland Green
860-871-7405
www.artsoftolland.org

Crandall Park
64 Cider Mill Pond Rd.
860-871-3610
www.tolland.org

Daniel Benton Homestead
154 Metcalf Rd.
860-974-1875.
www.tollandhistorical.org

Hicks-Stearns Museum
42 Tolland Green
860-875-7552
Facebook.com/HicksStearns

Old Tolland County Court House
53 Tolland Green
860-870-9599
www.tollandhistorical.org

Old Tolland County Jail
52 Tolland Green
860-870-9599
www.tollandhistorical.org

[Passport Stamp / Signature & Date Here]

Union

By Jeannine Upson, Union Historical Society

Union, the smallest town in the state, numbered only 913 souls in 2015 within its 29.9 sq. mi. Union is in northeastern Tolland County and has the highest elevation in the state east of the Connecticut River.

Last of the towns east of the Connecticut River to be settled because of its rough terrain and poor soil, Union was sold in 1720 by the Gen. Assembly to 12 proprietors for 307 British pounds. Before the town was incorporated in 1734, the proprietors established 200 acres for public use, with places for a meetinghouse, burying ground, and parade ground.

Forestry has always been Union's primary industry. There is no post office or bank. There is a free public library, town office building, highway garage, a picturesque white church set on the hill across from the Town Green, and the pavilion in the Town Grove.

Union provides unlimited opportunities for outside activities: hiking, biking, cross-country skiing, snowshoeing, boating, hunting, and fishing. One third of the town's area is set aside as park and forest land: Bigelow Hollow State Park, the Mountain Laurel Sanctuary, and Nipmuck State Forest. The Yale School of Forestry occupies another one fifth.

Interesting Places

Bigelow Hollow State Park. Consists of approx. 513 acres and contains the 30-acre Bigelow Hollow Pond and the 370-acre Mashapaug Lake. The beautiful scenery attracts many visitors to picnic, swim, boat, and enjoy nature. Located on Rt. 171.

Breakneck Pond and Cat Rocks. Located in the NE corner of Union within Nipmuck Forest, it is a lure for many hikers because of immense masses of boulders and precipices.

Laurel Sanctuary. Located on Rt. 190 in the Nipmuck State Forest, it consists of a 2-mile horseshoe-shaped road established in the 1930s by the Civilian Conservation Corps. June will find it blooming with Mountain Laurel, the Connecticut State Flower.

Nipmuck Forest. Surrounds Bigelow Hollow State Park, consists of 8,058 acres, most of it in Union. Located within the forest is Mt. Ochepetuck (Bald Hill) at an altitude of 1,286 feet.

Museum on the Green. A history museum of the Union Historical Society contains artifacts and information about Union. Open Tues. evenings from 7-9 PM or by appointment.

Town Green. In 1901 the foundation was laid for the Mothers' Soldiers' Monument, a cannon supported on a rough-finished dark gray granite base. A bronze plaque lists the names of Civil War veterans. Also on the Green is a granite tribute to veterans of WWI, WWII, Korea, Vietnam, and Persian Gulf wars.

Travelers Restaurant. The yellow-roofed building draws visitors from near and far. Turkey dinners are a specialty. Diners can choose a free book or two from an extensive collection. A used bookstore in the lower part of the building is a treasure trove.

Walking Tour. The Union Green Historic District was added to the National Register of Historic

The Union Green with the Union Historical Society (UHS) Museum (L) and the Congregational Church. UHS

Notes

Places in 1990. The route is marked by granite hitching posts. Booklets guiding the tour may be obtained at the Union Town Hall (860-684-3770), Union Free Public Library (860-684-4913), or Union Historical Society (860-684-7078).

At the Traveler Restaurant, diners enjoy burgers, steaks, fried seafood, beer, and free books. Traveler Restaurant

The historic 1910 Union Free Public Library is at 979 Buckley Hwy. Jerry Dougherty

Address Book

Town Site
www.unionconnecticut.org

Bigelow Hollow State Park
298 Bigelow Hollow Rd.

Breakneck Pond & Cat Rocks
Located in Nipmuck State Forest

Laurel Sanctuary
Rt. 190 in Nipmuck State Forest

Museum on the Green
1 Town Hall Rd.
860-684-7078
www.unionconnecticut.org

Nipmuck State Forest
166 Chestnut Hill Rd., Stafford Springs

Traveler Restaurant
1257 Buckley Hwy., Exit 74 off I-84
860-684-4920
Facebook.com/thefoodandbookpeople

Union Free Public Library
979 Buckley Hwy.
860-684-4913
www.unionctfreepubliclibrary.org

Union Historical Society
6 Town Hall Rd.
860-684-7078
www.unioncthistoricalsociety.org

Union Town Hall
1043 Buckley Hwy.
860-684-3770

Walking Tour of the Union Green Historic District
Booklet tour guides are available at: Union Town Hall, Union Free Public Library, or Union Historical Society

[Passport Stamp / Signature & Date Here]

Vernon

By Denise J. Stankovics, retired Co-Director, Rockville Public Library

Originally part of Bolton, Vernon, in Tolland County, contains the smaller villages of Rockville, Talcotville, and Dobsonville.

Vernon's claim to fame was its mills, the first of which was a cotton spinning mill est. in 1809 and powered by the Tankeroosen River.

The center of industry shifted to the town's northeast corner where the Rock Mill opened in the 1820s and gave its name to Rockville, later called the "Loom City." Powered by the Hockanum River's 254-foot cascade, it was the first of 12 textile mills built along the river. Rockville's population grew as workers were drawn to the mills which became internationally famous for their fine woolens. Fabric produced here was used in the presidential inauguration suits of Benjamin Harrison, William McKinley, and Theodore Roosevelt.

Abolitionist John Brown was hired by Rockville's mills to purchase raw wool in the west for which he was given $2,800, but he failed to follow through and still owed the money at the time of his death.

Rockville was incorporated as a city within the town of Vernon in 1889. A decline came in the 1950s when the mills closed and moved south. In 1965 the city ceased to exist when its government was consolidated with the town's.

The rest of Vernon remained rural until the 1940s and '50s when a highway, now I-84, was built through the town and the post-war housing boom began. The majority of the town's pop. of almost 30,000 now lives in the outlying area, which includes Vernon Center, Dobsonville, and Talcottville. Most residents are employed by companies based in greater Hartford.

Notable People

Vernon's famous residents include three graduates of Rockville High School. Still life painter Charles Ethan Porter (c.1847-1923), one of the few African-American professional artists of the 19th century, grew up in Vernon and studied abroad. After a promising start his career declined and he died in poverty, but fortunately a renewed appreciation of his work occurred late in the 20th century.

Rock and Roll Hall of Famer Gene Pitney (1940-2006), the "Rockville Rocket," lived in the area all his life. He had 16 Top 40 hits in the United States. An exhibit in Vernon's Town Hall honors his memory.

Virginia U.S. Senator and former governor, Mark Warner (1954-), a contender for the 2008 presidential nomination, was born in Indiana but moved to Connecticut and attended schools in Vernon.

Interesting Places

Fox Hill Tower (1939). The 72' Romanesque tower built of Tolland granite is a memorial for the town's veterans.

New England Civil War Museum. The museum is housed in the original Grand Army of the Republic Hall. Open Sundays except holidays, 12 Noon-3 PM.

Rockville Historic District. On the National Register of Historic Places, the area includes Greek Revival, Late Victorian, and Classical Revival architecture. Bounded by Snipsic St., Davis Ave., West St., and South St.

Rockville Public Library. The original part of the building, dedicated in 1904, was designed by famed New York architect Charles A. Platt. The white marble building is a memorial to mill owner George Maxwell. Mon.-Thurs. 10 AM-8 PM, Fri. and Sat. 10 AM-1 PM (Closed Sat. during July and Aug.).

Vernon Historical Society. Every Thurs. and 2nd and 4th Sundays, 2-4 PM.

Notes

The beautiful 72' Romanesque Fox Hill Tower was built in 1939 of Tolland granite to honor the town's veterans.
Denise J. Stankovics

Address Book

Town Site
www.vernon-ct.gov

Fox Hill Tower in Henry Park
120 South St.

New England Civil War Museum
14 Park Place
860-870-3563
www.newenglandcivilwarmuseum.com

Rockville Public Library
52 Union St.
860-875-5892
www.rockvillepubliclibrary.org

Vernon Historical Society
734 Hartford Tpke.
860-875-4326
www.vernonhistoricalsoc.org

[Passport Stamp / Signature & Date Here]

Willington

By Mark A. Palmer, Town of Willington Historian

In 1720, a patent for 16,000 acres lying east of the Willimantic River and north of the Mansfield town line was sold to eight men. One of the original patent holders, Roger Wolcott served as Governor of Connecticut from 1750 to 1754. The patent was a part of Wabaquasett Country that had been acquired by Major James Fitch in 1684. Wabaquasett country extended from Shenipsit Lake to the Quinebaug River and beyond, supposedly some 45 miles in breadth. On May 11, 1727, the Town of Willington was incorporated following the settlement of about a dozen families.

From descriptions in early town land records, this countryside was a mosaic of bare, plain or grassy hills, cedar swamps, woodland and meadow. The bare hills and meadows were likely a result of the seasonal burn of the countryside by Native American communities prior to and during initial English settlement. According to records, this Nipmuck country was a traditional hunting ground for the Shetucket, Wabaquasett, and Mohegan. Records note that in 1725 there were Shetucket and Wabaquasett still hunting and fishing in Willington. A historical salmon fishing place on the Willimantic River, adjacent to present day Cole Wilde Trout management area, was noted on Woodstock surveyor John Chandler's 1705 map of the Mohegan Sachems Hereditary Land.

The Colonial center of Willington was the 1736 Congregational Meeting House on Willington Hill. Several historical routes crossed the town such as the Hartford road shown on Chandler's 1705 map. The Windham and Mansfield Turnpike (Rt. 320), chartered in May 1800, and the Tolland County Turnpike (Rt. 74), chartered in May 1809, crossed paths near the 1815 Glazier Tavern, located on the west end of the Common on Willington Hill.

Water powered mills like John Cady's 1725 sawmill on Conant Brook in South Willington were important to the town's economy. Mills have defined the East Willington, Daleville, Forestville, Eldredge Mills, and South Willington parts of town from the early 1700s to the 1900s. Willington in the late 1800s was identified with Gardiner Hall's Thread Mill in South Willington.

Family farms, mills, forges, woodworking, shoe, and comb shops from the early 1720s and family-run businesses such as button shops in the 1930s, have provided Willington with the varied economic base typical of eastern Connecticut towns. Small family farms and businesses continue to do so today. With a population of just over 6,000, the landscape retains much of the mosaic of fields, meadows, ponds and streams found in this Mohegan reserved land of 300 years ago.

Willington is the birthplace and childhood home of Jared Sparks (1789-1866), historian, President of Harvard University and biographer of George Washington.

Places of Interest

Glazier Tavern (1815). At the west end of the Willington Green it is owned by Willington Historical Society. It serves as the town museum and educational center. Please check with the Willington

The Gardiner Hall Jr. Museum at The Mill Works is at 156 River Rd. (Rt. 32). Podskoch

Notes

Historical Society for events.

Masinda Ocean Pearl Button Co. The property, site of an 18th century sawmill, was purchased in 1903 by William Masinda and operated until 1938 when abalone shell imports from Australian and New Zealand ceased. The shop, with the original 80-year-old equipment, is once again making shell buttons as Masinda's Button Shop.

Gardiner Hall Jr. Museum. The Eastern Connecticut Center for History, Art, and Performance. creates the opportunity for the residents of Willington and surrounding towns to learn about the technical innovations, production methods, and the application of unique management practices that shaped the local area.

The Packing House. In 1860, Gardner Hall, Jr. built the first spooled-thread production facility in the U.S. It was valued at over $2,225,000 at the time of his death in 1915. This historic hall now provides an intimate environment for performance, events, and programs in acoustic music, dance, film, literature, and the visual arts.

Willington Common Historic District. For a map, visit willingtonhistoricalsocietyct.org

Fenton-Ruby Park and Wildlife Preserve. At the intersection of Burma and Moose Meadow Rds.

Trout Fishing on Roaring Brook. Please see the Connecticut Department of Energy and Environmental Protection web site for stocking information and maps: www.ct.gov/deep

Willington Public Library.

The c.1815 Daniel Glazier Tavern is at the west end of the Willington Green and owned and operated as a museum by the Willington Historical Society. Mark Palmer

Address Book

Town Site
www.willingtonct.gov

Fenton-Ruby Park
Burma & Moose Meadow Rds.
www.willingtonct.org

Gardiner Hall Jr. Museum
www.thepackinghouse.us/history

Glazier Tavern
Willington Green
www.willingtonhistoricalsocietyct.org

Masinda's Button Shop
213 Luchon Rd.
860-429-4988
Facebook.com/MasindaButtonShop

The Packing House
437 Pequot Ave., Ste. 1301
518-791-9474
www.thepackinghouse.us

Willington Public Library
7 Ruby Rd.
860-429-3854
www.willingtonpubliclibrary.org

[Passport Stamp / Signature & Date Here]

Windham
County
WOODSTOCK
THOMPSON
PUTNAM
ASHFORD
EASTFORD
POMFRET
KILLINGLY
CHAPLIN
HAMPTON
BROOKLYN
WINDHAM
SCOTLAND
CANTERBURY
PLAINFIELD
STERLING

CHAPTER 8

WINDHAM COUNTY

Ashford

By Joanie Bowley, President, Ashford Historical Society

Ashford, in Windham County, is in the northeast, or 'Quiet Corner,' of the state. In 2010 the population was 4,317. The town includes the hamlets of Westford and Warrenville.

Ashford was formerly New Scituate, and was settled in 1710. It was incorporated as a town in October of 1714. Eastford was part of Ashford until 1847 when Eastford separated and organized its own town.

During the Revolutionary War the famous Knowlton's Rangers were led by Ashford's Col. Thomas Knowlton who led about 75 men to Boston to fight the British at the Battle of Bunker Hill. He later fell in battle on Sept. 16, 1776, at Harlem Heights, on Long Island where he was covering a retreat of Washington's troops. Other famous men from the Civil War include Brigadier General Edward W. Whitaker (1841-1864) and Brigadier General Nathaniel Lyon (1818-1861).

Ashford has many beautiful old buildings dating back to the 18th and 19th centuries. The Village of Westford had a very prosperous glass factory in the late 19th century. In the early 18th century the center of Ashford, was located on "Pine Hill" east of Warrenville where the First Congregational Church stood. However, it was destroyed three times and never rebuilt. Warrenville then became the center of Ashford where a Baptist Church had been in the late 1700s.

Ashford was a farming community. Roads laid by committees elected at the Annual Town Meeting were configured to provide farmers with the fastest, safest routes to market and direct routes from Hartford to Boston and Providence. Taverns, hotels, and blacksmith shops grew up along the well-traveled highways. Tanneries and carpenter shops, gristmills, dairy and chicken farms, a glass factory and the production of local produce waxed and waned with the population. Following conflicts beginning with the Revolution, Ashford's population became aware of the possibilities of easier lifestyles elsewhere than those offered by farming in its rocky terrain and frosty winters. The population of Ashford has fluctuated from 2,286 in 1782, to 668 in 1910, to 4,349 in 2004. The early to middle 1900s brought an influx of Central Europeans who were eager to purchase land and establish themselves in dairy farming and later in poultry raising.

People who gravitated to NE Connecticut during the 1950s and 1960s because of the University of Connecticut or jobs in the insurance industry or at Pratt & Whitney, all contributed to the Ashford that we see today, a basically residential community.

Interesting Places

June Norcross Webster Scout Reservation. Has a traditional Summer Camp with programs for Boy Scouts, Cub Scouts, Venturers, Sea Scouts, and Fire Service Explorers.

The Hole in the Wall Gang Camp. Founded in 1988 by Paul Newman on the simple premise that every child, no matter what their illness could experience the transformational spirit and friendships that go hand-in-hand with camp.

Knowlton Memorial Hall.

The Babcock Library is located on the second floor of the rustic stone Knowlton Memorial Hall (1924) at 25 Pompey Hollow Rd. Jerry Dougherty

NOTES

Constructed in 1924 by Loud and Hebert as a government building. It is used as a library and city hall.

Westford Hill Distillers. An artisanal distiller that uses fruit as the main ingredient to make clear brandy.

Babcock Library. On the top floor of an unusual stone building called the Knowlton Memorial Hall.

Midway Family Restaurant & Pizza.

Henrietta House B&B.

River's Edge Sugar House.

Old Ashford Academy (1825). A historic school building.

Ancient Babcock Cemetery. Dates back to the 1700s. Intersection of Fitts Rd. and Rt. 44.

Tremko-Stebbins House (c. 1773). Future home of Ashford Historical Society Museum and Tourist Information Center.

Langhamer Property Hiking Trails. 100 Lustig Rd.

The Old Connecticut Path. Native American Trail from Boston to Hartford used by Thomas Hooker in 1630. The path crosses the Mount Hope River in Ashford.

St. Philip the Apostle Catholic Church, at 64 Pompey Hollow Rd. in Warrenville, was built in the 1930's of native stone through the efforts of local farmers who came from Slovakia. Jerry Dougherty

ADDRESS BOOK

Town Site
www.ashfordtownhall.org

Babcock Library
25 Pompey Hollow Rd.
860-487-4420
www.babcocklibrary.org

Henrietta House B&B
125 Ashford Center Rd.
860-477-0318
www.historichenriettahousebnbct.com

Hole in the Wall Gang Camp
565 Ashford Center Rd.
860-429-3444
www.holeinthewallgang.org

June Norcross Webster Scout Reservation
231 Ashford Center Rd.
www.gotowebster.org

Knowlton Memorial Hall
25 Pompey Hollow Rd. (Rt. 44)

Midway Family Restaurant & Pizza
174 Ashford Center Rd.
860-429-1932
www.eatatmidway.com

Old Ashford Academy
10 Fitts Rd.

River's Edge Sugar House
326 Mansfield Rd. (Rt. 89)
860-429-1510
www.riversedgesugarhouse.com

Tremko-Stebbins House
5 Town Hall Rd.
860-429-4568
www.ashfordhistoricalsociety.org

Westford Hill Distillers
196 Chatey Rd.
860-429-0464
www.westfordhill.com

[Passport Stamp / Signature & Date Here]

BROOKLYN

By Kathryn Stellitano, Brooklyn resident and writer

Brooklyn is a small town of rolling hills and beautiful stone walls, located in the center of Windham Co. in the "Quiet Corner" of Connecticut. Originally part of Pomfret and Canterbury, the residents were granted permission to build a separate meetinghouse in 1734. The town of Brooklyn was incorporated in 1786.

Brooklyn is noted for its historic churches. The Unitarian Meetinghouse in the center of town is an outstanding example of colonial architecture. It was completed in 1771 by the Congregationalists. In 1819 there was a split in the membership and it became the first Unitarian meetinghouse in Connecticut. Samuel May, an outspoken abolitionist, reformer, and supporter of Prudence Crandall, served as the first Unitarian minister during the 1820s. In 1871 Celia Burleigh, the first female minister in the U.S. was ordained in the meetinghouse.

Old Trinity Church, the oldest surviving Anglican church building in Connecticut, was also completed in 1771. Godfrey Malbone, one of the largest landowners in the parish, built Trinity rather than pay taxes toward the building of the new Congregational meetinghouse.

General Israel Putnam is Brooklyn's most illustrious resident. Putnam gained fame as a brave leader during the French and Indian War, a general during the Revolution, and for killing the last wolf in Connecticut. The equestrian statue of "Old Put" is located south of the Town Green.

Due to its central location, Brooklyn became the home of the Windham County Agricultural Society which was incorporated in 1820. Since that time the Society has held an annual agricultural fair which has become known as the Brooklyn Fair, the oldest continually running agricultural fair in the United States.

In 1820 Comfort Tiffany built the first cotton mills on the Quinebaug River in East Brooklyn. His son Charles would be the founder of Tiffany's in New York and his grandson Louis Comfort Tiffany would later be famous for stained glass and other decorative arts.

PLACES OF INTEREST

Israel Putnam Statue. Large equestrian statue sculpted by Karl Gerhardt and dedicated in 1888. It serves as a memorial to Putnam and is his final resting place. Rt. 169 south of the Brooklyn Town Green.

Brooklyn Historical Society Museum. It includes an Israel Putnam gallery and other changing exhibits of local interest. Open Wed. & Sun. afternoons June thru Sept. Directly behind the Putnam statue.

The Daniel Putnam Tyler Law Office. Daniel Tyler, a great-grandson of Israel Putnam, practiced law here from 1822 to 1875. Directly behind the museum.

Unitarian Meeting House. Town Green at the intersection of Rts. 6 & 169.

Town Hall. Constructed in 1820 as the Windham County Courthouse. It was here that Prudence Crandall was tried for breaking the Connecticut "Black Law," that prohibited a school from teaching African-American students from outside the state without the town's permission. Town Green at the intersection of Rts. 6 & 169.

The equestrian statue of General Israel Putnam, "Old Put," is south of the Town Green. Kathryn Stellitano

NOTES

Old Trinity Church. Intersection of Brown Rd. and Church St.

Brooklyn Fair. The Brooklyn Fair is held the weekend before Labor Day.

Creamery Brook Bison. Visitors may see bison in the field. Bison meat is available for purchase.

Brooklyn Riverside Park. Canoe and kayak launch, fishing.

Davis Forest & Disc Golf Course. Hiking along the Quinebaug River to Dyer Dam Mill site. At the end of Salmon Dr. off South St.

The 1820 Brooklyn Town Hall is on the Brooklyn Town Green at the intersection of Rts. 169 and 6. Jerry Dougherty

ADDRESS BOOK

Town Site
www.brooklynct.org

Brooklyn Historical Society Museum
25 Canterbury Rd.
860-774-7728
www.brooklynct.org

Brooklyn Riverside Park
18 Day St.

Brooklyn Town Hall
Intersection of Rts. 6 & 169

Creamery Brook Bison
19 Purvis Rd.
860-779-0837
www.creamerybrookbison.net

Davis Forest & Disc Golf Course
Salmon Dr., off South St.
www.dgcoursereview.com

Old Trinity Church
Brown Rd. & Church St.

Unitarian Meetinghouse
Intersection of Rts. 6 & 169

EVENTS

Brooklyn Fair
15 Fairgrounds Rd.
www.brooklynfair.org

[Passport Stamp / Signature & Date Here]

CANTERBURY

By Debbie Loser, Canterbury Historical Society member & Docent at Prudence Crandall Museum and Ellen Wilson, President, Canterbury Historical Society

Canterbury is in southern Windham County along the Quinnebaug River. The first inhabitants of the area were the Peagscomsuck Indians who traded along the Greenwich Path, an early Indian trail which became the first highway between Hartford and Providence. In 1697, Major James Fitch, a military and civil leader, built the first structure in the area. His large family and many acquaintances traveled through the area and established a path which connected to the Greenwich Path. The name Canterbury (from Kent, England) was given to the Fitch land and was part of the town of Plainfield. Canterbury naturally separated from Plainfield and became a town in 1703 with fifteen male inhabitants.

During the 18th century many settlers followed in Fitch's footsteps and established farms in the area. Canterbury grew to some 150 inhabitants in 1709 to over 2500 in 1782. Besides farming, the rivers and streams provided power for industry. A gristmill on Rowland's brook was established in 1703. In the early 1800s, Capt. Daniel Packer created a textile mill which grew to include tenements and stores called Packerville. By the early 1800s, Canterbury was a prosperous town, but later in the 1800s, the population fell due to westward migration and the emergence of the railroad. Moses Cleaveland, Canterbury resident and founder of Cleveland, Ohio, led one such expedition westward. In the later 1800s and the early 1900s, the immigrant population increased, and farming in Canterbury was reestablished. Numerous Finnish and German immigrants settled in Canterbury. The Finnish American Heritage Society at the Finnish Hall on Rt. 169 is still very active today.

The growth of education followed population growth. Many one-room village schoolhouses were established. In 1947 these schoolhouses were combined into the now Dr. Helen Baldwin School. In 1990, the Canterbury Elementary School was built to house the lower elementary grades with the Baldwin School becoming a middle school. Canterbury does not have a high school, so students may opt for area high schools and technical schools.

The famous teacher Prudence Crandall established the Canterbury Female Boarding School in 1831 which provided a varied curriculum for girls from the area. In 1833, when an African-American girl asked if she could attend classes, Miss Crandall accepted her. White girls withdrew from the academy and it became a school "for young ladies and little misses of color." African-American girls came from several states to attend the school until the Connecticut legislature passed the Black Law in 1833. The school was forced to close.

To date, Canterbury's population has recovered, family farms and several farm stores are thriving, and many new houses have been built. Along Rt. 14 visitors will find the Canterbury Town Hall and the Canterbury Public Library as well as several businesses. Many old homesteads, historic churches, and the town green with a one-room Green schoolhouse, built on land donated by the original Robert

Prudence Crandall Museum where Prudence Crandall (1803-1890) opened the first academy for African-American women, 1833-1834. Debbie Loser

Notes

Green family, also line the scenic roads through town.

Interesting Places

Prudence Crandall Museum. This National Historic Landmark is the site of the nation's first Academy for African-American young women, 1833-1834. Open May-Oct.

Cleaveland Cemetery. This historic cemetery includes the graves of Moses Cleaveland and other early Canterbury residents.

Quinebaug River. The scenic Quinebaug is excellent for canoeing, kayaking, and fishing. Robert Manship Park entrance is found on Rt. 14.

The gravestone of Moses Cleaveland. Born in Canterbury, he who founded the city of Cleveland, OH, while surveying the Western Reserve in 1796. Debbie Loser

Address Book

Town Site
www.canterburyct.org

Canterbury Public Library
1 Municipal Dr.
860-546-9022
www.canterburylibrary.org

Canterbury Town Hall
1 Municipal Dr.
860-546-9693

Cleaveland Cemetery
North Canterbury Rd., Rt. 169

Prudence Crandall Museum
1 South Canterbury Rd.
860-546-7800
www.cultureandtourism.org

Robert Manship Park
50 Lovell Ln.

[Passport Stamp / Signature & Date Here]

Chaplin

By Kitty Le Shay, Chaplin resident, freelance writer, and Member of Chaplin Historic District Commission

Chaplin is a small rural town located in the hills of northeastern Connecticut. Mansfield, Ashford, Eastford, Hampton, and Windham border it with the closest city being Willimantic. It is a natural wonderland in all seasons with nearly 30% of the land being preserved either in State Forest, Joshua's Trust, a private land and historic trust, and the Legacy Program, a state and federally funded land preservation program which purchases the development rights of private landowners. These properties (3700 acres) are defined as "protected open space."

Like most early communities the historical development of the town was directly connected to the building of the church. In the late 1700s Chaplin was part of Mansfield, Windham, and Hampton. People had to travel long distances to attend church. Benjamin Chaplin, who was a wealthy deacon of the Mansfield church built his home on the Natchaug River. Before he died in 1795, he gave $1,500 to finance a new meetinghouse (church) to be built about a mile from his home. The church was built between 1812-1815 and was followed by a 30-year building boom of homes on a one-mile loop off Rt. 198. The homes along Chaplin St. comprise what is known as "The Village." It is the Historic District with most of the homes being Federal or Greek revival in style. Most are wood frame homes with two being brick structures. Missing is the post office, country store, tavern, and businesses which comprised a village center 200 years ago, but this does not detract from the charm of a street seemingly suspended in time.

There are working farms operating in Chaplin, but most people commute to other towns to work, many employed at the University of Connecticut, a short drive from town. Chaplin has not experienced a building boom or population growth. The rural character has been maintained.

The business district is located from the intersection of Rt. 98 and Rt. 6 to the Windham town line.

Interesting Places

Diana's Pool. A deep-water pool in the Natchaug River located along the river off Diana's Pool Rd. It is a designated fishing location but people from all over New England travel to Chaplin to photograph the pool. Park and walk east on a trail along the river for a quarter of a mile.

The Village. It is an interesting walk on a quiet street. A trip back in time.

Airline Trail. This trail which extends from East Hampton to Thompson is completely finished on the Chaplin section. It is a wonderful place to hike, bike, and cross-country ski. It can be accessed from Lynch or Chewink Rd. Map at www.ct.gov/deep.

Edward Garrison Park. Recreation fields, playground, and picnic pavilion.

Hubbard Sanctuary & Agnes' Pasture. Joshua's Trust preserve hosts a variety of bird and animal life. The 1.3-mile yellow trail takes you through Garrison Park, loops up and through Agnes' Pasture, and Natchaug State Forest. Along the trail is an open habitat hayfield, two ponds, a young forest habitat within Agnes' Pasture, and mature mixed hardwood forests, offering a scenic experience for hikers, birders, and wildlife viewers.

Garrison Field, the Hubbard Sanctuary, and the Natchaug Forest are contiguous and offer miles of hiking. Park at the Chaplin Town offices on Rt. 198.

Notes

Diana's Pool is a favorite place to be in the summer. Kitty Le Shay

One of Chaplin's many historic homes and the 1812-1815 Congregational Church on Chaplin St. Kitty Le Shay

Address Book

Town Site
www.chaplinct.org

Diana's Pool
20 Dianas Pool Rd.

Edward Garrison Park
495 Phoenixville Rd.

Hubbard Sanctuary & Agnes' Pasture, Joshua's Trust
513 Phoenixville Rd.
www.joshuastrust.org

[Passport Stamp / Signature & Date Here]

EASTFORD

By Carol Davidge and Linda Torgeson, Eastford Historical Society

Eastford is a small town in northeastern Connecticut, in a region known as the Last Green Valley. Connecticut Magazine named it the best small town in the state in 1993. Eastford possesses scenic beauty, a low crime rate, excellent education, moderate home prices, access to nature and metropolitan areas, thriving small businesses, and dynamic community life.

Incorporated in 1847, it was originally the eastern part of Ashford. It was first settled in 1711 by John Perry, a post rider over the Old Connecticut Path, which crossed though the town at the southern end of Crystal Pond and served for years as the principal bridle path between Boston and Hartford. The other Native American trail used by colonists was Boston Post Road, remnants of which form the Boston Turnpike and Greenway. Three distinct villages emerged around ecclesiastical societies, stagecoach roads, and inns: Eastford Village, home to the Congregational Church; Phoenixville with its Union Society (a nondenominational group that met for spiritual and social activities); and North Ashford, home to the Baptist Church.

Much of Eastford's 28.6 sq. mi. is covered by two major forests. The Natchaug State Forest, a Native American word meaning "land between two rivers," offers fishing, hunting, hiking and horseback riding, with private campgrounds on the riverbanks along Rt. 198. The Yale Myers Forest (7,840 acres), is Yale University's main forestry training center and one of Connecticut's top ten birding sites on the blue-blazed Nipmuck Trail. Originally home to the Nipmuck and Mohegan tribes, the region is known geologically as the Eastern Uplands or Windham Hills. Pristine bodies of water include Crystal Pond, Halls Pond, the Still, Natchaug Rivers, and Bigelow Brook. Eastford is beloved among astronomers for its dark night skies.

Although Eastford began as a self-sufficient agricultural community, home to dairy and sheep farming, abundant water power by the Natchaug and Still Rivers gave rise to early industry. Mills sprang up along the riverbanks: grain, lumber, cotton, wool, and silk mills, as well as an iron foundry and a tannery. A clover-seed mill produced 20,000 pounds of clover seed annually. Manufactured goods included stoggies (shoes and shoe parts), palm leaf hats, cart wheels, cotton mattresses, carriages, wooden washing machines, twine, guns, furniture, wooden handles, and baseball bats.

A visitor to Eastford Center today will find artisans, attractions, and small businesses ranging from Bowen's Garage, the oldest family-owned Ford dealership in Connecticut (1930) to high technology at Whitcraft, LLC, a leader in aerospace manufacturing. Annual events include Earth Day, the Memorial Day Parade, Experience Eastford Day, a Frog Jump, Band Concert and Cakewalk, 5-K Cancer Benefit, Buell's Harvest Festival, Veterans Ceremony, and holiday events including a Live Nativity.

Eastford's most notable citizen was General Nathaniel Lyon (1818-1861), the first Union general killed in the Civil War. Fifteen thousand mourners attended his funeral. His grave and monument including a canon are in the General Lyon

The area around Crystal Pond was once the home of the Nipmuck and Mohegan tribes and later a Boy Scout camp. It is now a town park in Eastford & Woodstock. David Barlow

Notes

Cemetery in Phoenixville.

Places of Interest

Eastford Public Library. Open Mon. 3-8 PM, Tue. 10 AM-8 PM, Thur. 3-8 PM, Sat. 9 AM-1 PM.

Veterans Memorial Town Green. Adjacent to the library.

Crossroads Pizza & Restaurant. Open daily.

Buell's Orchard (1889). Open year-round. Gifts and seasonal Pick-Your-Own.

Florence Warren Latham Museum of Eastford History. Open 2nd & 4th Sun., May-Oct., 2-4 PM.

Crystal Pond Park. Disc golf, lake, year-round trails, event facilities.

Natchaug State Forest. Rt. 198.

Yale Myers Forest. Westford Rd. to Center Pike in Ashford.

Halls Pond. State boat launch.

Askew Trail along the Still River. Behind Eastford Elementary School. Guide and backpacks available at Public Library.

Boston Turnpike Trail & Greenway.

Old Town Pound. Erected c.1849 to hold wandering livestock.

Old Cemetery and Beaver Pond. John Perry, earliest grave, 1727. Westford Rd. (Rt. 198)

General Lyon Cemetery (1806-1930). 35 General Lyon Rd. in Phoenixville.

Grove Cemetery. Westford Rd. (Rt. 198). 20th-21st century.

The 1847 Ivy Glenn Memorial was a Methodist Church and later the Town Hall. It now houses the Eastford Public Library. Carol Davidge

Address Book

Town Site
www.eastfordct.org

Buell's Orchard
108 Crystal Pond Rd.
www.buellsorchard.com

Crossroads Pizza & Restaurant
192 Eastford Rd. (Rt. 198)
860-315-1244
/CrossingsEastford

Eastford Public Library
179 Eastford Rd. (Rt. 198)
860-974-0125

Florence Warren Latham Museum of Eastford History
65 John Perry Rd.

Frog Rock Rest Stop
212 Pomfret Rd. (Rt. 44)
//FrogRockEastfordCT

Old Town Pound
Town Pound Rd.

Hiking & Trails

Askew Trail
12 Westford Rd.

Boston Turnpike Trail & Greenway
86 John Perry Rd.

Crystal Pond Park
Weeks Rd. (Old Connecticut Path)

Halls Pond
80 Kennerson Rd.

Natchaug State Forest
Rt. 198

Yale Myers Forest
Westford Rd. to Center Pike, Ashford
www.environment.yale.edu

[Passport Stamp / Signature & Date Here]

Hampton

By Jean Wierzbinski, Hampton Antiquarian and Historical Society

Hampton is nestled in the Last Green Valley's "Quiet Corner" in northeastern Connecticut. For thousands of years, Nipmucs hunted and fished in the reedy swamp they called Appaquage, and cleared small areas for farming. Evidence of their presence has been found at the Cohantic Ledges on Rt. 97 and near Sand Hill Rd. in Howards Valley. Archeologists believe there may also be a site further north in the Hemlock Glen Industrial Archeological District.

Hampton's first European settlers came from Salem, MA in 1709, building a Puritan meeting house in 1725. Replaced in 1754 and remodeled in 1836 in accordance with the new architectural Grecian style, it is the now the second oldest continually operating church in Connecticut. During the Revolutionary War, many residents fought on the side of the colonists, including at Bunker Hill and under General Benedict Arnold. Hampton was officially incorporated as a town in 1786.

Historically, Hampton's economy was farm-based with supporting small scale industries powered by rivers. Hampton never saw the development of large mills that gave rise to the extensive mill housing and commercial growth seen in some other towns. In the early 20th century, it was a popular summer destination for "city folk."

Although small, Hampton has had many influential residents. Famous abolitionist Theodore Weld was born in Hampton. Connecticut Governor Chauncey Cleveland lived here, and Hampton was declared Connecticut's capital for one day during his tenure in the 1840s. Cleveland belonged to the newly formed Republican Party and was one of the original electors for Abraham Lincoln. Forester James Goodwin, a leader in early forest conservation and environmental movements, donated acreage from his farm to the State. It is now James L. Goodwin State Forest. Naturalist Edwin Way Teale wrote about his Hampton farm, Trail Wood, in his book A Naturalist Buys an Old Farm. Trail Wood is now owned by the Audubon Society.

Hampton also has a rich cultural history. Deaf artist John Brewster, Jr., known for his 18th century primitive portraits, was born in Hampton, and artist John Steward lived here for a time, serving as minister during the illness of the Rev. Samuel Moseley in the 18th century. Illustrator and painter Florence Pearl Nosworthy lived in the town in the early 20th century.

Ultimately, agriculture died out, the mills closed, and the population declined. Today, the center of town, with its diverse architecture, is the Hampton Hill Historic District. The town retains its rural character, with open fields and plentiful forests, reminding visitors of days gone by.

Interesting Places

The Burnham-Hibbard House represents a small farm and boarding house through various periods of history. Open during the afternoon on Memorial Day, the first Sunday in December, and by appointment.

James L. Goodwin State Forest. Offers walking trails and fishing in season. A museum commemorates the life and work of Goodwin. Foresters lead many walks and a

The 1834 Burnham-Hibbard House Museum is owned by the Hampton Antiquarian and Historical Society. Susan Hochstetter

Notes

conservation education center hosts various events throughout the year. On Potter Rd. off Rt. 6

Rad Ostby Memorial Forest. Owned by the Eastern Connecticut Foresters Association, has a trail leading to old foundations, a disused mill pond, and a unique stone bridge. East Old Rt. 6. (Approximately 1/2 mi. west from intersection of Providence Tpke. Rt. 6)

The James Goodwin State Forest Observation Deck on Pine Acres Lake. www.wikipedia.org

Trail Wood. Open to the public and sponsors many events throughout the year.

Hampton Community Center. Houses a variety of exhibitions and cultural events.

Fletcher Memorial Library. Historic Italianate structure dating to 1860 and donated to the Library in 1924.

Main Street and Hampton's back roads. A scenic drive, especially in the fall.

The Hampton Congregational Church was founded in 1723. Podskoch

Address Book

Town Site
www.hamptonct.org

Burnham-Hibbard House
185 Main St.
860-455-0783

Fletcher Memorial Library
257 Main St.
860-455-1086
www.fletchermemoriallibrary.org

Hampton Community Center
178 Main St.
860-455-9132
www.hamptonct.org

James L. Goodwin State Forest
23 Potter Rd.

Rad Ostby Memorial Forest
100 East Old Rt. 6

Trail Wood
93 Kenyon Rd.
www.ctaudubon.org/trail-wood-home

[Passport Stamp / Signature & Date Here]

Killingly

By Natalie L. Coolidge, Killingly Historical Society

The Town of Killingly includes seven villages: Attawaugan, Ballouville, Danielson, Dayville, East Killingly, Rogers, and South Killingly, and is in the northeast corner of Windham County 15 miles south of Massachusetts on the Rhode Island border. Major access is through I-395 which runs north/south through the western side of town.

Killingly owes its early prosperity to the establishment and growth of mills built along its waterways. The early sawmills and gristmills provided lumber to build homes and grain to feed families. By early 1800 attractive sites along the brooks and rivers were developed and dams were built. Killingly's factories were so successful that historian John Warner Barber reported the town as, "the greatest cotton manufacturing town in the state" in 1836. As the textile mills later moved south, the town was successful in attracting diversified industries to occupy the old mills and build newer, more modern ones. Killingly is an Eastern Connecticut Enterprise Corridor Community located in what is publicized as The Last Green Valley and active in the Northeastern Connecticut Chamber of Commerce with offices at 210 Westcott Road, Danielson, and is in the Killingly Business Association.

Interesting Places

Killingly Historical Society Museum. Built in 1902 as a public library by Edwin Bugbee, it now serves as home for artifacts and photos of the town's history. It is also a widely known and respected home for genealogical and biographical research. Open Wed. and Sat. 10 AM-4 PM.

Old Furnace State Park. Has beautiful scenery and plenty of hiking.

Danielson Ross Pond State Park. Invites hikers, hunters, and fishermen.

Quinebaug Lake State Park. Has something for everyone: park, reservoir and beach, fishing, and non-motorized boating.

Killingly Pond State Park. Offers boating, fishing and hiking.

The town also offers three other parks for enjoyment.

Davis Park. It is a beautiful place in the center of Danielson.

Owen Bell Park. It has a track, trails, tennis courts, basketball, ball fields, picnic area, playscape, skate park, and a splash park in the summer.

Cat Hollow Town Park. Wooded area for trail walking, fishing, and viewing the beautiful Whetstone Brook and falls.

Areas on the National Register of Historic Places include:

Dayville Historic District, Broad Street/Davis Park Historic District, Danielson Main Street Historic District, and Daniels Village Archeological Site in the Ballouville area. Other Historical Sites are the Elliottville Lower Mill (Peeptoad), East Killingly; Old Killingly High School, Danielson; Old Westfield Cemetery, North St., Danielson; Quinebaug Mill, Quebec Square Historic District, South Main St., Brooklyn; and Temple Beth Israel, Killingly Drive, Danielson.

Killingly Historical Society (KHS est. 1972) is in the Bugbee Memorial Library (1902) building at 196 Main St., Danielson.KHS

Notes

Address Book

Town Site
www.killingly.org

Cat Hollow Town Park
Cat Hollow Rd., Dayville

Danielson Ross Pond State Park
South Frontage Rd.
www.killinglyconservation.org/parks

Killingly Historical Society Museum
196 Main St., Danielson
860-779-7250
wwwkillinglyhistorical.org

Killingly Pond State Park
Quinn's Hill Rd., East Killingly
www.ct.gov/deep

Old Furnace State Park
South Frontage Rd.
www.ct.gov/deep

Owen Bell Park
19 Town Farm Rd., Dayville

Quinebaug Lake State Park
59 Shepard Hill Rd., Danielson
www.ct.gov/deep

Notable People

Charles Tiffany. Co-founder of Tiffany & Co. jewelery in New York.

Mary Dixon Kies. First woman to receive a patent for weaving silk with straw for making bonnets.

Dr. Emeline Roberts Jones. First woman to practice dentistry in the U.S.

William Torrey Harris. U.S. Commissioner of Education (1889-1906).

Dr. Sidney P. Marland, Jr. U.S. Commissioner of Education (1970-1972).

The Whetstone Brook flows through Cat Hollow Park that is off Cat Hollow Rd. in Dayville. The park has a half-mile road with a few narrow side trails that lead to some of the park's features, such as an old trolley bridge, the ruins of a mill, and a stone dam and waterfall. KHS

[Passport Stamp / Signature & Date Here]

Plainfield

By Ruth Bergeron, Plainfield Historical Society

Plainfield, incorporated in 1699, has been transformed from Indian country into a farming community populated by settlers of English origin, and then into a heavily industrialized town divided into four village communities: Central Village, Moosup, Plainfield, and Wauregan. People emigrated from other countries to work in the several mills and businesses located around the Moosup and Quinebaug Rivers and other waterways.

Today, the town, located in Connecticut's "Quiet Corner," is still growing and is one of the 35 Connecticut and Massachusetts towns that comprise The Last Green Valley National Heritage Corridor. Plainfield has rural areas, wooded and farmland places, in addition to the villages and Industrial Park.

The Quinebaug Valley State Trout Hatchery, located in Central Village, is open to visitors. It is surrounded by the 2,000-acre Quinebaug State Management Area with its open fields along the Quinebaug River considered to be a "birder's paradise."

The Moosup Valley State Park Trail, a 5.8 mi. walking trail on a former rail bed, originates in downtown Moosup and travels eastward to connect with rail trails in Rhode Island. www.ct.gov/deep

There are four National Register of Historic Places/Districts: Central Village, The Lawton Mills District, Plainfield Street, and Wauregan.

The National Historic Trail, the Washington-Rochambeau Revolutionary Route (W3R) travels through town, for the most part on State Rt. 14A from Sterling to Canterbury. In 1781 French troops marched from Newport, RI to Yorktown, VA via this route to help the colonists win the American Revolution. This route crosses State Rt. 12 in the Plainfield Street Historic District, an area of older homes and the old stone church. The Town Hall is in the former Recreation building of the Lawton Mills whose indoor swimming pool is still in use.

The Plainfield Historical Society (PHS) History Room is open by appointment.

Wauregan Mills, a cotton mill powered by the Quinebaug River, was constructed using local fieldstone c.1854. The company was well known for its woven cotton goods including various types of flannels. The mill closed in 1957. Jerry Dougherty

Notes

The beautiful stone First Congregational Church built in 1815 is at 519 Norwich Rd. in Plainfield. Jerry Dougherty

Address Book

Town Site
www.plainfieldct.org

First Congregational Church
519 Norwich Rd.
860-564-5932
www.fccplainfieldct.org

Moosup Valley State Park Trail
2-58 Withey Hill Rd., Moosup

Plainfield Historical Society History Room
www.plainfieldhistory.org

Plainfield Town Hall
8 Community Ave.
860-230-3001

Quinebaug Valley State Trout Hatchery
www.ct.gov/deep

Wauregan Mills
51 South Walnut St.

[Passport Stamp / Signature & Date Here]

Pomfret

By Walter Hinchman, Pomfret Town Historian and Pomfret Historical Society member

Pomfret is a truly rural town in the northeastern corner of Connecticut. Only a generation ago there were literally more cows than people in town. Most of the dairy farms have closed and the development rights to several thousand acres of that land have been purchased through cooperation between the town, the state, and several conservation organizations ensuring that the town will retain its rural character.

Our public school goes only through grade eight, and we have a volunteer fire department; however, there is no police department, and no town water or sewer.

The first Europeans came to Pomfret in the late 1600s and the Town Hall still has the original deed between Owaneco, the son of Uncas, and Major James Fitch in its vault. Major Fitch resold the land in 1686 to twelve "proprietors," primarily folks from Boston, some of whom settled here while others sold the land again. By 1713 Pomfret had grown enough to support a congregation whose members appealed to the colonial legislature for incorporation. In 2013 the annual town meeting, celebrating the 300th anniversary of incorporation, was held in the building (not the original) now used by the successors of that original congregation.

For many years Pomfret was home to subsistence farmers and small mill owners who sawed the timber and ground the grain produced on the local farms. General stores and post offices sprang up and five villages were founded within the town, Pomfret, Pomfret Center, Abington, Pomfret Landing, and Elliott. Following the Civil War, a railroad line connecting Boston to New York was completed and caused a major change in the character of the town. The rolling hills of Pomfret, and rumors of health giving properties of local waters, attracted wealthy families from Boston and New York who built elegant summer "cottages" which were the scene of glamorous summer parties and a source of employment for local families. Some of these mansions still exist as private homes or as parts of private schools.

In the mid-20th century transportation again changed the character of Pomfret as the construction of Rt. 52, now I-395 and the other parts of the Interstate system, connected the town to surrounding cities so that residents could commute to work in Providence, Hartford, New London, and Worcester, and Pomfret became a bedroom community as well as a haven for retirees searching for a quiet relaxed lifestyle.

Interesting Places

The Pomfret Historical Society works to preserve these two historic structures:

Brayton Grist Mill was built in 1890 and added to the National Register of Historic Places in 1986. The mill is located along Mashamoquet Brook, at the entrance to Mashamoquet Brook State Park, and features its original equipment and a collection of blacksmithing tools and equipment. It is open during the summer on Sunday afternoons from 2-5 PM. Admittance is free.

Pomfret Town House is a historic meetinghouse on 17 Town House Road in Pomfret. The building was erected in 1841 and was used for many years as the site of Pomfret's town meetings. The meetinghouse was listed on the National Register of Historic Places in 1989.

The quiet life continues and a visitor to Pomfret can enjoy outdoor recreation activities at:

Mashamoquet State Park. Visit "Wolf's Den" where Israel Putnam shot the last wolf in CT. Offers hiking, camping, fishing, and swimming for the whole family.

Notes

The Connecticut Audubon Center at Pomfret. Open daily, year-round, from dawn to dusk.

Wyndham Land Trust. Ten preserves in Pomfret for walks. www.wyndhamlandtrust.org

Airline Trail. Follows the route of the former railroad. Map at: www.ct.gov/deep

After a few hours of hiking, fishing in season, or exploring the wolf den, lunch can be obtained at:

Vanilla Bean Café. Where Coca-Cola introduced a new flavor, Vanilla Coke, to the world on May 15, 2002.

Grill 37.

Pizza 101.

The Bakers Dozen. Coffee shop and bakery.

The campuses of two noted independent schools, Pomfret School and Rectory School, which attract students from around the world, are along Rt. 44 in the center of town. Also, along Rt. 44 is Christ Church, which has a number of stained glass windows as well as a baptismal font attributed to Louis Comfort Tiffany.

The Pomfret School, founded in 1894, is an independent boarding school on Rt. 44 that attracts students from around the world. Walter Hinchman

Address Book

Town Site
www.pomfretct.gov

The Bakers Dozen
24 Mashamoquet Rd.
860-928-6469
www.bakersdozenct.com

Connecticut Audubon Center at Pomfret
218 Day Rd., Pomfret Center
www.ctaudubon.org

Grill 37
37 Putnam Rd.
860-315-5640
www.grill37.com

Mashamoquet State Park
147 Wolf Den Dr., Pomfret Center
www.ct.gov/deep

Pizza 101
16A Mashamoquet Rd., Pomfret Center
860-928-5566
www.pizza101menu.com

Pomfret Public Library
449 Pomfret St. (Rt. 169)
860-928-3475

Vanilla Bean Café
450 Deerfield Rd.
860-928-1562
www.thevanillabeancafe.com

[Passport Stamp / Signature & Date Here]

Putnam

By Kathy Naumann, former owner of Inn at Woodstock Hill

Welcome to the Town of Putnam! Located in the northeast corner of Connecticut, Putnam was voted one of the "Best 15 Small Towns To Visit in New England" by *Boston Magazine*. The once bustling mills, still perched near the banks of the Quinebaug River, defined and built the town. In 1955, Putnam was devastated by a flood from back to back storms, forever changing its landscape.

Today, there is much more to Putnam than its treasured antique stores as residents and visitors alike flock to the town for dining, shopping, culture, and festivals.

Named after Israel Putnam, a patriot and Revolutionary War veteran most famous for his bravery, Putnam offers alfresco dining at several Main Street restaurants, making for a lively atmosphere in season with multiple venues featuring live music and craft beers, year-round. Specialty retail shops, art galleries and a beautiful theater with productions from local talent that rival Off-Broadway, enhance the downtown experience. Putnam is a small town that thinks big: community cooperation chanting "I think I can, I think I can, I know I can, I know I can!", with no intention of slowing down.

Interesting Places

Rotary Park & Bandstand. Features unique and free, alfresco live entertainment organized by Putnam Parks & Recreation. Musical themes for all ages include opera, swing, big band, classical, and more.

Putnam River Trail & the River Mills Heritage Trail. A multi-use trail that follows the Quinebaug River offering beautiful historic and scenic views of Putnam and Cargill Falls, with convenient free parking, iron benches, a Story Walk for children, a small boat launch, the Farmer's Market, Dog Park, Bicycle Repair Spot, and Riverview Pavilion along the trail.

The Gertrude Chandler Warner Boxcar Children Museum. The museum is dedicated to the life and work of Gertrude Chandler Warner, the author of The Boxcar Children books. The museum is open on weekends from May through October and is housed in an authentic 1920s New Haven R.R. boxcar.

Bradley Theater. The Bradley Playhouse is a 114-year-old vaudeville theatre in the heart of the Putnam antiques and restaurant district.

Year Round Events

Fire & Ice Festival. As the largest single ice-block competition in the United States with more than three dozen ice carvings, this event takes place the weekend of Valentine's Day and includes a cake or chocolate sculpting and molding contest.

Putnam's Main Street offers alfresco dining at several restaurants. There are also specialty retail shops, antique stores, art galleries, and a theater with productions from local talent. Mystic Country Photo

Notes

River Fire. Illuminating the Quinebaug River with 20 wood bonfires that burn for 90 minutes after dusk, each River Fire is accompanied by music produced by local radio station, WINY, and preceded by a live musical performance.

Main Street Car Cruise. This annual event brings over 2,000 classic and antique cars to Putnam the second Sunday in August. The event brings thousands of visitors and offers food, music, raffles, and more.

The Great Pumpkin Festival. Putnam's annual Fall Festival is the third Sunday in October and includes a full day of events, such as a scenic train excursion, flea market, craft fair, pumpkin-carving contest, food court, art exhibitions, and live music.

Holiday Dazzle Light Parade. With as many as 100 brightly lit floats plus marching bands and walkers that travel the 1.5 mile route through downtown, kicking off the holiday season the Sunday after Thanksgiving. Several other events are offered throughout the year such as the 4th of July Fireworks and Concert and the O'Putnam 5K.

The town will continue with two big themed events this year including an International Day and a Comic Con Day. Please check the Discover Putnam website at discoverputnam.com/events.

Address Book

Town Sites
www.putnamct.us
www.discoverputnam.com

Bradley Theater
30 Front St.
860-928-7887
www.thebradleyplayhouse.org

Gertrude Chandler Warner Boxcar Children Museum
1 South Main St.
www.boxcarchildrenmuseum.com

Rotary Park & Bandstand
196 Kennedy Dr.

Events

4th of July Fireworks & Concert
Fire & Ice Festival
The Great Pumpkin Festival
Holiday Dazzle Light Parade
Main Street Car Cruise
O'Putnam 5K
River Fire

[Passport Stamp / Signature & Date Here]

Scotland

By Kevin Ring, Scotland Historical Society

The town of Scotland is in Windham County, approx. 6 miles east of Willimantic. It is a predominantly rural area with small farms. The population in 2010 was 1,726.

Scotland was settled in 1700 as the third ecclesiastical society of Windham. Isaac Magoon, one of its first settlers, named the settlement after his homeland of Scotland, because the geography reminded him of his origins. Scotland sought its independence from Windham and in 1857 was incorporated as a town. Today it is the eighth smallest town in Connecticut. Once a town with deep agricultural roots, it is predominantly a 'bedroom' community maintaining its picturesque rural beauty and quaint historic town center.

Within walking distance of the town center is the birthplace of Samuel Huntington, one of Scotland's most prominent citizens. Huntington was one of four Declaration of Independence signers from Connecticut. In 1781, while serving as a president of the Continental Congress, the Articles of Confederation were ratified which resulted in him becoming the first President of the United States in Congress Assembled. He returned to Connecticut and in 1786 was elected governor, a position he held until his death in 1796.

Interesting Places

Huntington Homestead Museum. It is Samuel Huntington's home and is open on many weekends from May to Nov.

D'Elia Antique Tool Museum. Contains one of the most extensive collections of woodworking hand planes in the nation displayed in the Scotland Public Library.

Edward Waldo House (1715). It was owned by the Waldo family from 1715 to 1975 and contains early 1700s furniture and personal effects of Waldo. It is operated by the Scotland Historical Society.

Scottish Highland Festival Association. New England's largest Scottish festival on its 20-acre property. It is held each Columbus Day weekend. Pipers, dancers, and athletes from all over the northeast come to compete.

Scotland Public Library.

Rock Spring Preserve. Owned by The Nature Conservancy, it has a 3-mile loop trail on its 475-acre property that has a natural spring and scenic overlook.

Spignesi Wildlife Management Area. A 137-acre preserve that offers trails for horseback riding and in season hunting and fishing.

Talbot Wildlife Management Area. Has 387 acres and a hiking trail along Merricks Brook, a well-known trout stream as well as hunting in season.

The 1867 Chapel and 1842 Congregational Church facing the beautiful Scotland Town Green with a cannon monument. Kevin Ring

Notes

Huntington House was the birthplace of Samuel Huntington (1731-1796) who was a leading Patriot and was a delegate to the Continental Congress where he signed the Declaration of Independence. Kevin Ring

Address Book

Town Site
www.scotlandct.org

D'Elia Antique Tool Museum
21 Brook Rd.
860-456-1516
www.deliatoolmuseum.com

Edward Waldo House
96 Waldo Rd.
860-423-1547
www.scotlandhistoricalsociety.org

Huntington Homestead Museum
36 Huntington Rd.
860-423-1547
www.huntingtonhomestead.org

Rock Spring Preserve
288 Pudding Hill Rd.

Scotland Public Library
21 Brook Rd.
860-423-1492
www.scotlandpubliclibrary.org

Scottish Highland Festival Association
96 Waldo Rd.
www.scotlandgames.org

Spignesi Wildlife Management Area
220 Pudding Hill Rd.

Talbot Wildlife Management Area
269 Bass Rd.

[Passport Stamp / Signature & Date Here]

Sterling

By Megan McGory Gleason, President and Ron Marchesseault, Curator of Sterling Historical Society

Sterling is a Connecticut border town, located in the southeast corner of Windham County. Any farther east and you would be in Rhode Island. Sterling is nine miles long, north to south, and has an average width of three miles. The population was 3574 in the 2010 census. The town has two village centers, Sterling and Oneco. It has a relatively new elementary school, opening in 2006, and shares a high school with the neighboring Town of Plainfield.

In 1794 Sterling was incorporated after separating from Voluntown. By the early 1800s it was a prosperous small town with multiple textile factories, highlighted by the discovery and development of "Sterling Fast Black" dye by James Pike and his son William. In 1880 James Pike organized the Sterling Dyeing and Finishing Co., bringing into use the bleaching of cloth by chlorine as well as dyeing fast black.

Sterling was also noted for its quarries, which produced the finest grained bluish-gray colored granite. The quarry operation soon became one the largest employers in the area, at its peak, employing over 200 men, and shipping granite as far away as England. History of the quarries remains memorialized by the "Great Wall" located in the village of Oneco. It is 15' wide and used waste stone from the quarry.

Another attraction in Sterling is "Ye Old Voluntown Pound," located between the villages of Sterling and Oneco, one of the few left in the state. It was built in 1722 by a vote of the citizens to confine roaming sheep and stray cattle. At the time the only fences built were to keep animals out of the home and garden. Strays were impounded, the owner was notified, and charged for the animal's stay.

Sterling is also the home of "Pharisee Rocks." This is a huge chain of rocks that extend about one-half mile from the highest peak and gradually tapers off into what is known as "The Narrows." Native Americans used these rocks for a lookout. By climbing to its highest peak, they could trace their game to learn the exact herding locations. Many pow-wows were held here as it was a meeting place for several tribes.

Sterling was the birthplace of Charles H. Dow, who, along with Edward Jones, founded the Wall Street Journal in 1889 and originated the Dow-Jones Average.

Sterling is a place where history, scenic beauty, and friendly folks come together. Any visit to Sterling would be incomplete if it did not include a fine home-cooked meal at a local Church or Grange. Plan ahead, you won't be disappointed.

Interesting Places

Sterling Hill Historic District. Located along scenic Rt. 14-A, the district includes picturesque colonial homes and is a part of the 680-mile historic Washington-Rochambeau Revolutionary Route. Follow in the steps of George Washington as the march route along Plainfield Pike (Rt. 14A) has its own historic designation on the U.S. National Register of Historic Places.

Pachaug State Forest. Several hiking trails are located in the southern end of town as a part of the largest state forest which covers 26,477 acres in six different towns.

"Ye Old Voluntown Pound" at the corner of Sterling Rd. (Rt. 14) and Providence Rd. was where stray livestock was held in the stone enclosure, until the owner claimed them. Ron Marchesseault

Notes

Moosup Valley State Park Trail. A partially-paved walking and biking path that follows the old New Haven Railroad line from Moosup through to RI, where it connects with the Coventry Greenway.

Sterling Family Day. Held the second Sat. of September, includes fun, food, and fireworks.

Ekonk Community Grange #89. The Grange, a staple of Sterling life since its organization in 1888, hosts many events in the community throughout the year, but is probably best known for its dinners. Whether you're looking for corned beef and cabbage for St. Patrick's Day or turkey at Thanksgiving, you can find a hearty meal and a warm atmosphere in the Grange.

Sterling Public Library. Hosts different talks and fun activities for both children and adults.

Weidele's Pizza & Pub.

Ekonk Hill Turkey Farm. Homemade ice cream, turkey pies, baked goods, and a corn maze in the fall.

An Anatolian Shepherd guardian dog named "Blue" watches over a free-range turkey flock at the Ekonk Hill Turkey Farm. Winter Caplanson, ***Connecticut Food & Farm***

Address Book

Town Site
www.sterlingct.us

Ekonk Community Grange #89
723 Ekonk Hill Rd.
www.ekonkgrange.org

Ekonk Hill Turkey Farm
227 Ekonk Hill Rd., Moosup
860-564-0248
www.ekonkhillturkeyfarm.com

Sterling Historical Society
1183 Plainfield Pike, Room 19
www.sterlinghistoricalsocietyct.weebly.com

Sterling Public Library
1183 Plainfield Pike, Oneco
860-564-2692
www.sterlingct.us

Weidele's Pizza & Pub
901 Sterling Rd.
860-564-6680
/weideles.pizza.pub

[Passport Stamp / Signature & Date Here]

Thompson

By Joe Lindley (1955-2019), Thompson Historical Society

Thompson is in the northeast corner of Connecticut, locally called the "Quiet Corner".

The Nipmuck Indians, the Fresh Water People, settled the area several thousand years ago. They established several major settlements to include Quantisset on Thompson Hill, and Maanexit in the village of Quinebaug. They constructed a large fort on what is now Fort Hill Farms. There are an abundance of cairns, monuments, and settlement remains to be found.

The area, considered "wilderness" by the Europeans was settled c.1709. It became the North Parish of Killingly c. 1727 and an independent town in 1785 and took the name of one of its early non-resident landowners, Major Robert Thompson of England. Like many English landowners, Thompson never saw the land. Ten villages make up the larger town of Thompson: Thompson Hill, Mechanicsville, West Thompson, East Thompson, North Grosvenordale, Grosvenordale, Wilsonville, Quaddic, Quinebaug, and Fabyan.

Thompson's beauty is in its rolling hills, water, and rocks. Three major rivers, the Quinebaug, French, and Five Mile (Assawaga) pass through its hill-and-valley villages with the Quinebaug and French Rivers joining just below the West Thompson Dam at a place the Native Americans called "Nashaway." Severe flooding in 1936, 1938 and 1955 resulted in this U.S. Army Corps of Engineers' mammoth dam designed to withstand a 100-year flood event. It is one of Connecticut's most scenic and extensive recreation areas. Complementing the rivers are numerous brooks and streams, passing through the villages that may have more stone walls than any other area in Connecticut.

During the mid-1800s, the three rivers provided enough power to transition Thompson from an agricultural community into an industrial powerhouse. Villages and neighborhoods sprang up all over Grosvenordale and North Grosvenordale to accommodate immigrants. Neighborhoods like Three Rows, Greek Village, and Swede Village are among the more important communities that shaped Thompson's story.

Many of Thompson's once-mighty mills are now silent, but the most significant, the Grosvenor-Dale Mill, at the heart of North Grosvenordale village and listed on the National Register of Historical Places, is still host to a number of businesses.

During the height of New England's industrial age, no town in Connecticut had more train stations and depots than Thompson. Building upon ancient Native American pathways, first as colonial roads and then as rail lines, Thompson became a high-traffic crossroads for travel between Boston, Hartford, New York, Providence, and Springfield. The East Thompson train station was the site of the famous 1891 Great East Thompson Train Wreck, one of the very few four-engine train wrecks in American history. The old rail bed has been converted to a bucolic walking trail.

Thompson Common, located on Thompson Hill, was once the center of town due to the intersection of two major colonial highways. After the mills were constructed and the railroads built, the heart of the town moved west to Grosvenordale and North Grosvenordale. Thompson Hill then evolved into a summer location for a number of wealthy

An early 1940s photo of automobile racing at the Thompson Speedway. Thompson Historical Society

Notes

men, to include Norman Ream and John Doane. The Common still retains its unique charm with many of its original houses, to include the home of Ellen Larned. The Congregational Church and Vernon Stiles Inn are among the most photographed Early American structures in New England.

Interesting Places

Tourtellotte Memorial High School (1909). Tourtellotte Memorial Room, managed by the Thompson Historical Society and the Tourtellotte Board of Trustees, is the largest public school museum in the country .

Thompson Historical Society Museum at the Ellen Larned Memorial Building.

Thompson Common. A National Historic Register & Historic District. Site of Quinnatisset, a major settlement area of the Nipmuck Indians. Other attractions include the Vernon Stiles Inn and the Old Thompson Town Hall (1842).

West Thompson Dam (U.S. Army Corp of Engineers).

Thompson Speedway Motorsports Park. In 1940 it was the first paved-banked oval racetrack in the U.S. In 1953 the first purpose-built sports car track in the country was added.

Fort Hill Farms.

Raceway Golf Club.

Quaddick State Park.

The 1902 Ellen Larned Memorial Building was the former town library and is now operated as a museum by the Thompson Historical Society. The steeple of the Congregational Church is in the background. Joe Lindley

Address Book

Town Site
www.thompsonct.org

Fort Hill Farms
260 Quaddick Rd.
860-923-3439
www.forthillfarms.com

Old Thompson Town Hall
815 Riverside Dr.
860-923-9561

Quaddick State Park
818 Quaddick Town Farm Rd.

Raceway Golf Club
205 E. Thompson Rd.
www.racewaygolf.com

Thompson Historical Society at the Ellen Larned Memorial Building
339 Thompson Rd.
401-208-6051
www.thompsonhistorical.org

Thompson Speedway Motorsports Park
205 E. Thompson Rd.
860-923-2280
www.thompsonspeedway.com

Tourtellotte Memorial High School
785 Riverside Dr., North Grosvenordale
860-923-9581

West Thompson Dam
449 Reardon Rd., North Grosvenordale

White Horse Inn at Vernon Stiles
351 Thompson Rd.
860-923-9571

[Passport Stamp / Signature & Date Here]

WINDHAM

By Bev York, Museum Educator at The Mill Museum

Windham lies in the heart of eastern Connecticut. The original 1692 settlement is Windham Center Green (Rts. 14 and 203), which retains its early charm and architecture. Nearby on Rt. 203 is the historic burying ground and on Rt. 14 is Frog Pond, the setting for the 1754 incident where a huge noisy ruckus in the night led the militia to grab their muskets thinking the town was being invaded only to find in the morning 'thousands' of bullfrogs in the drying drought-ridden mill pond. Apparently, some sort of frog turf war had broken out and the carnage was excessive. It was the cacophony of that battle they heard.

The villages of North and South Windham were bustling industrial sites during the early 19th century. The industry-changing Fourdrinier papermaking machine was one of the early patented products.

The Willimantic section developed in the early 1800s and grew rapidly as textile industries harnessed the water power of the Willimantic River. For 180 years "Thread City," in addition to clothing and bedding, the mills produced thread for tea bags, baseballs, ribbons, seatbelts, parachutes, and thousands more. The largest company, Willimantic Thread, was renowned for spooled thread, innovative company housing, and Mill No. 4, the first factory designed for electric lighting. The industries provided jobs for immigrants who built churches and social clubs making an ethnically rich community. J. Alden Weir, famous American impressionist painter, summered in town and painted the Factory Village and The Red Bridge among other works. The community is rich with amenities such as The Chronicle newspaper, WILI Radio, Windham Airport, Windham Hospital, and Eastern Connecticut State University.

Interesting Places

The Mill Museum and Visitor Center (Windham Textile & History Museum). Open Feb. thru Dec. Fri., Sat., Sun. 10 AM-4 PM.

Connecticut Eastern Railroad Museum. Open Saturdays, 10 AM-4 PM, May-Oct.

Jillson House Museum and Windham Historical Society. Historic house museum of early cotton industrialist William Jillson. Open seasonally for events.

Willimantic Whitewater Park. An urban waterfront and whitewater park along the Willimantic River.

The East Coast Greenway Trail and Air Line Trail. Goes through town. www.willimanticriver.org

'Willibrew' Willimantic Brewing Company. Award-winning Restaurant and Brew Pub in old post office building.

The Harp on Church. Irish pub and restaurant.

Ethnic Flavor. There are many small restaurants which feature authentic ethnic foods. For a complete listing contact the Mill Museum.

Willimantic Food Co-op. Downtown grocery, organic foods.

The America Museum. Stories of contributions and sacrifice to American freedom.

Four giant bronze 10-foot frogs perched atop 12-foot tall spools of thread keep watch over the Thread City Crossing Bridge in downtown Willimantic. Bev York

Notes

WindhamARTS Coffee Break Gallery.

Swift Waters Artisans' Cooperative.

Chocolate Festival and Romantic Willimantic. Mid-Feb. Main St.

Hop Fest. Annual Beer Fest. June. 627 Main St.

Third Thursday Street Festival. Food, music, and vendors. May thru Sept. Main St.

Willimantic Farmer's Market. Sat. mornings, June thru Oct. 28.

Fourth of July Boom Box Parade. World's largest People's Parade. Radio station WILI plays marching band music on the air, while thousands march and watch, loudly playing their personal boom boxes. Anyone can march in the Boom Box Parade. 11 AM on Main St.

Railroad Days. Sat. of Labor Day weekend, 11 AM-3 PM.

Nightmare on Main at the Mill Museum. Haunting experiences from history. Sept. and Oct.

Tree Lighting and Lighted Fire Truck Parade. Fri. after Thanksgiving. Main St.

Address Book

Town Sites
ww2.windhamct.com
www.windhamrec.org
www.willimanticdowntown.org

The America Museum
47 Crescent St., Willimantic
www.americamuseum.org

Coffee Break Gallery
47 Crescent St., Willimantic
www.windhamarts.org

Connecticut Eastern Railroad Museum
55 Bridge St., Willimantic
www.cteastrrmuseum.org

Jillson House Museum and Windham Historical Society
627 Main St., Willimantic
www.windhamhistory.org

The Harp on Church
69 Church St. #1, Willimantic
860-423-8525

Mill Museum & Visitor Center
411 Main St., Willimantic
860-456-2178
www.millmuseum.org.

Stone Row Kitchen & Bar
948-956 Main St., Willimantic
860-423-4243
www.stonerowkb.com

Swift Waters Artisans' Cooperative
866 Main St., Willimantic
860-456-8548
www.swiftwaters.org

The Mill Museum and Visitor Center. Bev York

Trigo Wood Fired Pizza
744 Main St., Willimantic
860-377-6255
ww.trigokitchen.com

Willimantic Brewing Company
967 Main St., Willimantic
www.willibrew.com

Willimantic Food Co-op
91 Valley St., Willimantic
860-456-3611
www.willimanticfood.coop

Willimantic Whitewater Park
28 Bridge St., Willimantic
www.willimanticwhitewater.org

EVENTS

Chocolate Festival & Romantic Willimantic
/RomanticWillimantic

4th of July Boom Box Parade
/WiliBoomBox

Lighted Fire Truck Parade & Tree Lighting
Main St.

Nightmare on Main
411 Main St.

Railroad Days
55 Bridge St.

Third Thursday Street Festival
www.willimanticstreetfest.com

Thread City Hop Fest
627 Main St.

Willimantic Farmer's Market
28 Bridge St.
www.willimanticfarmersmarket.org

[Passport Stamp / Signature & Date Here]

Woodstock

*By Zachary Lamothe, author of **Connecticut Lore and More Connecticut Lore***

Bucolic Woodstock, with images of autumn's changing leaves, creeping stonewalls bisecting the woodlands, and acres of farmland, is arguably Connecticut's prettiest town. Located in the NE section of the state, Woodstock initially was a possession of Massachusetts. In the mid-1600s, the land which is now Woodstock was established by an English missionary, John Eliot, as a praying town called Wabaquasset. The purpose of this town was to convert Native Americans to Christianity and to rid them of their customs and traditions in favor of the English way of life. After the outbreak of King Phillip's War in June 1675, the praying town was abandoned.

In 1686, Woodstock was founded as New Roxbury by men from Roxbury, Mass. Its name was changed to Woodstock four years later, and in 1749 it became the property of Connecticut. Much like today, Woodstock was agrarian in nature although industry did grow in town during the 19th century. A visit to the Chamberlin Mill showcases this side of Woodstock. In addition to agriculture, the 21st century Woodstock is best known for its scenic beauty, quaint boutiques, and historic sites. The Woodstock town green is bordered by Roseland Cottage, summer home of wealthy entrepreneur Henry Bowen. Built in 1846 in the Gothic Revival style and painted a striking pink, the home is available for tours. As well as his business endeavors, Bowen published the anti-slavery newspaper The Independent. Also, flanking the green is Woodstock Academy, the area high school founded in 1801. The main classroom building which is topped by a clock tower dates from 1873. Woodstock Cemetery just south of the academy has well-preserved stones from the town's early years. Its villages include North Woodstock, South Woodstock, East Woodstock, West Woodstock, Woodstock Valley, and Woodstock Hill.

Northeastern Connecticut is known as the Quiet Corner with Woodstock being its crown jewel. To witness the glory of the town, make sure to head down Rt. 169, one of two National Scenic Byways in the state. Each place of interest is along it. It is a worthwhile drive any time of the year, but is especially magical on a clear autumn day.

Interesting Places

Roseland Cottage (1846). Woodstock native Henry Bowen returned to his hometown after establishing a successful business in New York City. He used Roseland Cottage as a place to entertain friends and political connections, including four U.S. presidents. The picturesque landscape includes original boxwood-edged parterre gardens planted in the 1850s. The estate includes an icehouse, aviary, carriage barn, and the nation's oldest surviving indoor bowling alley. The house is instantly recognizable for its pink exterior, but it also has an equally colorful interior, featuring elaborate wall coverings, heavily patterned carpets, and stained glass. The house is a National Historic Landmark. Tours: Wed.-Sun., June to Oct., 11 AM-4 PM.

The Bracken Memorial Library. Visitors will be amazed at the beautiful interior. The library serves both the high school for The Woodstock Academy and as one of the four public libraries in Woodstock.

The 1856 Roseland Cottage offers hourly tours of the magnificent home and gardens from June to October. Jerry Dougherty

Notes

Woodstock Historical Society. Collections of agricultural artifacts, personal items, books, documents, photographs and historic buildings including the Quasset School, the Red and White School, and Palmer Hall.

Woodstock Fair. This northeastern Connecticut tradition harkens back to 1860. Today's fair is an agricultural showcase, with amusement rides, games, crafts, and entertainment. The fair occurs each Labor Day weekend. Woodstock Fairgrounds.

Woodstock Orchards. Pick your own or buy apples, cider, pumpkins and more at the small farm store. Make sure to try the cider donuts!

Sweet Evalina's. A no-frills eating establishment with diner style food, a convenience store, and ice cream stand.

Inn at Woodstock Hill. A mansion built in 1816 for the Bowen family is a quintessential country inn with a sophisticated dining room.

The Christmas Barn. This converted barn is the place for autumn and Christmas décor.

On the Woodstock Green is the 1873 Woodstock Academy high school classroom building, is topped by a clock tower. Zachary Lamothe

Address Book

Town Site
www.woodstockct.gov

Bracken Memorial Library
57 Academy Rd.
860-928-0046
www.woodstockacademy.org

The Christmas Barn
832 Rt. 169
860-928-7652

Inn at Woodstock Hill
94 Plaine Hill Rd. (Rt. 169)
860-928-0528
www.woodstockhill.com

Roseland Cottage
556 Rt. 169

Sweet Evalina's
688 Rt.169
860-928-4029
www.sweetevalinas.com

Woodstock Fair
281 Rt. 169
www.woodstockfair.com

Woodstock Historical Society
523 Rt. 169
www.centerforwoodstockhistory.com

Woodstock Orchards
494 Rt. 169
www.woodstockorchardsllc.com

[Passport Stamp / Signature & Date Here]

INDEX

O

P

Q

R

S

T

Join Our Contact List

Be among the first to get CT 169 Club news, and information about the Annual Dinner, books signings, and talks!

To Register, visit the <u>NEW</u> www.martinpodskoch.com

Or send your name, address, email, and phone no. by U.S. mail to:
Marty Podskoch, 43 O'Neill Lane, East Hampton, CT 06424

/connecticut169club   Also on Facebook, "Connecticut 169 Club - Share Your Stories"

Connecticut 169 Club Annual Dinner

Each Fall, a dinner will be held for members or friends to share their stories and adventures. It is not restricted to those who have visited all 169 towns, but open to all. It will also be time to honor those who have visited all 169 towns and cities and they will be awarded the "Leatherman Award" patch.

More books from Marty Podskoch

Podskoch Press offers a variety of books about the history of the Adirondacks and Catskill regions. The Adirondack Stories: Historical Sketches I & II tell interesting stories through the comic sketches of Sam Glanzman, well-known *DC Comics* and *Outdoor Life* illustrator. The Fire Tower books tell photo-illustrated stories that Marty gathered while traveling throughout the region, which led to the development of his Adirondack CCC Camps book detailing the area's growth after the Great Depression. He has also written about the CCC camps in Connecticut where he now lives. These **autographed** books make perfect gifts for those who love the region's history.

Order yours today!*

Adirondack Stories: Historical Sketches		$20.00
Adirondack Stories II: 101 More Historical Sketches		$18.95
Adirondack Stories Two-Volume Set (includes vol. I & II)		$34.95
Fire Towers of the Catskills: Their History and Lore		$20.00
Adirondack Fire Towers: Their History and Lore The Northern Districts		$20.00
Adirondack Fire Towers: Their History and Lore The Southern Districts	HARD COVER	$24.95
Adirondack Civilian Conservation Corps Camps: History, Memories, & Legacy of the CCC		$20.00
Connecticut Civilian Conservation Corps Camps: History, Memories, & Legacy of the CCC	 HARD COVER	$24.95 $29.95
Adirondack 102 Club: Your Passport & Guide to the North Country	HARD COVER	$20.00

43 O'Neill Lane, East Hampton, CT 06424
podskoch@comcast.net 860.267.2442

*Book prices listed on this page do NOT include shipping and postage. Contact Podskoch Press for total price.

About the Author

Marty Podskoch was a reading teacher for 28 years at Delaware Academy in Delhi, NY. He retired in 2001. Marty and his wife, Lynn, raised their three children, Matt, Kristy, and Ryan, in a renovated 19th c. farmhouse along the West Branch of the Delaware River. He became interested in fire towers after climbing to the fire tower on Hunter Mountain in the fall of 1987. He met the observer, who was in his 60s, chatted with him, and listened to his stories. Marty was hooked. He set out on a quest to find all he could about the history and lore of the fire towers.

In 1997 Wray Rominger of Purple Mountain Press asked Marty to write about the history of the Catskill fire towers and the restoration project that was occurring in the Catskills.

After interviewing over 100 observers, rangers, and their families, Marty had gathered hundreds of stories and pictures about the 23 fire towers in the Catskill region. In 2000 his book, *Fire Towers of the Catskills: Their History and Lore*, was published by Purple Mountain Press, which also published his second book, *Adirondack Fire Towers: Their History and Lore, the Southern Districts*, in June of 2003 and his third title, *Adirondack Fire Towers: Their History and Lore, the Northern Districts*, in November of 2005.

Marty also wrote a weekly newspaper column, "Adirondack Stories" in five area newspapers. Sam Glanzman, a noted comic book illustrator for the past 50 years, illustrated the stories. After five years of weekly columns Podskoch Press published 251 illustrated stories in two volumes, *Adirondack Stories: Historical Sketches* and *Adirondack Stories II: 101 More Historical Sketches.*

In 2011 Podskoch wrote and published *Adirondack Civilian Conservation Corps Camps: History, Memories & Legacy of the CCC.*

In the fall of 2013 Podskoch received the "Arthur E. Newkirk Education Award" from the Adirondack Mountain Club for his work in preserving the history of the fire towers and Civilian Conservation Corps Camps in the Adirondacks and Catskills.

Adirondack 102 Club: Your Passport and Guide to the North Country was published in 2014. It is a comprehensive guide to travelers listing the history and interesting places to visit in all 102 towns and villages in the Adirondacks. It is also a journal and passport, a place to get each town stamped or signed by a store or resident and the chance to discover the secret and lovely places that the main roads do not reveal. Those that achieve this goal receive a "Vagabond Award" patch.

After eight years of research, his book *Connecticut Civilian Conservation Corps Camps: History, Memories & Legacy of the CCC* was published in 2016.

In 2018 Podskoch published *Connecticut 169 Club: Your Passport and Guide to Exploring Connecticut.*

Presently he is writing books on the CCC Camps of Rhode Island and The History of East Hampton/Chatham.

Marty Podskoch and family at his lake house in East Hampton, CT. Front row: Kira & Lydia Roloff.

Travel Log / Notes

Travel Log / Notes

Travel Log / Notes

Travel Log / Notes